The Kingdom of Coal

Fourty years I worked with pick & drill
Down in the mines against my will,
The Coal Kings slave, but now it's passed;
Thanks be to God I am free at last.

From the tombstone of an anthracite miner
in St. Gabriel's Cemetery, Hazleton, Pennsylvania
Quoted from George Korson in Black Rock.

The Kingdom of Coal

Work, Enterprise, and Ethnic Communities in the Mine Fields

Donald L. Miller
Richard E. Sharpless

upp

University of Pennsylvania Press

PHILADELPHIA   1985

Library of Congress Cataloging in Publication Data

Miller, Donald L., 1944–
  The kingdom of coal.

  Bibliography: p.
  Includes index.
  1. Coal trade—Pennsylvania—History.   2. Coal
miners—Pennsylvania—History.   3. Ethnology—
Pennsylvania.   I. Sharpless, Richard E.   II. Title.
HD9547.P4M55   1985   306′.09748   85-1153
ISBN 0-8122-7991-3
ISBN 0-8122-1201-0 (pbk.)

Printed in the United States of America

Contents

Illustrations

Acknowledgments

We are indebted to a number of individuals and institutions for assistance in the writing of this book. For assistance in our research we would like to acknowledge the staffs of the Lackawanna Historical Society; Elutherian Mills National Library; the Anthracite Museums, Scranton, Pa., Eckley, Pa., Ashland, Pa.; the Historical Society of Schuylkill County; the Wyoming Historical and Museum Commission; the Bethlehem Public Library; the Easton Public Library; the Historical Society of Northampton County; the Library of Congress; the National Archives; the Balch Institute for Ethnic Studies; the Pennsylvania Historical and Museum Commission, particularly Carl Oblinger for assisting us with their collection of W.P.A. materials; the Pennsylvania Canal Society, particularly Lance Metz, an astute student of the region's history; Skillman Library, Lafayette College, particularly Richard Everett who was of continuing and valuable assistance to us throughout this entire project, and Dorothy Siles, who helped us with the illustrations.

Our special thanks to David Johnson, Charles Best, and Donald Sayenga for reading parts of this book in manuscript form and to the students in the Regional Studies Seminar at Lafayette College for helping us to piece together the history of the anthracite region.

A number of friends and colleagues provided help at various stages of this project: Dan Rose, Harold Aurand, William Gudelunas, John Bodnar, Mary Ann Landis, David Salay, Alan Johnson, John Steber, Keith Standbridge, John McCall, John N. Hoffman, Craig Bartholomew, Rev. Joseph K. Hammond, Archibald MacDonald, Louis Poliniak, Anthony F. C. Wallace, Stephen R. Couch, Basil Borota, Irene Daleker, Jim Clarke, M. Mark Stolarik, Joseph Anderson, Tom Beck, Michael Korb, Jerry Bastoni, Karen Fried, Elizabeth R. Jewell, Tom Clark, Joe Malacavich, Tom Norton, Robert Chase, Richard Faas, Bruce Conrad, Margaret Fasulka, Jule Majikas, Frank and Ann Katrinak.

Part of the research that went into this book was supported by a grant from the Committee for Advanced Study and Research, Lafayette College.

We are especially indebted to Hilda Cooper, who typed and proofread this book in its various versions, and to Marcia Brubeck, who was our splendid copyeditor.

Two extraordinary men were of great assistance to us in telling this story of the anthracite people: William Whyne, a miner, gave us an education in anthracite mining and Steve Nelson, a former labor organizer in the region, gave us a first-hand account of the struggles of the anthracite people during the Great Depression. These two men symbolize what the region has come to mean for us.

Finally, we owe an enormous debt to Malcolm Call, who believed in this book from its inception.

Introduction

At least if there's a war they won't bomb us. The planes will look down and think we've already been bombed.

Darryl Ponicsan, *Andoshen, Pa.*

In one corner of Pennsylvania under the low skies of winter, the scarred and violated land lies exposed, a hundred and some years of industrial history bared to the leaden light. In the waste piles of slate and rock, low scrub and scrawny trees are stripped of covering green, and the mountainous black banks of coal refuse stand stark and forbiddingly barren.

Everywhere there are gigantic pits and craters, the work of bulldozers and dynamite and of power shovels as big as small buildings. Surrounding these vast holes are heaps of clay, crumbled rock, and slate; just beyond, oily-black brackish ponds give off the smell of sulfur. In places, acrid white smoke rises from the ground, eerie evidence of fires raging far below in the coal seams. There are occasional fires, too, on the towering piles of discarded slate and low-grade coal, fires that burn on and on, even through days of drenching rain.

In winter, the coal breakers, vast factories for processing coal, seem even more imposing against the barren landscape. Most stand silent now, more than 100 feet tall, rotting remnants of a once-dominant industry. Not far from every breaker and pit head are the simple homes of the people who remain in the region. The buildings are strung together in long rows, and some of them are sinking into the earth. They are cleaner now, these homes, for poverty and decline have at least brought purer air. Yet many of the older homes in the older patch towns have been indelibly colored by grimy coal dust, smoke, and soot. If it were not for the snow—and snow falls often in these raw, rugged hills—almost everything would be colored a dozen shades of black and gray.

Nevertheless, winter in the region has a strange beauty. The traveler advances slowly along the broken back roads, stunned into fascination by the destruction, al-

Shenandoah during the Great Depression.   Courtesy of the Library of Congress.

most haunted by the desolation. This is anthracite country. American industry was born here. This is all that remains.

*   *   *

Coal was once king in northeastern Pennsylvania. Within an area of little more than 1,400 square miles, hard coal—anthracite—gave rise to one of America's first gigantic industries, with its powerful coal bosses, stupendous technological achievements, and bloody labor struggles. Beginning in the early 1800s, lasting a full century and then some, anthracite reigned in the region. The overlords who controlled this industry owned almost everything of great value in northeastern Pennsylvania—including, some people said, the souls of the men they paid to go into the earth to get the coal.

But the industry's influence extended well beyond the borders of Pennsylvania. In the opening decades of this century newspapers spoke of an anthracite empire, and powerful reform interests in Congress tried again and again to break it up. Only oil, a new fuel of far greater value, would be able to do so. Like all extractive industries, anthracite mining took from the earth and gave nothing back. When the huge profits had been made and coal had started to yield to other fuels, the larger companies abandoned the anthracite region, leaving behind a trail of destruction.

In anthracite country the industrializing process assumed its most nakedly brutal form. The land was savaged almost beyond repair. On the eve of the Civil War, only thirty years after the opening of the coal lands, the region's forests had been stripped completely of their timber stands. Streams and rivers had been dangerously contaminated by raw sewage from coal settlements and by acid seepage from the mines. Visitors to the area reported seeing the busier towns of this furiously growing area blanketed by far-spreading clouds of coal dust and grit. After the war, the growth and the devastation really began as more big money rolled in to reap the big profits in coal. In an age of steel, one writer observed, men esteemed coal more highly than rubies.[1]

Anthracite mining also came at a terrible human cost. Deep in the earth men and boys from Wales, Ireland, Poland, and Germany worked in total darkness, often knee deep in water, at the most dangerous job of the day. They learned to live with accidents and to accept the risk of death as part of the job; and few miners, if they lived long enough, escaped the dreaded black lung disease. "Miner's lung," they called it, and its victims found their last years more terrible than death. No other American industry inflicted more heedless destruction on men and the environment than anthracite mining.

Yet the shiny "black diamonds" the miners pulled from the earth broke the country's dependence upon foreign coal and helped to trigger a national industrial explosion. At the turn of the century, when Theodore Roosevelt intervened to end

An abandoned coal breaker in anthracite country.   Photograph by Dan Rose.

Breaker boys at the height of the anthracite boom, 1911.
Courtesy of the National Archives.

the great anthracite strike of 1902, Pennsylvania's clean-burning anthracite was the Northeast's chief domestic fuel and a fuel for industry and transportation as well. When America entered the First World War the same industry, now a sprawling financial combination of mines and coal-hauling railroads ruled by the nation's largest investment houses, was producing 100 million tons of coal yearly and was employing a work force of nearly 180,000 men, almost all of them members of the largest labor union of the day, the United Mine Workers of America.

Today, more than a half century later, with production below 6 million tons a year and a work force of barely 3,000, anthracite accounts for only 1 percent of the nation's coal supply and about 7 percent of Pennsylvania's production. Anthracite is not even a strong local industry. The region's thinly populated towns and abandoned mine sites are poignant reminders of the time when coal was king.

This book describes the rise and decline of anthracite. It is the first comprehensive history of the industry and of the unique regional culture that grew up with it. *The Kingdom of Coal* is, however, more than an industrial history. It is the story of the rich and the powerful, the poor and the powerless, the people whose struggles changed this land of low mountains and winding valleys just as the land and their exploitation of it changed them. Coal was their life. This is their story. It is a story, in small, of America's industrial revolution, of its origins and impact, of its costs and consequences.

The Kingdom of Coal

1. Anthracite Pioneers

MORE THAN 200 YEARS AGO, MUCH OF ANTHRACITE COUNTRY WAS KNOWN AS Saint Anthony's Wilderness. Count von Zinzendorf gave the region that name while traveling through it in 1742. At the time it was a rough and roadless land. Even the Indians rarely ventured there; to them it was *Towamensing*—the wild place. The cautious Germans and Scots who opened the rich farmlands to the south and east hesitated to move across its first barrier of mountains. Yet it beckoned, as do all mysterious places, a forbidding land of temptations and promises.[1]

The first white explorers entered a dense, tangled wilderness of narrow, thickly grown valleys and steep, heavily forested mountains. It was a green and lovely land, but the soil almost everywhere was hard and sterile. Only in the northern reaches, where the Susquehanna flows, was the land suitable for farming. In that fertile area, the valleys broaden, breaking the prevailing pattern of elongated parallel ridges and deep intervening troughs. This northern region, the wide Wyoming Valley, was once known as America's garden spot. Yet this verdant land lured few settlers before the age of coal and iron. In 1828, a traveler passing through the valley on his way to Wilkes-Barre reported seeing only three crude dwellings in thirty-five miles.[2] The lands to the south were even more sparsely settled. The Indians said spirits dwelled there; it is still a place where tales and legends abound—only now these tales are of miners and Molly Maguires.

Some place names were provided by the Indians and early white settlers: Panther Valley, Bear Run, Rattlesnake Ridge, Shickshinny, Oneida, Schuylkill. Minersville, Coaldale, and Port Carbon would be named later. The first white settlers coming from the south, from well-established places such as Reading, Easton, and Bethlehem, entered the region through gaps in the mountain wall chiseled out eons past by rapid-running rivers. Settlers from the Connecticut Valley entered the Wyoming region through the thick forests and rolling hills of the colony of New York. These founding families moved into an area that Pennsylvania's proprietary government, in a swindle comparable to the purchase of Manhattan Island, had bought from the tribes of the Six Nations for about $2,000. The buyers did not know that they had purchased almost all of Pennsylvania's anthracite. Hunters, farmers, and blacksmiths soon discovered the coal, and not long thereafter geologists began to tell interested investors just how much of it there was and where it could be found. From that point forward, coal defined the region's boundaries. The area became coal country, "the anthracite region," as it is known to the people who live there today.

The anthracite region is bounded on the north and west by the branches of the Susquehanna River, on the east by the Lehigh River, further north by the Delaware, and to the south by the first ridges of the Blue Mountains, part of Pennsylvania's

Appalachian Mountains. The area is a small piece of America; yet it contains three-quarters of the earth's hard coal deposits. The rest of the planet's anthracite is found in several other states and in a scattering of European and Asian countries.

All of Pennsylvania's anthracite lies in four separate fields or basins. Nature dictated these physical boundaries; settlers accepted them; and each of the four fields acquired its own identity. The Northern field, shaped like a long canoe, stretches from Forest City on the Lackawanna to Shickshinny on the Susquehanna. In the other three anthracite fields the coal lies in sharply pitched veins and is heavily faulted, making mining extremely difficult and hazardous. But the subsurface coal beds in the Wyoming Valley lie almost horizontally until they pitch upward to outcrop halfway up the mountains that rim the valley. These flat-lying beds are easier to mine than beds to the south. But here nature laid a trap for the unsuspecting miner. During the Ice Age, a glacier cut through the basin a valley that was later covered over by layers of earth and stone. The Susquehanna River flows directly over this "Buried Valley of Wyoming." In the nineteenth century, mining operators penetrated the hidden valley. In 1885 the walls of the valley broke open and flooded a mine at Nanticoke, killing twenty-six men. Their bodies were never recovered.[3]

The Northern field has the deepest anthracite deposits and the coal with the highest carbon content. It was the last field to be exploited because it is far from Philadelphia, without a passable river connection, but it became in time the most prosperous of the anthracite fields. In the peak years of mining, one-half of Pennsylvania's anthracite was shipped from the field; and its commercial centers, Scranton and Wilkes-Barre, have long been the region's largest, most important cities.

Just fifteen miles south of the Northern basin is the Eastern Middle, or Lehigh, field, the smallest of the four fields. It is really a group of parallel basins that sit on a high plateau bordered by Spring and Green mountains. Hazleton, its chief city, was the home of some of the most powerful coal families of the region, including the Markles and the Pardees. Most of the early coal from this region was shipped down the Lehigh River to Philadelphia.

Southwest of Hazleton is the Western Middle field, located between the Susquehanna and Little Schuylkill rivers; and just south of this field is the long Schuylkill basin, stretching from the town of Jim Thorpe (Mauch Chunk) on the Lehigh River southwestward for seventy miles almost to the Susquehanna River in Dauphin County. It is an area of narrow valleys and steep jagged mountains, and it is drained by the Schuylkill River, which flows southward through Pottsville, the Gibbsville of John O'Hara's fiction, to Reading and Philadelphia. During the development of the coal trade the four fields were reclassified as three: the Northern became the

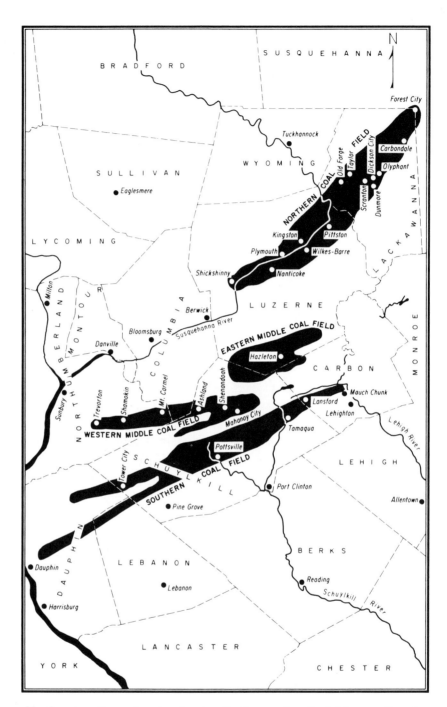

Northeastern Pennsylvania, showing the four anthracite fields as well as the principal cities and towns. Before the coming of the railroads, coal was shipped over canals along the river routes.   From Michael Novak, The Guns of Lattimer *p. 3. © 1978 by Michael Novak. Reprinted with permission of Basic Books, Inc., Publishers.*

Wyoming-Lackawanna; the Eastern Middle, the Lehigh; and the Western Middle and Southern were joined to become the Schuylkill field.

*   *   *

Anthracite is an underground industry, and its story begins in the earth itself. All of Pennsylvania's coal—anthracite and bituminous—was formed at approximately the same time, more than 250 million years ago during the Pennsylvania period of the Paleozoic era. Then the state was a flat, hot, moist plain, covered with steamy swamps thick with tall trees and wide-spreading ferns. As the giant plants and ferns of this tropical age decayed and died, they fell to the bottom of the swamps, where they mixed with the remains of the animal life—fish, amphibians, reptiles, and insects. This mass gradually formed a spongy, brown vegetable matter called peat. Over millions of years this peat was squeezed down and sealed off from the air by mud, sand, and new debris carried in by the periodic eastward movement of the vast, shallow inland sea that covered the middle of the continent. The resulting increased pressure combined with heat rising from the earth's core to drive off moisture and gases and transformed the peat, over millions of years, first into lignite, then into bituminous, or soft, coal.

The relentless, eons-long, natural process created, in parts of Pennsylvania, as many as 100 superimposed beds of coal, reaching a total thickness of 3,500 feet and separated by vast sedimentary layers of sandstone, shale, clay, and limestone. In the western part of Pennsylvania the bituminous coal is deposited relatively close to the surface in flat-lying beds. But in northeastern Pennsylvania subsequent upheavals of the earth, known as the Appalachian Revolution, reared up the flat plain and folded the earth's crust, creating the mountains of the anthracite region. Here the additional pressure caused by the earth's convolutions produced coal of unusually high carbon content.[4] The average fixed carbon content of anthracite is 86 percent; volatile matter amounts to only 4.3 percent. Anthracite is therefore more difficult to ignite, but it burns longer and cleaner than bituminous coal, making it more attractive for domestic use. It also is easy to store and is more resistant to deterioration.

Yet the very geological pressures which produced this high-quality coal also restrict its wider use. Anthracite often lies in severely pitched beds, or veins, which frequently reach beneath the area's water table, making anthracite more difficult and dangerous to mine than bituminous. Bituminous coal thus has the advantage in today's energy market of being both cheaper and safer. Anthracite, however, was the first widely used American coal for domestic and industrial purposes. For more than half a century it was America's most important coal. Its history, from early discovery

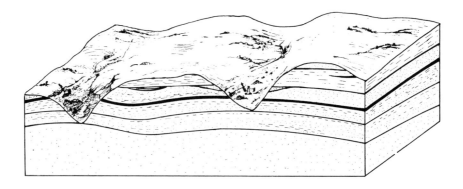

and exploitation by small, risk-taking capitalists to monopoly domination of the industry by the big railroad companies and New York banking houses, replicates the major developments of the American industrializing process.

*   *   *

The present-day anthracite region was first settled by Yankee farmers from Connecticut. Armed with copies of Connecticut's royal charter of 1662, which defined that colony's western boundary as the Pacific Ocean, an exploring party came into the Wyoming Valley in 1750. Other settlers followed as reports of the long green valley filtered back to Connecticut. Word filtered back, too, of the existence of coal deposits in the area, although coal was not believed to be a great find. The Indians probably told their new neighbors about the hard rock that burned. But even the British, who were already using great amounts of coal, were not excited by the discovery. A decade before the American Revolution, Thomas and Richard Penn of London, descendants of the original proprietor, were informed by James Tilghman of Philadelphia that large deposits of "stone coal" had been found in the Wyoming Valley near one of the area's major rivers. The Penns may not have been impressed, but Tilghman thought that the coal alongside the Susquehanna "may some time or other be a thing of great value."[5]

Many of the coal outcrops in the Wyoming Valley followed winding creeks that flowed into the Susquehanna. They were easy to work—it was not necessary to go into the earth to get the coal—and the coal was easily shipped on the river, so many local blacksmiths began to experiment with anthracite in spite of the abundance of wood. Adapting the fuel to forges took some doing, however, for the "stone coal" was exceedingly difficult to ignite. But in 1769 the brothers Obadiah and Daniel Gore used it successfully at their workplace in Wilkes-Barre. They then demonstrated its

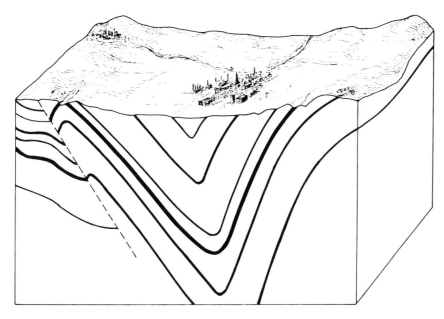

*Facing page and above: Bituminous and anthracite coal beds. The sloping
of the anthracite beds was caused by intense pressure and upheavals
of the earth's crust. The convolutions also gave hard coal its
unusually high carbon content.*

use to other blacksmiths, who preferred to use anthracite because the intense heat generated by its burning melted iron much faster than charcoal, the usual fuel. The limited local markets sustained anthracite production on a limited scale until the larger markets in the big eastern port cities were opened decades later.

In 1776 Wyoming Valley anthracite contributed to the American struggle for independence. That year two Durham boats, shallow-draft cargo carriers of twenty-ton capacity originally developed for the Delaware River trade, were loaded with coal from a mine owned by Matthias Hollenback, located at Mill Creek above Wilkes-Barre. Hollenback, a merchant and land speculator, was the Wyoming Valley's largest coal land owner and one of the first coal barons, with holdings of almost 50,000 acres. The coal from his mine was floated in the boats down the Susquehanna over 100 miles to Harris' Ferry, now the state capital, Harrisburg. From there it was transported overland by wagon another twenty-five miles to Carlisle, where it was used in the forges of gunsmiths manufacturing arms for the Continental Army. In 1780 other shipments from the Mill Creek mine were sent to Carlisle for the same purpose.[6]

As fate had it, someone looking for something else stumbled upon the first rich coal find in the Lehigh region. Philip Ginter, an immigrant German miller who served the farmers of the Mahoning Valley, on a day in 1791 was searching for the conglomerate rock consisting of quartz embedded in siliceous cement that made the best millstones. Coincidentally, it also formed the base of all anthracite beds. While stopping to examine a boulder on Sharp Mountain, near present-day Summit Hill, Ginter noticed a black substance beneath it. Curious, he broke off a piece and held it up to the light for examination. Since he had heard rumors and legends concerning the presence of stone coal in the area, he decided to carry the lump back with him. He took it to Joseph Neyer, a blacksmith friend, who tossed it onto his charcoal hearth. After what seemed an interminable time, the coal finally ignited. Joe's laconic response, in Pennsylvania Dutch dialect, was: "I guess it's coal all right."[7]

Ginter carried some specimens of his find to Colonel Jacob Weiss, the most prominent settler in the area. Originally from Philadelphia, Weiss had been deputy quartermaster general for the patriot forces during the War for Independence. After retirement from the service, he purchased some 700 acres of timberland from the Moravian church—his own denomination—on the Lehigh River north of Blue Mountain near what is now Weissport. He was a man of affairs with good connections in Philadelphia, a shrewd businessman involved in logging, farming, and general merchandise trade. There is evidence that his blacksmiths had used coal for making horseshoes and nails as early as 1785, making him one of the earliest users of anthracite in the Lehigh Valley region. He sensed immediately the importance of Ginter's discovery.

Weiss took the coal to Philadelphia, where he had its value and potential assessed by the best scientific counsel available. He then consulted with Michael Hillegas, his cousin, a leading merchant, and first treasurer of the United States, and Charles Cist, his brother-in-law and an important Philadelphia printer and publisher. The group met with John Nicholson, comptroller general of Pennsylvania and speculator, and other merchants, on January 19, 1792, and agreed to form a company. On February 13 a general public organizational meeting of the Lehigh Coal Mine Company was held. Within a week every share in the venture was subscribed.[8]

Enthusiasm ran high because of the mounting demand for coal in Philadelphia. In the postwar era the port city experienced an economic boom sustained by a burgeoning population and its role as the new nation's capital. Craftsmen were attracted by its economic potential; they, in turn, became increasingly dependent upon coal to fuel the industries they developed. Since before the War for Independence coal had been used in the city. By the 1790s more than a thousand tons were being consumed annually. Much of the supply came from Scotland, Wales, and Ireland; some came from Virginia. The possibilities of eliminating the dependence upon imported coal by developing nearby sources, and simultaneously monopolizing local markets, were not lost on the Philadelphia investors. For his trouble, Weiss received ten of the original fifty shares in the company, plus other concessions. He remained an active participant in the company, helping it to acquire an additional 10,000 acres of coal lands reaching from Mauch Chunk across the mineral-rich Panther Valley to Tamaqua.

The new company's directors authorized Weiss to pay Ginter for showing him where he found the coal, but Ginter refused any financial remuneration. Instead he sought Weiss's influence in expediting a claim through the Land Patent Office to 308 acres adjoining the miller's property in Penn Township. Weiss agreed to help but apparently lacked the influence Ginter thought he had. The patent was not granted for six years—not until 1797—and by that time Ginter was too old for clearing land and breaking in new soil. He soon sold the tract. Ginter passed into legend almost a decade later when, as a very old man, he was turned off the land where his gristmill was located by a stranger who claimed the property on the basis of an earlier survey. A folktale has it that a despondent Ginter, possibly cheated and certainly forlorn, wandered off to disappear forever in the great coal lands to the west.[9]

Every important area of the coalfields had its own Philip Ginter, its original folk hero who supposedly first found coal in the vicinity. In Schuylkill County he is Necho Allen, who, it was rumored, decided to spend the night at the base of Broad Mountain (near Pottsville) after hunting one day in 1790. He lit a fire under a protecting ledge and fell asleep next to it. Sometime in the middle of the night he was awakened by a bright light and heat. Jumping up in surprise, he discovered, as he said later, that "the mountain was on fire." When daylight came he found that what he thought was a rock ledge was actually an outcrop of coal, which his campfire had ignited. The fire forecast events to come.

Allen, unlike Ginter, apparently realized from other discoveries in the area that he had happened upon a valuable commodity. Eventually he successfully prospected for coal, obtained warrants for coal lands in Schuylkill County, and operated a small mine as well as a tavern on Broad Mountain and a sawmill in Mount Carbon. He lived into the 1830s but, as with Ginter, the circumstances of his final years and death remain a mystery.

Another traditional tale concerns one John Charles Fitzgerald, a Conyngham blacksmith. John Charles, as he was known, was out hunting in 1826 near Cranberry when he came upon what looked like a groundhog hole. The burly smith laid aside his rifle and, more courageous than wise, reached into the hole. What he grabbed, perhaps fortunately for his hand, was not a weather prophet but a lump of anthracite. Subsequent explorations in the area resulted in the formation of the Hazleton Coal Company in 1836.[10]

By this time most of the richest deposits had been discovered and marked on maps, not by buckskin-clad hunters and trappers, but by teams of trained geologists working for the U.S. government or for interested investors. It was not, however, a quick, easy step from discovery to widespread use. Though the blacksmiths of the anthracite region and nearby Lehigh Valley gradually adopted hard coal, they provided at best a limited local market. Sizable problems had to be overcome before the vast potential of the fields could be tapped and before the large eastern markets could be opened. This was the work of adventuresome pioneer entrepreneurs. They were among America's first industrial capitalists, and their enterprise carried the country into an industrial age.

A major problem was the public's resistance to anthracite. Hard coal was almost impossible to ignite in the open fireplaces commonly used in the eighteenth century. Though Oliver Evans of Philadelphia reportedly burned hard coal in an open grate without an artificial draft in 1800, and Dr. Thomas James of that city heated his living room with it in 1804, these isolated successes failed to convince a wary public. "If the world should take fire, the Lehigh coal mine would be the safest retreat, the last place to burn," an early experimenter with anthracite exclaimed. And on one occasion the public's resistance to anthracite almost cost the life of a vigorous promoter. In 1812 Colonel George Shoemaker carted nine wagonloads to Philadelphia and talked himself hoarse trying to persuade homeowners to buy it. He finally sold two wagonloads and gave the rest away. But when it would not ignite, the colonel was nearly lynched by an irate mob that denounced him as a "swindler and imposter." Fortunately for Shoemaker's reputation, some of his coal found its way to a rolling mill in Delaware County, where, after some experimentation, it was used successfully.[11]

There were always fears about the unhealthy effects of burning coal in homes. "Scientific" reports about its disadvantages continued to appear in popular magazines well into the nineteenth century. One magazine claimed that hot air from anthracite fires "destroys" the "delicate" health of women and children, "contributes largely to our cemeteries, increases the number of bald heads, decayed teeth and black-craped [sic] hats."[12]

One of the difficulties was that the stoves then available were not suited to burning hard coal, though some could be used for the more commonly known bituminous fuel. Technical innovations that assured a continuous draft of heated air were required. Until grates or stoves that provided this draft were available, widespread use of anthracite as a heating and cooking fuel was not possible.

Another problem was transportation. The few roads of those days hardly deserved the name; most of them were virtually impassable for much of the year, especially in the wild and sparsely populated anthracite region. Transport by wagon was limited and inordinately expensive. Though the major highways for bulk commodities from the interior to the coastal cities were the rivers, the major rivers flowing from the region—the Susquehanna, Schuylkill, and Lehigh—were shallow, rock-strewn, and treacherous, even during high water when most shipments occurred. Substantial improvements had to be made before they became major arteries for moving coal in large quantities. The government of Pennsylvania did encourage efforts to improve the rivers for commerce as early as 1791, for example, on the Lehigh. But this and other efforts were largely unsuccessful. It became evident to individuals engaged in the coal trade that adequate transportation systems held the key to development of the anthracite industry.

As with any great enterprise, vision, tenacity, imagination, and good luck—not to mention a strong dose of greed—were required. And as it happened, scores of Pennsylvania men possessed all of these qualities in the age of spirited entrepreneurial capitalism and rapid change. The first important breakthroughs came from the Wyoming Valley. There, in 1788, Judge Jesse Fell of Wilkes-Barre used anthracite in the manufacture of nails. Not content with this industrial application, he experimented with coal for home heating. Most of his efforts occurred at night because he did not want to arouse the scorn of his neighbors for attempting to burn stone coal in an open grate. Finally in 1808 he devised an L-shaped grate made of simple iron bars spaced several inches apart, which he inserted in his home fireplace. On it he placed wood, which he ignited, and then a quantity of coal. A practical man, he did not wait to see the coal ignite but went to bed. When he awakened the next morning, the fire was still giving off a warm, friendly glow. A revolution in home heating had begun.

The judge's discovery caused a great deal of local excitement. If an early history is believable, the event stimulated more discussion at church that week than the sermon. As for Jesse Fell, he simply wrote: "Made the experiment of burning the common stone-coal of the valley, in a grate, in a common fire-place in my house, and find it will answer the purpose of fuel, making a clearer and better fire, at less expense, than burning wood in the common way."[13]

A follow-up experiment came quickly from Abijah and John Smith, originally from Connecticut, who had purchased coal lands at Plymouth, just below Wilkes-Barre, and engaged in the precarious business of mining and marketing coal. In 1807 they had taken an ark with fifty-five tons down the Susquehanna but, finding no buyers, were compelled to dump the cargo at Columbia. The following year, convinced that coal would find a market, and buoyed by Fell's success, they sent several more arks down the river, accompanied by masons who would adapt grates and demonstrate to potential customers how the coal should be burned. The effort succeeded because people were willing to pay ten dollars for a ton of coal that was the equivalent in heating value of two and one-half cords of the best hardwood, burned cleaner and longer, and was more efficient to use.

The Smith brothers gradually expanded their trade along the river to the Chesapeake Bay and Baltimore. By 1812 they had penetrated the New York City market, where the firm of Price and Waterbury, acting as agents, took 220 tons. The coal for New York was loaded in coastal schooners at Havre de Grace, Maryland, and was then taken on to New York. Despite the difficulties and distances involved, the coal sold profitably in the city for $16.67 per short ton.[14] The success of the Smiths attracted other enterprising investors to the trade. By 1830 more than 100,000 tons of Wyoming anthracite had been shipped, most of it down the Susquehanna in the great flat-bottomed arks.

The arks themselves were an innovation developed to meet the needs of transport on the broad but often shallow and rock-filled Susquehanna. Piloted by a rough breed of rivermen, they went down stream on "freshets" following heavy rains and were sold for lumber after the coal had been delivered. Constructed far upstream near abundant forests, the arks were ninety feet long and sixteen feet wide, with a four-foot draft. Mounted amidship was a small cabin for the crew. Each ark carried about fifty tons of coal. Manned by four men who worked in pairs, the arks were steered by thirty-foot oars, one mounted in the stern and the other in the bow. The journey to tidewater took about a week. Since they usually traveled at high water, many arks started off together, forming a procession that diverted and delighted the riverside towns and settlements. Yet piloting was a dangerous occupation, for the river took a toll of one ark of every three.[15]

Another of the pioneer shippers and developers of the Baltimore market was Jacob Cist of Wilkes-Barre. Cist was a son-in-law of Matthias Hollenback, a merchant and the owner of the largest amount of coal land in the Wyoming Valley. He contributed more than any other single person to the early promotion of anthracite, and he must be counted among the decisively important forerunners of the American industrial revolution.[16] Born in Philadelphia in 1782, Jacob was the son of Charles Cist and the nephew of Jacob Weiss. Since both his father and uncle were among the first shareholders in the Lehigh Coal Mine Company, Jacob's interest in coal began early. His father sent him at the age of twelve to the Moravian Academy in Bethlehem, an excellent school for young men interested in business, where Jacob received sound instruction in writing, mathematics, languages, and geography. He also trained in drawing, which served him well in future years. Many of his drawings of early industrial technology, of his own inventions, and of the geological formations of the Wyoming coalfield survive and provided, at the time they were made, a wealth of information to people interested in coal.

After marrying Hollenback's daughter, Jacob Cist moved to Wilkes-Barre in

1811. As a member of the local elite with good connections among Philadelphia's leading families, he was in an excellent position to further the interests of people wanting to develop anthracite's markets. Unlike many of his contemporaries, however, he approached his business in a studiously scientific manner. He was a young man of wide learning (he was said to possess the best library in the Wyoming Valley) and he had a terrific desire to excel in a number of areas. Before his untimely death at age forty-three in 1825, he had made a reputation as a businessman, a scientist, an inventor, a public official, and an economic visionary. He knew more about the natural configurations of the Wyoming coalfield than anyone else and corresponded on the subject with the foremost scientists at home and abroad. His conception of a wide-spanning canal and railroad network linking the fields with their markets was prophetic. He practiced, according to his biographer H. Benjamin Powell, "the essential virtues of the Protestant ethic—hard work, diligence, patience, prudence, and frugality." He was anthracite's perfect propagandist and promoter.[17]

Cist's opportunity came during the War of 1812. The British blockade of American ports, combined with the increasing costs of firewood because of the scarcity of readily accessible supplies near the large eastern cities, provided a chance for hard coal to capture new markets in the midst of America's first fuel crisis. The potential for profits was considerable. A Baltimore merchant who handled Wyoming coal reported to Cist that a sixty-ton shipment sold for $1,320, with a profit of nearly $1,000. The merchant estimated that the city consumed 7,000 to 10,000 tons annually in 1813. Though Virginia bituminous was the preferred product in the city, he believed that the uncertainty of supply enhanced hard coal's possibilities. So Cist moved quickly, not only to continue supplying Baltimore, but to open new markets in Philadelphia as well.[18]

Cist organized a partnership that utilized Wyoming Valley capital and labor to tap resources located in the Lehigh field, the field closest to Philadelphia. From the Lehigh Coal Mine Company, which despite the efforts of Jacob Weiss had failed to develop a successful venture, Cist and his Wilkes-Barre partners Charles Miner and John Robinson obtained a ten-year concession to mine coal, construct roads, and use timber for arks. In return they agreed to ship a specified amount of coal annually. The company was quite willing to make such an agreement because any successful effort would increase the value of its holdings. Furthermore, Cist was a major stockholder in the company because he had inherited his father's shares; the enterprise thus linked Wilkes-Barre and Philadelphia interests.

Cist's enthusiasm was infectious. When he organized an expedition of workers in Wilkes-Barre to send to the Lehigh, one of his employees wrote that, "beside the anticipated golden harvest, the whole thing was a romance. Here was a chance for adventure well suited to their prolific imagination, beside an eternity of glorious

post-humous fame." The workers marched off that summer of 1814 as if to war, singing "The Girl I Left Behind," while their wives and sweethearts waved tearful
goodbyes.[19]

The work at the mine site, however, was enough to dampen the most lively spirits. The area was remote and wild, with only a few scattered farms and settlements.
Since they had no quarters, the workers stayed at a makeshift lodging house, where
they slept in cramped quarters and subsisted on basic provisions sent overland from
Wilkes-Barre. The mine at Summit Hill was no more than an open pit about sixty
feet deep. The mining itself involved simple techniques. But it was brutal pick and
shovel labor. The coal was quarried in much the same manner as stone; then it was
loaded into wheelbarrows and pushed to wagons that would carry it on the treacherous eight-mile trip to the Lehigh River.

Difficulties appeared at every turn. Severe weather hampered operations and
often made the single road all but impassable. Horse and wagon teams were expensive and hard to attract because of the difficult nature of the work. Cist had to send
teams from Wilkes-Barre and had to pay much higher rates than he expected. Labor
eventually also became difficult to recruit. Finally, the building and preparation of
arks proved to be the most expensive part of the operation and a steady drain on
scarce capital. Work continued nonetheless, and by the summer of 1814 the partners
were shipping limited amounts of coal overland into the nearby Lehigh Valley. Most
of the sales were made to blacksmiths and gunsmiths who had previous experience
with anthracite. They took enough coal to keep expectations high.[20]

Meanwhile, in Philadelphia, the full impact of the fuel crisis hit in the winter of
1813–1814. In March 1814 Cist reported that he had sold 100 tons and ordered the
coal to be readied for the trip down the rivers. The coal sold for $2,700, yielding a
profit of $1,650, or about $550 per partner.[21]

On August 9, 1814, following heavy rains, the partners sent off their first ark,
guided by the best Susquehanna and Lehigh pilots they could find. They were barely
under way when the ark struck a rock that broke a hole in its bow. The crew fran-
tically stuffed their extra clothes into the leak and continued on their way. By night-
fall they had reached the Delaware River, fifty miles away at Easton. Four days later
they were in Philadelphia. During the following weeks other arks were sent down
the rivers. By late September the partners had delivered almost 150 tons of coal to
the city.[22]

Though the Summit Hill mining venture did not immediately pay off for him,
Cist was encouraged by his first penetration of the Philadelphia market. He began a
campaign to demonstrate anthracite's qualities to potential customers. Leaving operations on the Lehigh in the capable hands of his friend and partner, Isaac Chapman,
Cist embarked on a systematic, finely orchestrated marketing effort in the Phila-

delphia area. Though there was a fuel crisis in that city, he could not succeed simply by making coal available; he had to show customers how they could use it in their homes and businesses.

In the ponderously methodical manner with which he approached everything he did, Cist made a precise inventory of enterprises requiring heat for manufacturing. He then contacted craftsmen who had successfully used anthracite and asked them about their methods. He was aided in his efforts by the wide network of influential merchants and craftsmen with whom he and his family had had dealings over the years. Since blacksmiths were his best potential customers, Cist recruited smiths from the Wyoming Valley who were experienced in anthracite and brought them to Philadelphia to demonstrate their techniques. He and his crew went from shop to shop, arguing the benefits of hard coal and offering practical advice on how to use it. He even bribed journeymen to experiment with the unfamiliar product, figuring that workers would put pressure on their employers if they found it easier to use hard coal.

Cist's campaign extended to nail and wire works, rolling and slitting mills for agricultural implements, steel foundries, steam producers, and glass manufacturers. When he found the existing technology inadequate for adapting anthracite, he drew up plans for new furnaces, complete with detailed drawings and illustrations. He used his knowledge of mineral science to develop plans for utilizing hard coal in limekilns (for making fertilizer). He even designed a fairly elaborate new still, hoping to make inroads in an important and widespread industry during that hard-drinking age.

Cist's principal advertising device was the testimonial. Whenever a blacksmith, ironmaster, or other manufacturer experimented successfully with anthracite, the promoter encouraged him to write about it in detail. The testimonials were then printed as handbills and circulars and were distributed widely, often by street urchins who ran from place to place for a few pence. Cist also wrote articles for newspapers and magazines extolling the virtues of his product and the best ways of using it. In 1815 he wrote and published a pamphlet titled *On the Importance and Necessity of Introducing Coal, Particularly the Species Known as Lehigh Coal, into Immediate and General Use.* Intended principally for craftsmen, the pamphlet was often reprinted and was used for many years afterward by other promoters of the coal industry. It was the most complete statement of the time on the subject. Cist argued that hard coal burned longer and provided more regular heat, that its efficiency as a fuel allowed for an increase in production, and that the absence of smoke and fumes improved working conditions and thus benefited the workers as well. He favorably compared anthracite to Virginia bituminous coal, claiming that the former permitted the user to realize a considerable cost savings. Since he was also concerned about pollution, he noted that using anthracite assured a clean environment, an important consideration in a growing industrial city like Philadelphia.[23]

Nor did Cist ignore the potentially vast domestic market. A calculation by James Ronaldson in 1815 estimated that Philadelphia's 16,000 households paid out approximately $1.1 million annually to heat their homes. When households were combined with businesses and industries, the city's total fuel bill for wood came to about $2 million a year. Coal offered an attractive alternative to increasingly expensive hardwoods for fuel and cooking. Here also Cist realized that he would have to educate the public. To do so he designed several stoves for burning anthracite and contracted with a Bethlehem manufacturer for their construction. He had his stoves assembled in the homes of several prominent citizens, in businesses and banks, and even in a jail—in places where a good many people might be expected to see them. He wrote more newspaper articles explaining that anthracite gave off a constant, regular heat that required little attention and that its clean-burning qualities reduced the chances that chimneys and stovepipes would catch fire. He also calculated the costs of heating an average-sized room for a year, the quantity of coal required, and the cost-savings benefit when compared with wood.

Cist's promotional methods and similar efforts by others gradually paid off. As one author noted, "Motivated by desires for profit and pride in accomplishment, capitalist, speculator, retailer and politician enlisted the aid of scientist, geologist, political economist and journalist in a successful campaign to educate the public in the virtues of anthracite, 'the most despised of the combustibles.'"[24]

Who, after all, could resist the lyrical enticement of:

> But if your coals a quick ignition take!
> And being lighted, show a lambent flame,
> Of yellow, orange, or rose-colored taint,
> Still playing calm and gentle o'er the surface,
> Like smiles upon the gentle face serene;
> And if the ashes prove, instead of white,
> A reddish brown, soft, fine, impalpable;
> And if the fire, once lit, continue long,
> Glowing and lively, sending forth the heat;
> The coal is good and fit to warm the hearths,
> Of honest men. Make haste to purchase more,
> If more there be, and you are not supplied.[25]

Jacob Cist was representative of a new type of American capitalist. Such a man combined theoretical knowledge with a wealth of practical skills; he was at once a businessman, an inventor, a salesman, and an engineer. Risk taking and versatility were his hallmarks. Not content merely with investing and speculation, he and men like him mastered every aspect of an enterprise and developed it with their own work and imagination. And they inspired others with equal intelligence, persistence, and vision. Jacob Cist's story is the story of a thousand other upstart entrepreneurs who led this country into the period of its greatest growth.

2. The Anthracite Canals

O N AUGUST 13, 1814, A COAL ARK THAT SURVIVED THE PERILOUS PASSAGE DOWN the Lehigh and Delaware rivers from the mountainous wilderness near Lausanne landed at Philadelphia. The exhausted and bedraggled leader of the flotilla was only too happy to sell the cargo of stone coal for $18.50 per ton. Two of his customers were Josiah White and his partner, Erskine Hazard, who bought the coal as an experimental fuel for their nail and wire mill at Manayunk on the Schuylkill River, also near Philadelphia. Their purchase had a profound effect on the course of American history. It was to make White a pioneer in the development of the river transportation of anthracite, the first great energy source of the nation's industrial revolution.[1]

White, a devout Philadelphia Quaker with an inventive mind and an inborn talent for business, had early been an advocate of American manufacturing. He knew from afar the impact that the industrial revolution was having on England's power and prosperity, and he deplored the fact that America was still locked into an eighteenth-century agrarian economy "under the sway & influence of Mercantile operations, as the only avenue to fortune."[2] He had expressed his views on a number of occasions. In 1812, in an unsigned letter to the *Philadelphia Aurora*, he urged his fellow citizens to turn to manufacturing for themselves rather than rely on imported English goods. "Our countrymen possess an ingenuity, skill and industry equal to those of the inhabitants of the old world! I know very well the sort of objections which are daily made to manufacturing for ourselves. Prejudice and ignorance operate together on this subject."[3]

White had been born in 1780. Apprenticed to an ironmaster at the age of fifteen, he later went into the hardware business and made a fortune there and in other investments before he was thirty. His fascination with manufacturing continued, however, and eventually he formed a partnership with Erskine Hazard, scion of a prominent Philadelphia family, who had similar interests. Hazard had conceived the idea of building a wire works at the falls of the Schuylkill utilizing the water power of the river. White bought the falls and in 1810 began the work of harnessing the river. He soon developed a plan for damming the Schuylkill which proved successful. A lock for the passage of boats was built on one bank, and a millrace for the wire mill on the other. Though attempts to leash the water power from the millrace were unsuccessful, the partners' manufacturing enterprise flourished.

Overleaf: A canal boat on the Lehigh Canal, circa 1920. The anthracite canals formed America's first comprehensive transportation system. They made the coal boom possible, and several of them continued to operate into the twentieth century. Courtesy of the Pennsylvania Canal Society Collection, Canal Museum, Easton, Pa.

Josiah White.
Courtesy of the Pennsylvania Canal Society
Collection, Canal Museum, Easton, Pa.

Erskine Hazard.
Courtesy of the Pennsylvania Canal Society
Collection, Canal Museum, Easton, Pa.

They devised several technological innovations, including a universal mill to roll nails on four sides simultaneously and a method for casting iron draw plates. They made iron wire fences in an attempt to open a new market and built a footbridge over the river suspended from iron wire catenaries, following a method commonly used later for all suspension bridges.[4]

Then disaster struck. A fire severely damaged the mill in 1815, and its rebuilding put the partners deeply in debt. Both men were discouraged and ready to give up their manufacturing business. At this point they accidentally made the discovery that reversed their fortunes and sent them and the nation off in a new, more prosperous direction.

White and Hazard, like other iron makers, knew of anthracite and tried to make it burn in their furnaces as a substitute for expensive charcoal but without good results. During one of these efforts with the coal bought from Cist's coal ark, White, Hazard, and their workmen labored unsuccessfully with the fuel for hours one day. Finally they slammed shut the door of the furnace containing the coal and went home in disgust. Not a half hour later one of White's workmen was pounding on his door. The man excitedly explained that he had returned to the mill to retrieve a forgotten coat and had found that the furnace with the anthracite was white hot. White rushed back to the mill where he found the fire burning inside the furnace with a pale blue flame that gave off no smoke or smell. The coal was burning like no other coal he had seen burn before. This was it! He had accidentally discovered the secret for burning anthracite in an iron furnace: the furnace door had to be closed and the draft made to pass through the fuel rather than over its surface. White made four "runs of iron" before the fire began to subside. That night fuel was found for the furnaces of American industry.[5]

White immediately began to seek a way of obtaining an adequate supply of the coal. It was still exceptionally expensive because of the fuel crisis and because it had to be transported overland by wagons. He turned his attention first to the Schuylkill because of the large coal deposits that existed far up that river. An appeal to the management of the recently chartered Schuylkill Navigation Company for rights to make temporary improvements in the river channel for the movement of coal arks failed, however, and White, in a fury, exclaimed, "This ends our using the Schuylkill! I'll go to another region! The . . . Lehigh . . . I'll make the Lehigh a rival to the Schuylkill!"[6]

White's desperate financial situation reinforced his determination. The mill on the Schuylkill was heavily mortgaged. Joseph Gillingham, a major financial backer, refused to invest in any further anthracite ventures. "Nothing but Ruin," White wrote, "seemed to present to me, unless I could leave the Falls and support my family elsewhere."[7] Facing bankruptcy, White borrowed a horse and started a journey up the Lehigh in December 1817 accompanied by one of his employees and George Hauto, an erudite fraud who passed himself off as an heir to a German barony and an intimate of wealthy Philadelphians.

White's first visit to the Lehigh convinced him that his hunch about using the river was correct. He inspected the mine Jacob Cist had opened at Summit Hill, and in 1818 he, Hazard, and Hauto took over its management from Jacob Cist. Then he developed a plan to improve the nine-mile road from the pit site to the river so that a railroad could ultimately be constructed on it. In order to deepen the river to handle coal arks, he devised a scheme for channeling the water by constructing a series of wing dams that would ensure the necessary depth of fifteen to eighteen inches. The idea was to form pools behind the dams, then periodically to release the water and allow the arks to move downstream on the artificially created freshet. Details as to "the plan of Locks & gates for letting out the freshet in a proper manner I took for granted I could devise," wrote the confident White.[8]

Following his return to Philadelphia, White formed a company with his old partner Hazard and new-found friend Hauto. White was in charge of plans and construction; Hazard was "Skribe & a good mechanic & excellent councellor"; and Hauto was fund raiser, because "Hoto assured us the larger the plan the easier it would be for him to Raise the money, through his Ritch friends."[9] The group obtained a twenty-year lease on the Summit Hill mine and 10,000 acres of coal lands for one ear of corn a year and the promise to deliver 40,000 bushels of coal annually to Philadelphia after three years. They then petitioned the state legislature for navigation rights on the Lehigh. In these negotiations Hauto provided his only real service. He spoke fluent German and managed to convince the predominantly German-speaking legislators that the new scheme was harmless, insane, or both, and in that spirit the legislature granted thirty-six-year rights to the group in March 1818.[10] When Hauto failed to raise any money, however, White and Hazard managed with difficulty to find a group of investors who put up about $50,000. Since some of the investors were interested only in the possibilities of river trade, and others only in the mining operations, two separate companies, the Lehigh Navigation Company and the Lehigh Coal Company, were formed in the fall of 1818.

The previous spring White and Hazard had surveyed the Lehigh route using borrowed instruments because they did not have the money to purchase any. For six days they had camped along the ice-fringed river while they completed their work. They had concluded that White's plan was feasible, and in August 1818 the two men left Philadelphia for Lausanne to commence work on the river. Before the river froze over, halting work for the winter, a series of wing dams was constructed at shallow spots on the river from the Nesquehoning Creek to the Lehigh Gap. In 1818–1819 a road, "built as regularly as the ground would admit of and to have no indulation," capable of handling wagonloads of four to six tons, also was constructed from the mine to the river.[11]

A severe drought in the spring of 1819 made White realize that there might not be enough water available to fill the eighteen-inch by twenty-foot channel he was constructing. To solve this problem he invented a hydraulic sluice which permitted a sudden release of water impounded behind a dam. The sluice, called a "bear trap," was operated by water pressure and closed automatically. When it was opened, it produced an artificial flood that augmented the flow of the river and carried the coal arks from one dam to the next. Twelve such dams and sluices were built on the Lehigh that year, as well as two large stone and cribbage dams equipped with lift locks to provide additional control of the river.[12]

White and Hazard employed more than 200 men on their construction works in a wilderness where few settlers lived. Men working on the river lived in scows about thirty feet long by fourteen feet wide which were moved downstream as work progressed. The workers, White wrote, came "from all nations and [were] Strangers to us." They were also a wild and undisciplined lot. When the first group of workers gathered at Lausanne, White reported,

the Hands on First Day (being a day of leisure) as usual must needs kill time with sport, as usual. a number of them got drunk & then quarrel'd, drove the Landlord out of his House broke his Windows &c &c Hauto until then allways when he Rode out on Horsback had a pr of hosslers & Pistols on the saddle and shew'd a very Military defence, but on this occasion was wise enough to keep those weapins out of sight.[13]

Guards had to be posted on the kitchen scow to prevent the workers from looting the provisions. A rule was made that "any Hand that took more Victuals on his plate than he coul Eat, was t be cobed, he was also to be cobed for Running or going any way uncivel to his meals."[14] White took the precaution of leaving his gold watch chain at home and paid the men with checks drawn on an Allentown bank to prevent attacks on him for money. The checks were signed by White and another foreman so that no one man could be coerced into signing. When White and his foremen ventured into the surrounding countryside they dressed in rough frontier clothes so as not to arouse any undue suspicions among the inhabitants.

The temperament of the workers was hardly improved by the nature of life and work on the river. Forty to sixty men slept in bunks of rough pine boards, most without even straw for a mattress, on the portable A-frame rafts that were built to replace the original scows. They spent as many as seven or eight months working in water. Their clothes consisted of red flannel shirts, coats and trousers of coarse cloth or buckskin tanned in oil as crude waterproofing, and caps and heavy shoes with holes cut in the toes to let out the water. White stated that he was in the water as much as out of it for three working years and was dry only in the evenings when he changed clothes. While he was in the river he maintained his circulation by moving about constantly.[15]

The hardships on the river were compounded by other difficulties. Hazard lost his entire fortune when the mill on the Schuylkill failed. Hauto was finally exposed as an imposter. Timberlands on the upper Lehigh for the construction of arks had to be purchased by White alone, entirely on credit. The two large stone and cribbage dams cost $40,000 to build. As usual, however, luck rode with White. The city of Philadelphia purchased the falls of the Schuylkill for $150,000, allowing him to pay his debts and to retain more than $45,000 for the works on the Lehigh. He had just enough capital to finish the job.[16]

In 1820 the first regular shipment of 365 tons of anthracite was shipped down the Lehigh and Delaware rivers to Philadelphia. According to historian Alfred D. Chandler, that event marked the real beginning of the industrial revolution in America.[17] White had also won his race against the Schuylkill Navigation Company; in entering the coal trade he preceded the competitor by several years.

With the river route open, White next turned his attention to marketing and raising much-needed working capital. He advertised and distributed pamphlets on how to use anthracite with testimonials from satisfied customers. He made coal competitive with other fuels by fixing the price at $8.40 per ton. Gradually the public was converted. The shift in popular opinion in turn attracted new investors. Hauto's share was bought out, and in 1821 the new Lehigh Coal and Navigation Company was organized. It was incorporated the following year. White and Hazard were two of the five controlling shareholders. In order to maintain close supervision over their new enterprise they moved, along with their families and their best employees, from the falls north to the Lehigh, where Mauch Chunk, a new company town, was laid out and built at the juncture of the mine road and the river.[18]

After 1824, when the Lehigh Coal and Navigation Company shipped more than 9,000 tons of coal, the market for the new fuel expanded rapidly. With both the Lehigh and Schuylkill routes open in 1828, more than 77,000 tons were shipped that year; by the early 1830s Philadelphia took 200,000 tons annually.[19] For the anthracite shippers the major problem was how to meet the rising demand for coal along the eastern seaboard. A more efficient method had to be found for transporting the coal. Ark building had continued at a furious rate; Lehigh Coal employees had perfected a method of constructing one of the boats in forty-five minutes. The arks were sixteen to eighteen feet wide and twenty to twenty-five feet in length. In the first years two of them were joined together by hinges which allowed them to move up and down when passing the sluices. Eventually, as the channels were straightened and the oarsmen became more expert in steering, arks were joined together to make a string sometimes as long as 180 feet.[20]

But construction needs had strained available lumber supplies. The company had purchased additional timberlands fourteen miles up the Nesquehoning Creek and had dredged a channel to facilitate the movement of logs downstream, but this solution was only temporary. Furthermore, the arks were for downstream navigation only; on arrival in Philadelphia they were broken up for sale, and their crews had to walk or ride back to Mauch Chunk. White, with characteristic foresight, had been aware of the need for both descending *and* ascending navigation as early as 1819. When the Commonwealth certified the Lehigh channel for descending navigation in 1823, he and Hazard began plans for their most daring project of all. Increasing competition from the Schuylkill Navigation Company also compelled them to move rapidly.[21]

Considered in retrospect, the plan made by White and Hazard was no less than astonishing in its vision and originality. The two men proposed to the state legislature that the Delaware be dredged with a channel for the development of a deepwater ship navigation system that would allow the passage of steamboats with a capacity of 150 tons, or steam tugs, with tows, all the way from tidewater to the anthracite region and back. The interior of eastern Pennsylvania would thus be opened to oceangoing traffic. White and Hazard expected their proposal to be approved, and in anticipation they constructed on the lower Lehigh two huge slack-water dams equipped with large locks and hydraulic sluices that were capable of handling boats of as much as 150 tons in capacity. The locks worked so well that they could be filled or emptied in three minutes.[22] When first put into operation, they were far in advance of canal technology anywhere.[23]

The bold plan, however, encountered the canal-building mania that was sweeping the nation. In 1825 the Erie Canal opened and gave New York a competitive edge in the race for western trade. The Pennsylvania legislature, casting about for an alternative solution, passed a series of canal bills, one of which was for the building of a canal along the Delaware from Easton to Bristol, just above Philadelphia. New Jersey also got into the act; plans were laid for the building of canals from Easton to Newark, and connecting Trenton with Perth Amboy, both to supply the New York market. In addition construction began on a sea-level canal linking the Delaware and Chesapeake bays, which would open Baltimore and Washington to the anthracite waterborne trade. All this activity effectively negated the scheme advanced by White and Hazard.

The partners gave up their deep-channel idea but immediately turned their attention to the construction of a combination slack-water and parallel canal on the Lehigh for both descent and ascent, using mule tows in the manner of other canals. The canal was to extend from Mauch Chunk to Easton, where it would connect with the state-constructed Delaware Canal. Canvass White (he was unrelated to Josiah), a brilliant young engineer from the Erie Canal who had extensive knowledge of the latest English canal technology, was employed to carry out the project. By coincidence, he had already patented a method for making waterproof cement from crushed limestone, a material found in abundance in the Lehigh Valley.

Construction began in midsummer of 1827. The canal was 60 feet wide at the top, 45 feet wide at the bottom, and 5 feet deep. It extended 36.01 miles in length; another 10 miles was slack water on the river. A towpath ran the entire length. A total of fifty-six locks—forty-eight of the lift type and eight guard locks—were built. The locks were 22 feet wide by 100 feet long except for four at Mauch Chunk, which measured 30 feet by 130 feet. The lifts were from 6 to 9 feet. Four aqueducts and twenty-two culverts were constructed along the route to allow passage over creeks and streams. Nine supply dams of timber and stone, varying in height from 5 to 15 feet, were also built. The drop in elevation over the route from Mauch Chunk to Easton was 354.7 feet.[24]

The project took two years to complete. The workers used the simplest tools: picks, shovels, wheelbarrows. Earth-moving equipment consisted of scoops pulled by horses or mules. The workmen were "Yankees" and Pennsylvania Germans from the surrounding towns and countryside or, in increasing numbers, immigrants from Ireland. The Yankees and Germans were praised for their thrift and steadiness. The Irish, on the other hand, were frequently criticized for their behavior. Many were itinerant workers who drifted from one canal job to another, living and laboring in the most wretched conditions. Mrs. Anne Royall, a contemporary observer, wrote:

> But the Teagues, poor fellows, they are strung along the canal, scarcely alive, stupid from drink. The poor fellows, fleeing from oppression to be free, grow rich in our country, make short life, and a merry one of it. I have been informed that they generally live about 18 months after coming to this country, and work and drink most of the time. They care little about eating, provided they get whiskey. In many instances on some of the canals, they die so fast, that they are thrown into the ground from four to six together, without coffins.[25]

Mrs. Royall, who apparently traveled along the canal route, went on to warn: "If you ever see a man with a rusty crown-cracked hat, short legs, tattered clothes, and dirty face, standing before you in the road, you may expect a Pat in the stage." She added that he was almost certain to be mud-covered, stinking, and drunk.[26]

There is no question that accidents and disease took a high toll of the workers. Some were killed, like the workman who went to investigate a fuse that had supposedly gone out; it suddenly went off and the blast blew him into the river. Others died of epidemics. A "fever" thought to have originated from the vast quantities of upturned earth killed a number of people near Bethlehem in August and September 1828 during a heat wave.[27] Bad drinking water, poor food, and unsanitary conditions in the work camps undoubtedly contributed to the high rate of sickness and death.

When the Lehigh Canal opened for navigation in June 1829 it was expected to link up with the Delaware Canal. Shoddy construction, however, delayed the Delaware's opening. Furthermore, no dams had been built to supply water. Lehigh Coal proposed to remedy this problem by constructing a dam on the Lehigh; but when water was let into the Delaware Canal, it leaked so badly that it soon ran dry. White was appointed to the Pennsylvania Canal Commission and was asked to supervise repair of the waterway. Canvass White's patented cement was used to patch the porous sections, and the Delaware Canal finally opened in July 1832. Its completion, along with that of the Morris Canal, which ran across New Jersey from Phillipsburg on the Delaware, opposite Easton, to the port of Newark, linked Lehigh Coal to the major anthracite markets of Philadelphia and New York. By 1840 the company was shipping 280,000 tons of coal along the various canal routes.[28]

Once the Lehigh and Delaware navigation system had proved viable, the company had no problem raising capital among Philadelphia investors through the sale of stock. Capitalization, however, had been set by the legislature at $1 million by the act of incorporation, and this money had been spent on the transportation works. As the demand for coal continued to increase, White and Hazard were prompted to make improvements close to their mining operations. In order to raise the needed funds, they petitioned the state legislature to increase the capitalization of the company. This effort failed because of strong opposition among both the lawmakers and the public. The legislature refused to consider any change in the charter or capital of the company unless it was willing to relinquish some of the river concessions granted earlier. Hearings in the state senate and public meetings in Allentown decried Lehigh Coal's monopolistic hold on river transport. A pamphlet issued after the Allentown meeting noted that granting "property in a great public watercourse is . . . selling the people's birthright for a mess of pottage."[29]

The company was also charged with preventing the development of other coalfields by setting toll charges so high that independent operators could not market their coal profitably. It was noted that Lehigh Coal charged $1.04 a ton for transport on the Lehigh Canal, while the longer, state-owned Delaware Canal cost only $0.30

The coal mine at Summit Hill, 1821.
From Richard Richardson, Memoir of Josiah White *(Philadelphia, 1873), 48.*

The inclined plane and loading docks of Hazleton Coal Company, c. 1860. Inclined planes
were among the first railroads in the United States.
Courtesy of the Pennsylvania Canal Society Collection, Canal Museum, Easton, Pa.

per ton.[30] Despite state senate investigating committees, various proposals for breaking the monopoly, and public hostility, Lehigh Coal firmly held onto its privileges. It
solved its capitalization problem by borrowing heavily. This outcry against the
power of a coal transportation company in the late 1820s and early 1830s, however,
would be heard again and again throughout the nineteenth century. It was an indication of the decisive position that the carriers held—and would hold—in the
industry. Lehigh Coal's ability to fend off efforts to limit its monopoly also demonstrated the influence of big capital in the Commonwealth even at the earliest stages
of the industrial revolution.

White and Hazard completed their first major project at the coalfields in 1827
with the building of a railroad running from Summit Hill to Mauch Chunk. It too
was a pioneer effort, probably the first commercially successful railroad in the
United States.[31] As usual White had done painstaking planning before construction

began, even to the extent of building and experimenting with toy models. On the railroad, a string of wagons, each containing a ton and a half of coal, moved by gravity down the nine-mile route on wooden rails with iron strap facing. The speed was controlled by one man, who operated a hand brake. At the terminus the cars ran onto a chute located some 700 yards from the riverbank. The cars were raised and tilted and the coal released into the chute. It then traveled downward over sizing screens into waiting canal boats. Mules pulled the empty cars back up to the mine. For the sake of efficiency, White designed a special car that allowed the mules to travel down with the train. They were fed on the journey, which prompted Solomon Roberts, one of White's relatives, to declare years later that the line had "the first railroad dining-car! The first transportation of cattle by railroad!"[32] In the 1840s the railroad was modified and the mules eliminated by construction of a series of inclined planes that allowed the cars to run by gravity back to their point of origin. This was accomplished by a series of "switchbacks," or zigzag switches, located in a nearby valley. The backtrack became known as the Switchback Railroad and was used for many years by the company.[33]

In the hope of exploiting the full potential of the Switchback, White and Hazard explored the feasibility of driving into coal deposits that they were convinced lay under the mountain along the route. Between 1824 and 1827 they drove the Hackleburnie Tunnel 790 feet into the mountain. It was later extended, mostly for drainage, to more than 2,200 feet. Though the building of another railroad to more accessible deposits in a nearby valley largely ended the need for large-scale extraction, it was the first big underground mine tunnel dug in the United States.[34]

In 1830 a second railroad was begun to carry coal from new mines in the Room Run Valley north of Mauch Chunk. This line had an inclined-plane return track, something originally devised by the English and used successfully to carry boats over high ground on several American canals, including the anthracite-carrying Morris and the Delaware and Hudson. It was the only method of ascending steep grades before the invention of the steam locomotive in the 1830s. On the Room Run railroad, movement was controlled by powerful stationary steam engines with cables attached that were hooked to coal cars. As the loaded cars descended they pulled the empties back up the plane on the second track. One of the disadvantages of the system was the high cost of maintaining the power transmission lines, since the hemp ropes and iron chains frequently broke. The undaunted White solved the problem by inventing a method using iron bands which wound on huge drums, like a giant watchspring.[35]

In the 1830s Lehigh Coal embarked on its final major transportation project. The original charter of the company called for completion of navigation upriver to

Stoddardsville, and with time running out that section was begun in 1835. When the so-called Upper Grand section was completed in 1838, it extended 26.06 miles— 20.54 miles of slack water and 5.52 miles of canal—from Mauch Chunk to Port Jenkins and by descending navigation another 12.2 miles to the Great Falls at Stoddardsville. The route not only allowed transport from the new Beaver Meadow deposits but also provided a natural outlet for the production of the middle anthracite, or Lehigh, field that had been discovered in 1826. During the 1830s the state had allowed the incorporation of seventeen mining companies in the area; some of them built railroads to connect with Lehigh Coal on the river. A final link that carried Lehigh Coal's transportation system entirely across the anthracite region was completed at the same time. The Lehigh and Susquehanna Railroad between White Haven on the Lehigh Canal and the North Branch Division of the Pennsylvania Canal at Wilkes-Barre in the Wyoming field was constructed. This 19.7-mile road was notable for the remarkable inclined Ashley Planes, powered by steam engines like the Room Run railroad, which remained in continuous use from 1843 to 1948.[36]

The completion of the Lehigh-Delaware navigation system ushered in an era of prosperity for Lehigh Coal. Tolls on the Lehigh and Delaware canals rose almost annually into the 1850s, and revenues exceeded $757,000 in 1866, one of the peak years.[37] In that year the profits from the Lehigh Canal alone were greater than $480,000. Though coal was the principal commodity moved, the system became a major transporter of lumber, iron and iron ore, limestone, and other products for an industrializing America. White's and Hazard's vision, imagination, and hard work had paid off handsomely. The company of which they were the moving spirits had conquered a wilderness, had demonstrated technical virtuosity, became a model corporation of the early industrial era, and played a major role in the economic transformation of an entire region.

White's engineering accomplishments at Mauch Chunk and on the Lehigh attracted a steady stream of visitors. Many were businessmen and politicians interested in ways of applying the technology elsewhere. Some observers were merely curious, drawn to works which were considered marvels of the age. A favorite of everybody was the "Gravity Road," and so loud was the clamor to ride on it that White ordered a special car to be built for tourists. "So long as it doesn't interfere with business, they may go!" he exclaimed. As White's biographer noted: "The conductor had the time of his life, as fancy city-folk clutched each other, screaming in terror and delight at the terrific speed [40 mph] of wagons swooping down the road." One passenger declared: "The pleasure of the traveler . . . is mingled with a sense of danger. . . . The nine miles from Summit Hill are frequently made in twenty minutes!"[38]

*The Switchback railroad at Mauch Chunk was first
used to carry coal from the mines to the canal and
was later turned into a tourist attraction.*
Courtesy of the Library of Congress.

Another delight of travelers was the packet line established on the canal. Passengers could forgo the arduous overland journey by stagecoach or wagon and could instead glide smoothly on water from Philadelphia to White Haven. A man who took a packet boat from White Haven to Mauch Chunk in 1844 wrote of his experience:

> The descent of the Lehigh is interesting, both on account of the almost gigantic construction of the canal and the magnificent wildness of the natural scenery. . . . Beneath me, the Lehigh either reposed in a black, glittering sheet, or bounded over its rocky channel in wreaths of snow-white foam; about me, on every side, for hundreds of feet, rose the pine-capped mountains, here, dark, jagged and precipitious, interspersed only with occasional

forest trees. . . . Everywhere the mountain sides were spotted with tall, gaunt, leafless trunks of withered pines, blasted by lightning, or scorched by the hand of man. . . . Along the course of the river, not a single rod of arable land is to be perceived; the mountains sink sheer to the water's edge. In wild magnificence of scenery, I have seen nothing to compare with the banks of the Lehigh.[39]

The canals created a thriving local economy along their routes. Employment in maintenance, on the locks or on the boats themselves, was provided for the inhabitants of nearby settlements and farms. Stores and inns appeared on the waterway to service crews and passengers; local farmers sold produce to boatmen or moved their products more readily to distant markets. Lumber yards and iron works were located near the canals for convenient access to cheap and reliable transportation. A major industry that developed to support the canal was boat building. Large yards at Weissport, Bethlehem, Easton, and other towns constructed Lehigh Coal's boats with their famed red "bulls-eye" identification markings. One of the canal boat building contractors was Asa Packer, who later built the Lehigh Valley Railroad and became one of the area's great industrial barons.

A canal boat passing through a lock of the Lehigh Canal at Mauch Chunk.
Courtesy of the Historical Society of Schuylkill County, Pottsville, Pa.

While White and Hazard were developing their route on the Lehigh and Delaware, the Schuylkill Canal—soon to become the busiest waterway in the United
States—was under construction to the south. Since colonial times far-sighted Philadelphia citizens such as Benjamin Franklin had fixed their attention on the Schuylkill River as a potential passage to the western frontier. In their imaginations the
river would be the key link in a system of transportation that would draw trade from
the west through Pennsylvania and into Philadelphia. It would also provide an
outlet for the agricultural and lumber products of the rich Schuylkill Valley. The
formidable task of taming the wild river dampened all dreams, and Philadelphia
capital continued to seek investment opportunities elsewhere. Finally a group of interested upriver inhabitants took matters into their own hands. In 1813 some German settlers gathered in Reifsnyder's Tavern in Orwigsburg, Schuylkill County.
Following a wet and tumultuous meeting, they voted to send a petition to the state
legislature. What they wanted was better access to the Philadelphia market.[40]

In 1815 the governor signed an act of incorporation of the Schuylkill Navigation
Company. Work on the river began the following year. Philadelphians invested
heavily in the new company, as they had with the Lehigh project. One major stockholder was the Philadelphia merchant and banker Stephen Girard, who provided
needed funds during the difficult years of building and who took a first lien mortgage on the company for $230,000 to complete the section between Reading and
Hamburg. In his honor the portion starting below Reading and ending at Philadelphia was named the Girard Canal. But the initial stock issue of $500,000 was not
enough to complete the works. Eventually $2.2 million was raised to finish the sys-
tem, much of it from among the settlers along the route. The shrewd and frugal
Pennsylvania German farmers knew a good thing when they saw it; families of little
means from Reading to Pottsville bought stock with their meager savings. They also
found employment digging the canal and as boatmen, lock tenders, and maintenance workers when it was finished. The men did not relinquish their attachment to
the soil, however; even when they went into canaling, mining, or railroading, they
held firmly to farms inherited from eighteenth-century ancestors. The women and
children worked the land while the men went off to labor in the new enterprises.[41]

The Pennsylvania legislature, made wary by earlier unfulfilled schemes of internal improvements, had insisted that construction go forward from both ends simultaneously. The system therefore was built in two parts: from the mouth of the
Mill Creek, above Pottsville, to Reading and from Reading to Philadelphia. Total
length was slightly more than 100 miles. Less than half consisted of slackwater
navigation on the river; the remainder was mule-tow canal. A major obstacle was
overcome when a 450-foot tunnel was driven through a mountain near Auburn in
Schuylkill County which had blocked the canal's path. It was the first tunnel of its

type in the United States and was considered one of the greatest engineering feats of the time. Like White's and Hazard's railroad, it attracted visitors from far and wide.[42]

Though the canal had originally been conceived as a route for the movement of general merchandise, by the time of its opening in 1825 coal was expected to provide the most important freight. In 1817 the Schuylkill's managers modestly hoped that traffic in coal might reach 10,000 tons annually. In 1842, after fourteen years of transportation monopoly from the Schuylkill field, the canal actually moved more than 490,000 tons, making it by far the busiest of the anthracite-carrying canals. The profits from the coal trade produced substantial returns to the company's stockholders. Between 1835 and 1839 dividends averaged between 15 and 19 percent annually, and the value of a share of stock rose from $50 to $175. In the 1830s the

The Blue Mountain Dam and lock, Schuylkill Navigation,
Hamburg, Pennsylvania, 1913.
Courtesy of the Pennsylvania Canal Society Collection, Canal Museum, Easton, Pa.

Schuylkill Navigation Company was considered one of the best and safest invest-ments in America.[43]

The canal contributed decisively to the prosperity of an area that had been con-sidered little more than a wilderness only a few years earlier. Fortune hunters and entrepreneurs rushed in to exploit the mineral wealth of the Schuylkill field. Start-ing up in mining in that era required little more capital than did farming; in fact, many of the first coal operators had been farmers. As a result the Schuylkill field from the outset was dominated by a large number of independent operators. As early as 1833 there were 47 separate coal operators shipping over the canal; another 225 bought coal from miners and were engaged only in transport. By the end of the decade almost 600 boats plied the waterway. More than 500 of them were owned by individuals.[44]

The Schuylkill Company soon became a major competitor of other anthracite carriers in eastern markets. Boats arriving in Philadelphia were towed by steam tugs up the Delaware to Bordentown, New Jersey, then were moved through the Delaware and Raritan Canal to New Brunswick, and were again towed by tugs to New York. In 1839 Asa Packer, who started as a boat builder on the Lehigh, designed and built the "Packer Boats," sixty-ton barges equipped with covered hatches and outfitted for coastal navigation, which were pulled by steam tugs in a string of fif-teen or more from Philadelphia to the New York area.[45]

The race to capture a share of the coal market created the third great anthracite canal, the Delaware and Hudson. During the War of 1812 two Philadelphia dry goods merchants, Maurice and William Wurtz, made a move like that of White and Hazard. The Wurtz brothers owned forest lands near Carbondale in the northern Wyoming-Lackawanna field that they knew contained anthracite. In 1816 they mined some coal, dragged it overland to the Delaware, and floated it downstream on rafts to Philadelphia—where the coal failed to sell. Convinced that coal had a future, the brothers again returned to their mine and this time sent 100 tons downriver. When they arrived with their shipment they discovered that White and Hazard had already appeared with their own coal, which had been sold at the price of $8.40 per ton, or below the Wurtz brothers' cost. The Wurtzes then decided that their best hope was to supply the New York market.[46]

Fortunately for the brothers, public confidence in canal enterprises was high when they floated the first stock issue of the Delaware and Hudson Canal Company. On January 8, 1825, $1.5 million worth of shares were offered at the Tontine Coffee House in New York City. Before two o'clock in the afternoon the entire amount was subscribed. The stock attracted investors not only because of potential profits from the canal but also because the company's charters from Pennsylvania and New York allowed it to purchase coal lands and engage in banking, too. The Delaware and

Hudson's entry into the Wyoming-Lackawanna field set a pattern of big-company domination that would characterize that field throughout its history.[47]

Construction began in July 1825. The company attempted to keep the exact route of the canal secret so as to encourage property owners to make gratuitous offers of land. Yet the project, which was sublet to contractors in half-mile sections, assumed such a scale that secrecy became impossible. The entire enterprise was notable for being "the largest undertaking that had ever been entered into upon the continent by any [private] corporation." In 1826 more than 2,500 men—paid wages of $12 to $14 a month—and 200 teams were working on the canal. The project was rushed to completion in 1829, when the first canal boats arrived at tidewater. The work was so costly, however, that the state of New York had to bail out the company with a loan of $500,000 in 1827. As with other internal transportation improvements in the country at the time, this represented a convenient marriage of private enterprise and state government.[48]

The completed canal ran from Honesdale, Wayne County, along the Lacka-waxen River to the Delaware. At Montgap on the Delaware another sixty-five-mile section linked with Roundout on the Hudson. From this point boats floated down river to New York. There was no slack-water navigation as on the Lehigh and Schuylkill canals. A notable feature of the system was its inclined-plane railroad, which transported coal from the Lackawanna Valley over Fairview Mountain to the terminal at Honesdale. Cars were lifted from the mines near Carbondale 1,900 feet up a series of five planes with intervening level stretches. At the top of each plane a steam engine powered large drums around which the pulling chains turned. As with the railroad at Mauch Chunk, one end of the chain was attached to loaded cars and the other end to descending empties. Switching devices on the plane ensured that one string of cars moved into a turnout at the proper moment to avoid collisions. On the descent to the east the cars went down three more planes by gravity. The speed of the loaded cars was partially braked by the ascending empties attached to the other end of their chains. The track, made of wooden rails overlaid with iron, ran for nearly seventeen miles.[49]

Like its sister companies to the south, the Delaware and Hudson became a prosperous enterprise. It made improvements on its canal and railroad that allowed for the movement of ever-increasing tonnages of coal. The company also expanded its coal landholdings until it became one of the biggest operators in the Wyoming-Lackawanna field. Like the Lehigh and Schuylkill companies, it had a near monopoly on coal movements from the northern part of the region. The three great anthracite canal companies together, in fact, demonstrated the commanding position that transportation companies occupied in anthracite. It was a lesson well learned for individuals who later sought to control the industry.

The Lehigh, Schuylkill, and Delaware and Hudson were the key components of what became, in the 1830s, the nation's largest canal network. Taken together, the canals that owed their existence to anthracite constituted the first major inland transportation system in the country. Over the Delaware and Hudson route anthracite moved to the New York market and intermediate locations. From the Lehigh and Schuylkill it went to Philadelphia and then by sea to New York, New England, and southern ports or across New Jersey on the Morris and Delaware and Raritan canals. From the North Branch of the Pennsylvania Canal with its major terminal at Nanticoke, near Wilkes-Barre, it went north to Buffalo in New York state or south to Baltimore. The canals made the anthracite industry possible; hard coal, in turn, created the prosperity that contributed importantly to the economic development of the nation in the decades before the Civil War.[50]

For the farmers and small-town inhabitants who lived along the routes, the canals opened up possibilities of employment and adventure hitherto only dreamed about. Many a young man, looking up from his plow on a Pennsylvania farm, saw

The Delaware and Hudson Canal connected the coal regions to the Hudson River and New York City. Freight boats like these were used to carry coal.
Courtesy of the Pennsylvania Canal Society Collection, Canal Museum, Easton, Pa.

the passing canal boat as his ticket to a life of excitement and travel to faraway places. Perhaps at night, in a canal-side tavern or general store, he listened with envy to exciting tales of high times on the water told by unimaginably experienced boatmen. If his courage were high enough, he might leave home to take work for a couple of seasons as a driver boy. If he survived the grueling eighteen-hour days on the towpath, the ornery mules, and the pomposity of the captain—and actually enjoyed the life—he might decide to take out a company boat. He did not really need any money to start. He was sure to be grubstaked for a round trip by a storekeeper who had a company's guarantee of payment from the captain's earnings.

The independent boat owners on the Schuylkill and the company boatmen on the Lehigh began their runs in April, after the ice broke on the rivers and canals. Except for Sundays, when they tied up to observe the mandatory day of rest, they plied the waterways continuously until November. The captains hired their own crews, consisting of bowsmen and drivers. They also supplied their own mules and upkeep for both crews and animals; storage facilities for provisions and feed were aboard. Mules were furnished by the companies to individuals who did not own them; the animals were paid for in installments taken out of the captain's pay. The captains were paid on a ton-mile basis from loading dock to tidewater, with rates for intermediate stops based on the distances. But earnings were seldom enough to keep men with families. Most had other occupations during the winter months. Some owners were employed as lock tenders and had older sons operate the boats. Other boatmen used members of their families, including wives and children, as crew. Many canalers got their start driving mules for their fathers, went on to become captains of their own boats, and passed on the occupation to their children.[51]

The life of a canaler, however, was anything but romantic, though it did offer a certain amount of independence and mobility. Hours were long, boats moved in all but the worst weather, and there were plenty of hazards—for example, men were sometimes thrown off a badly steered boat and crushed in a lock between the wall and the hull. On the Schuylkill the working day began between three and four in the morning. The bowsman prepared breakfast while the driver boy fed, curried, and harnessed the team. The captain's order, "Gear up your team fust; then you'll get your breakfast," established the order of priorities. By four the boat was usually on the move, the way lit by the "nighthawk" kerosene lamp on the bow. Stops were infrequent, except for waiting to get "locked through" or perhaps to trade some coal for homemade bread and pies at nearby homesteads. As the boat approached the locks the captain announced its coming by sounding a horn or a seashell, called a conch. On an average day the boat traveled about twenty-five miles before being tied up for the night at about nine. Perhaps the hardest job fell to the driver. He was often a boy no more than nine or ten years old, who walked—often barefoot—with the mules throughout the long days. On the Schuylkill there were usually three mules in a team: the lead mule that led and pulled, a middle mule that pulled, and the "shafter." The towline tended to pull the shafter toward the canal, and it was this animal's job, while being pulled sideways, to keep the other mules from going into the water. The driver's job was to walk behind the mules and keep them in line. He often did this with a whip—not to beat the mules but to give them direction. Some drivers became so proficient with their whips that it was said they could flick flies from the lead mule's ear.[52]

Various types of boats were used on the canals. On the Lehigh the most common were hinge boats, or "snappers." They were eighty-seven and one-half feet long and approximately ten feet wide. They came in two sections—hence their name—for ease in loading and unloading. Loaded to capacity of ninety-five tons per section, they drew about five feet of water.[53] Single-piece barges were called "stiff boats." All the boats had cabins aft that were entered by a ladder. Cabins on the Lehigh boats were no more than eight feet by ten feet. They contained two wooden bunks, one above the other, built into the side; a cupboard across one corner; a table that folded against the wall; and a small coal or oil stove for cooking and heat. During the warmest months the stove was usually set up on deck, often beneath a canvas canopy.[54]

Though most boatmen traveled without their families, it was not unusual for a captain to take his wife and several children along during the season. The practice did save on the cost of crews. The wives did the cooking, tended the children, and often steered. The older children helped on the boat and worked as drivers. Sleeping accommodations were limited and living conditions crowded. But the older children could sleep on deck in the summer or in the feed bins. Privacy, however, did not exist. There were no toilet facilities on board. A slop bucket served in the cabin at night; otherwise, there was always a convenient bush along the towpath. Water for cooking and washing was drawn from springs along the way or even from the canal itself. There was no premium on excessive cleanliness, though it was said that some captains took great pride in their snappy appearances.

Storage facilities for food were limited. Provisions had to be purchased in general stores along the way or from farmers. Since no baking was attempted on board, and much of the food was bought in prepared form, costs were generally higher than on land. Boatmen, however, were not reluctant to trade some coal for vegetables and fruits or even to engage in petty larceny. Chickens that wandered onto the towpath were always fair game; on the Morris Canal, as the saying went, "the first five corn rows along the towpath belong to the canaler."[55] The most notable thing about the fare, however, was its sameness. Salt mackerel was a common breakfast food, consumed with bread and strong black coffee. On Sundays roast beef was a special fa-

A canal boat on the Delaware Division Canal, circa 1890. Most boatmen traveled with their families.
Courtesy of the Pennsylvania Canal Society Collection, Canal Museum, Easton, Pa.

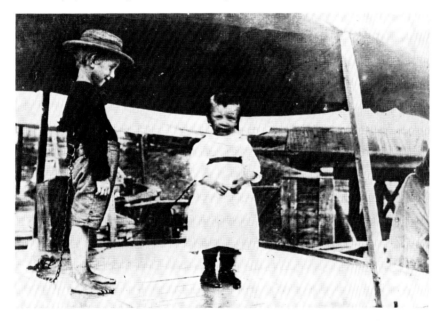

Small children were sometimes fastened to the decks of canal boats for safety.
Courtesy of the Pennsylvania Canal Society Collection, Canal Museum, Easton, Pa.

vorite. But mostly the meals were stews, soups, or boiled and fried combinations. Isabelle Lenstrohm Mann, who was born and raised on the Morris Canal, tells about canalers' soup:

> We made soup called pork float. . . . Everybody made that and it was made from salt pork and our meat was almost always salted because you couldn't keep it unless it was salted. . . . And we used to sauté the pork a little bit before we put it in the soup and the potatoes, onions and tomatoes. Some people like corn in it but we never did. . . . Pepper, salt and a little parsley and a sweet majoram . . . , and it was really delicious. There was bean soups we made and corned beef and cabbage.[56]

Mrs. Mann remembered that another Sunday treat was "Hunks-A-Go-Pudding," made from a batter of flour, salt, milk, and eggs cooked in the grease left over from the beef roast.[57]

Recreation was mostly limited to Sundays when the boats tied up. The adults rested while the children found whatever diversions they could. Marbles, dominoes, and checkers were played, and dolls made from clothespegs, corn husks, and dried apples. Swimming in the canal was a favorite sport for the children. Since youngsters often fell overboard, they almost all learned to swim at an early age. The smallest children usually had ropes tied about their waists so that they could readily be hauled back on the ship. When several boats tied up together there was sure to be music and singing. Many boatmen became accomplished musicians, having taught themselves to play during the long days on the water. When they met at gatherings, impromptu concerts were held with accordions, fiddles, Jew's harps, and even empty beer bottles played with a stick. The made-up songs were often about life on the canal. "Go Along Mule," one of the favorites, goes in part:

> I've got a mule, she's such a fool,
> She never pays no heed.
> I'll build a fire beneath her tail,
> And then she'll show some speed.
>
> > Go along mule.
> > Don't you roll those eyes,
> > You can change a fool, but a doggone mule
> > Is a mule until she dies.
>
> I'm going down to the river now,
> To lay me down and die.
> But if I find that the river's wet,
> I'll wait until it's dry.[58]

Boatmen, of course, were often subjected to ditties of another sort, sung by kids from the shore:

> You rusty canaler
> You'll never get rich
> You'll die in a cabin
> You son-of-a-bitch.[59]

The boatmen were a tough and independent breed not particularly noted for their gentleness. In the early days it was relatively easy to get a boat, a fact that attracted the footloose and irresponsible types found in abundance in the booming coal region. The hoodlums, drunkards, and ne'er-do-wells tended to give the occupation a doubtful place in the public's eye. Insults were frequently exchanged between passing boats; at locks fistfights often broke out over which boat was to go through first.[60] But even the most peace-loving canalers were ready for anything, including piracy. In Philadelphia a gang known as the Schuylkill Rangers was notorious for attacks on canal boat crews. One night, however, the gang made the mistake of attempting to rob the canal boat *Rattlesnake*. Captain Peter Berger, who had a reputation as a fighter, drew a pistol and shot one of the would-be robbers dead. A magis-

Burrowing animals sometimes caused banks to wash out, giving the railroads another advantage over the canals. Courtesy of the Pennsylvania Canal Society Collection, Canal Museum, Easton, Pa.

trate subsequently freed the captain with the remark, "Your pistol did not work well this time. You only killed one man." [61]

There were boatmen, of course, who tried mightily to follow the Christian Way. One of these was the legendary William "Billy Black" McCullough, who worked as a captain on the Lehigh and Morris canals in the latter half of the nineteenth century. As Billy Black himself said, he was the "wildest kind of an Irishman. My uncle was good, my aunt was good. I had no need to go. But I did not wish to be controlled. I was a wayward child, I would not be controlled." He left home at sixteen for life on the canals. Until he was twenty-six he had a fondness for strong drink. Then, suddenly, he found religion and gave it up. But it was hard. There were other distractions. He continued to live in "a wild, rough, uncultivated state," with Sabbath-breaking, swearing, chewing tobacco—"slobbering around"—his special vices. "I was not a robber," he said, "nor a murderer; but I was full of dirt and filth and foolish talk." Like most boatmen, he could discuss mules for hours on end; but, he said, "when the Lord saved me, He put me to talk about other things—the things of His Kingdom. The less you have to do with the animal kingdom, the sweeter will be your spirit." Billy went off to fight in the Civil War. When he returned he brought a strong inclination to drink home with him again. His wife, however, caught him in time. "William," she said, "you were a sober man when I married you, and if you take to drink, I won't live with you." Billy pondered her words and finally came to a decision. "I thought much of her, and would rather part with the drink than with her. A woman has a wonderful influence if she uses it for good, and she has a wonderful influence if she uses it for bad. A woman can do more with a man than a man can do with a woman." [62]

*   *   *

New York and Philadelphia capitalists financed the canal companies that penetrated the anthracite region in the 1820s, but the real pioneers were the men who dug them. When this motley assortment of Irishmen, Pennsylvania Germans, and down-on-their-luck Anglo-Saxons breached the Appalachian wall, they entered a sparsely populated wilderness of forests and mountains. In the entire region only the Wyoming Valley had a settlement—Wilkes-Barre—of any size, and it was little more than an overgrown trading village clinging to the banks of the Susquehanna River. Elsewhere there were a few scattered inns along rough roads like the Easton-Sunbury "turnpike" and isolated communities of a few families whose oldest members dimly recalled the days of Indian attacks. A handful of coal prospectors there might be, but they could only look wistfully at the unpromising rivers and the impossible trails and wonder what to do with their black rocks. If the diggers of the canals chanced to glance up from their back-breaking work, they must have ques-

A mule driver appears to the left of the canal boat. Boatmen were a hardy, independent breed. Drivers were often boys as young as 6 years old and often walked thirty miles a day or more.   Courtesy of the Pennsylvania Canal Society Collection, Canal Museum, Easton, Pa.

tioned why anyone would pay good money to drive a ditch through a place where there were more bears and mountain lions than people. Yet when the canals were finished and coal moved out, people moved in, first by the dozens, then by the hundreds and thousands. Within the lifespan of a generation after 1830, mining towns and settlements spread across all four of the anthracite fields.

The canal companies promoted settlements along their routes; first the supply and labor camps for their construction crews, then the docking and loading facilities for coal at places like Nesquehoning, Summit Hill, and White Haven on the Lehigh. A few houses were built for resident workers, perhaps an inn, sometimes a lumberyard, forming the nucleus of a village. Upstream at the heads of navigation the companies built terminals with wharves, warehouses, storage areas, stables, boatyards, and housing. Here the first real urban centers in the region took root: Pottsville, near the Schuylkill Canal; Mauch Chunk on the Lehigh; Wilkes-Barre on the Northern Branch of the Pennsylvania Canal; and Carbondale on the gravity railroad leading to the Delaware and Hudson. Their locations made them natural points of entry into the surrounding coalfields.

Had the region not possessed coal, it would have remained undeveloped and underpopulated for decades longer. Except for the Wyoming Valley, much of it was unsuitable for agriculture. Before the discovery of coal only the hardy and the strange ventured there. According to legend the first white residents of what became Pottsville were members of the Neiman family, who put up a hut and attempted farming in a place described by an early history as "a veritable mud hole." Local Indians murdered the family, not for intrusion on tribal hunting grounds, but because anyone who chose to dwell in such an unlikely spot had to be crazy and unsafe to be at large, even among red men.[63] As late as 1862 woodcutters at the present site of Shenandoah sometimes fought with local bears for the right to their dinner pails.[64]

Coal made all the difference, of course, and the opening of the canals set off a wild rush to find the black diamonds in the anthracite wilderness. The most frenzied activity occurred in the Schuylkill field. Up north in the Lehigh and Lackawanna fields Lehigh Coal and the Delaware and Hudson, along with Boston, New York, and Philadelphia land companies, bought up a lot of good coal lands even before they proved commercially viable. The same was not true in the Schuylkill, where the canal company was prohibited from owning coal lands. The field appeared to offer unlimited opportunities for individuals. When the canal unlocked the field, speculative fever swept over it. Eli Bowen, a contemporary observer, reported that the Schuylkill was a "gambler's den during the years of feverish land speculation" in the late 1820s and early 1830s, that it "stood in a position equally as tempting to the people of surrounding states, and especially to those of our own [Pennsylvania] as California [during the gold rush]." Joseph Neal, an unsuccessful mine operator, made another comparison: "Young and old were smitten by the desire to march upon the new Peru, rout the aborigines, and sate themselves with wealth." The speculators, half of whom were under twenty, were "in no mood for trifling." They were determined to make a killing. Up the Schuylkill Canal they came, "the grave Quaker, the ejaculating Methodist and the sober Presbyterian," all determined to outwit Lady Chance and each other. Armed with picks and shovels they scoured the mountains surrounding Pottsville by day, furiously traded in real and fictional coal lands by night, and grabbed a few hours sleep on barroom floors, which they rented by the square foot. Along with the gamblers came the miners, "hordes of Tartar-looking people cohabiting together in shanties or tents, ready to engage in the laudable business of penetrating the bowels of the earth."[65]

The great coal rush emptied as many dreams as it did pockets. Many of the confident young men who rode in style up the canal from Philadelphia walked dejectedly back along its route, harassing Pennsylvania German farmers along the way for the remains of supper and a night's sleep in a barn. The more determined set off in search of other coal lands, toward Shamokin and the Susquehanna, up to Hazleton and beyond to the Wyoming and Lackawanna. Those with nothing to lose or no place to call home stayed on, working for others and keeping dim hopes alive. They and the skilled miners from Scotland and Wales settled the rough mining towns.

Within a decade after the canal's opening the Schuylkill field was the region's most populous and productive. Towns and villages appeared virtually overnight. Port Carbon had a single family in 1829; a year later it claimed 912 residents. Minersville, New Castle, St. Clair, Tamaqua, and other settlements experienced the same rapid growth. Between 1826 and 1829 the number of buildings in Pottsville increased sixfold; its population twenty-seven times. And between 1829 and 1844 the number of inhabitants doubled again.[66] As a transportation center and county seat Pottsville became a prosperous boom town, its economy bolstered by the canal and railroads, coal mining, iron manufacturing, brewing, banking, and a host of commercial and mercantile activities. A local capitalist elite formed around land-owning families like the Potts, Pattersons, and Eckarts, families whose men were the first to open coal veins and sink shafts, and found outlying towns like Frackville, Taylorville, and Cressonville. They promoted the canal and railroads, wielded financial, political, and social power, and made their neighborhood around Mahantango Street the business, professional, and intellectual nerve center of the Schuylkill. They established a board of trade in 1832 to further their interests and backed the *Miners' Journal*, which under the editorship of Benjamin Bannan became the leading voice of the anthracite industry, probusiness, pro-Whig, and pro–Anglo Saxon in orientation.[67] By 1850 Pottsville had 7,500 inhabitants, making it the largest mining town in the region and the keystone of the Schuylkill coal trade.

Though the field held the promise of opportunity, the reality was something else. The fortunate speculators and small companies that managed to obtain and exploit coal lands fared poorly. They never accounted for more than a small percentage of the coal mined. Most were marginal operators who failed quickly: 78 percent within five years, 87 percent within ten. They were undercapitalized and inexperienced and used wasteful and inefficient techniques. As Eli Bowen complained in the mid-1850s: "Mining as an art and distinct branch of human industry is scarcely understood at all by a large number of those engaged in the Trade. Probably not one in five has been brought up to the business—many were doubtless never inside of a regularly wrought mine before they found themselves embarked in its affairs."[68] The exhaustion of easily worked veins near the surface and the introduction of deep-shaft mining below the water table, which required expensive technology, also worked against the small operators. As a result, production in the Schuylkill gradually became concentrated among a few major producers. Of more than 100 firms, 16 mined one-half of all coal as early as 1833; by 1868 one-third of the operators had

The terminus of the Schuylkill Canal was Port Carbon.
From Frank Leslie's Popular Monthly, *3 (1877): 125.*

produced three-fourths of the total annual tonnage. The concentration of production capacity roughly paralleled concentration of coal land ownership.[69]

Pottsville's capitalist elite, though dominant in the town, never owned more than a third of the coal lands in the Schuylkill field. Mining did form the original basis of their wealth, but members of the elite diversified their investments in other activities. Most of the coal lands in the field were owned by investors living outside the region: New Englanders William Eaton, Leverett Saltonstall, William Chapman; New Yorkers Cadwallader Colden, Frederick Geisenhaimer, Warren and Franklin Delano, and others; and by far the largest group, Philadelphians such as John Biddle, Joshua Lippincott, Lloyd Wharton, Stephen Girard, and Henry C. Carey. Investors such as these did not mine coal themselves because their state-granted company charters forbade them to be both operators and carriers. They frequently worked through land companies that located the coal veins, improved the land, laid railroads, and built or bought canal boats. They then leased the coal lands to tenant operators, who did the actual mining. While the outside investors did not maintain control over actual mining operations, they nevertheless exerted tremendous influence through their ownership of land.[70]

An example of this type of holding was the coal lands of Stephen Girard, Philadelphia merchant and banker. Girard became interested in the coal trade at an early date. He provided financing for the Schuylkill Canal during a difficult construction stage; later he promoted railroad building in the field. In 1830 he acquired more than 22,000 acres of land in the "middle" anthracite field near Shenandoah. After his death in 1831 the coal lands became part of the Girard estate, controlled by the city of Philadelphia, profits from which were used for an institute for orphaned boys (Girard College) and other benevolent purposes. The Girard estate was divided into tracts which were leased to coal operators for exploitation. The terms of the leases ensured substantial returns. The first lease, for example, was signed with Colonel James J. Connor in 1862. It was for five years with royalty payments on prepared coal of twenty-five cents per ton and ten cents on chestnut coal. The lessee was required to build a breaker that prepared for market no fewer than 100,000 tons annually; erect twelve blocks of tenant houses, with each block containing two two-story houses with attached kitchens; pay for 50,000 tons of coal each active year of the lease; and receive reimbursement of $20,000 maximum for any improvements constructed under the terms of the lease.[71] Eventually ten tracts were leased. Between 1863 and 1884 the lessee coal companies shipped 18.3 million tons of anthracite and paid royalties of more than $5 million dollars to the estate.[72]

Many of the "independent" operators who leased lands in the Schuylkill were Philadelphians; others were backed by Philadelphia financiers. As a result, the field even in its earliest years became to a large degree an internal colony exploited by outside interests. Profits made in the field, like its coal, went elsewhere. The local capitalists participated in the coal trade, controlled secondary activities such as iron manufacturing and banking, and invested in the canal and railroads but did not dominate the field. They could not, later in the century, prevent the great "land grab" by the Reading Railroad or its virtual monopoly over transportation, nor could they break their area's dependence upon one industry by significantly diversifying its economic base. In the long run Pottsville lost its position as the region's leading urban center and became something of an economic appendage to Philadelphia. The downriver city of Reading surpassed it as a major manufacturing center of iron products, railroad equipment, and textiles.

The other towns of the Schuylkill field became to an even greater degree dependent upon the coal trade. Like mining towns throughout the anthracite region, they owed their existence solely to the presence of collieries and the workers employed by them. Many of the smaller villages, or "patches," were owned by the coal companies, like the one built by Colonel Connor on his Girard estate tract. In the company towns, services for the residents were provided by itinerant peddlers or company-owned stores. A small merchant class developed in the larger freehold towns, but it could not become wealthy or powerful enough to challenge the coal companies. As happened elsewhere in the region, local coal operators or businessmen who accumulated capital often moved to Pottsville, to other regional centers, or even outside the region. An example was George H. Potts, who from 1834 to 1845 was the largest individual coal operator in the country. Potts was a man of unusual enterprise: he installed the first steam engine for pumping that allowed mining below the water table; built the second coal breaker in the region; constructed the first boat for carrying coal directly to New York; and invested in successful early experiments in making anthracite iron. Yet he eventually merged his interests with the big coal and iron firm of Lewis Audenried and Company and in 1853 moved to New York to direct it. Potts's career illustrates the pervasive power of multiregional interests in the Schuylkill at an early date. The failure of Pottsville's capitalist elite to control the field's mining, transportation, and many coal-related industries meant, in effect, loss of control over its economic future. The Schuylkill Canal, like the other anthracite canals, opened the region not only to markets for its primary export but also for the outside capital that ultimately made the region an internal colony.

3. Anthracite Ignites an Industrial Revolution

IN 1826 ABRAHAM POTTS BUILT A NEW CONVEYANCE FOR HAULING COAL AT HIS Black Valley mine in Schuylkill County. The contraption attracted a lot of attention because anything that made it possible to bypass the terrible roads in the Schuylkill wilderness was guaranteed to arouse considerable interest. Eventually news of Potts's innovation reached Philadelphia, and a group of Schuylkill Navigation Company officers came into the region on a canal boat to investigate. When they arrived they saw thirteen loaded coal cars standing on wooden rails that extended from the head of canal navigation at Mill Creek to the mine a half mile away. The affable Potts quickly offered a demonstration. He hitched up a single horse to the lead car, ignored some skeptical wisecracks from the group, and had the animal rather easily draw the ton-and-a-half load over the rails. He then informed the canal men that within a decade they would see coal from the region travel to Philadelphia entirely by rail. As they stepped onto their boat for the return trip, the company officers promised to lock up Potts as a lunatic should he ever venture into the City of Brotherly Love.[1]

Potts turned out to be more far-seeing than the skeptical canal managers. He was off the mark by only a few years. On New Year's Day 1842 the Philadelphia and Reading Railroad officially opened the last stretch of its track linking Philadelphia and Pottsville. The event marked the beginning of a new era in anthracite. The canals' near monopoly of coal shipping was broken as the railroads began their amazingly rapid climb to domination, not only of transportation, but of the anthracite industry itself. America's railroads had their real origins in Pennsylvania's anthracite region. The railroad industry developed in the area's difficult mountainous terrain, carrying coal to and from towns and pit sites that canals could not reach. By trial and error, railroad engineers worked out construction techniques and operational methods, invented mechanical devices, and established customs and rules that became part of railroading everywhere.[2]

The first lines were actually part of the canal system, feeder railroads for carrying coal directly from the mines to the canals. Built in the late 1820s and 1830s, they were simple extensions of the rails outside the mines. The railways were made of timber and were secured on notched crossties and bound with iron strapping spiked to the rails. Horses or mules pulled the cars. As more mines opened, lateral lines were built that picked up cars from the feeder lines of collieries along the route. The lateral roads, chartered by the state as public highways, charged tolls (usually a cent and a half per ton per mile) for use of the track. They were built as cooperative

Overleaf: On August 8, 1829, the Stourbridge Lion became the first steam engine locomotive to run in the United States. It was purchased in England by the Delaware and Hudson Canal Company.   Courtesy of the Historical Society of Schuylkill County, Pottsville, Pa.

ventures by groups of mine owners who shared in stocks and profits or by independent promotors who made arrangements with mine owners to have secure outlets to the canals.[3]

The first steam-powered locomotive in North America was purchased by the Delaware and Hudson Canal Company. In 1828 John B. Jervis, head of the company, sent Horatio Allen, an ambitious twenty-five-year-old engineer, to England to size up the possibilities of the new iron horse that Americans were reading about in the newspapers. Greatly impressed by what he saw, Allen placed orders for four iron horses, and in the spring of 1829 the first four-wheeled locomotive arrived in New York City. It looked, said one observer, like a giant grasshopper. "Its driving wheels were of oak-wood, banded with a heavy wrought-iron tire, and the front was ornamented with a large, fierce-looking face of a lion, in bold relief, and it bore the name of 'Stourbridge Lion.'"

That summer Allen sent the locomotive by river and canal to Honesdale, Pennsylvania; and in early August he was ready to test it. Many people worried that the Stourbridge Lion would break the cracked and warped timber railway that ran to the coal mines at Carbondale, or that it would jump the tracks and plunge into the creek. "My reply to such apprehension," Horatio Allen remarked later, "was that it was too late to consider the probability of such occurrences; that there was no other course but to have the trial made of the strange animal which had been brought here at such great expense, but that it was not necessary that more than one should be involved in its fate; that I would take the first ride alone."[4]

As he placed his hand on the handle of the throttle valve, Allen recalled that he "was undecided whether I would move slowly or with a fair degree of speed; but believing that the road would prove safe, and preferring, if we did go down, to go down handsomely and without any evidence of timidity, I started with considerable velocity, passed the curve over the creek safely, and was soon out of hearing of the cheers of the large assemblage present. At the end of two or three miles, I reversed the valves and returned without accident to the place of starting, having thus made the first railroad trip by locomotive on the Western Hemisphere."[5] The experiments with the Lion, however, proved ultimately unsuccessful. The primitive rails were not sufficiently firm to carry a heavy locomotive. Nor was the engine constructed well enough to pull laden coal cars. But Allen's ride on the Lion inaugurated a transportation revolution in America.

Allen soon took his skills to other railroads further west. Ingenious, risk-taking engineers and craftsmen like him and Matthias W. Baldwin were most responsible for the spectacular rise of the railroads in the period before the Civil War. By the 1840s, as Dee Brown has noted, Baldwin and other locomotive builders had transformed the original primitive engines into "the powerful Behemoth that would

*The Rocket, weighing eight and a half tons, was the first locomotive used on the Reading
Railroad. Built in England, it made its first American run in 1838. The Rocket was
used until 1879.   Courtesy of the Historical Society of Schuylkill County, Pottsville, Pa.*

change the face of the earth. The vertical wine-bottle boiler became horizontal;
flanges were placed on the wheels instead of on the tracks; flexible beam trucks were
designed to prevent binding or derailment when the engine rounded curves; a pilot
or cowcatcher was placed on the prow; a weatherproof cab sheltered the engineer
and fireman from the elements; flared spark-arresting smokestacks shaped like bal-
loons, sunflowers, and cabbage heads replaced the straight stacks; boxed oil head-
lamps embellished with elaborate designs made night travel possible; brass-capped
domes filled with sand to give traction to spinning wheels appeared behind the
smokestacks; mellow-toned bells and melodious whistles added both safety and
charm."

Men compared such iron horses to the "wings of the wind," feeling they would
take them anywhere they wanted to go. Orators predicted that railroads would ring
the entire continent and would make America the greatest power on the earth. In
honor of the new technology, cities built lavish new railroad stations in classical
styles; and railroad terms slipped into everyday language. People talked about
"building up a head of steam" or of getting "untracked" or "uncoupled." And what "a
heck of a way to run a railroad"! In small and large towns, rushing down to the sta-

tion to see the train come in was an exciting diversion. Even Henry David Thoreau was impressed by the railroad that ran past Walden Pond. "When I hear the Iron Horse make the hills echo with his snort like thunder, shaking the earth with his feet, and breathing fire and smoke from his nostrils (what kind of winged horse or fiery dragon they will put into the new mythology I don't know) it seems as if the earth had sent a race now worthy to inhabit it."[6]

Much of the earliest railroad construction occurred in the anthracite fields. There men dreamed of building fortunes on the coal trade, now that coal could be moved to market quickly and cheaply. The Schuylkill field was the center of much railroad expansion, and in this field there occurred one of the short, furiously pursued battles between canals and railroads that canals simply could not win. The Schuylkill Navigation Company, unlike its counterparts in the Lehigh and Wyoming-Lackawanna fields, was chartered as a general traffic canal and did not have both transportation and mining rights. Since the company could not mine coal, it kept its tolls low enough to encourage investment in mining by independent operators, who still had to ship over the canal route. The result was a frenzy of speculative activity in the field. The price of coal lands soared from a few cents an acre in 1825 to more than $250 an acre by 1829. Investment capital poured into the field from Philadelphia and the southeastern part of the state. As mining activities expanded into Schuylkill, Columbia, Northumberland, and Dauphin counties, the railroads followed. By 1842 in Schuylkill County alone there were sixty-five miles of incorporated railroads, built at a cost of $650,000, and forty miles of individually owned roads costing $90,000. Most of the lines in the field were later absorbed into the Philadelphia and Reading system.[7]

One of the pioneering figures of the fast-arriving railroad age was the German émigré Frederick List, a scholar-businessman who became one of the foremost promoters of early American industry. His lectures and essays in favor of tariffs to protect young industries gained him a wide following, as did his important book *The National System of Political Economy*. In the late 1820s while List was the editor of the German-American newspaper the *Readinger Adler* ("Reading Eagle"), he predicted that railroads would play a pivotal role in the development of the anthracite industry. And he gambled his own money on it, buying coal lands along the Little Schuylkill River near present-day Tamaqua and persuading a group of prominent Reading citizens to organize a railroad company which would link these coal purchases with the Schuylkill Canal. When construction costs outran the ability of the Reading investors to raise capital, List turned to Philadelphia, the nation's financial center, and interested Stephen Girard, America's wealthiest man, in the project. With the help of Girard and other Philadelphia financiers, the Little Schuylkill Navigation, Railroad, and Coal Company, linking Tamaqua with Port Clinton, was completed in 1831. It was one of the first railroad corporations chartered in Pennsylvania.[8]

As anthracite shipments on the Schuylkill Canal increased and the company prospered, investors and owners of coal land, like Girard, cast covetous eyes on the trade, well aware of the financial success of the British coal-carrying Stockton and Darlington Railroad. Soon talk of a through road linking the mines with tidewater, and competing directly with the canal, was heard in Philadelphia. Plans already were under way for a railroad from Philadelphia to Reading. The completion of the Little Schuylkill meant that a distance of only fifty-four miles would separate the two railroads. Philadelphia financial groups were active in both enterprises, and in 1833 the two lines merged to form the Philadelphia and Reading Railroad Company.[9]

The Reading became the largest of the great anthracite railroads, one of the most powerful railroads in all of America. Its managers and technicians were the first to face and solve many engineering and financial problems of the early railroad industry. Under the hard-driving, sometimes reckless leadership of men like Franklin B. Gowen, the Reading came to dominate the entire Schuylkill field. There, within a half century of its organization, it effectively eliminated the competition of the canal, gained a near monopoly of coal transportation, became the major holder of coal lands, and, in its relations with labor, government, and the public, demonstrated the gathering power of large business enterprise.[10]

The Reading, however, began its rise to power inauspiciously. It was chartered as a corporation at a time of Jacksonian outrage over the shipping monopolies of the Delaware and Hudson and the Lehigh Coal and Navigation companies. The public and the press were complaining that these giant companies charged excessively high rates and stifled fair competition. Both companies were also buying large tracts of coal land. Sensitive to these pressures, the state legislature refused to grant the Reading the right to own or operate coal mines, chartering it purely as a transportation company with capital stock fixed at $1 million. The company ran into other problems. The panic of 1837 created a gloomy investment climate and, as a result, the Little Schuylkill Railroad was unable to complete its project of linking the Reading's lines with the coalfields. This difficulty undermined the Reading's original purpose. Finally there was opposition from turnpike and canal interests, who lobbied in financial circles and government agencies against the new railroad company.[11]

That the Reading was able to survive at all was testimony to the imagination and tenacity of its managers and other individuals who believed in the future of railroads. Nothing could be done about the prohibition against owning coal lands, but efforts could be made to improve the financial situation. Intensive activity took place on several fronts. The railroad persuaded the state legislature to amend its charter to allow it to build a connecting line from Reading to the edge of the coalfield

at Port Clinton. The Bank of the United States was drawn into the project; it provided help during the financial panic, became a major stockholder, and served as the
Reading's fiscal agent. The railroad's managers persuaded the stockholders to grant
them powers to borrow all necessary funds. The managers made connections with
New York banking interests and through them tied into the world's leading financial circles in London. The English banking firm of McCalmont Brothers and
Company became the Reading's financial agent, purchased stock, and subsequently
played a leading role in the railroad's finances for four decades. Despite these efforts,
however, the Reading remained on the brink of bankruptcy during its early years.
First and then second mortgages were held on it; its bonds at times sold for under 75
percent of par or less, and its debt was so huge that few expected it to survive. By the
early 1840s its creditors were so dismayed that they began slapping judgment after
judgment on the company. Its locomotives were often seized by sheriffs to satisfy
creditors' claims; wages and salaries were used to pay bills and redeem attached
property. Working for the Reading became as great a speculative adventure as investing in it.[12]

Most of the opposition to the Reading came from canal interests. Philadelphia
capitalists with holdings in the Schuylkill Navigation Company mounted a campaign of vilification against the railroad designed to discourage investors. They
claimed that the railroad would never be solvent. Soon the newspapers and magazines were filled with charges and countercharges by the champions of the two
routes. The battle even reached the Bank of the United States. Nicholas Biddle, the
bank's president, claimed that a stockholders' committee investigating its management practices was inspired by Joshua Lippincott, its chairman and president of the
Schuylkill Navigation Company, who opposed the bank's support of the railroad.[13]
When Robert McCalmont, the head of the London banking firm, came to investigate
the Reading's loan request for the building of a second track, the canal company's
managers attempted to dissuade him. McCalmont was told that the railroad's plans
to move 300,000 to 400,000 tons of coal a year would wear out the rails in three
years and would cripple the carrier. The shrewd McCalmont listened quietly and
then replied: "Gentlemen, you have entirely removed the only doubt I ever had of
the safety of my investment. You admit in all your arguments that there are 300,000
or 400,000 tons of coal to be carried. That has been my only doubt. If the railroad can
get the tonnage, I will see to it that it charges enough to buy new rails as fast as they
are needed."[14]

When the Reading opened its route to the Schuylkill field in 1842, competition
with the canal escalated from words to rate war. Both transportation companies dramatically cut shipping charges. An agent of the Reading wrote: "If we can't bring
coal down *a dollar and a quarter cheaper* than the Schuylkill Navigation *we are*

broke." To this statement a representative of the canal company responded, "There is not in the State of Pennsylvania a professional engineer who will now affirm that the Reading . . . can maintain a successful competition with the Schuylkill Naviga-tion."[15] The words of the Reading agent were more prophetic. The railroad boldly slashed its rates to fifty-four cents a ton for coal shipped from Mount Carbon to Philadelphia, thirty-six cents per ton lower than the prevailing canal rate. This was a daring ploy, given the precarious financial condition of the company. But it worked. By 1845 the Reading was shipping 820,000 tons of anthracite, as compared with slightly more than 263,000 tons for the canal. After only three years of direct competition, the Schuylkill Navigation Company had lost 40 percent of its coal busi-ness and more than 30 percent of its total tonnage to the railroad.[16]

Still the canal company fought on. In 1846 it made extensive improvements of the navigation system intended to increase its tonnage capacity. But these failed to restore its competitive position. Their cost brought the canal company to the brink of bankruptcy, and it was forced into a cooperative pooling arrangement with the Reading. Despite some recovery of its financial situation in the 1850s, the Schuylkill Navigation was never really competitive again. In 1870 the canal's final demise was

One of the Reading Company's iron horses that pulled loaded coal cars to the canal dock, circa 1887.   Courtesy of the Historical Society of Schuylkill County, Pottsville, Pa.

assured when the Reading took possession of its property and works in a leasing arrangement, "thus terminating in a friendly spirit . . . a rivalry that had existed so many years."[17]

The triumph of the anthracite railroads over the canals could not have happened without a revolution in American iron making. The most important equipment the railroads used—boilers, locomotives, carriages, wheels, couplings, rails—were made of iron, iron capable of withstanding enormous stress. Before the 1840s American iron makers had difficulties making such products. Compared to the British, who made the best iron in the world, the American industry was pathetically primitive. Most iron was still made on so-called "iron plantations" located in remote rural areas close to ore deposits and ample supplies of wood for making charcoal. The technology on the plantations had advanced little since the eighteenth century. Wood was reduced to charcoal by a long, tedious burning process. The fuel was then heated in furnaces to proper temperature by blowers driven by water-powered wooden machinery. Output was small. Few iron furnaces produced more than twenty or twenty-five tons weekly. Their locations also were a drawback. In Pennsylvania iron was made before the War for Independence in the southeastern part of the state, but the industry gradually shifted to central and western counties during the early nineteenth century. Newly discovered ore deposits and large forest lands assured the supply of raw materials, but the furnaces were far from good transportation routes and forges where iron products were manufactured. For all these reasons American blacksmiths and manufacturers relied upon cheaper, higher-quality British iron.

A major problem for early railroad builders was obtaining good iron rails in large quantities. Americans simply did not produce them. The old wooden rails with iron strapping proved inadequate as loads grew heavier and volume increased. Josiah White and Erskine Hazard were forced to turn to England for rails for their Ashley Planes inclined railroad. Other railroad builders did the same. In the early 1840s the New York and Erie Railroad was desperate for rails to complete a track from Port Jervis to Binghamton. But English production could not keep up with both domestic and foreign demand. As the railroad building boom got under way, the American iron industry simply had to modernize its method for producing iron products. The key was to find a cheaper, more abundant, and efficient fuel for making iron.

English and American ironmakers had been experimenting with anthracite as a substitute for charcoal since the 1820s. The success of blacksmiths and manufacturers of iron products in using hard coal to reheat iron encouraged them, but they could not make the breakthrough required to produce the basic product. The difficulty lay in creating a high and constant temperature inside the furnace sufficient to reduce the raw materials to molten iron. Frederick W. Geissenhainer, an American clergyman, successfully accomplished this goal at his Valley Furnace on Silver Creek in Schuylkill County in 1836, but he died before he could begin commercial production. David Thomas, a Welsh ironmaster, became the first person to make anthracite iron in large quantities.

In 1837 Solomon Roberts, Josiah White's nephew, was in Britain inspecting rails for Lehigh Coal's Ashley Planes railroad. News reached him of the successful smelting of iron ore with anthracite. Roberts immediately visited the ironworks belonging to George Crane at Yniscedwin in Wales, where the new anthracite furnace was located. After inspecting the operation and talking with Thomas, Crane's ironmaster, he reported back to his uncle. White and Hazard had been trying to make iron with anthracite for years, but rather than waste time on further efforts, the partners decided that Hazard should go to Wales and persuade Crane to come to America and build a furnace for them. Crane refused to leave his flourishing business, but he suggested that Thomas go instead. It was Thomas, after all, who had built the furnace.

After drawn-out contract negotiations that would eventually make him a wealthy man, Thomas agreed to emigrate. On his arrival in the United States he immediately began building furnaces for the new Lehigh Crane Iron Company, organized by White, Hazard, and a group of other Philadelphia investors. The works were located on the banks of the Lehigh River at Catasauqua, near Allentown, Pennsylvania. On July 3, 1840, the first furnace was successfully blown in by Thomas; the following day its first cast was made. The furnace produced fifty tons of good foundry iron weekly. Along with the four other furnaces Thomas built at the works, it made the Lehigh Crane Iron Company the first in America to achieve commercial success using anthracite to make iron. This was a monumental breakthrough for American industry.[18]

White and Hazard strategically located Lehigh Crane to take advantage of natural resources and transportation. Nearby in the Lehigh Valley were substantial deposits of iron ore and of limestone, which was used for flux in the furnaces. The furnaces stood above the Lehigh Canal, which brought coal from the fields just to the north and which carried the iron on to the big eastern markets.

Thomas's furnaces at Catasauqua employed a hot-blast method originally conceived by James Neilson and two associates in Scotland in 1828. He adapted Neilson's concept of heating air in a chamber before it was blasted into the furnace. This technique required much less fuel to raise the temperature to the melting point of the ore and reduced fuel consumption in the furnace. The first furnace he constructed for Lehigh Crane was similar to traditional charcoal furnaces, except for the addition of a hot-blast stove placed on the ground next to it. The stove consisted

A thriving iron industry grew up along the anthracite canals. Under David Thomas, the Lehigh Crane Iron Works in Catasauqua on July 3, 1840, became the first anthracite furnace to smelt iron commercially.
Courtesy of the Pennsylvania Canal Society Collection, Canal Museum, Easton, Pa.

of four chambers, each with twelve U-shaped pipes manifolded together so that the cold blast air passed through each pipe in succession. The air became progressively hotter as it passed through the pipes before entering the furnace. The air originated in specially manufactured iron blowing cylinders. The power for the blast was provided by a large breastwheel propelled by water from the canal. Eventually powerful coal-fueled steam engines replaced the water source.[19]

Thomas's success at Catasauqua was soon duplicated elsewhere. In 1842 William Henry made pig iron with anthracite at a site in the Lackawanna Valley of northeastern Pennsylvania. Henry, a geologist, had purchased land in the Lackawanna for a blast furnace because he believed the valley contained the right combination of water power, iron ore, limestone, and coal. Despite the inaccessibility of the area, he persuaded Seldon Scranton, his son-in-law, and George Scranton, Seldon's brother, to invest $20,000 in the venture. The Scrantons, who operated the Oxford Iron Works in Oxford, New Jersey, made the equipment for Henry's furnace and sent it to him for assembly.[20]

Since there was little demand locally for iron, the major problem was transporting it to outside markets and selling it at competitive prices. With no solution in sight, George Scranton took over from Henry and reoriented the business. If he could not sell pig iron, he would sell nails. To do so, however, he would need to purchase a rolling mill and nail factory, which would cost another $86,000. Once again the Scrantons tapped their family resources. Joseph and Erastus Scranton, two cousins and prosperous merchants of Augusta, Georgia, put up most of the required funds; the remainder was obtained from the New York merchant John Howland. By 1843 the Scrantons were producing nails. But once more reality defeated optimism. The nails were too brittle because of the low quality of the Lackawanna ore; furthermore, overland transport by wagon to Carbondale on the Delaware and Hudson Canal, and Pittston on the Susquehanna River, raised costs prohibitively. The nail business went the way of the pig iron.

The desperate Scrantons took a long shot. Since they could not sell pig iron or nails, maybe they could sell rails. At first glance, the idea appeared preposterous. English iron makers produced the best rails in the world and completely dominated the American market. In addition the Scrantons would have to borrow another $90,000 just to build a rail mill. Yet luck was on their side again. The New York and Erie Railroad could not obtain rails for its route from Port Jervis to Binghamton, which was located not far from the Lackawanna Valley. Somehow the Scrantons persuaded the directors of the railroad not only to give them the contract for the rails but also to advance the money for the mill.[21]

The Scrantons now faced the daunting task of constructing a mill and making thousands of tons of rails, something no American had done before. First they had to learn to make rails, then they had to manufacture the proper machinery. They then had to import large quantities of iron ore and limestone from downstream counties on the Susquehanna because the geologist Henry had misjudged the quality and quantity of local ores. For that purpose they had to construct a flotilla of barges. Finally they had to organize large numbers of wagon teams and improve roads so that they could cart the rails overland through the wilderness to the construction site. All the while they wasted valuable time reassuring their New York investors, who not surprisingly developed cold feet. But the work went on, and astonishingly, on December 27, 1848, just four days before the railroad's charter expired, the Scrantons completed the project.[22]

During the dark days of the early 1840s, George Scranton described himself as "worried most to death for fear we can't meet all [financial obligations]. I cannot stand trouble & excitement as I once could. I don't sleep good. my appetite is poor & digestion bad. . . . If we can succeed in placing Lacka.[wanna] out of debit it would help me much."[23] George's nerves undoubtedly improved after fulfillment of the Erie contract. The family's fortunes took off in subsequent years. Debts were paid off, Scranton holdings expanded, and a lucrative business built up. In 1853 the Scrantons incorporated their $800,000 Lackawanna Iron and Coal Company with the help of New York capital. That year they also completed two railroads, one running north from Scranton to connect with the Erie in New York state, the other running east to the Delaware River at Stroudsburg. These roads, eventually consolidated into the Delaware, Lackawanna, and Western, provided both a market for the products of their iron company and an outlet for coal from the mines which they soon opened.

The successes of David Thomas and the Scrantons opened a new era for American industry. The availability of abundant, inexpensive, good-quality iron spurred the development of the railroad and metalworking industries. Anthracite broke the dependence on wood and water as energy sources in manufacturing, and its use in iron making permitted the adaptation of machinery such as steam boilers. The ease with which anthracite could be used encouraged the growth of factories, large-scale production, and industrialization generally. With Americans able to produce large quantities of high-caliber iron and the fabrication plants it made possible, the development of modern industry was assured.

Hard coal from northeastern Pennsylvania was responsible for the transformation of American manufacturing in the 1830s and 1840s. Anthracite had begun moving over wagon roads and river routes to eastern markets in some quantities during the 1820s. Its advantages as a clean, long-burning, and cheap fuel were evident to metal manufacturers even then. A ton of anthracite selling for $7.50 to $8.00 in the metalworking center of Philadelphia did the work of 200 bushels of charcoal at $0.06 to $0.08 a bushel. Metalworkers using Virginia bituminous found that savings of as much as 50 percent were made by substituting anthracite. In those years furnaces and foundries in eastern Pennsylvania, New Jersey, and New York widely adopted hard coal for the reheating and working of pig iron, even in rural areas near iron plantations where charcoal was comparatively cheap. Then, in the 1830s, with the opening of the canals, anthracite production and shipments increased dramatically as investors rushed into the booming region to start new mining operations. In 1828 hard coal production stood at more than 91,000 tons. By 1835 it had increased to more than 670,000 tons, and it passed the 1-million-ton mark in 1840. Only nine years later production tripled to more than 3 million tons. As increasing quantities of coal moved to cities and industries along the canal routes, to the big urban centers of Philadelphia and New York, and to New England and other coastal locations, its price continued to fall. In 1842 it dropped to less than $4 a ton and remained in that range until the mid-1850s. No other available fuel could compete in either price or quality; American industry had found a new source of power.

"The sudden availability of inexpensive anthracite during the 1830s," historian Alfred Chandler writes, "had a profound effect on the output, technology, location and organization of several major American industries."[24] As early as the 1820s most eastern blacksmiths were already replacing wood and bituminous with hard coal. It was cheaper and gave off less sulfur and other fumes that tended to contaminate the iron being processed. For these reasons nail and wire manufacturers also adopted the fuel for reheating wrought iron. In the 1830s technical innovations were introduced that permitted manufacturers of iron products to refine wrought iron from cast pig iron by using anthracite in the puddling and rolling process. With more cheap fuel becoming available than ever before, rolling mills using wrought iron were able to cut production costs substantially. In 1840 the success of the Lehigh Crane Iron Company in using anthracite to make pig iron gave a new impetus to the industry. Production of pig iron soared as new furnaces were built. There were 6 anthracite furnaces in the United States—all in Pennsylvania—that made iron at the end of 1840. Six years later there were 42 such furnaces in Pennsylvania and New Jersey. And by 1856 there were 121 anthracite furnaces in the country—93 in Pennsylvania—with many more built in the following years. Pig iron production is estimated to have increased nationally from approximately 220,000 tons in 1842 to more than 750,000 tons in 1847. By the mid-1840s anthracite-produced pig iron was being made in Pennsylvania for $12 a ton, compared with $16 for charcoal-made pig.[25]

The introduction of the hot-blast method of making pig iron from anthracite resulted in a major relocation of iron production in the United States. New iron furnaces were built along the Susquehanna in the Wyoming-Lackawanna area and in the Schuylkill and Lehigh valleys. The location of these works astride or near the great anthracite fields assured an abundant supply of cheap fuel. Their product was shipped over the canals, and later railroads, to the new rolling mills and fabricating plants built along the transportation routes in cities like Allentown, Bethlehem, Reading, Norristown, Phoenixville, Philadelphia, and Wilmington. The cost-saving advantages to the iron industry of using anthracite were increased even more by low transportation rates. Iron was shipped from eastern Pennsylvania to New York and Philadelphia for about one dollar a ton, compared with five to eight dollars a ton for charcoal iron from the older furnaces in central Pennsylvania.[26]

By the 1840s anthracite had made possible the widespread adoption of steam engines for power in both iron making and manufacturing. The bellows and other machinery in the new Pennsylvania furnaces were powered by steam, as were almost all the new plants making iron products. The ample supplies of fuel, new sources of iron, and use of steam technology allowed for greatly expanded production. The modern factory system of manufacturing came in, with its large labor force, standardization, subdivision of functions and continuous operation. The old-style metalworking plant that turned out a small volume of a diversified line of products was gradually replaced by the specialized mill that manufactured a large quantity of a standard product. In the sector of the iron industry that manufactured for the railroads, specialized factories made rails, locomotives, wheels and axles, steam engines, and other equipment. As the factory system spread throughout the metalworking industry, and the method of fabricating and assembling interchangeable metal parts took hold, specialized manufacturers appeared that made a wide array of products—from steam engines to stoves, from agricultural equipment to firearms. These large metalworking enterprises created the demand, in turn, for a machine tool industry. In the 1840s and 1850s, a period of significant innovation in machine tool design and development, manufacturers who made tools for other industries were established in Hartford, Providence, Springfield, and Philadelphia.[27]

Other fuel-intensive industries basic to industrialization, such as food processing, breweries, glass, paper making, textiles, ceramics, chemicals, and india rubber, benefited from anthracite. Like the metalworking manufacturers, these new large-scale factories clustered in the towns and cities of the Northeast, close to their biggest markets and to transportation systems that brought them coal and other raw materials and carried off their finished products. Anthracite mining itself changed

An anthracite colliery in Centralia, probably in the 1880s. Such collieries were vast factories for the mining, processing, and shipping of coal.   Courtesy of the George Bretz Collection, Albin O. Kuhn Library, University of Maryland, Baltimore County.

Coal refuse plane of a breaker probably in the 1880s.
Courtesy of the George Bretz Collection, Albin O. Kuhn Library, University of Maryland, Baltimore County.

with the new technology. The use of steam power for pumping water and for lifting and driving air fans, and the availability of mass-produced iron rails, made it possible to drive deep mines below water levels. Since greater capital investment was required by the new technology, along with the acquisition of extensive coal lands, anthracite mining became increasingly concentrated in big companies which employed large numbers of wage workers and a new strata of managers and supervisors.[28]

After mid-century the combination of anthracite, iron, and railroads propelled Pennsylvania's Lehigh and Lackawanna valleys into the industrial age. Lehigh Crane's commercial success prompted the founding of other iron companies along the Lehigh and its tributaries. Eventually the construction of feeder railroads and their connection with the big anthracite carriers and the canal allowed ironworks to locate close to ore deposits. Iron production in the valley soared. In 1850 five companies operated thirteen anthracite blast furnaces at Glendon, South Easton, Allentown, Catasauqua, and Coplay on the Lehigh. A decade later there were six companies operating thirty-three furnaces, and by the end of the 1860s, with the completion of the railroads, ironworks were under construction in half a dozen towns and hamlets away from the river. By 1873 the Lehigh Valley was the biggest producer of anthracite iron in Pennsylvania, which led all other states with 49 percent of total production. That year the valley's forty-seven furnaces produced 390,000 tons.[29]

The railroads were the major beneficiaries of the anthracite iron industry, though the growth of one would have been impossible without the other. For many years the railroads consumed as much as 50 percent of the iron and steel industry's total output in the form of rails, locomotives, cars, and railroad bridges. But anthracite iron making also spawned a multitude of other related industrial activities in the valley. Surrounding the iron works in the cities and towns were manufacturing concerns that turned out boilers, pumps, tools, fencing, rails, pipes, structural iron for bridges and buildings, and a variety of other products. Clay deposits in Allentown created a brick-making industry that supplied firebricks for blast furnaces and later for new factories and houses for the expanding work force. Limestone discovered by the builders of the Lehigh Canal formed the basis of a major cement industry. The limestone was used first to make "cement rock" as a masonry sealant in canal locks, then in the iron furnaces, and finally as a construction material in the valley's great housing boom of the 1860s. The rapid urbanization of Allentown, Bethlehem, Easton, and surrounding areas that accompanied industrialization spurred demand for all sorts of lumber materials—and for the builders and craftsmen who turned them into finished products. With the completion of branch railroads in the 1860s the new slate industry in the northern reaches of the valley began to flourish. Finally, the exploitation of zinc deposits led to the manufacture of paint, zinc sheeting, and zinc galvanizing of iron and steel.[30]

Farther to the north in the Lackawanna Valley, Scranton emerged as the major industrial center of the anthracite region. The original 500-acre tract of land, for which the Scrantons had paid Henry $8,000, was worth many times more than that by mid-century—for the coal under it and the improved land on the surface. The Scrantons exploited its full potential, laying out streets, selling lots, building company houses for workers and mansions for themselves. They encouraged outsiders with capital and entrepreneurial talent to settle there, often recruiting them personally. They wanted bankers, merchants, agricultural processors, real estate developers and the ever-necessary lawyers. Since Scranton's population grew by almost a thousand persons annually during the 1850s, investors from nearby towns like Towanda and Montrose needed little prompting. The money went into coal and coal-related industries, such as engine manufacturing, lumber, and gunpowder works. But the newcomers also founded diversified enterprises which established Scranton as a major manufacturing center. One example was Thomas Dickson, an English immigrant who came by way of Carbondale. With the financial backing of the Scranton family he started a foundry and machine shop in 1856; by 1863 his Dickson Manufacturing Company, capitalized at $800,000, was making locomotives, railroad cars, engines, and other iron products. He later joined a group of Scranton capitalists who organized the First National Bank, the largest and most important financial institution in the city.

Scranton grew spectacularly between 1850 and 1880, its population jumping from 1,000 to 45,000. It became known as the "Anthracite Capital of the World." But its reputation also rested on manufacturing. The city's factories produced everything from mining and railroad machinery to food products, stoves, iron goods, building materials, carriages, and apparel. The Woolworth family and its partners, the Kirbys, got their start there with the merchandising techniques that made them world famous. Four major anthracite railroads built terminals and maintenance yards, establishing the city as a leading transportation center.

The attitude of the Scrantons and the group associated with them was decisive in making the city the largest industrial center in northeastern Pennsylvania. They were venture capitalists willing to take enormous risks and not simply transfixed by coal. In many ways they were classic nineteenth-century liberals, open to new ideas, fascinated by material growth and progress, encouraging of new endeavors. As a capitalist class they did not close themselves up in an exclusive domain but remained willing to take in new men. They built industry but also a city and endowed it with parks, a hospital, a library, and modern urban services. Though aggressive defenders of their order and interests, they made a place for others. When immigrants swelled the city's working class, the elite reached accommodations in the political arena. In 1880 Terence V. Powderly, national president of the Knights of Labor, became the Irish mayor of Scranton.[31]

*   *   *

The combination of coal, iron, and railroads created vast opportunities for men of enterprise willing to take risks. Every part of the anthracite region had such men. They started with virtually nothing and built industrial empires. Several were remarkable in their achievements. One such man was Asa Packer. In the winter of 1833 Packer rode into Mauch Chunk on a sled, looking for a job. The twenty-eight-year-old carpenter had heard that men were wanted to run boats on the recently opened Lehigh Canal. To that point in his life, Dame Fortune had not exactly courted Packer; the Connecticut native had worked as an apprentice tanner, had tried farming, and had plied his carpenter's craft in New York City and along the Pennsylvania frontier—without apparent success. The little town of Mauch Chunk must have looked good to him, even in the dead of winter.

View of Mauch Chunk, an anthracite boom town, circa 1860.
Courtesy of the Pennsylvania Canal Society Collection, Canal Museum, Easton, Pa.

Packer got his job and returned to Mauch Chunk from his Susquehanna County home in the spring of 1834 when the ice broke on the canal. He took boats down to Philadelphia and was so impressed by the potential of the coal trade that he persuaded James Blakslee, his brother-in-law, to join him. The following year he contracted for two boats, one of which he placed in command of Blakslee. Packer guarded his profits closely, but he was willing to take chances. Within two years he had enough money to purchase a general store on the banks of the Lehigh which sold supplies to boatmen and miners. As soon as the business was established, Packer made Blakslee the general manager, then turned to a new enterprise.

Packer had the good luck to arrive in Mauch Chunk just as it became Pennsylvania's most famous boom town. White's and Hazard's decision to headquarter the Lehigh Coal and Navigation Company there had transformed the little river outpost in the mountainous wilderness into a thriving transportation and mining center serving the Lehigh field. When Lehigh Coal opened the company town in 1831 in order to spur its development, outsiders like Packer saw their chance. With coal production in the surrounding mountains increasing and work begun on the expansion of the canal upstream, there were plenty of opportunities. Packer recognized the growing need for canal boats and he finally put his carpentry skills to good use by establishing a boatyard. Soon afterward he began building canal locks for Lehigh Coal on the upper Lehigh. By 1840 the boatyard was so successful that he decided to open another on the Schuylkill Canal near Pottsville. In partnership with his brother he built larger, seaworthy boats capable of making the run down the canal and directly on to New York across open water.

These sundry enterprises brought Packer substantial profits, but his ambition was not sated. Back in Mauch Chunk in the early 1840s, he purchased coal lands on the Nesquehoning Creek. When the coal company he established began production, he shipped coal from his mines and those of neighboring operators on his boats. His practice of bringing brothers, nephews, brothers-in-law, and other kinsmen into his businesses, or helping them get started as merchants and coal operators, made Packer the head of an extensive financial network tied together by family, friendships, and interlocked interests. By 1850 Packer was the richest man in Mauch Chunk.[32]

Newcomers like the "Yankee" Packer clan and the Pennsylvania Germans helped Lehigh Coal make Mauch Chunk a center of mining, transportation, merchandising, banking, and small manufacturing by the mid-1840s. It was not long before the town attracted the attention of eastern money interests. In 1846, as the Reading began to demonstrate the profitability of railroads in the anthracite industry, a group of Philadelphia investors led by Edward R. Biddle obtained a charter to build a rival line farther north. They planned to run it through the Lehigh Valley and on to Mauch Chunk in order to tap into the transportation area largely monopolized by the Lehigh Canal. Packer and his associates, who saw a clear advantage in breaking Lehigh Coal's hold, immediately invested in the new railroad corporation. Faced with the possibility of dangerous new competition, the canal company did not sit by idly; it played a role in convincing suspicious Philadelphia capitalists that building a railroad into the mountainous mining area was an extremely difficult and costly venture. As a result, stock in the multimillion-dollar enterprise did not sell well.

With construction delayed, Packer waited until the railroad company's charter was due to expire in 1851. Then he marshaled his resources and those of his family and friends to purchase a majority of the outstanding stock. His decision to build the railroad in the face of widespread investor skepticism was a major gamble. To that time only big financial groups in cities like Philadelphia and New York could raise the millions needed for canals and railroads. Those interests controlled the transportation routes; they usually left it to the smaller local entrepreneurs to develop the products that were shipped. From the outset there was considerable doubt that Packer could do the job. Few people realized then what a determined man he was.

Packer threw his entire personal fortune into the enterprise, as well as substantial sums of his associates. He borrowed heavily in tight money markets, putting up railroad stock as collateral. Yet it was hardly enough. Time after time in the early 1850s, as one problem after another arose during construction, Packer danced on the edge of bankruptcy. Building costs soared as the right-of-way was pushed beyond the Lehigh Gap between the soaring mountains and winding river. The cost of materials suddenly shot up. A cholera epidemic swept through his construction crew. Nervous bankers shut off lines of credit. Rumors flew in financial circles about the impending failure of the venture. But somehow Packer held on. He pulled his backers in so deeply that they had to give him more time and risk even more money. He wheeled and dealed with other carriers, especially the Central Railroad of New Jersey and its president, John Taylor, a personal friend he appointed to his board of directors. At critical moments Packer always managed to scrape together enough funds to stave off disaster. Finally, in 1855 the forty-six-mile main line of the Lehigh Valley Railroad between Mauch Chunk and Easton was completed. Packer and his adopted town had a rail outlet through Easton via the Central of New Jersey and the canals to New York and Philadelphia. The railroad also passed through the growing iron-making center of the Lehigh Valley.

Packer soon made the line profitable by shipping coal from his own lands and those of his relatives and friends. With chief engineer Robert Sayre (whom Packer lured from the rival Lehigh Coal) in charge, feeder lines were pushed into newly opened coal lands to the west and north. Shipping rates were kept competitive; by

1868 the Lehigh Valley carried more than twice the amount of coal and freight as its chief competitor, the Lehigh Canal. That year the railroad's stock was worth a phenomenal $16 million. Packer's gamble had paid off. He had become one of the wealthiest men in Pennsylvania, had made others rich, and had transformed Mauch Chunk into one of the most important towns in the anthracite region.[33]

From the 1850s on, the character of Mauch Chunk changed appreciably. The gritty little company town became a prosperous shipping center. It boasted more concentrated wealth than any other town in the Lehigh field; in 1870 it probably had the highest mean per capita income of any city in the United States. Fifty of its residents were each worth more than $50,000; Packer's holdings and personal wealth exceeded $10 million.[34] Money flowed in from coal, transportation, and services. It built impressive new buildings, including Lehigh Coal's massive brick headquarters and a collection of fine homes along "Millionaire's Row" on a ridge overlooking the town. Mauch Chunk's scenic location added to its attraction. The railroad brought affluent tourists from New York and Philadelphia to this "Switzerland of America." They disembarked from the train at the foot of a new resort hotel, eager to take the mountain airs, ride the scenic gravity railroad, see and be seen in the new opera house, and bask in the warm, self-congratulatory atmosphere of capital gains.

Packer himself began to practice the good life. He enjoyed the diversions of political office. As a state legislator in the 1840s he secured an act that made Mauch Chunk the seat of Carbon County. He earned the title of "Judge" Packer, as he liked to be called, by serving five years as an associate county justice. In 1852 he was elected to Congress, and he served for two terms. He had the reputation in Washington of being a party "regular," always voting with the majority and supporting incumbent presidents Pierce and Buchanan, "sound" men like himself. In 1868 the Pennsylvania delegation to the Democratic convention nominated him for president; the following year he was the party's nominee for state governor. He capped his political career in 1876 when he was named to the prestigious Commission of the National Centennial Exhibition.

On a hill above Mauch Chunk Packer built a grand Victorian mansion, some say on the very spot where Josiah White first had his house. The tycoon filled the spacious rooms with the best furnishings from Europe and America. Skilled craftsmen were imported from Italy to add the finer touches. In line with Packer's practical side, most of the architectural additions had a clear function. He had a glassed-in cupola added at the very top of his house, connected to the floor below by a winding staircase, at the foot of which sat a young boy expressly hired for the purpose. Packer sat up there sometimes with a gold watch, timing the arrivals of his trains at the station in the town below. If an engineer brought a train in late, the boy was dispatched to bring the unfortunate worker in for a full explanation.

By the 1860s, however, Mauch Chunk had literally become too small for its new men of wealth. The two square-mile town was wedged in a ravine between imposing mountains; its flats along the river were already crowded. There was simply no room to expand, to build the new industries and manufacturing works; or, for Packer, to raise the headquarters of his railroad. So he and other Mauch Chunk millionaires began to cast their eyes on the Lehigh Valley, just over the mountains to the south.

The broad Lehigh Valley, located some fifty miles north of Philadelphia and astride the main transportation route from the upper Schuylkill and Lehigh coalfields to New York, eighty miles to the east, was an obvious magnet for investors. It contained substantial deposits of iron ore and limestone, crucial to industrialization, access to eastern markets, a rich agricultural base, and a thrifty, hard-working population. In the eighteenth century it developed as a hinterland of Philadelphia, settled by a scattering of English Quakers, Scotch-Irish, and a large number of German Protestants. These mutually suspicious groups carved out prosperous farms and generally kept to themselves in small, close-knit communities, held together by ethnic and religious preferences. In 1741 a group of Moravians came from central Czechoslovakia. These pious, devotionalist Protestant dissidents developed a communalistic system of shared labor, wealth, and living and for a century excluded outsiders from Bethlehem and Nazareth, the towns they founded. Until the mid-nineteenth century, the only urban center of any significance was Easton, located at the eastern end of the valley near the juncture of the Lehigh and Delaware rivers. Its mostly Scotch-Irish merchants, craftsmen, and shopkeepers tied the economy of their town to Philadelphia, transferring and shipping goods that moved along the rivers, and providing banking, transportation, government, and other services for the northeastern Pennsylvania frontier.

The opening of the Lehigh, Delaware, and Morris canals encouraged the development of an export economy based on grain, lumber, distillery products, and charcoal iron. After mid-century, anthracite iron and railroads pushed the valley into the industrial age. In 1854 a Moravian bank president sold more than 100 acres of the community's land in South Bethlehem to Easton speculator Charles Brodhead. A distant relative of Asa Packer, Brodhead wanted to establish an iron foundry on the property and hoped to make it a terminus for the Lehigh Valley and Northern Pennsylvania railroads. Brodhead perhaps did not know that Packer and his associates, persuaded by chief railroad engineer Robert Sayre, had already purchased land in South Bethlehem on which they planned to build their railroad depot and, just across the way, their mansions. In any case, Brodhead went ahead with his plans. In association with Moravian August Wolle, who owned local iron mines, he organized the Bethlehem Iron Company in 1860; Asa Packer was appointed to the first board of directors of the incorporated firm. By 1863 Bethlehem Iron was rolling rails exclusively for the Lehigh Valley Railroad. In that decade and the following it built new furnaces, and in the 1870s it adopted the Bessemer and open hearth processes for making steel. The company eventually became the valley's largest iron and steel maker, a multimillion-dollar firm second in size only to the Lehigh Valley Railroad.[35]

The close relationship between the iron and railroad companies prompted several leading families of the Packer group to relocate from Mauch Chunk to South Bethlehem in the 1860s. They became shareholders in both Bethlehem Iron and the Lehigh Valley; several of them went on to hold high positions in one or the other of the firms. Children of the families linked to the Packer group and Brodhead also intermarried. They too worked in the main enterprises or subsidiary companies or founded new firms connected with the coal, iron, or railroad industries. The group made South Bethlehem a major regional industrial center, which contributed to the growth of nearby Bethlehem and Allentown. The residents of those towns worked in the railroad and iron concerns; their businessmen provided local services. Packer and his associates dominated South Bethlehem and its environs while retaining their far-reaching influence in the coalfields to the north. They not only built industries; they endowed churches, hospitals, and educational institutions. Packer himself founded Lehigh University, which, like Easton's Lafayette College, became an important source of technical and managerial talent for the iron and coal industries.[36]

Packer's career illustrates how outside financial interests, which originally made money in coal, developed major industries, which, in turn, spurred urban growth. The Philadelphia-controlled Lehigh Coal and Navigation Company first provided the catalyst for industrialization by promoting and supporting communities such as Mauch Chunk, Catasauqua, and South Easton. Later the anthracite-carrying railroads, the Central of New Jersey and Lehigh Valley, gave a similar boost to industrialization and population growth. By 1880 Philadelphia interests that owned Lehigh Coal and part of the Lehigh Valley Railroad controlled the three largest iron companies in Allentown, one in Catasauqua, and another in Phillipsburg, New Jersey. A Boston group owned the Glendon Iron Company, one of the major producers in the valley. New York and Philadelphia investors owned the big Pennsylvania and Lehigh Zinc Company, while the giant Lehigh Portland Cement Company, heavily capitalized from the outside, rose to dominance in that industry.[37]

The effect of this pattern of development was to create core areas of heavy industry and transportation, generally located in or close to the largest towns of the valley: Allentown, Bethlehem, and Easton. Surrounding these cores were an array of locally owned smaller manufacturers and service activities, which depended upon the main industries. Farther out on the periphery were the extractive industries,

The Glendon Iron Works, near Easton, on the Lehigh Canal.
Courtesy of the Pennsylvania Canal Society Collection, Canal Museum, Easton, Pa.

such as mining, and the valley's farming areas, which supplied the urban-industrial cores with agricultural goods. This pattern was not unusual in itself; it was characteristic of industrialization generally. The result, however, was the attraction to the booming industrial cores of the region's most enterprising people and of much of its capital and resources. Older communities tended to languish over time. Furthermore the continuing well-being of the outlying, peripheral areas came to depend upon the health of the cores. In this case, the key industries of the core areas were largely controlled by outside, multiregional financial interests, and by local groups closely associated with them. The Lehigh Valley industrial region itself became an economic periphery to the capital centers of New York and Philadelphia.

The development of the anthracite iron industry and the railroads opened to full exploitation the last and most productive of all coalfields in the Wyoming Valley. Located just south of the Lackawanna Valley along the Susquehanna River, the Wyoming is hemmed in to the east by a series of formidable mountains. Though coal shipments began in the first decades of the nineteenth century, a major problem was finding a cheap, reliable means of getting the product to the big eastern markets. Overland routes were prohibitively expensive; the Susquehanna not only was long and dangerous but emptied into the Chesapeake Bay, inconveniently distant from Philadelphia and New York. The completion in 1834 of the North Branch Canal, which linked the Wyoming Valley with the east-west Pennsylvania Main Line

Canal via Harrisburg, provided an outlet to Philadelphia, but the results were dis-appointing. The Philadelphia market was already adequately supplied by the Schuylkill and Lehigh fields. To the north in the Lackawanna Valley, the Delaware and Hudson Canal had locked in the New York trade. If the Wyoming was to grow, alternate outlets for its coal had to be found.[38]

The opportunity came with the appearance of anthracite iron furnaces down-river at Danville, Bloomsburg, and Sunbury. Not content to wait for outsiders to finance rail lines, or to rely solely on the North Branch Canal, Wyoming coal mer-chants raised several million dollars locally to build two anthracite carriers in the late 1840s and early 1850s. By the end of the latter decade their Delaware, Lacka-wanna and Wyoming Valley, and Lackawanna and Bloomsburg railroads were haul-ing more than 70 percent of the Wyoming field's coal. The coal production boom that followed prompted three other major carriers to build lines into the field, with termi-nals at Wilkes-Barre. With outlets via these roads to New York City, New England, Buffalo, and the Great Lakes region, the growth and prosperity of the Wyoming field was assured.[39]

The men who originally promoted the coal trade in the Wyoming Valley were not newcomers to the area. They and their offspring had built the village of Wilkes-Barre on the Susquehanna into an important trading center in the late eighteenth century. They hauled goods by horseback from Philadelphia through the Pennsyl-

A late nineteenth-century anthracite town and coal operation.   *Courtesy of the George Bretz Collection, Albin O. Kuhn Library, University of Maryland, Baltimore County.*

vania wilderness and sold them to agricultural communities up and down the river. As traders, they recognized the importance of transportation, so they pushed hard through their representatives in Harrisburg for internal improvements such as the turnpike to Mauch Chunk and Easton and the dredging of the Susquehanna for navigation. When the Wyoming Valley began to shift from agriculture to anthracite export in the first part of the nineteenth century, original settler families such as the Hollenbacks, Butlers, Denisons, and Stewards moved easily from mercantile activities into coal land speculation, mining, transportation, and banking. These founding families formed a local capitalist elite like the Packer group, bound together by marriage and common business interests.[40]

Until the railroads opened up new markets and greatly increased demand, coal operations were largely family enterprises scattered in towns and villages across the Wyoming Valley. The capitalization and technological levels of these collieries were relatively low. Stimulated by the need to increase production, and perhaps also by the fear of New York financial interests, Wilkes-Barre's capitalists in the 1850s began to move to gain control of their primary industry. Their method was the incorporated company, which could not only pool capital and resources to provide economies of scale but would also effectively centralize regional operations in Wilkes-Barre. Beginning in 1849 and continuing to the end of the century, the city's capitalists led the way in organizing more than twenty-five major coal corporations that dominated the industry in an area extending from the Susquehanna around Wilkes-Barre through Hazleton to the south and to the edge of the Schuylkill field. The biggest and most important of these companies had their headquarters in Wilkes-Barre; the city's elite occupied more than 100 seats on their boards of directors and the 30 top executive posts. The effect was to make the city dominant in the Wyoming field and to guarantee powerful influence over the development of the industry.[41]

The long-term advantages to be gained by merger and consolidation encouraged the Wyoming Valley's independent operators to incorporate their holdings. When they did so they moved with their families from outlying towns like Plymouth and Nanticoke to the expanding Wilkes-Barre. The communities they left behind remained little more than extensions of their corporate networks, mining towns feeding coal to the outside world and profits to Wilkes-Barre. Through their control of the twenty coal companies headquartered in the city, another in Kingston, and five in Hazleton, Wilkes-Barre's capitalists exercised pervasive control over the principal industry of virtually every town in their region. Their power was such that they were able to resist to a considerable degree intrusion by outside corporate interests, including the major anthracite carriers. Yet while they were locking the Wyoming Valley into dependency upon a single specialized industry, subject to the hazards of economic fluctuations in markets outside of their control, they reinforced the domination of their city by investing their coal profits in lumbering, mining machinery, textiles, banking, utilities, and city transportation. Few activities of any economic importance escaped their grasp; indeed, they made sure that no one could compete with them.[42]

Wilkes-Barre's capitalists demonstrated an amazing unity and single-mindedness of purpose in making the field they controlled the most productive in the anthracite region and their city one of the two largest and most prosperous in the area. They did so because of a commonality of interest, sustained by a commonality of culture and family relationships. They invested in each other's companies, sat on each other's board of directors, and married into each other's families. They created a relatively closed world of business and society which outsiders penetrated only with extreme difficulty. Most members of the class were of English origin, descendants of old stock colonial families. They were overwhelmingly Episcopalian or Presbyterian by religious preference. Two-thirds came from families that had originally settled the Wyoming Valley and its hinterland. A significant percentage were graduates of Ivy League colleges or of colleges with high-quality engineering programs, such as Lafayette. Those from outside the Wyoming Valley who gained entry into the elite were of similar background. Though some were of German descent and came from southeastern Pennsylvania, they shared the common interests, views, and prejudices.[43]

This inbred group of coal entrepreneurs and lawyers maintained an iron grip on all important public and private organizations and institutions. They controlled both political parties and groomed their own for local, state, and national offices. In Harrisburg they promoted the interests of Wilkes-Barre to the detriment of other rival cities such as nearby Scranton. They succeeded in excluding outside investors from establishing industries not under their control. In the exclusive comfort of their private clubs—Cheese and Crackers, the Malt, the Wyoming Historical and Genealogical Society—they decided who would rise and who would fall, which companies would flourish and which would languish. They created a closed social and economic order that affected the fate of thousands, and they did it in accord with the demands of their own narrow class interests. They believed that they had the right because they had the might, and many of them no doubt came to believe that it was even God-given.

From the first days of the trade, Wilkes-Barre's coal barons managed to protect and steadily enlarge their domain. Yet they remained essentially conservative men, reluctant to admit outsiders to their closed circle of money and power. Nor did they show much interest in broadening their activities or encourage others to do so. They did invest in the urban services that supported their city's growth, but their attention remained fixed on coal. While they promoted railroads, lumbering, and mine

A coal country mansion.   Courtesy of the George Bretz Collection,
Albin O. Kuhn Library, University of Maryland, Baltimore County.

machine industries, these really were subsidiary to their main concern. They did not, like the Packer group, diversify into iron and steel. One industry dominated Wilkes-Barre, as it did every other community in the Wyoming Valley. A comparison of employees engaged in coal and manufacturing in Luzerne County in 1880, for example, shows that 92.2 percent were in coal, while only 7.8 percent worked in manufacturing.[44] Wilkes-Barre's elite reaped its profits primarily from coal; from the security of its mansion-lined enclave along the city's river common its members watched the iron ore barges pass upstream to the rival city of Scranton.

By the 1860s the five great anthracite railroads—the Philadelphia and Reading, Lehigh Valley, Delaware and Hudson, Delaware, Lackawanna, and Western, and Central of New Jersey—were in place, along with several smaller roads. They carried the fuel that heated the homes of the Northeast and fired the furnaces of America's new industries. Their reach extended beyond that of the canals, whose monopoly they broke and whose final demise they assured. In their ascendancy the anthracite railroads created a new transportation monopoly and opened a new era for the industry.

They certainly brought greater order and stability to the industry. Here they followed the practices of their rivals, the first big canal companies. The anarchy of production that characterized the first decades of hard coal did not well serve the canals. The companies sought to ensure regularity of tonnage by acquiring their own coal lands, and later they discriminated against independent operators in order to protect their own mining interests. After the railroads gained transportation supremacy they followed the same practices or fixed rates in such a way that they stimulated production without making independent coal operators overly prosperous. The frenzy of the operators to raise production and the intense competition among them led to periodic cycles of overproduction and depression. The public clamor for regularity of supply and price in the coal trade broke down resistance to the fear of domination of the industry by giant companies.

Pottsville, the Gibbsville portrayed by novelist John O'Hara, at the height of the anthracite boom. Anthracite spurred both industrial and urban growth.   Courtesy of the Historical Society of Schuylkill County, Pottsville, Pa.

A coal train leaving a small mine operation in Scranton.   Courtesy of the Library of Congress.

After the Civil War the railroads moved to extend their lines and acquire vast tracts of coal lands. An 1868 Pennsylvania law allowed for the consolidation and merger of coal companies and permitted the railroads to expand their landholdings. They did so in order to reduce competition and to guarantee the source of the product they carried. They also understood the profit-making potential of large-scale mining operations. Another law passed the following year under pressure from railroad interests allowed the joint ownership of railroad and mining enterprises. Soon the railroads formed their own subsidiary coal companies. An example was the Reading, which under the leadership of Franklin B. Gowen acquired 100,000 acres of prime coal lands in the Schuylkill field and engaged in mining. Between 1869 and 1874 the anthracite carriers gained control of the greater proportion of coal lands in the region. Their rate-fixing practices and the competition of their heavily capitalized and technologically advanced coal companies forced many independent operators to sell or go out of business. Strong independent operators like those around Hazleton and in the Wyoming Valley were forced to make long-term cartage contracts for their coal, which effectively gave the railroads almost complete control of supplies going to markets. The domination of the railroads over the anthracite industry raised competition for coal markets to another level, but consumers did not benefit. The railroads learned that rate and price wars hurt only themselves and that if they combined in pooling agreements to limit production and carve out exclusive markets they would have the public at their mercy.[45]

The railroads brought the anthracite industry to maturity in the decades after the Civil War. Big capital and big companies came to rule supreme in the region. Individual entrepreneurs such as White and Hazard, the Scrantons, and Asa Packer had developed coal, iron, and railroads and fostered industrialization and city building. But they had not done their work alone; behind them was money from New York and Philadelphia. Gradually, as industrialization spread and a national market formed, as technological advances required greater investments, as competition intensified and compelled larger and larger operations, they or their descendants sold out to, invested in, or were absorbed by bigger multiregional capital. Those who held out, like the independent coal operators, though strong in their regions, became dependent on markets over which they had no control. In the end, New York and Philadelphia capital, decisive from the beginning, asserted its domination. Descendants of the Packer group moved to Philadelphia's Main Line; those of the Scranton group lost control of their hometown industries or squandered their money in New York and Paris; the Woolworth and Kirby progeny found more lucrative investments outside the region. By the early 1900s the biggest name associated with anthracite was New York's J. P. Morgan.

Behind the rising wealth and the staggering changes one thing remained the same. Coal continued to be mined by men who never even dreamed of rising to the status of a Packer or a Pardee. Their work was difficult, dangerous, and sadly unrewarding. But without it, as every coal overlord knew, there could be no anthracite empire.

4. Working in the Black Hell

PART FROM THE LURE OF PROSPECTING, NO ONE ENTERED THE MINE IN CIVILIZED states until relatively modern times except as a prisoner of war, a criminal, a slave. Mining was not regarded as a humane art: it was a form of punishment: it combined the terrors of the dungeon with the physical exacerbation of the galley." These are the words of the social critic Lewis Mumford.[1] Most miners in the anthracite country saw their work a little differently.

"You ask me if I like working in the mines? Well it is my opinion that no one ever really liked work, especially when performed for someone else. But life is a struggle for existence and one can become interested in any work that will supply his bread and butter. I have always worked in and about the mines—I know nothing else—and while some places are gassy, wet and dangerous, there are other places which are not so bad. Mining is in my blood."[2] Chester Siock, a miner and the son of a miner, described the attitude of the men who worked anthracite. They did it because they had to do it, because they knew nothing else, and because, finally, it became a way of life, something more than a job. Chester Siock and the men who went underground to dig coal probably would have scoffed at the notion that they did something special, yet there is no denying that it was special. Their work was neither easy nor commonplace. It required not only brawn and muscle and certain skills but also a special kind of courage to spend long hours in a world without sunlight, where time and the rhythms of nature were meaningless and dangers ever present.

Deep in the earth they worked in small teams of two, three, or four men, in damp air with the acrid smell of coal dust always in their nostrils, in silence complete except for the loose coal crunching beneath their boots or the dull clinking of their tools. But for the faint light from their lamps shining on the black, glossy coal, they worked in total darkness. They drilled holes into the coal seams, tamped in the explosives and fired them from a safe distance, always alert for the deadly fumes of "rotten gas" and "stink damp," for the creaking of timbers overhead, for falling rocks, or even for the sudden scurrying of rats—for miners, a sure sign of an imminent cave-in. When a bad accident occurred, death sometimes came mercifully quickly, but for others hopelessly entombed, there was the agony of burial alive.

In the residential blocks of many mining towns not a single family had been spared the loss of some member in the mines—father, son, brother, uncle. When they emerged from underground at the end of their shift, their faces and hands blackened, their clothes clotted with sweat and dust, their bodies weary from labor and tension, they felt a surge of relief: they had survived another day without mishap. They had their pints of ale and porter and then trudged home. If asked about their

Overleaf: A nineteenth-century miner. Courtesy of the National Archives.

A miner working alone, ankle deep in water, in the steeply pitched coal seams
of the southern anthracite region.
Courtesy of the Historical Society of Schuylkill County, Pottsville, Pa.

work they would reply like Chester Siock, without pretension, yet knowing that in the morning they would go down again for all the obvious reasons, but also because the mining of anthracite defined them, made them what they were. It was in their blood.

The anthracite industry both inspired and experienced a technological revolution in the course of its history, yet the method of extracting hard coal from the earth changed remarkably little over time. It was always done by men using a few simple tools. The technology used to support the workers in the mines, to remove, sort, and transport coal, would become more sophisticated, but the actual labor of removing the coal from the seams remained, for the most part, in the hands of skilled individuals working almost alone. The nature of the anthracite seams dictated the removal process. Unlike many of the bituminous deposits, the hard coal seams were seldom flat or horizontal. They pitched to more than 2,000 feet beneath the surface and climbed hundreds of feet up inside mountains, often to outcrop on the sides or tops. Until well into the twentieth century, modern coal-cutting machinery could not be used to get the coal, and the mining of anthracite remained a craft or "cottage" industry, requiring hand labor and skilled workers. Laboring in small teams in tight underground passages and galleries, the work of miners was not closely supervised by management. It could not be. As a result anthracite mining was different from other types of industrial work, and anthracite miners were different from other types of industrial workers.

In the industry's earliest days, the men who dug anthracite were rarely skilled miners. They were hunters, trappers, lumbermen, and small farmers scratching out a living in a soil-poor and sparsely populated region. Or they were Pennsylvania Germans from the rich farmlands just eastward over the mountains who went in to dig the black rock in the Schuylkill wilderness for a few months every year. Or sometimes they were ne'er-do-wells and bankrupts looking for better days.

The methods they used for "cutting" the coal were simple, even primitive. Wielding picks and shovels, helped perhaps by some powder, they dug the coal where it was most easily reached. They mined outcroppings on the surface, then quarried or stripped the coal as they followed the seams into the ground. Where the seams outcropped on the sides of mountains, they drove openings directly into the coal at a slight upward pitch to permit natural drainage. These tunnels were known as "drifts" and seldom required elaborate timbering support to keep the passageways clear. Since much of the work was done in the open, the earliest mining was a fair-weather occupation. The coal was broken up and stored on the ground until the dirt or timbered roads were passable. Then it was loaded into sledges or wagons and was pulled by oxen, horse, or mule teams to deposit sites on the river banks.

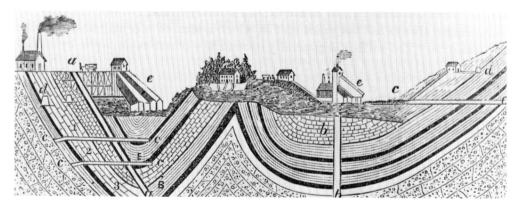

An early illustration of the three types of underground mining. At the left (a) a slope; at center (b) a shaft; and right (c) a drift. All openings were designed to drive through multiple veins of coal (darkened lines).
From Samuel H. Daddow and Benjamin Bannan, Coal, Iron and Oil *(Pottsville: Bannan, 1866).*

As the market expanded in the 1820s and 1830s, thousands of new workers were attracted to the booming region. They included skilled miners and mechanics from England, Scotland, Wales, and Germany, men who knew the latest mining technology and freely adapted it to the conditions of anthracite. Aided by abundant investment capital, these men soon devised the means to drive underground mines deep beneath the water level and to hoist heavy loads of coal up several hundred feet in one lift. Where the seams ran upward inside the mountains, they first drove tunnels at various levels through alternate layers of rock and coal, then passages or "headings" into the seams at angles, removing the coal as they went. To reach seams in hilly areas beneath the surface but too far underground for surface mining, they dug slanted tunnels or "slopes" down through the seams. As the mechanization of the steam age took hold, and powerful pumps and lifting engines were developed, the men of anthracite excavated holes, or "shafts," straight down to the coal seams that lay far beneath the surface. They then opened horizontal entries through the seams of coal so that the coal was mined through tunnels spreading out from the shaft. Elevators or "cages" lowered or lifted the miners and equipment and carried the loaded coal cars to the surface.

In the Schuylkill and Lehigh fields, where the outcrops were on the mountaintops, stripping or quarrying was used. Slopes were then cut into the mountain where the pitch of the seams was steep and outcrops frequent. In the Wyoming field the upper seams were exploited by drifts and slopes until exhausted. The rich, deeplying Wyoming seams were then mined primarily by shafts, which sometimes reached well over a thousand feet beneath the surface. By the end of the nineteenth century, when the anthracite industry reached maturity, most of the easily available seams or beds had been worked out, and the most common type of mine was either the shaft or the slope. Today most mining in the region is done on the surface by huge shovels or "drags," which literally move mountains.

But for almost a century, anthracite mining was underground work, in a world where daylight had been abolished. Awakened before first light by colliery whistles or church bells, the miner arrived at the pit site dressed in rough coveralls and rubber boots, with a lamp atop his cap, his multilayered lunch pail in hand. There he met his helper, and with other men he stepped into the elevator cage at the top of the shaft. A bell rang and overhead the massive iron sheave wheels began to turn, lowering the thick, greasy steel cable attached to the top of the cage into the black depths. Slowly the cage began its descent, passing the slimy, moss-encrusted, dripping granite blocks at the mouth of the shaft, then faster past the soil walls held by wooden cribbing. Daylight disappeared as the cage plunged with extraordinary speed to the accompaniment of creaking machinery and groaning timbers, the only light provided by the flames of miner's lamps, flames that "fluttered and flew and

A late nineteenth-century stripping, or surface mining, operation.
Courtesy of the Wyoming Historical and Geological Society, Wilkes-Barre, Pa.

struggled like tied birds to release themselves from the wicks."[3] Down went the cage into the black void on a journey that seemed endless.

Above, in the hoisting room, the engineer watched the "depth gauge" and responded to a signal from a foreman below to stop the cage at a "level." The pale light revealed tunnels extending into the darkness from two sides of the cage and several loaded mine cars standing on a narrow-gauge railroad, waiting to be pushed onto the rails of an ascending cage. Here several men got off and were soon lost to sight. The cage again began its descent, stopping at other levels hundreds of feet beneath the surface. Suddenly, more than 1,000 feet down, the platform slowed, then jarred to a final stop. The miner and his helper stepped off into the gloom, their nostrils filling with the dank smells of rotting mine timbers, wet rock and earth, carbide gas, and sulfuric acid. Their lungs began to labor with longer respirations despite the strong, cold downdraft of air at the bottom of the shaft. The thumping of powerful water pumps in the sump throbbed in their ears.[4]

The miner and his helper entered one of the tunnels, or "gangways," that extended from the shaft. They walked along the tracks and sometimes stepped into a ditch filled with brackish water to pass mine cars. Now there were few sounds except the crunching of boots on coal dust, the trickle of water, and perhaps in the distance the rumble of mine cars or the ominous thud of an explosion. The flickering orange and yellow lamplight played off the damp rock walls and massive timbers, bedecked with a gruesome white mosslike fungus, occasionally catching streaks of coal that shone like black diamonds. The men walked silently and purposefully, aware of the unimaginable weight pressing down on the roof just inches above their heads. They instinctively recoiled from the thought of touching it or the oozing, jagged walls and crusty timbers, as if fearful of disturbing the alien, imponderable mass.

Miners in the cage waiting to be lowered into the earth.
Courtesy of the Wyoming Historical and Geological Society, Wilkes-Barre, Pa.

The long, heavily timbered gangway, the main haulage tunnel of an anthracite mine.
Courtesy of the Burg Collection, MG-273, Pennsylvania State Archives.

A thirteen-year-old nipper (door boy) at his lonely job a quarter of a mile underground at
Pittston, 1911. The massive wooden doors controlled the flow of air in the mines.   Courtesy
of the Lewis Hine Collection, Albin O. Kuhn Library, University of Maryland, Baltimore County.

Some distance along the gangway they came upon a ponderous wooden door which regulated the flow of air into the mine. The attendant or door boy opened it and allowed them to pass. They trudged on perhaps another mile or more until they came to a small shed built into an alcove carved in the rock where the inside fore- man had his "office." There they checked in with the "fire boss," the man responsible for the safety of everyone in the mine. The fire boss entered the mine each morning before the shift and made a thorough inspection of all working areas, checking for gas and ensuring that the ventilation system was working properly, measuring the amount of fresh air, testing the roof with his drill for the "ping" that told him the roof was safe or the "pong" that indicated loose rock overhead. On his return from his rounds, the fire boss marked down conditions in each area on a slate which the miner always checked before going to work. If there was an accumulation of "bad air," the miner and his laborer waited until their working chamber was cleared by the "bratticeman," who manipulated the ventilating system to drive out the gas. When the "slate was clean," work could begin. The miner then hung his numbered

A fire boss testing for gas before the miners begin their shift.
Courtesy of the Wyoming Historical and Geological Society, Wilkes-Barre, Pa.

brass check on a pegboard marked with the area in which he was working. His helper also hung a slightly different check on the same peg. By this system the exact location of every miner and helper was known at all times. The miner also received instructions from the fire boss about setting up additional props for roof protection or taking down any loose or threatening pieces of rock.[5]

The miner and laborer resumed their journey along the gangway, the main "highway" of the mine. They now carried all that they needed for their day's work: pick, shovel, bar, drill, powder, fuses, ax, and lumber. When they arrived at the work site the method of mining depended upon the angle or "pitch" of the coal seams. If the seams were relatively level, they used the "pillar and breast" method. At intervals along the gangways, chambers, known as "breasts," were opened at right angles to the gangways into the coal seams. The inner end of the breast, which continued to advance as the coal was extracted, was known as the "working face," or

Miners at the face, 1844. The miner in the middle is using a patent drill or coal auger to bore a hole for the placement of explosives. This photograph by George Bretz of Pottsville is one of the first to show the interior of an American coal mine illuminated by electric light. Courtesy of the George Bretz Collection, Albin O. Kuhn Library, University of Maryland, Baltimore County.

A hand mining drill machine.   *Courtesy of the Wyoming Historical and Geological Society, Wilkes-Barre, Pa.*

simply the "face." A number of breasts were worked together, connected at intervals by openings called crossheadings, which also served as air passages. The walls between the breasts formed "pillars," the thickness of which depended upon the condition of the roof. In dangerous mines the pillars were as wide as the breast, so that only half the coal was taken out. As soon as the breasts were opened sufficiently, a track, called a "buggy road," was laid for the passage of the mine cars, or buggies. The track advanced as the face was worked.

At the "face" the only light came from lamps attached to the workers' caps. In the early days the lamps were round, flat-bottomed tin containers, which burned crude oil. Later, a much safer carbide lamp was developed; today the miner's lamp is electric, the current carried by a line connected to a storage battery attached to the miner's belt.[6] The miner's real work began when he reached the breast. The first thing he did on entering his work place was to test the roof. If there were any loose or hanging pieces he took them down. Then he put up new props to further secure the roof. Next he drilled his holes and began firing. Twentieth-century miners work with jackhammers and electronic detonators, but over the entire history of anthracite mining, the work underground has changed little.

The nineteenth-century miner opened holes for explosives with hand drills or augers and filled them with squibs and fuse. Many miners made their own squibs

Moving a coal car weighing one and a half tons.   Courtesy of the Library of Congress.

from rye straws filled with powder, but they were usually made of paper and were dipped in a resinous mixture to make them waterproof. The squib was inserted into the hole leading to the explosive charge, usually black powder. After ignition the squib burned slowly until the powder was reached; then it burned swiftly until it ignited the explosive. Fuses and blasting caps were generally used to fire in wet places and in rock. The fuse consisted of a central core of fine-grained gunpowder around which threads of jute, hemp, or cotton were wrapped and made up in spools, which permitted it to be cut off at the desired length. A detonator cap was placed over one end of the fuse and was inserted into an explosive cartridge, which was placed in the hole with the fuse extending beyond its mouth.[7] At no time in the history of mining was "firing" a safe or easy job. Dominick Just, an Italian miner, employed in the Rock Vein at the Monarch mine in the 1930s, said that blasting in water was especially dangerous. "I worked there three months in one-and-a-half-foot of water. When you drilled a hole in the water you had to be ready to put your explosive in just as you pulled your bit out. You had to be quick at tamping it and firing."[8]

After the charge was fired, the miner used a pick to break off loose pieces from the face and to separate slate from the coal. The laborer then loaded the coal into the buggies. The miner occasionally helped out, but it was customary for him to go home after he had cut his quota of coal. The laborer broke up the blasted coal, separating

In most anthracite mines, mules were used to haul coal to the surface.
Courtesy of the Wyoming Historical and Geological Society, Wilkes-Barre, Pa.

A company man and miners' representative taking a miner's tickets, which were used
to identify the coal that the miner and his crew had mined on their shift.
Courtesy of the Wyoming Historical and Geological Society, Wilkes-Barre, Pa.

out the rock and refuse before shoveling it into the buggy. The finer coal from the bottom of the chamber was loaded first, then the larger chunks were placed along the sides and ends of the buggy, building up an extension over the top of the car called "topping." Since slate and refuse inevitably mixed with the coal, the topping ensured that the buggy was loaded to the proper weight. When the buggy was loaded a number was chalked on it for identification and credit, a mule was hitched up, and the buggy was pulled through the gangway to the shaft, where it was lifted to the surface. The laborer tossed the refuse on a pile called a "gob," then cleared the chamber in preparation for the next day's work.

Few of the anthracite seams were level, especially in the Schuylkill field, where they often pitched at steep angles. When working these, the miners first opened a breast at the gangway, then worked upward into the seam, allowing the loosened coal to move downward by gravity through the natural chute that was formed. At the bottom of the chute a wooden barrier was constructed with a gate that controlled the flow of coal into the cars on the gangway. After the seam had been worked for some distance, the loosened coal was allowed to pile up behind the barrier gate. The miners then opened parallel passageways, called "manways," up along both sides of the seam. These allowed the men access to the advancing face. This work was tedious and time-consuming because they had to drag timber up the steep manways, building wooden ladders into the rock as they went. Along the way and at the face they timbered and propped the roof, precariously clinging to the walls of the mine as they worked. The seams often went upward at dizzying angles for several hundred feet. By the time the miners had reached the working face with their timber and tools, they were already on the "down side" of their shift. The miners climbed slowly upward, one team in each manway, pausing every several yards to test for gas with a special lamp. When they reached the face they stood on the backed-up, loosened coal from previous firings and drilled their holes. After the charges had been placed, the men went into their manways to ignite them.[9]

The gangways and breasts followed the bending and winding course of the coal seams. The distance that the breasts could be worked depended upon the seam of coal. It could run to a boundary line, an outcrop, or an arch where the seam pitched down, and there was the danger that further work might cause flooding in the mine. Alternatively the seam could thin out until the rock wall and rock floor came together. The seam might also hit a "fault," where the strata had been disturbed and the seam broke off and disappeared. When seams in a section of the mine worked by the pillar and breast method were exhausted or could no longer be worked, the last stage of mining had been reached, "robbing the pillars." This stage was extremely dangerous because coal was removed from the support pillars to the last limit of safety, and the roof was allowed to settle behind the workers.[10]

A more recent method of extracting anthracite is the "long-wall" system. In long-wall mining a long block of coal is taken out in a single operation, with the face advancing in a single, unbroken line. At the Marvine mine in the 1930s, for example, a block of coal 300 feet long, extending from one gangway to another, was extracted in this manner. One shift of workers, using an undercutting machine with a six-foot cutter bar, undercut the full length of the face. Drillers prepared the holes, and propmen and chutemen moved the props and the shaking chute which removed the loosened coal. Every day a six-foot cut was taken out. The roof of the working area near the face was supported by two rows of collapsible steel jacks running parallel to the face. Each night one row of jacks was removed and reset to keep up with the advancing face. The shaking chute carried the coal directly to cars on the gangway, where they were loaded and topped off by a crew of two or three men.[11]

The skilled miner was master of his solitary underground domain. He contracted with the operator to work the breast at a certain price per car; he supplied

Men and boys waiting for the cage to take them to the surface at the close of their shift. The cage is entirely open on two sides and not well protected on the other two. Courtesy of the Lewis Hine Collection, Albin O. Kuhn Library, University of Maryland, Baltimore County.

*Mule drivers, door boys, and spraggers at the close of a day in a mine, 1915.   Courtesy of the
Lewis Hine Collection, Albin O. Kuhn Library, University of Maryland, Baltimore County.*

the tools and powder and paid his laborer, his "butty." It was the miner's job to direct
the opening and advance of the breast, to cut the coal and to prop the roof. And of
course he had to supervise the work of his butty, making certain that the car was
loaded with as much clean coal as possible. The miner learned his skills on the job.
He had to have at least two years' experience as a laborer before taking the required
state examination for a skilled miner's certificate. Before a state-appointed board,
he had to answer, in English, at least twelve questions on the practical business
of mining.[12]

The miner and his laborer were the key workers underground, but in the anthracite mines of the late nineteenth and early twentieth centuries, before the electric motor and other mechanical machinery had eliminated some occupations, there
were numerous other jobs as well. Workers were employed as runners, drivers, door
boys, masons, carpenters, repairmen, company laborers, barn bosses, fire bosses,
foremen, bottom men, engineers, pumpmen, and blacksmiths.

Young mine workers, Nanticoke, Pennsylvania, 1911.   *Courtesy of the Lewis Hine Collection, Albin O. Kuhn Library, University of Maryland, Baltimore County.*

One fascinating, and dangerous, job was performed by the runner, a boy or young man who had to be lightning quick of hand and foot, capable of maneuvering in low and narrow places between moving mine cars and the "rig" or walls of the mine. His job was to control the speed at which the cars moved down inclines. Many of the gangways pitched up and down ten degrees or more. On upward grades a trip of loaded cars moved at the pace of the mule team which pulled them. But when the cars reached the top of a grade the mule team was unhitched "on the fly" and turned quickly into a crosscut so that the cars could move downward by their own momentum. As the cars started rolling, the runner, kneeling beside a pile of "sprags," placed one in each wheel to stop its motion as it sped past him. If he missed too many wheels the cars might fly out of control and topple over or jump the track and smack into the mine wall.

It was usually easy to sprag the first half of the trip, but as the trip gained speed, placing sprags in the wheels of the last cars required great skill and preci-

sion. Often the runner had to chase after the last car, sprags in hand, dodging low
roofs and narrow places, leaping over debris and splashing through water as he
tried to make a perfect score. Miners working on planes always sought the best runners because a poor runner would spill a lot of top coal, for which the miners were
docked. On very steep inclines two runners were used, one on each side of the trip, so
that all the wheels could be stopped if necessary. In addition they put sand on the
rails to increase friction, a procedure that sometimes wore down the iron wheels of
the cars.

Occasionally the mules were not turned off in time at the summit of a plane, or
the leather stretcher that attached the mule to the car was too tight for the driver
boy to unhook it. The mules would then be dragged along with the fast-moving cars
and would be either crushed to death or badly injured. To prevent such injury, large
wooden blocks were placed at the top on the incline so that the driver had to bring
the trip to a complete halt before unhitching the mule team. But since the blocks
meant more work for the driver, he often ignored the safety procedure if no one in
authority was present.[13]

A mule about to be lowered into a mine shaft.
Courtesy of the Wyoming Historical and Geological Society, Wilkes-Barre, Pa.

Mules provided the locomotive power in the mines before the introduction of the electric motor. They were highly valued because they were more sure-footed, more powerful, and sturdier than horses and less susceptible to illness. Usually they were kept underground in a widened section of the gangway known as the "barn." Their care was supervised by a "barn boss," who saw that their drivers cleaned out their stalls, fed and watered them daily, combed them, and cleaned the harnesses. The attention they received caused some miners to feel that the mules were valued more than the men.

Mule drivers were generally boys in their early teens who enjoyed the job because it gave them freedom of action. The boisterous and aggressive drivers, who already had several years' experience underground, learned the quirks and idiosyncrasies of individual mules—and the mules of the boys—so that sometimes the mules responded to the commands of only one particular driver. Frequently mules shared driver's lunches or developed a taste for tobacco. It was not unusual for a driver to pull a plug of tobacco from his pocket, give a bite to his mule, and jam the remainder into his mouth.

The boys used no reins to drive the mules. The drivers sat or stood on the front bumper of the car and either shouted commands or directed the mules with a "black snake" whip made of braided leather attached to a short, stout stick for a handle. The whips had "crackers," or tassels made of hemp, on their tips which made sharp reports when the whip was swung in the air and jerked back abruptly. The mules learned what the crack of the whip meant and were directed accordingly. Sometimes the drivers simply led the mules, harnessed either singly or in tandem, the lead animal with a miner's lamp attached to its head or hung from its collar.

Robert Reid of Dickson City, a mine worker for more than fifty years, drove mules in the early part of the century. He had to take care of thirteen working places with one mule, and each chamber had to take six cars. "If you accomplished this by quitting time," he recalled, "all well and good; if not you had to stay until the work was done and received no extra pay for the additional time required."[14] The mules had to be cleaned, harnessed, and out of the barn by 7:00 A.M. Reid usually took four empty cars and distributed them at chambers along his route. At each chamber the mule was unhitched from the trip, rehitched to one empty, and led into a chamber. "Where we could not get the car up into the chamber far enough," Reid said, "we simply turned the mule around and it pushed the car up the required distance with its breast. The mule was trained to do that work." After the empties were distributed, he brought loaded cars back to the place where they were sent to the surface. Reid observed that the work was not without its difficulties: "There was always the danger of being crushed between the cars or between the cars and pillars and props, and that of being kicked or bitten by vicious mules. Not only did one have to learn to drive but had to learn how to govern his mule and keep out of harm's way."[15]

The mules, notoriously stubborn creatures, had the same independent spirit as the mine workers. Accustomed to pulling a certain number of cars, they simply would not move if an extra one was hitched up. They sometimes stopped work instinctively at quitting time, even in mid-trip, and nothing short of dynamite could move them. Curses and beatings from drivers only elicited a swift kick in return. Mules that spent years in the mines would tremble and became nearly delirious with joy when they were finally brought to the surface and exposed to sunlight, grass, and fresh air. Some memory of the dread darkness below would remain, and at times nobody could force or entice them back down.[16]

The mules were esteemed for their instinct of self-preservation. In the 1850s at Spencer Slope Mine near Black Heath, Schuylkill County, an explosion and fire ripped through the workings. Had some of the miners been able to reach the sump and bury their faces in the water, the oxygen in the water might have sustained them for a while. But only a little black mule reached the sump. It plunged its snout into the brackish water and then, revived, raced up the plane to the surface, where its singed body gave the first alarm of the inferno raging below.[17]

Driver boys and their mules suffered the same fate when accidents occurred. One poignant story relates how a slight and frail boy, who had grown deeply attached to one of his mules, disappeared toward the barn when told that a cave-in had blocked any hope for escape. Though some of the men were eventually rescued, the boy was found lying dead beside his mule, his arms wrapped around the animal's neck in a final embrace.[18]

Eventually mules and driver boys were replaced by electric "trolley" locomotives equipped with wire rope or cables to pull cars out of chambers and about the mines. They required brakemen and "motor runners" to throw switches, drive the trains, care for the motors, and keep sufficient sand, for preventing the wheels from slipping, in the boxes mounted on the locomotives. The electric locomotives naturally speeded transport in the mines, but the exposed overhead wires that carried the current for the trolleys created their own hazards. Chester Siock, who worked as both a brakeman and motor runner, explained, "I got plenty of electric shocks especially when I was a brakeman. When your feet were wet and you grabbed the cable on the reel you got a shock. Once I grabbed the trolley wire and was almost electrocuted. The black damp was so bad that my lamp went out when I was coming out on the head end of the motor. I was using the reel coming out of the chamber and tried to unhook the cable."[19]

The vital flow of air in the mines was controlled by wooden partitions built across gangways, in which a door was constructed. The doors were kept closed at all times so that the good, incoming air would be forced into the working places. They

Mule drivers in a typical anthracite patch town.
Courtesy of the Historical Society of Schuylkill County, Pottsville, Pa.

were opened only to allow cars to pass. All the doors were built to swing open against the air current and were therefore self-closing. The job of opening the doors at the approach of cars was assigned to door boys, called "nippers," usually aged twelve to sixteen years. The work was not very difficult, but they sat alone on a crude bench in the darkness and silence, with only the mine rats for company most of the time. Not infrequently the boys fell asleep at their posts, with disastrous results when mine cars crashed into the closed doors. Yet the job provided the boys with their first real experiences working underground, and many of them, fresh from years of grinding labor in the breakers, looked forward to it. Joe Mataconis, a Lithuanian miner, remembered his days as a door boy with affection: "I got a thrill on my first day as a nipper in the mines. At last I felt I was a man and was working with others of the neighborhood in which I lived. Everyone soon came to know me

and all had a friendly word. I was often called upon to perform little jobs or acts of
favor for the other workers, who greatly appreciated it, and generally addressed me
as 'nipper.'"[20]

Other underground workers such as carpenters, masons, and blacksmiths
worked at jobs similar to those performed on the surface. In addition repairmen and
"company laborers" were occupied in maintaining timbering, in laying and repairing tracks in gangways, in moving water toward the sump, in clearing debris, and in
performing similar duties to ensure the safe and continuous working of the mine.
All of these men were paid hourly wages.

The underground supervisory force included the mine foreman and his various
assistants. They were "company men" who were paid on a monthly basis; by the
latter half of the nineteenth century they were usually Anglo-Saxon and Irish in
national origin, drawn from the ranks of skilled miners with years of experience.
They were charged with the safe, efficient, and profitable working of the mine, but
their tasks were far from easy. It was practically impossible for the foreman and his
assistants to make more than brief daily visits to all the working areas of an average coal mine; they had to depend to a large extent upon the responsibility, skill, and
good working habits of the men under their supervision. The foreman's job was further complicated by the miner's independence and resentment against taking orders
from superiors, the result of the circumstances in which he worked as well as a long-
standing tradition of hostility toward people in authority. This attitude was best ex-
emplified by the miner who told his newly landed "hunky" laborer: "Come here,
Frank. Here's the boss. Don't work. Always sit down when the boss is around."[21]

The foremen had the power to hire and fire all the men working underground.
He assigned the work and told the men how it should be performed. By law he or his
assistants were required to visit daily all the working places of all the miners. In the
average mine this task required miles of walking every day, since the mine was a
vast underground city, or even crawling on hands and knees through debris-filled
cross-cuts. On his rounds he checked everything, ordering props to be stood here or a
bad roof pried loose there. In the labyrinthine workings of the mine he had a thousand details to take care of, and nothing but his memory to rely on. For apart from
payroll and weight reports, almost no written records were kept. The mine foreman,
always in a hurry, had little time to see that his orders were carried out. He could
only check and recheck and rely upon his close knowledge of the mine and all aspects of its work—and his position as "final authority"—to see that the mine was
kept safe and the work properly performed.

Men working underground required air, vast quantities of it—by law no less
than 200 cubic feet per minute per person. Without this amount of air, gas and dust
would accumulate and, if it did not explode and turn the mine into an inferno, they

would suffocate every living thing inside the mine. A mine had to breathe, to take in fresh air and expel the bad. Its lungs were the ventilation system.[22]

Until late in the nineteenth century most anthracite mines were poorly ventilated. Though the English had invented an advanced system of mine ventilation earlier in the century, which made their accident rate far lower than that in the anthracite fields, the Americans resisted adopting it because of its cost. During the era of intense competition in the Schuylkill field, for example, profits in the best-run mines were seldom more than 10 percent per ton of coal; in most mines the profits tended to be marginal. As the surface seams were exhausted and operators had to go deeper the cost rose—and the operators tended to cut back on safety technology. Utilizing the English system of double shafts for ventilation simply added to operating expenses. As a result of inadequate ventilation, "firedamp," or methane gas—which is lighter than air—tended to accumulate in pockets high in the manways. When ignited, usually accidentally by a miner's lamp, it exploded, killing the miner and his laborer and any other people nearby. The annual toll in human lives from this type of accident was high and constant, but since only a few men were involved at a time, demands for greater safety were generally ignored. The operators, of course, blamed the accidents on the miners' carelessness rather than on their own failures to follow the best ventilation practices.[23]

By the end of the nineteenth century, most mines had at least two shafts, one for hoisting and the other for air. At the top of the air shaft there were huge fans resembling rimless wheels with broad blades like those on a side-wheeled steamboat; these were kept turning day and night. They created a vacuum at the top of the air shaft; the weight of the atmosphere drove fresh air down the hoisting shaft, while stale, gas-laden air was drawn up the air shaft. If the fresh air flowing down the hoisting shaft was allowed to follow its natural course, it would immediately flow into the air shaft and rush into the fan-created vacuum at the top. It was prevented from doing so by the use of doors, brattice-work "curtains," and air bridges which controlled the flow of air in the mine and directed it into the working areas.

Parallel to the gangways and some distance from them smaller tunnels called airways were driven, which were connected to the gangways at intervals by short tunnels called crossheadings. The airway tunnels opened into the air shaft, and as "used" air was drawn out through them, fresh air rushed through the gangways from the hoisting shaft. Its flow into the crossheadings was controlled by partitions, so that it entered the airways only at the desired crossheadings. Entry occurred at a point that ensured a maximum flow of air past and into the working breasts. If the breasts were worked only a short distance, the strong current of air sweeping past their entrances was sufficient to ventilate them, especially since the miners had the habit of "brushing" out the powder smoke by swinging their coats over their heads.

As the breasts advanced, however, and new crossheadings were opened to connect them, partitions of gob were built in the airways, and the air directed into one breast, then through the new crossheadings into the next, and so on. If the breast was very gaseous, a brattice of boards, or "brattice cloth," was built to force the air to pass close to the working face. Since the air had to reach every part of the mine, it was often necessary for one air current to cross another. This was accomplished by an air-tight box called an air bridge, actually a tunnel carrying one current of air over another. Each current of air was called a "split," and the law required that no more than seventy-five men work in one air split.[24]

Even the most efficient ventilation system could not keep the mine completely free of dust and gas. The mine workers faced constant hazards as a result. The exhalations of men, animals, and the ever-present coal dust polluted the air. Coal dust is particularly dangerous because it gradually clogs the lungs. Three out of every four miners who survived the normal hazards of working underground could look forward to being disabled by the black lung disease, which is incurable and slowly kills a man.

In the mines workers were threatened by several dangerous gases given off by coal. The most abundant is methane gas (CH_4), known to the miners as "firedamp." About half the weight of air, it rises and accumulates along the roofs of chambers. At times it suddenly issues from cracks in the coal wall, spewing out in a stream called a "blower." When a miner's lamp came into contact with a large volume of gas, a tremendous explosion destroyed everything in its path. Miners who survived the initial blast threw themselves on the mine floor and buried their mouths, noses, and eyes in the damp dirt to escape the flames and searing heat. They waited until the gas burned itself out, then quickly scrambled to their feet and fled, for the by-product of firedamp was an even more deadly gas known as "afterdamp." This is carbonic acid mixed with some nitrogen. It is heavier than air and gathers along the floor. A single inhalation of afterdamp in its pure state results in unconsciousness and certain death. A constituent of afterdamp is "blackdamp," pure carbonic acid gas. It is given off by coal in the same manner as firedamp and frequently the two mixtures evolve together. Also a heavy gas, it gathers along the floor of the mine. Inhalations of small quantities of blackdamp dull the mind and numb the body. In larger quantities it brings sudden death.

Though its presence is less frequent than the others, the most dangerous gas is carbonic oxide, known as "whitedamp." It is odorless and tasteless and usually cannot be detected until it does its fatal work. It is formed when carbonic acid passes through ignited carbonaceous material and is produced by smoldering gob fires, burning wood in the mines, or as a result of explosions of firedamp or blasting powder. Miners who had the good fortune to escape explosions of firedamp and the other toxic gases had little chance for survival if they encountered the dreaded whitedamp.[25]

Miners fought their battles against gas in several ways. In the early days dogs were sometimes lowered into suspected gaseous areas. If the dog was not breathing when he was hauled to the surface, the miners figured his death had saved their lives. Miners also carried caged canaries into their working places; the theory held that the small lung capacity of the birds would cause them to be overcome first if gas were present. Eventually a safety lamp, called a "Davy," was developed to test for gas. The lamp flame was enclosed within a fine wire gauze; if gas were present, small quantities seeped through the gauze, causing the flame to flare up. Similar but more sophisticated versions of this type of test lamp have been used since the Davy was introduced in the nineteenth century.[26]

Exposure to deadly gas was but one of the dangers the miner faced. In reality he

A mine rescue worker with an oxygen helmet. 1911.
Courtesy of the Lewis Hine Collection, Albin O. Kuhn Library,
University of Maryland, Baltimore County.

was surrounded by them. If a man worked in the mines for twenty-five years, he could expect to suffer several serious injuries during that time. The cuts, bruises, dislocations, and minor burns that frequently occurred in the normal course of his work were hardly noticed. Every miner really worried that he would not come out of the mine alive. On the average, one miner was—and is—killed in America every day. Since the turn of the century almost 102,000 men—and women now, too—have lost their lives in the nation's mines. In the nineteenth century, when safety was often ignored and the enforcement of regulations lax, the toll of dead and injured was appalling: three miners were killed every two days in the anthracite fields, and tens of thousands were seriously injured and maimed. Some of the fatalities were caused by great disasters that claimed scores of lives; most died in accidents involving one or two men. The monotonous day-to-day toll of lives went largely unnoticed by the public, but the total over time was grim evidence of the human cost of mining coal.[27]

A roof fall. The scene shown here was probably arranged by photographers of the Kingston Coal Company in the area of an actual roof fall. Courtesy of the Wyoming Historical and Geological Society, Wilkes-Barre, Pa.

The character of the work contributed to the high accident rate. Strict supervision was difficult; the number of competent supervisory personnel was always inadequate. In their haste to complete their day's work the miners themselves often took unnecessary chances. Dangerous pieces of roof rock might not be taken down, or adequate support props might not be placed. In the case of Slavic or Italian miners, instructions given in English by foremen might be understood badly or not at all. Then, if an accident occurred, and the victim was a foreigner with no relatives in America, the boardinghouse owner might refuse to receive the body, saying, "Dead Hungarian no good." The corpse was usually dispatched to a medical college for the dissecting table.[28]

The most frequent accidents were caused by roof falls. With startling frequency the overlying layers of rock and soft slate above the veins came down, splintering timbering and props and crushing men's bodies. The weight of such roof falls was sometimes so great that men were literally flattened and ground into the damp mine floor. Their bodies had to be scraped up with shovels. Those who survived such falls were frequently horribly mangled, with crushed spines and splintered limbs that could not be properly set or required amputation.[29]

The black powder used for blasting also took a heavy toll of lives. The fuses used before the introduction of electric detonators were not always reliable; the fuse might simply smolder inside the tamped hole rather than ignite the powder. The miner waited for a time; then, thinking that the fuse had gone out, went into the breast to pull the charge. At that moment the smoldering fire might finally reach the powder, greeting the miner with a blast that sent hundreds of pounds of coal hurtling upon him. Fine particles of coal dust were frequently blown into his unprotected eyes, causing blindness.

Working in near darkness contributed to the high accident rate. The dim light from the miner's lamp illuminated only the area directly in front of him. He might fail to see or hear approaching mine cars and be crushed between them and the rib or supporting timbers. Sometimes while riding atop a moving mine car he did not see a low approaching roof cross-support and he would be caught and "rolled" as the car moved along beneath him. The introduction of electricity for lighting gangways and powering locomotives increased the incidence of accidents. Many motormen were electrocuted when they inadvertently touched the live trolley wire just a foot or so above their heads. Other workers stood up in the cars at the wrong moment, or stumbled over cross-ties and touched the exposed electric power cable.[30]

The major losses of life were usually caused by explosions and mine fires which swept through the workings. Great quantities of highly volatile coal dust collected on every surface in the mines. When coal was blown from the face in a very dry area, millions of particles of coal dust were left suspended in the air. A spark of a lamp flame might ignite the dust, and then, with a tremendous roar, it exploded, sending flames through the dust-filled air. "Flashing like lightning and booming like massed cannons," chainlike, explosion after explosion raced through headings, breasts, and gangways. The effect was like that of a fiery hurricane. Debris, coal, timber, tools, empty mine cars, animals, and men were blown through the air like pellets shot from a gun. The great amounts of wooden timbering often caught fire. Sometimes a seam was ignited, and the resulting sulfurous fumes contaminated the mine. Those who escaped the explosions might die of suffocation.[31]

The most disastrous mine fire in anthracite history occurred at Avondale, near Wilkes-Barre, on September 6, 1869. At that time a fire was kept burning at the bottom of shafts to help form a draft which, in addition to fans, kept air circulating through the workings. The Avondale colliery had been closed by a strike and the fire had been allowed to go out. When it was relit at the resumption of work it flashed out of control, igniting timbering and other debris. The flames roared up the ventilator shaft and into the engine hoisting room, located in the breaker built directly over the shaft. The hoisting machines, the only means of escape for the men working below, were completely destroyed. The only way to get air into the shaft was through the main opening—the *only* opening—and as the flames spread this also was partly filled with burning timbers. Desperate efforts went on for two days to control the fire and rid the mine of gas. When rescuers finally reached the trapped workers more than 300 feet below the surface they found no one alive. All 108 men and boys had died. The scene where most of the workers were found was described by the rescuers:

> Fathers and sons, they said, lay clasped in each other's arms. Some of the dead were kneeling; some were sitting hand in hand, as if they had vowed to live and die together; some lay on the ground, as if they had fallen while fleeing; and others lay as if pressing their faces into the earth in the hope of extracting from it a breath of pure air. . . . In one chamber every man had stripped off his clothing to use it in stopping the crevices of the embankments, and one man was in the attitude of pushing his coat into a crevice. . . . the foul gas rushed in and overcame him.[32]

Water also posed a major danger to miners. Shafts or slopes were driven beneath the natural water level, causing downward seepage. Mines were generally graded so that water would accumulate at the bottom of the shaft, where the sump was located. From there it was pumped to the surface by powerful steam engines through a timbered compartment of the shaft known as the pump way. At the turn of the century the most powerful pumping engines extracted 1,200 gallons of water per minute. Seldom in the anthracite region did the tonnage of water pumped from a mine fall below the tonnage of coal hoisted; in the Lehigh field there were mines

In some anthracite mines eight to ten tons of water were removed for every ton of coal extracted. Courtesy of the Wyoming Historical and Geological Society, Wilkes-Barre, Pa.

Jumbo pumps removed water from the mines.
Courtesy of the Burg Collection, MG-273, Pennsylvania State Archives.

where eight to ten tons of water were pumped for every ton of coal extracted. In active workings every effort was made to control the amount of water, but abandoned workings at a higher level often filled with water. Until accurate underground survey maps were required, miners unaware of the exact location of such workings would sometimes break through a barrier pillar and would suddenly be swept away as the water broke through with irresistible force.

At Jeansville, a mine patch south of Hazleton, such an accident occurred on February 4, 1891. Two miners were firing near an abandoned slope that had been flooded several years before. Their mine map indicated that they were about sixty feet from the slope, but they were actually only five feet away. When their blast went off it opened the old workings and the water poured in with flood force. The two miners were in the gangway and the water swept them to a place where they could swim to safety. But seventeen other men working nearby were not so fortunate; they drowned in the rush of water. Emergency pumps were installed that raised 2,000 gallons of

Robbing the pillars caused the section of track and ground shown here to collapse, probably in the 1880s.   Courtesy of the George Bretz Collection, Albin O. Kuhn Library, University of Maryland, Baltimore County.

water per minute, but it was several days before the water level was sufficiently low so that rescuers could descend. Then they had to make their way through the flooded and rock-clogged workings on a raft. After twenty days five men were found alive in a breast; they had managed to survive by eating parts of their clothing and by chewing bark from the timber. Eventually six bodies also were discovered, eaten by rats almost beyond recognition.[33]

Disasters sometimes occurred as a result of unsuspected geological conditions. A Susquehanna Coal Company miner working near Nanticoke on December 18, 1885, broke into a geological depression, or pocket, filled with water, quicksand, and culm. Within minutes, twenty-six men and boys had lost their lives. Though efforts to reach the flooded and clogged part of the mine went on for weeks, the quantity of water and debris was so great that the rescue attempt had to be abandoned.[34]

Until the Avondale disaster aroused public opinion and resulted in the passage of legislation regulating some aspects of mining operations, safety was at the discretion of individual operators. Since Avondale, laws regulating almost every aspect of mining with reference to the health and safety of mine workers have been passed. Breakers must be located a safe distance from the mouths of shafts; every mine has to have at least a second opening for escape purposes; mines must be ventilated by fans rather than by dangerous furnaces; the amount of powder that can be stored underground is limited; there must be sufficient support timbering; and laws regulate the working of breakers and other machinery. The legislation regarding safety is enforced by state mine inspectors from the Pennsylvania Bureau of Mines.

The state also requires operators to provide first aid facilities at the collieries. This requirement was intended to meet a need that existed from the very first days of anthracite mining. In the early years medical care was haphazard at best. Injured miners were simply deposited at their homes; the care they received was administered by their families. Operators assumed little or no responsibility for men injured in their mines. In the decades after the Civil War the operators provided company physicians, with fees for their services deducted from the workers' pay. But in the nineteenth century medical care was rudimentary. The variety of saws and similar appliances found in company physicians' bags looked like carpenter's tools rather than medical instruments. Some of the larger operators eventually did provide facilities for medical care. The first of these in the region was the so-called Drifton Hospital, established by the Coxe family at their holdings near Hazleton. A commentator, however, suggested that it seemed more like a place for dying rather than a place for getting well.

The first miners' hospital was built at Ashland about 1878. Another institution with facilities specifically intended to treat mine injuries was the Hazleton Hospital, which opened in February 1891. It was also financially supported by the Coxe

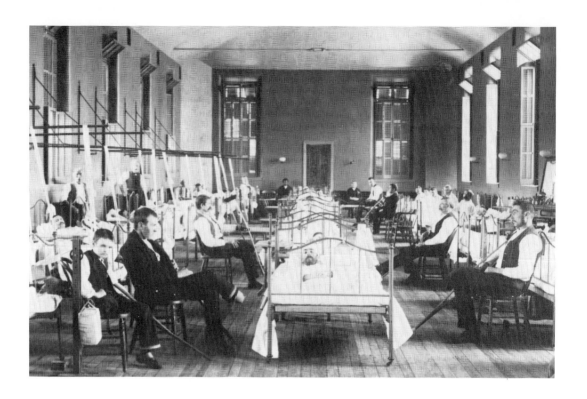

Above: A miners' hospital ward, probably in the 1880s. Courtesy of the George Bretz Collection, Albin O. Kuhn Library, University of Maryland, Baltimore County.

Left: The victim of a mine accident. Courtesy of the Burg Collection, MG-273, Pennsylvania State Archives.

Facing page, top: An ambulance at a mine shaft near Wilkes-Barre. Miners called these ambulances Black Marias. Courtesy of the Wyoming Historical and Geological Society, Wilkes-Barre, Pa.

Facing page, bottom: The funeral for a victim of a mine tragedy, probably in the 1880s. The empty casket indicates the victim's body was not recovered. Courtesy of the George Bretz Collection, Albin O. Kuhn Library, University of Maryland, Baltimore County.

family. The injured were brought to the hospital in mule-drawn covered wagons large enough to accommodate two patients, an attendant, and the driver. The hospital authorities invoked the "next of kin" rule, and after the patient had been taken to the facility, the ambulance drivers had to drive to the injured man's home to inform the family of the victim's injury or death. As soon as the ambulance appeared in a patch, a crowd gathered to follow the wagon. Children would anxiously call out to the driver: "Hey, mister! Hey, mister! Who was hurt? Was it my pop? Was it my pop?" The driver, faced with the threat of losing his job, could not tell, since the wife, or widow, as the case might be, was notified first.[35]

The high incidence of injuries and death engendered feelings of fatalism and resignation in the mining communities. The shrill blast at an odd hour from the colliery whistle warning of an accident below, and the appearance of ambulances or the dreaded "Black Marias" with their cargoes of corpses, were expected occurrences. Still, the anguish of the victims' families and friends was no less intense. In this hour of grief, the community came together. When the broken body of a miner was deposited on the porch or in the kitchen of his house, the neighbors came immediately to help the family wash the corpse and prepare for the wake and funeral. The families of dead and injured men received contributions of food and money from neighbors and special parish funds. In many collieries a "keg fund," consisting of payday contributions deposited in an old powder keg, was established for the victims of accidents.

Before workmen's compensation laws were enacted, or union-negotiated benefit packages established in the twentieth century, most disabled miners or the families of those killed could look forward to a life of penury. Seldom did community contributions or insurance funds from the beneficial societies stretch very far. Mining companies did sometimes make lump sum payments to the victims or their families, but the amounts seldom exceeded several hundred dollars, and smaller sums were much more common. Disabled workers, widows, and children had to manage as best they could. They were usually evicted from company housing soon after the accident; eviction was expected. One crippled miner actually remembered with gratitude that the operator allowed him to remain in his company house for an entire month after the nature of his accident was known. As a result every mining community had an area of dilapidated housing, sometimes called "widow's row," where the families of accident victims eked out a meager existence.

Miners cutting coal at the face and the other workers underground were complemented by men and boys who performed a variety of jobs in and around the complex of colliery buildings located near the mouth of the shaft. They were called surface workers; their jobs involved supporting the men underground and transporting and processing the coal that was brought up from the mine. Unlike the contract miners, they were company employees and were paid an hourly wage; if they were bosses, they were paid on a monthly basis.

The colliery superintendent, who reported directly to the operator, was responsible for all operations, including the office staff. Working under him was the outside foreman, who saw that the coal moved swiftly from the shaft to the head of the breaker. He dealt with the multitude of problems involved in the transportation, grading, cleaning, and loading of coal for shipment to market. His assistant was the breaker boss, who was in charge of the building where the coal was processed and prepared for shipment.

At the bottom of the shaft a crew of men, usually four or five, called bottom men, kept loaded cars moving onto the cage and took empties off. At the shaft mouth a crew of similar size, called top men, raised the latticelike gate which protected the shaft opening, pushed off the loaded cars and coupled them to other loaded cars for transport to the breaker, then pushed empty cars onto the cage. At a signal the engineer operating the hoisting machinery lowered the cage into the shaft. The hoisting,

Surface workers at an anthracite colliery.
Courtesy of the Library of Congress.

A young mine worker.   Courtesy of the Burg Collection, MG-273,
Pennsylvania State Archives.

pumping, and fan engines were powered by steam generated in boilers fed by firemen with coal from the mine. All of the machinery, including that in the breaker,
was maintained by skilled machinists.[36]

A miner was experienced in many skills, including dynamiting, rock drilling,
masonry, carpentry, ventilation, drainage, mechanics, and, in the twentieth century,
electricity. He learned all of them on the job as he worked toward the coveted "title"
of miner under the guidance of more experienced men. For many it was commonplace to start working lives in the breakers before "graduating" to other jobs, first on
the surface, then underground. Dominick Just went through such a cycle. After a
time as a breaker boy, he worked outside at different laboring tasks, including saw-
ing mine props in the colliery lumberyard, unloading lumber, and loading prepared
coal into railroad cars under the breaker. He shoveled coal into the steam boilers
that provided energy for the colliery machinery, then worked in the car shop repairing mine cars. Eventually he was broken in as a hoisting engineer, which he considered an exciting job. "The mine carriages or elevators were operated by steam
Corliss hoisting engines with large drums, operated by a steam throttle and a reverse lever. It took me a number of days to learn," he said. "One had to become thoroughly familiar with its every operation before he was allowed to hoist coal. . . . I
eventually became master . . . and we hoisted 700 to 800 mine cars every day." Just
later went on to become a first assistant to the outside foreman and a carpenter boss
in charge of construction before finally going underground. Even then he worked for
a time putting up support timbers before actually learning mining.[37]

A nineteenth-century coal breaker.   Courtesy of the George Bretz Collection, Albin O. Kuhn Library, University of Maryland, Baltimore County.

The interior of the top of a breaker, where coal cars bring coal for processing, probably in the 1880s.   Courtesy of the George Bretz Collection, Albin O. Kuhn Library, University of Maryland, Baltimore County.

Coal waste from the breaker was deposited on towering black mountains called culm banks.   Courtesy of the Burg Collection, MG-273, Pennsylvania State Archives.

A breaker operation. Older and disabled miners often worked with the breaker boys, hence the miners' saying—"twice a boy and once a man is the poor miner's life."   Courtesy of the George Bretz Collection, Albin O. Kuhn Library, University of Maryland, Baltimore County.

The cycle of a miner's life began early. Every fourth worker was a boy. He usually started out in the breaker, sometimes at age six but normally at eight or nine. The breaker was a towering structure that loomed 100 to 150 feet above the other colliery buildings and machinery. It was the most important building, and its peculiar design made it unlike any others. Its architectural form followed its function, though its shape—like that of a truncated, stepped pyramid or giant praying mantis—gave it a menacing air. Coal brought up from below was carried to the top of the breaker in mine cars along an inclined plane; the coal was tipped from the cars into revolving cylinders which crushed and screened the coal, separating it into various sizes. The coal was then fed downward through a series of chutes. Boys sat crouched on narrow planks over the moving coal, their feet in the chutes to slow the flow. Below them in tiers were other boys, each responsible for picking out the slate and refuse missed by those above. Sometimes old men or injured miners who could no longer work underground labored as "breaker boys," hence the popular regional refrain: "Twice a boy and once a man is the poor miner's life."

In the industry's early days the breaker boy's work day averaged ten hours, a work week six days. The daily wage was forty-five cents. Before water was used in cleaning and processing, the screening room where slate was picked was so thick with dust that the boys could hardly see beyond their reaches. They wore handkerchiefs over their noses and mouths and often chewed tobacco to keep from choking. Later mechanical breakers were somewhat cleaner, but the noise was horrendous and the whole building shook from the movement of the belts and chains that pushed the coal along. The novelist Stephen Crane, on one of his visits to the anthracite region, wrote that the boys "live in a place of infernal dins. The crash and thunder of the machinery is like the roar of an immense cataract. The room shrieks and blares and bellows. All the structure is a-tremble from the heavy sweep and circle of the ponderous mechanism."[38] The windows in these breakers often were broken, and in winter icy air swept in, while in summer stifling heat caked coal dust on sweat-soaked bodies. Even after gloves were introduced many companies forbade them, and bleeding fingers—a condition known as "redtop"—were common. Oldtimers claim that the paths the boys took home after work could be followed by the drops of blood in the snow.[39] "Over the Coals," a poem by James Sweeny Boyle, catches something of the pathos of their lives:

> Over the ice they pull the coals,
> Their fingers rent by a hundred holes;
> You may trace the path torn digits tread
> By the crimson stream on the iced chutes shed.

Their heads are bowed and their bodies cramped.
A painful look on their features stamped;
Their knees are pressed against aching breasts
Till bones are bent in their chambers tight. . . .

In sorrow they slave where the massive screen rolls,
So fearfully, tearfully over the coals.[40]

In the deep snows of winter, fathers carried smaller boys to the breakers on their backs in the predawn darkness, or mothers would take the younger boys and return to wait for them at the end of the shift. A story from the World War I era in Wilkes-Barre relates how a mother carried her son's lunch pail to the breaker for him because he was too small to handle it himself. After steam-powered mechanical chutes were introduced, many boys who fell into the chutes were killed, their bodies horribly mangled by the rollers. There is a ballad about a mother who went insane when her son was crushed by the rollers. She returned to the breaker day after day, always walking home alone.

At the end of their shifts the boys clambered down the rickety stairs of the breakers, happy to be free, their teeth gleaming in coal-dust-blackened faces. After a wash and supper, they sometimes ran off to night school, where all ages were taught by a single teacher, with light coming from a lamp carried by each boy. In some schools the history and geography lessons were sung in improvised verses that the teacher invented. Most teachers, male and female, seldom lasted long in one school. They usually were not tough enough to deal with the boys.[41]

Work discipline in the breakers was enforced by foremen who used clubs or leather switches to keep the boys at their work and to enforce order. Whippings and similar harsh treatment frequently resulted in spontaneous strikes, slowdowns, and sitdowns. But usually these strikes were short-lived as bosses went after the boys with whips, a practice known as "whipping them in." Still, the boys remained contemptuous and rebellious, shouting and swearing like troopers above the noise as they developed the independence and scorn for the bosses that they would later show in the mines. The brutality of breaker bosses sometimes led to more direct action.

At the "Muskrat" breaker near Moosic in the early part of the century, barbarous methods backfired on a breaker boss with a wooden leg.

The boss, whose name was Bill, had forty or fifty boys under him. As an old-timer who worked for him said, "And when I say that he had those boys under him, I mean just that! For a man with a wooden leg he could skip and hop over those seats and chutes with the speed and accuracy of a squirrel flying from limb to limb. And if he found a single piece of rock, slate or bone in any chute about to enter the coal pocket, he proceeded in a methodical and efficient manner to make every boy on that chute of coal realize the grave necessity of clean coal."[42] Bill's methods were "cruel

Breaker boys at their work, Eagle Hill Colliery. George Bretz's photographs, taken in the 1880s, include some of the earliest depictions of child labor in the anthracite region.   Courtesy of the George Bretz Collection, Albin O. Kuhn Library, University of Maryland, Baltimore County.

and unique. He would raise that wooden stump and give each boy a prod in the back, or use it as a club to inflict punishment on little backs already aching from the constant bending of the body above the chutes of coal. Or, he would come up from behind a boy and take him by both ears and lift him a foot or two above his seat."

One sunny July afternoon after work the boys met at a nearby swimming hole and decided that they would spend the following day swimming rather than report for work. They realized that this was a grave offense; some of the more timid ones pointed out that they would receive far greater punishment at home for "playing hookey" than even Bill could inflict. But the leaders convinced them that their parents need never find out, at least until payday, and by then they might have devised a good excuse. The next day all the boys except three or four—who were promptly denounced as scabs—assembled at the swimming hole. They were soon confronted by the furious Bill, the colliery superintendent, and the outside foreman, who stood on a natural rock overhang above the pool and demanded that the boys return to work. While the bosses were exhorting the boys, two of them suddenly rushed upon them from a clump of bushes. They slammed into the unsuspecting Bill from behind and went sailing off the ledge with him. As the three bodies hit the pool with a mighty splash the other boys dove into the water and surrounded the puffing, sputtering breaker boss. They dove under him and pulled him down, and when he reached the surface again, gasping for air, they splashed water into his face. It took a full fifteen minutes before the other two bosses could pull the half-drowned Bill from the pool. Negotiations then began. The boys stationed themselves on the other side of the pool from the bosses and demanded that as a condition for their return to work, Bill be relieved from his duties as breaker boss. The superintendent finally gave in and the boys triumphantly returned to their places on the coal chutes.

Breaker boys were used in the mine fields until well into the twentieth century. The Pennsylvania legislature in 1885 made it illegal to employ boys under fourteen inside mines or under twelve in surface jobs. In 1903 these limits were raised to sixteen and fourteen, respectively. But the laws were seldom enforced. Parents eager for additional income filed false affidavits on a boy's age with local magistrates, who

Angelo Ross, breaker boy, Pittston, 1911.
Courtesy of the Lewis Hine Collection, Albin O. Kuhn Library,
University of Maryland, Baltimore County.

collected a twenty-five-cent fee for each document processed. The mining companies did not object because they paid the boys so little.

Young boys made up approximately one-sixth of the anthracite work force at the turn of the century, and a large number of these boys were under legal age. It is extremely difficult to determine the exact number of boys and their ages because 75 percent of them were foreign born. We do know, however, that as of 1905, 75 percent of the state pickers killed were under sixteen.

From their first days in the breakers the boys quickly picked up habits that lasted a lifetime. One of these was the "knockdown," the practice among mine workers of deducting a certain portion of their wages from their pay envelopes without telling their mothers or wives. It was a custom in the region as old as coal mining itself. Though the companies used various systems of payment over time, none was ever so complicated that the wily workers could not somehow circumvent it.

For workers such as breaker boys, door boys, drivers, and laborers, whose wages were based on a set daily or weekly rate, the knockdown was usually confined to a certain part of any overtime pay. But for contract miners, knocking down had a considerably broader scope. Since the miner might make more money on one day than on another, there was no way for his wife to check his wages. He might also charge his wife at the company store for lamp oil that was never purchased or have false charges made to the "book" for blasting powder or blacksmith work. A frequent practice was for the miner to empty his pay envelope, with the amount inside clearly marked on an outside corner, and substitute it for a borrowed company man's envelope, which showed a lesser amount. One St. Clair miner who married an unsuspecting girl from New Jersey devised an ingenious method of knocking down. He told his wife that he earned $5.96 a day but on payday gave her his pay with $0.20 deducted for each day worked. He explained that the company charged $0.10 fare each way for riding up and down the shaft.[43]

"A miner is his own boss." This statement, repeated time and again, was literally true for miners working at the face. There was little doubt that the miners themselves believed it. They showed it by their independence, their attitude toward authority, and their resistance to anyone who attempted to bring them under close supervision and control. They practiced a kind of "miners' freedom" in a work environment different from that of other industrial laborers.

Anthracite mining remained a "cottage" industry during the course of its history. In this case the cottage was the working breast. Work in the anthracite cottage was characterized by contract miners working almost alone, with little outside direction, and relying on skills, judgment, and knowledge acquired through years of practicing their craft. They had control of the pace of work in their immediate surroundings, the techniques used for doing the work, and all decisions affecting it.

Men at work in a mine gangway, probably in the 1880s. Miners had to be men of many skills.
Courtesy of the George Bretz Collection, Albin O. Kuhn Library, University of Maryland,
Baltimore County.

They relied on their own initiative, motivation, and sense of responsibility. They depended upon no one else in doing their work at the face; indeed, others—their laborers—depended upon them. Like any master craftsmen they took pride in their abilities and staunchly defended their right to work as they pleased.

The miners' freedom was a by-product of the geography of the workplace in the mines. The pitching nature of the anthracite seams usually rendered it impossible for coal-cutting machinery to be used; the assembly line techniques of the modern factory could not be employed. Though pneumatic drills and electronic detonators replaced hand drills and powder fuses, the work at the face still had to be done by individual miners. With hundreds of men working underground in separate chambers at various levels over miles of distance, close supervision was extremely difficult. Under these conditions the most expeditious method of ensuring production was to pay miners by the ton of coal produced, on what amounted to a piecework basis. The miners, who contracted with the operators to cut coal at so much per ton, thus were responsible for their own production. This autonomy further decreased the need for supervision. Since miners were largely on their own in the working place, even many operators were loath to interfere with the way in which the work was done. Foremen in the mines were often more arbiters of disputes or expediters than overseers.[44]

The miners' independence was perhaps best expressed by their attitude toward authority. Through their informal conduct they simply resisted any formal authority in the mines. In some respect they saw themselves as the stars of the show and tended to look upon other workers and even supervisors as mere stagehands. A master mechanic in a mine expressed the miners' feelings about authority:

> The men [i.e., the miners] don't want supervisors who are driving. Some of them have been in the mine for twenty or more years, and they don't like any fellows telling them how to get off. They don't produce for a tough foreman. They don't give a damn. After they've been here for awhile, they don't worry about anything.[45]

A work crew resting with a load of coal at the head of a slope mine, circa 1911.   Courtesy of the Lewis Hine Collection, Albin O. Kuhn Library, University of Maryland, Baltimore County.

Another miner said: "New men in the mine are nervous; they are always looking over their shoulder for a boss. They learn differently in a few days."[46]

Most miners learned independence and disregard for authority early. It was part of a tradition that they picked up, first in the breaker, and later as they continued through the succession of jobs leading to that of contract miner. They learned the tradition just as they learned mining—on the job, in the mine, from skilled miners. They also learned it wherever miners met: in their homes, the saloons, the fraternal halls, the patch towns. The tradition made even the youngest workers bold. At the Lincoln Colliery in Schuylkill County a mine superintendent caught a door boy smoking.

"Boy, don't you know you ain't supposed to smoke here?" thundered the superintendent.

"Yah, I know it," responded the boy, "but I watch out for the bosses. They won't catch me at it."

"I'm the superintendent!"

"Well, you've got a helluva good job," answered the door boy.

The superintendent just shook his head and walked away, laughing.[47]

The miners showed their independence by refusing to conform to a planned work schedule. They appeared ready for work at the start of their shift, loaded their assigned quota of cars—and God help everyone if empties were not available—and went home when their day's work was done. It did not matter if they were on the job six hours or eight. Working only long enough to meet their obligations was one of the most closely guarded traditions. They defended it against the companies' efforts to impose a standard work day, and insisted that their union not negotiate the right away. "We quit when we're through," was the miners' refrain.[48]

Even during World War I, when they were under pressure to extract every ton of coal, the miners refused to abandon their tradition of quitting after they had met their quota. When one mine superintendent put out an order that, except for sickness or injury, men would only be hoisted at noon and at the end of the standard shift, an incensed miner sent a loaded coal car to the surface with the following message chalked on its side:

> I'll have you know Mr. Dunne,
> That with this car my day is done.
> If you don't like my work or poem,
> You can go to hell, I'm going home![49]

"Down here we have no rules." Acting on this attitude, miners influenced other underground workers as well. Men were assigned to do jobs or were sent to help work teams without receiving specific instructions. A track-laying crew, for ex-

Three miners, Pottsville, 1891. Courtesy of the Historical Society of Schuylkill County, Pottsville, Pa.

ample, might be told to lay track without being told when to complete the job. The foreman might come by at the end of the first day's work, ask how the job was going, and inquire about the possibility of finishing it in a week or so. Someone would answer, "Maybe. If we get cooperation."[50]

Though the miners forcefully upheld their independence, they did not generally act irresponsibly. They seldom left jobs uncompleted. For them, jobs had a beginning and an ending. They also were quick to help their fellow workers, even if doing so meant working at jobs considered to be the domain of others. "One day we had trouble with the shuttle-buggy," a miner recalls. "Old Bull [the foreman] came in to see what it was. He said, 'Let's tear it off and put it together,' and we did so in less than an hour. If we had waited for the mechanics, it would have taken three to four hours."[51] The irregularity of the mine workers' day also gave them a chance to relieve one another. They often rotated jobs without consideration for the prestige or skill level involved. In this way, mine workers were able to master a variety of skills.[52]

In the informal atmosphere of the mine, grievances were expressed directly. If a foreman had something to say to a miner he confronted him face to face and used unadorned language. The miners expressed their feelings in the same way. As might be expected, there were sometimes serious differences. One miner, instructed to wade through a pool of water to reach a work area, refused, claiming the water was six feet deep. When the foreman vigorously insisted, the miner heaved the man into the pool to prove his point.

Observers of miners' behavior inside and outside the mine have commented on their devil-may-care attitude. This outlook arises from conditions inside the mine, the most dangerous of all industrial environments. Mine workers almost expected to be injured. As one brakeman put it:

> In this place it stands to reason you got to be lucky if you're going to get out O.K. Some old timers, like Joe ——, got out well. It's always there. You got to think all the time. Down here nothing gives. The cars are made of iron, and the floors are rock. You've got to give. . . . It stands to reason it's going to get you in the end. You are going to get careless sometimes.[53]

A miner added: "You know about that fellow last night? The roof fell in on him. He wasn't doing anything. He couldn't do anything about it."[54]

Men, however, could not concentrate on their work if they were continuously distracted by fears and anxieties. Their sense of resignation had to be tempered by some hope that they would come out all right. As a result miners held beliefs which strengthened their expectations that they would not be injured or killed, beliefs expressed in stories and folklore passed down by word of mouth. Many of these tales are about the rats which infested the mines. Their aggressiveness was legendary. They overran the feed boxes of the mules, sometimes tearing the animals' snouts in a contest for the hay. When the workers sat for lunch the rats gathered, peering at the eating men with beady eyes through the gloom, occasionally diving right into the open lunch pails. The miners put up with them because they gave the men a certain feeling of security. Miners believed that the rats had a finely honed sense of impending disaster. They could tell, for example, when the roof was ready to fall, and their scurrying exodus gave warning to the men.[55]

Another set of beliefs involved the ever-ominous roof. Miners knew that hundreds, even a thousand or more, feet of rock and earth precariously separated them from the surface. Their great fear was of being trapped underground, and they gave constant attention to the condition of the roof. Though they knew that rock falls were largely unpredictable, they did believe that sometimes the roof gave out a warning. A creaking from above, a falling rock—the roof's way of "talking"—told them to beware. Miners believed that they could in some measure control their fate by propping in order "to hold back the roof." The men knew, of course, that propping could not prevent a serious cave-in and that its main function was to give warning of

Miners setting timber.   Courtesy of the Wyoming Historical and Geological Society,
Wilkes-Barre, Pa.

Removing the body of an entombed miner near
St. Clair, December 1954.
Courtesy of the Historical Society of Schuylkill County, Pottsville, Pa.

a fall when the pressure from above caused the timbers to bulge, spread, and creak. Yet the miners placed singular importance on propping because it gave them some feeling of control and security. They insisted that the prop man be strong and highly skilled, and they went out of their way to admire and comment on his work. They also told stories about how single props had saved lives; one of these was about a last prop in a mine that was so strong and well placed that after it was removed the entire mine caved in from the surface down.[56]

Many miners' legends describe the courage of men who work below ground. One of these concerns a miner who lost his way in the workings many years ago. When parts of his skeleton were eventually found there was speculation about how he had died. Finally it was determined that he had snapped a dynamite cap between his teeth rather than await a slow, agonizing death by starvation. The man was greatly admired as "a guy with guts"; he had chosen to die in his own way.[57]

There are also tales about the strange sights and sounds of the spooky anthracite mines, of gurgling, moans, hisses, whines, and moving, luminous lights—of "ghosts." A miner working alone 1,600 feet down at the Wadesville Colliery years ago opened a draw hole leading to a gangway and saw a bright light. He called out but there was no answer. Suddenly the light spread out like a flame and a smoky wraith in the shape of a man and woman appeared and then vanished just as suddenly. The miner left the draw hole and took a deep breath. "Am I seein' things?" he said. "I knew I wasn't drinkin', and I knew sure enough I didn't have a hang-over. But I finally got nerve enough and went in!"[58]

Some of the miners played upon the fear and superstitions of newcomers. A Pennsylvania Dutch miner named Elias, who was expert at throwing his voice, decided to have some fun with recent Polish immigrant workers at the old Lincoln Colliery. Elias was about to climb a chute up into a breast when the foreigners stopped him and explained, "No, Elias, not go up there. Man got killed there. Name Andy Shalinsky." "Well, I'm going up there anyway," said Old Elias, and he disappeared up the chute. After a time an eerie moan came from the breast. "What goes on there," demanded one of the men on the gangway. "Whoo, whoo, whoo, this is Andy Shalinsky," moaned Elias's disguised voice. "Me come back finishin' breast." The foreigners rushed for the shaft, shouting to be hoisted to the top. They were not going to work, they said, with a ghost.[59]

Despite their independence, miners were noted for their group solidarity. Highly individualistic though they might be, the working conditions of the mines forced them into close dependency on each other. They had to cooperate under dangerous circumstances. And miners expressed their solidarity in various ways. If a miner was injured, his friends took up a collection for him, sometimes even among workers on another shift. Occasionally when a miner was badly injured the other workers

Merritt Bundy, miner. *Courtesy of the Library of Congress.*

walked off the job in protest or simply in sympathy for the injured man. According to one of the most noble traditions, miners immediately volunteered for rescue operations, no matter how hazardous they might be. A miner who was trapped expected others to rush to his rescue and to persist until all hope was lost; he knew that others expected the same from him as well. For miners who did not conform to these unwritten rules working conditions could be made intolerable. Such men were given the silent treatment or, worse, found themselves without help when they needed it.[60]

The miners' attitudes and behavior underground extended to their lives on the surface. They felt that the dangers of their mining allowed them to "raise hell" off the job and to be "the boss" at home. Generally, they were more extroverted, spontaneous, and independent than the average industrial worker. They were often criticized for their swearing, drinking, gambling, and seeming unconcern with how they spent their money. They excused themselves by claiming that they worked hard at a dangerous job and earned the right to enjoy themselves. Even their wives accepted this behavior. As one observer put it: "The wives don't argue. The miners are tough birds. They [the wives] have to take it."[61]

The miners took pride in the fact that they did "men's work." And they felt that they worked harder and better than any surface workers. Their pride made them motivated workers in the mines; supervisors rarely complained about laziness. The tradition of giving a good day's work was passed from generation to generation. Miners felt it gave them certain "rights," which even the toughest supervisors came grudgingly to accept: the right to work as they pleased without undue interference; the right to control their tools and their machines and not to be controlled by them; the right to control their work schedules and even to work irregularly and be absent if they pleased; and finally, above all, the right to be independent, individual *men*.

5. The Molly Maguires

O N THE EAST WALL OF CELL 17 OF THE CARBON COUNTY JAIL IN MAUCH CHUNK there is a faint outline of a human handprint. It is visible despite numerous repaintings and an attempt by a jailer to chip it out many years ago. According to legend it was placed there by Alexander Campbell, who declared angrily, "That mark of mine will never be wiped out. There it will remain forever to shame the county that is hangin' an innocent man." On the morning when he supposedly put his mark on his cell wall Campbell died on the gallows with Michael Doyle, John "Yellow Jack" Donahue, and Edward Kelly.

That Sunday, in nearby Pottsville, the seat of Schuylkill County, a similar drama was being enacted. While an emotional crowd of 2,000 family, relatives, and friends clung to the hills surrounding the prison yard, six more men went to their deaths. All marched to the gallows stoically, seemingly indifferent to their fates but to the end protesting that they were not guilty. The first to mount the double gallows were Hugh McGeehan and James Boyle, McGeehan clutching a crucifix in one hand and a small statue of the Virgin in the other, while Boyle held a blood red rose. Before the trap was sprung Boyle shouted to McGeehan, "Goodby, old fellow, we'll die like men!" Then the hangman summoned James Carroll, a father of four children, and James Roarity, a recent immigrant, who had received a letter from his father in Ireland just days before, declaring belief in his innocence and entreating him to trust in God's mercy. Finally Thomas Munley and Thomas Duffy died, despite the protests of a Roman Catholic priest, Father Daniel McDermott, who swore that Duffy, and probably Carroll too, were innocent. For the Irish it was "Black Thursday," June 21, 1877, "Pennsylvania's Day of the Rope."

Within the next year and a half ten more Irishmen died on the gallows, convicted, like those before them, in controversial and patently unfair trials, of murder and other crimes against mine company bosses and local law officials. The hangings brought to an end the Molly Maguires, the alleged secret society charged with conducting a reign of terror in the anthracite fields for more than a decade. The day after the first hangings leading newspapers throughout the country bannered headlines about justice being achieved at last and ran stories about the destruction of an "organized society of murderers whose track had been marked with bloodshed, incendiarism and robbery." One New York paper, however, the *Irish World*, claimed that the men had been unfairly tried, and questioned whether there even was a secret society known as the Mollies.[1]

The conflicting accounts opened a debate that continues to this day. Heated dis-

Overleaf: Pennsylvania's Day of the Rope, June 21, 1877. This engraving, from Frank Leslie's Popular Monthly *shows six alleged Molly Maguires being led to the gallows in the prison yard at Pottsville. Courtesy of the Historical Society of Schuylkill County, Pottsville, Pa.*

cussions still rage in the region, not only as to whether or not the Mollies existed but also about the nature of their deeds. They are seen as either heroic champions of a brutally exploited underclass, avengers of the oppressed, or merciless criminals who violated the laws of society and in the end got what they deserved.

On the question of the very existence of a society called the Molly Maguires, even professional historians have been unable to give an incontrovertible verdict. The controversy continues because so few written records survive. There are no membership lists, correspondence, or minutes of meetings. The trial transcripts have been recovered recently, but these stand mostly as testimony to flawed and ir- regular justice. They do not demonstrate the existence of the Molly Maguires. And as to whether the anthracite Irishmen were class heroes or cutthroat vigilantes con- cerned more with getting even than with getting a measure of fair treatment for their brethren—well, the answer still depends, in the region at least, on which side your ancestors took. For this was a blood struggle that tore apart entire commu- nities, dividing men and women along ethnic, class, religious, and sometimes even family lines. It wasn't just the Irish against "the rest of them."[2]

The details that are known with certainty concern the hanged men themselves. All were Irish either by birth or descent. All were Roman Catholic in faith. All were either miners or small businessmen in mining communities. And they were mem- bers of the Ancient Order of Hibernians (AOH), the largest Irish beneficial society in North America. Whatever the truth about the Mollies as an organization, there is no question but that the brutality of life and work in Pennsylvania's anthracite country contributed to the violence for which all who hanged were held responsible.

The Irish arrived in the anthracite region in great numbers in the 1840s and 1850s in response to the expanding labor demands of one of the country's fastest growing industries. Most were recent immigrants, driven from their home soil by a series of devastating natural and man-made catastrophies. When James Joyce's character Stephen Dedalus remarks in *Ulysses*, "History is a nightmare from which I am trying to awake," he describes the years of the Irish exodus to America.

Most of the more than 1 million Irish who emigrated to America in the two dec- ades before the Civil War were peasant villagers, tenant farmers, and cottiers on English-owned estates—rustic, ill-lettered people who subsisted largely on the po- tatoes they dug on their meager plots. For more than 100 years the Irish peasantry had been afflicted by periodic failures of their staple crop, but in 1845 disaster struck. In that and succeeding years the plant disease known as potato blight wiped out virtually the entire crop. The English overlords of Ireland, reconverting the land from tillage to pasture, allowed nature to take its course. Without money to buy food even when it was available, men, women, and children in the tens of thousands died from starvation and disease; for hundreds of thousands more the only recourse was emigration. Even after the potato famine the exodus continued as the English evicted their tenants, tearing down their peasant hovels and driving the desperate cottiers away. Bloated corpses lay in the fields for weeks, and the streets of villages, observers noted, were "black with funeral processions."[3]

This reign of oppression was nothing new. Since the middle of the twelfth century, when Adrian IV, a good English pope, gave Ireland to Henry II, the Irish had suffered under the British. In the sixteenth century the English extended their domination, and then in 1649 Cromwell swept Catholic Ireland with "fire and sword." In the decade of his invasion more than one-third of the population of Ireland died, most of them from starvation and disease—almost three-quarters of a million people, somewhat less than the number that died in the Great Famine two centuries later. The English decimated the Irish landholding classes, seized the land, and reduced most of the people to a condition of complete destitution. The Penal Laws, begun in Elizabethan times, were reinforced during the reign of Cromwell and developed to their fullest after the victory of William of Orange at the Battle of Boyne in 1690.

In addition to the land confiscation, all priests were required to register their names and their parishes under penalty of being branded with a hot iron. Public crosses, which stood in every village in Ireland, were torn down. All bishops were banished under penalty of being hanged, or drawn and quartered. Friars and monks were also banished. No Catholic chapel could have a belfry, a tower, or a steeple. Catholic pilgrimages were outlawed. Catholics were prohibited from sitting in Parliament, from voting for members of Parliament, or from serving on grand juries, the local organs of government. Catholic schools were outlawed; nor could the Irish send their children abroad for a Catholic education. Catholics were forbidden from marrying Protestants, and any priests caught performing such a marriage were to be sentenced to death. Catholics were excluded from the legal profession; they could not be members of municipal corporations; they could not serve in the military forces, bear arms, or own a horse worth more than five pounds. And the Gaelic language was outlawed. Lord Chancellor Bowes summed up the situation when he said, "The law does not suppose any such person to exist as an Irish Roman Catholic." The Earl of Clare, his successor, called Catholics "the scum of the earth."[4]

Periodically the Irish struck back. But their uprisings and rebellions, most of them led by vigilante groups, were quickly and ruthlessly cut down. The English, however, could never feel completely secure. Landlords and officials were harassed and sometimes murdered by bands organized as secret societies seeking revenge for injustices. In nineteenth-century Ireland there were numerous such groups intimidating officials and mounting raids against the evictors of tenants: the Whiteboys fought against tithing, the Oakboys against forced labor on the roads, and after them, the Peep O'Day Boys, the Thrashers, Caravats, Shanavest, Rockbites, Ribbonmen, and Defenders. One such group was said to be named after its leader, Molly Maguire, a huge woman who reputedly wore pistols on her thighs and led a band of young Irishmen, disguised as women and brandishing staves, on sweeping night raids against government agents.

On the eve of immigration, the Irish, as one historian writes, "lived in an atmosphere of violence." An old Irishwoman put it best: "Ten o'clock in the morning and not a blow struck yet!"[5] In the face of English power, such resistance was heroic but fruitless. Then when the Great Famine hit in the 1840s the fabric of Irish society came unraveled. In one decade Ireland lost 2.5 million people, while the British did almost nothing to save them. In fact, the British continued to export wheat and other farm products from Ireland and to evict tenants from the land.

Sir Charles Wood, chancellor of the exchequer, perfectly described the "unofficial" British position when he wrote to an Irish landlord: "I am not at all appalled by your tenantry going. That seems to me a necessary part of the process. . . . We must not complain of what we really want to obtain." While in London the *Times* editorialized that the native Irishmen would fortunately soon be "as rare on the banks of the Liffey as a red man on the banks of the Manhattan."[6]

By the thousands the Irish flocked to the ports and emigrated to cities like Liverpool and Glasgow or to other places across the seas. Some went to English colonies in Canada and Australia, but the majority, perhaps tempted by faint rumors of "America the Golden," set sail for the United States. They left a dispirited, blighted island, where in some counties the only remaining lucrative trade was the manufacture and sale of coffin mountings and hinges.

The voyage across the Atlantic matched the horrors left behind. Since few Irish passengers could afford decent accommodations, they were crowded by the hundreds into steerage, the cheapest quarters available. In the gales of the North Atlantic many ships foundered or ran aground. In bad weather the emigrants were confined to stinking, fetid holds. After weeks at sea, food and water were in short supply. Under such conditions disease ran rampant among the already weakened passengers. The numbers buried at sea will never be known. Thousands who rode in these aptly named "coffin ships" found themselves bound for an unexpectedly longer journey than they were ticketed for. At Grosse Isle, near Detroit, a plaque reads: "In this secluded spot lie the mortal remains of 5,294 persons who, flying from the pestilence and famine in Ireland in the year 1847, found in America but a grave."

Immigrants who reached America alive faced, once again, a harrowing struggle for survival. At the port of entry, surly, fast-talking officials hurried the bewildered recent arrivals through a round of inspections and registrations. The ill and infirm in New York port were separated out and were confined to miserable quarantine on Staten Island. Individuals who were processed through were dumped unceremoniously onto the streets of the ports, where often the first persons they met took advantage of their ignorance to swindle them of the little money they had.

In the cities the new arrivals crowded into tightly packed slums, where entire families shared tiny, vermin-infested rooms not unlike the dank, mud-floored cabins in which they had lived under British rule in Ireland. Some built shacks of scrap lumber on the outer fringes of the growing cities, earning for themselves the opprobrious label "Shanty Irish." The muddy, sewage-filled streets provided some refuge in warm months, but they were filled with dangers as well. "Irish towns" became a term synonymous with crime and violence as despair and alcoholism overtook many dispirited immigrants.

Work was often harder to find than the new arrivals had expected. In a city like Boston, without heavy industry, there simply were not enough jobs. Vast numbers of Irishmen left their families behind and took to the roads, walking great distances in search of work while living off the land. Some found their way to the anthracite counties from Philadelphia and Baltimore after first walking from Boston. For others there was employment digging canals or laying the track of the new railroads. In the anthracite fields there were, of course, many such jobs, and throughout the century the Irish filled the employment rolls of the region's big transportation companies, manning the most dangerous and lowest-paying jobs.

The Irish in the region and elsewhere encountered difficulties of other kinds. They were Catholics in a prevailingly Protestant country, the first great influx of Catholics to North America. And they were "paddies," as the Protestant press stereotyped them—coarse, loud, hard drinking, and clannish. But their faith, more than anything else, turned native-born Protestants against them. In large eastern cities Irish churches, convents, and schools were attacked and firebombed, and there were numerous street fights between Irish and Protestant mobs.

Many felt that the Protestant republic was in danger from Rome. Feeding on these fears, native-born Protestants formed a secret Order of the Star-Spangled Banner, with elaborate rituals and rigid discipline. Members, when questioned by outsiders, answered, "I know nothing." Candidates secretly nominated by the organization showed surprising strength at the polls. In the election of 1854 the Know-Nothings elected a new legislature in Massachusetts, which conducted investigations of Catholic schools and convents. In Baltimore, they organized "plug-uglies," gangs of hoodlums who patrolled the polls with carpenter's awls, to "plug" voters who did not give the password. In some Baltimore wards, loaded swivel guns were placed at the polls to intimidate the Democrats, the party of the Irish.

A best-seller of that day was *Awful Disclosures* (1830), Marie Monk's account of her conversion to Catholicism and her stay in a Montreal convent, where the nuns lived in "criminal intercourse" with priests who crawled through secret passageways connected to their rooms to meet at night. The children born of these scandalous liaisons were baptized and immediately strangled, their bodies buried in mass convent graves. Nuns who refused to cooperate were murdered.

The book, apparently ghosted by a professional writer, had a tremendous vogue. But then Marie's mother disclosed that her daughter had never been a resident of the convent described in the book and that she had instead been in a Catholic asylum for delinquent girls and had run away with her boyfriend, the probable father of her child. Marie was further discredited when she bore a second illegitimate child, although the Protestant press claimed that this latter pregnancy was arranged by the crafty Jesuits to besmirch Marie's reputation. Years later Marie was arrested for picking the pockets of men in a whorehouse, and she eventually died in prison. But the book outlived her. It went through twenty printings, sold 300,000 copies, and until the Civil War served as the "Uncle Tom's Cabin" of the nativist movement.[7]

Anthracite miners in the Schuylkill field, the center of Molly Maguire activity.
Courtesy of the Historical Society of Schuylkill County, Pottsville, Pa.

When the Irish came to the anthracite fields, they found little relief from the vicious religious and ethnic prejudice they encountered in the seaboard cities. And here, as back on the home sod, the Protestants, many of them of English origin, were on top. They owned and controlled the major mine and transportation companies; they dominated local politics and local organs of opinion; they were the chief mine supervisors and superintendents; and they did the most highly skilled and best-paying work in the mines. Everywhere the Irish went in anthracite country—in the mines and in the patches, in the streets and stores, in the banks and public offices of the new coal towns—they encountered Protestant power and Protestant prejudice.

Many Irish moved into new mining towns like Pottsville, St. Clair, and Mahanoy City, where they lived side by side with the English and Welsh. But large numbers found themselves in company-owned "coal patches" directly adjacent to the mining operations. The coal companies completely dominated the life of these isolated communities, which were built to attract and house labor in a still remote and wild region. The company towns were "total communities"—everything was owned by the coal companies. Community laws were laid down by the company, obedience enforced by company police, and the feared "black list" was used on those who did not fall into line. The coal companies extended their social and economic control through ownership of almost all property. They owned the land, streets, houses, stores, schools, churches, and any community buildings. Usually the villages bore the name of the nearby colliery, though independent operators sometimes gave names to their patches.

The company store, where the residents of the village were usually expected to trade, was an integral part of these communities. Generally it was the only outlet for foodstuffs, miner's supplies, and merchandise in the area, and, most important, it extended credit, payment being deducted from paychecks. Though practices varied with different companies, many insisted that families in the village buy all their necessities at the store as a condition of housing and employment. Prices in these "pluck me" stores, as the miners sometimes called them, were often set artificially high. After charges at the store had been deducted from a miner's pay, he sometimes received what was called a "bobtail check," a stub indicating that rent and the cost of supplies added up to the total of wages due, leaving nothing to show for work.

The companies also provided their own security forces. Later institutionalized as the Coal and Iron Police, these privately hired police patrolled the villages and had the right to enter houses at any time to check on things. Their most important function, however, was to deal with labor troubles. Since they were recruited from among the Pennsylvania Germans and other groups outside the region, they had little in common with the ethnically different miners. They owed primary allegiance to the coal operators.

The early villages were simple, usually little more than a row of shacks and houses along a single, narrow road. Over time a few side streets might be added. The layout often reflected the class and ethnic composition of the society. At the head of the street were larger, more substantial houses belonging to the mine bosses and supervisors. Since they were Protestants, there might also be a Presbyterian church if the village's size warranted. Next came the miners' houses, sometimes single but usually duplex, each side consisting of two rooms down and one up. At the bottom of the street or on side streets were habitations for laborers and other unskilled workers, which were little more than shacks. In the middle of the village was the company store and perhaps a community center which occasionally served as a makeshift school. If a Catholic church existed, it lay at the workers' end of the village. Looming over the entire community was the immense black bulk of the coal breaker, surrounded by railroad tracks, a mule yard, and machine shops.

The houses of the first arrivals were constructed of scrap lumber, with tar paper nailed over it. A contemporary account described these dwellings as unfit for human beings, "repulsive to all sense of decency and unfavorable to the cultivation of domestic virtues." Later houses were made of unfinished hemlock boards with weather stays over the cracks. Inside there were no ceilings or wallpaper. Furniture was rudimentary—a rough bedstead, a table, some chairs, and a small coal stove for cooking, heating water, and heat. As many as fifteen or twenty people lived in the two lower rooms and the attic above. For those who could not share the bed, coarse mattresses were rolled out on the floor. Between the houses or on narrow strips behind were summer garden plots to supplement the family's bland and monotonous diet of foods like potatoes and cabbage. Wild berries gathered by women and children from the surrounding mountains were a summertime luxury. In a small shed some chickens and a pig might also be kept. Water for domestic use was drawn from a well or pump located somewhere in the village. Young children, few of whom attended school regularly, were usually assigned the task of carrying it.

Rent, often artifically high, was deducted from the miner's pay, and leases were often short-term, sometimes on a day-to-day basis. Troublemakers in the mine or community faced swift and summary eviction. Mine agents simply deposited a family's belongings on the road outside the door. Later in the century the mine owners pushed through the legislature a bill that made it possible to dispossess a worker from a company house on ten days' notice if he failed to fulfill the terms of his contract.[8]

Family life was a cycle of daily drudgery revolving around the start-and-stop whistles from the mines. The men, including male children as young as seven or eight years, trudged off with their lunches in the predawn darkness. The women then turned to household chores, for which they had total responsibility. They did the shopping, cooking, laundering, gardening; they cared for sick children or injured workers. They often used their skills with ingenuity, taking in laundry, tailoring, and sewing to supplement family incomes. Often they had complete control over the family budget.

Women also gathered firewood and scrounged lumps of coal from the culm banks of mine waste. Toward evening they went out to meet the traveling beer wagon so they would have buckets of beer ready for the returning men. When the men arrived in the house they would strip and the women would pour hot water over them and scrub them down. At night the mattresses and bedrolls were spread out in any available space. Young children usually slept with parents for warmth. The daily cycle of incessant work ended with exhausted sleep.[9]

Women drawing water from a patch town hydrant. Twenty-five families were supplied by this hydrant.   Courtesy of the Burg Collection, MG-273, Pennsylvania State Archives.

A gathering of miners' wives.
Courtesy of the Historical Society of Schuylkill County, Pottsville, Pa.

Another responsibility, the most terrible of all, fell on the women. When, at an odd hour of the day, shrill, continuous whistle blasts announced that an accident had occurred down below, the women rushed to the mine head, often waiting long, agonizing hours while rescue operations proceeded. If luck held, there were only injuries. Too frequently, however, dirt-caked, mangled, and burned bodies were brought up. A company wagon then carted the corpses to the miners' homes, sometimes depositing a body unceremoniously on the kitchen floor. Women then had the responsibility of washing and preparing their men for burial. Certain formalities were required. The corpse, sometimes packed in ice, was laid out in the front room in a crude pine coffin, propped up on two chairs in a corner. Preparations, including food and drink, were made for the wake. Friends and neighbors always helped out. Then through the long night before mass and burial, a steady stream of people came to pay last respects. Women and children kneeled and prayed over the candlelit remains, while the men sat at the table in the kitchen, drinking and reminiscing.

Though accidental death was commonplace, the cycle of labor always began again and went on. The coal had to be dug. Death provided the respite, as indicated by these words on a miner's tombstone:

Fourty years I worked with pick and drill
Down in the mines against my will
The Coal King's slave, but now it's passed;
Thanks be to God I am free at last.[10]

The families of Irish immigrants were large, in keeping with the peasant traditions of Europe. Five or six children were common. Births were assisted at home by midwives or by a company doctor if one was available. Rarely did all the children survive until adulthood. Diseases like measles, dysentery, diphtheria, and pneumonia carried off many in their early years. Later they were prone to fall during one of the epidemics that periodically swept the region. Medicine was, at best, primitive, and home remedies often the only recourse.

Childhood was brief and brutal. Clad in ragged hand-me-down clothes, and going barefoot most of the time (shoes were reserved for best occasions and had to last for years), children early learned the discipline of work. If they were lucky, they received a few years of rudimentary education, taught in one-room shacks by ill-prepared teachers paid paltry sums by the parents when they could afford it. Instruction was by rote memorization, since there were few books; behavior was enforced by the rod. Most boys left school at the age of about eight or nine to begin work in the breakers. Girls helped out with chores at home or went into the houses of the bosses as servants. For them marriage, often arranged, came early—sometimes at age thirteen or fourteen. By twenty, under the burdens of childbirth and housework, they appeared years older than they were. Beauty was not important in a miner's wife, only strength, skill, and durability. Women were often the only force in the household. The men, worn by the drudgery of the mines, seemed to come alive only when they were drinking.

There were always many widows in a coal town. If they were still young, with few children, they might find another husband, sometimes one of the boarders who were taken in to supplement family income. Other widows struggled desperately to keep households together by any means, including dependence on working children or neighbors' charity. Numerous widows operated taverns or other small enterprises. Still, the number of homeless orphans increased as the century wore on; they were victims of the dissolution of families. The fortunate might be taken in by relatives or neighbors; others went into harsh orphanages or survived by the limited charity available. The lives of widows and orphans were as precarious as any in the coalfields.

Though life was hard and monotonous, and vacations from the long, six-day work weeks unheard of except for periodic layoffs, there were various diversions. Certainly one of the most important institutions was the tavern, and there were many of them. Some of the larger towns were said to have one drinking establishment for every twenty-five or thirty inhabitants. In the smaller patches beer and whiskey were often made by the miners themselves.

Among the Irish, accustomed to hard drinking in their native land, alcoholism became a problem. Even contemporary observers were surprised by the amount of alcohol consumed in the fields. Until the 1850s alcohol was sold at many collieries, but pressure from miners' wives and the realization by coal operators that drinking affected production resulted in prohibition there. Some of the villages owned by Protestants with puritanical leanings outlawed drinking altogether. But the miners simply walked several miles from a "dry" patch to a "wet" one for a drink or sent young boys with buckets to fetch beer from nearby taverns or from the itinerant beer wagons.

The taverns and porches of general stores were scenes of much tough and raucous entertainment. There the miners regaled each other with stories, tales, ballads, and songs which expressed their thoughts and feelings, wit and humor, hopes and fears. Since the Irish were superstitious, the ghost story always was a favorite. Legends abounded about departed miners who suddenly appeared to help a former companion out of a tight spot or came back to haunt the living in return for some past misdeed. Strange sounds in the mines like mysterious tapping, wailing, and groaning caused by mine settlement, air circulation, or gas seeping through crevices were the sources of other tales. Miners exchanged heated opinions as to which charms, amulets, or religious symbols provided the best protection against such things. They debated the relative merits of different "wise women," who sought to heal mental and physical afflictions through their secret knowledge of roots, herb barks, and plants; they believed that some women were to be avoided because they had the power to cast the "evil eye" and to bring about misfortune.

The tales themselves led to long-standing traditions. After a miner was killed, his companions immediately dropped their tools and refused to return to work until after the funeral. Sometimes whole operations were shut down after a major accident. Miners believed that, until all the bodies were recovered, ghosts would haunt the workings. Miners who put away their tools after a day's work could not be persuaded to take them up again, for fear of courting death. It was believed, however, that the contents of miners' lunch pails had curative powers, and it was common for children to wait outside the pithead and beg some leftover scraps when the men emerged.[11]

Favorite visitors to the taverns and patches were roving minstrels, who wandered through the region singing ballads, telling stories, and dancing. Though often profligate and irresponsible, they were welcome at every social gathering. Tavern keepers amply supplied them with drink because of their drawing power, and no wedding, christening, or wake would be complete without them. Strumming banjos or playing fiddles, the minstrels sang about events like the great Avondale mine disaster, the Molly Maguires, or simply the woes of working down below. Often they improvised ballads or stories about local happenings or people. Coins tossed into a hat were their pay. Their verses and music "exuded sweat and blood, echoed every colliery sound, captured every colliery smell."[12]

The Irish miners loved competitive sports, especially those in which they could display their strength and gamble on the outcome. Sizable purses went to those who could run the fastest, lift the heaviest weight, jump the farthest, or beat any man in the tavern—bare knuckles, fight to the finish. Old-country sports like soccer and rugby were played on Sunday afternoons, and betting ran high if rival ethnic groups such as the Scottish or the Welsh made up the other team. Cockfighting was a common pastime; money changed hands until the wee hours in saloon garrets or remote barns as game roosters spilled their blood.

Certain days had special significance. June 25 was celebrated by the Irish and others from the British Isles as Mid-Summer Day. Old flour or cracker barrels filled with excelsior and other flammable materials were stacked around a tall pole and were ignited after twilight. Singing and dancing went on around the huge bonfires that lit up the countryside. Single girls were supposed to see the faces of their future husbands in the crackling flames. On St. Patrick's Day no Irishmen would work. After attending church, they paraded through town behind the church's green banner, which was their symbol and their pride. In the evenings they usually held a banquet, which was followed by speech making, singing, and humorous stories about the foibles of their people. The Irish also turned July 4 into a great holiday of their own. Since it was the celebration of America's independence from England, the Irish joined in with special glee, parading in their best dress with every available member of the community.[13]

In the evenings miners and their families gathered together in the patches, against a backdrop of colliery buildings and culm banks, to sing, to listen to storytellers, and to play folk games. A sheet of iron borrowed from the colliery provided an improvised dance floor for reels, jigs, and breakdowns as the fiddler scraped out a tune. Even underground, miners entertained themselves. On their breaks they congregated at the turnout, and danced on an old door formerly used to control ventilation, in a vault lit only by the pale yellow flames sputtering from their teapot-shaped lamps.

Catholic holy days, weddings, and wakes also provided diversions. Women were more active socially than men, especially in church affairs. But the men also had their fraternal and beneficial organizations, which had chapters in every town of reasonable size. Weddings, which sometimes lasted for days and went on in shifts to accommodate the work rhythm of the mines, were fine excuses for drinking and rollicking.

Some of the larger towns developed unusual institutions which rendered both community and sportive services. In Mahanoy City, which was divided like other mining communities into sharply defined ethnic neighborhoods, the Protestant Welsh and Germans had a combined gang, known as the "Modocs," which organized a fire brigade. The Irish also had a fire brigade. Each brigade served its own end of town. Problems occurred when a fire broke out in the center of town. Then both brigades responded and a royal melee broke out as the two outfits tried to determine which should put out the fire. Fists flew while the fire raged. It has even been suggested that fires were started purposely in order to give the boys a chance to have a little fun.

The one unifying experience in the lives of the miners was their work, the most dangerous job of the day. In the residential blocks of many mining towns every family had lost some member in the mines—father, son, brother. To the hazards underground was added exploitation of other kinds. Miners were paid for the coal they cut, by the cubic foot, carload, or ton. Possibilities for cheating abounded. Unscrupulous company employees "short-weighed" miners' production or claimed there was too much slate in the coal. The miners paid for their own helpers and for the powder, tools, and supplies they used. The operators forced the miners to buy materials from company stores as a condition of employment—at prices fixed by the operators. When deductions were made for helpers' pay, supplies, and rent for the company house, a miner could take home less than one-fourth of what he had earned for the amount of coal actually dug. In addition, the Irish, newcomers to the fields, faced discrimination in the mines and in the communities. As unskilled laborers who frequently spoke only Gaelic, they were cheated of wages by skilled English, Welsh, and Scottish miners. Even after they had become miners they were often assigned to the hardest and most dangerous workplaces. In the patch towns the Irish were given the worst housing, shanties thrown up in back alleys or in fields behind the main street. Their habits, customs, and religion were mocked and derided. To the Anglo-Saxons they were "micks," "paddies," "papists," ne'er-do-wells and drink-sodden wastrels, their women ignorant wantons and their children dirty ragamuffins.

The Irish miners fought back as best they could. In the tradition of the nineteenth-century immigrants, they banded together for mutual comfort and protection, seeking in unity solace, self-help, and defense. They organized mutual aid and beneficial societies, in which old customs were kept alive. These societies helped newcomers to find employment and housing and to prepare themselves for citizenship. The largest of the Irish societies—and the largest in America at mid-century —was the Ancient Order of Hibernians, with branches on both sides of the Atlantic. Its purpose was to promote "friendship, unity, and true Christian charity" among its members, but it was also a center of Irish-American labor and political action.

In keeping with the traditions of their English-dominated homeland, AOH members were deeply suspicious of outsiders, using passwords and special signs, like two fingers placed in a certain way at the throat, to identify fellow members. These practices were not unique, however, in working men's organizations of that period. In an atmosphere intensely antagonistic to organized labor, precautions were necessary to protect members from exposure, firings, and blacklisting.

The Irish also turned to politics as a method of self-assertion. In the decades before the Civil War the five anthracite counties voted Democratic, following the party to which the Irish flocked. They elected their own people as local school directors, councilmen, magistrates, county commissioners, and police officials. John "Black Jack" Kehoe, hanged in 1879 as an alleged leader of the Molly Maguires, was an elected constable in Mahanoy Township.

Though the majority of its members in the region were German Protestants, the Democrats were more willing to accommodate newcomers of different ethnic and religious backgrounds. The other major party at the time, the Whigs, the party of the English and the Welsh, was staunchly anti-Catholic and nativist. It supported sabbatarianism and temperance, the latter a movement deeply rooted in anti-Catholicism.

The principal newspaper of the Whigs and mine operators in the region was the *Miners' Journal* of Pottsville, edited by Benjamin Bannan. Bannan, a militant Welsh Presbyterian, not only vigorously defended the interests of coal capital but also launched ugly attacks against the Irish. In the 1850s he charged that the majority of paupers in Schuylkill County were Irish and that the cause of their condition was intemperance. He noted that the county had 636 taverns, one for every nine voters, most of them frequented by the Irish. For Bannan drinking was "moral leprosy." He also railed against the Irish for disrespect of the Sabbath, and attacked Catholic parochial schools. With Bannan and the other Whig leaders championing anti-

Catholicism and supporting the interests of the coal owners, it is no wonder the Irish voted Democrat overwhelmingly.

Beneficial societies and politics could not, however, deal with the root causes of exploitation. The Irish turned naturally to trade unions, which they joined in large numbers at every opportunity. In fact, the Irish became so militantly prounion that some employers refused to hire them because of their justly earned reputation for being the first to insist on higher wages and the first to strike.

Early attempts at unionization in the coalfields, however, resulted in multiple failures. In 1835 boatmen on the Schuylkill Canal formed a "Committee of Vigilance" and struck, but this organization soon disbanded. In 1842 the first recorded strike in the anthracite fields broke out and involved more than 2,000 men, but it was a spontaneous effort that failed to produce a permanent union. Then in 1849 John Bates organized what became known as the Bates Union and called out 2,000 men to protest payment in scrip, redeemable only at company stores. The Bates Union lasted less than a year, to be replaced by ineffective local unions and associations.[14]

In the late 1850s a wave of anti-Catholic and nativist sentiment swept over the region. On Saint Patrick's Day, 1857, Irish paraders in Schuylkill County found an effigy of their saint hung from a telegraph pole with a string of potatoes around its neck. In that same year the Molly Maguires appeared in print for the first time. Bannan identified them as an Irish secret society being used for political purposes by the Democratic party.[15] The combination of anti-Catholicism, ethnic hostility, and class antagonism produced violence during the years of the Civil War—much of it blamed by the press on the Mollies. The Irish were frequently opposed to the conflict, which they called a "rich man's war and a poor man's fight." They viewed abolitionism as an English conspiracy that, in alliance with capital, sought to bring freed Negroes to the North as cheap labor to replace white workers who were struggling for higher wages. There were incidents in the coalfields in which Irish miners stopped trains filled with conscripts and went into the collieries to disrupt military recruitment.

Such antiwar sentiment, compounded by ethnic and class tensions, resulted in more than forty killings during the war years, all of them unsolved. Bodies turned up at the bottom of mine shafts or along lonely country roads. Though it is unknown exactly how many killings were directly related to labor strife, the majority certainly were. They followed a revealing pattern. For example, mine foreman F. W. Langdon, notorious for "short weighing," was openly stoned to death at a July 4 picnic in Carbon County in 1862, and mine owner George Smith was shot by a group of men in the presence of his family. In the summer of 1865 a mine superintendent in Schuylkill County was ambushed and killed in broad daylight. After the war the violence went on. In Schuylkill County alone during the first three months of 1867 there were five murders, six assaults, and twenty-seven robberies.[16]

Labor-related terrorism, however, could not solve the fundamental problem of labor. Most Irish workers turned to unionism, not vigilantism, to improve their conditions. During the economic dislocation following the Civil War, when working conditions worsened and wages were cut, the miners once again began organizing. This time they found a charismatic leader who was able to unite them in a strong organization.

John Siney, the son of an Irish militant who had been evicted from the land and moved to England, received his education as a labor agitator at a young age in the textile mills of Lancashire. In 1862 he emigrated to St. Clair, just north of Pottsville, and found work in the mines. At the Eagle colliery in 1867 he organized several hundred workers in a successful strike against wage cuts. Encouraged by this victory and the rising tide of labor dissatisfaction in the fields, he managed to bring local organizations together in 1868 in a union called the Workingmen's Benevolent Association, which he headed. At the peak of its strength the WBA had some thirty locals and 30,000 members, or four-fifths of all workers in anthracite.

John Siney, leader of the Workingmen's Benevolent Association of St. Clair, the first effective union of anthracite miners, pictured in 1868.   Courtesy of the Historical Society of Schuylkill County, Pottsville, Pa.

Franklin B. Gowen, president of the Philadelphia and Reading Railroad and the man who crushed the Mollies.   Courtesy of the Library of Congress.

Though Siney achieved an unprecedented organizing feat, he was unable to forge a completely unified organization embracing all workers. He had much more success in the southern field, where there were many individual operators engaged in fierce competition with each other, than in the northern fields, already dominated by giant transportation companies like the Delaware, Lackawanna, and Western Railroad and the Lehigh Coal and Navigation Company, organizations which practiced determined antiunion policies. He also found it tremendously difficult to persuade miners from the different fields to act as one. Several strikes in the late 1860s failed because miners in one field refused to join strikers in another.

Yet Siney did manage to achieve some success. In 1869 he forced operators in the Schuylkill and Lehigh areas to accept a sliding scale of wages tied to the price of coal. Miners were to receive an increasing percentage as the market price of coal rose, with a set minimum if the cost of a ton fell below a certain level. Siney and the WBA also carried their battle to the state legislature, gaining the passage in 1869 of a law allowing the workers to form and join organizations for their "benefit and protection." Previously individuals who made such efforts had been subject to prosecution for conspiracy under state law. In the same year the legislature also passed a mine regulation and inspection bill. Though it was limited at first to one county, its coverage was expanded throughout the region after the great Avondale mine disaster, which claimed 109 lives.[17]

If the limited victories of the WBA raised some optimism among the miners, they generated considerable alarm among the operators. Though the smaller mine owners in the southern field might recognize the union and make concessions, the big companies were intransigently unwilling to give way. They lacked only a plan of action and someone ruthless enough to carry it out. Unfortunately for the miners, there was a man willing to do the job.

Franklin Benjamin Gowen became president of the Philadelphia and Reading Company in 1870 at the age of thirty-three. The son of an Irish Protestant merchant who had made a fortune in Philadelphia selling groceries, liquor, and wine, Gowen had the benefits of an excellent education—the prestigious John Beck's Boys' Academy—and an elite background. He was deeply read in history and classical literature and, unlike many of the sober captains of commerce of that era, had a talent for histrionics that caught attention and inspired awe—and sometimes fear. "I'll turn Schuylkill County into a howling wilderness before I give in to the miners," he is reputed to have said during one of the mine strikes he tried to crush. His oratorical skills were legendary. On occasion he would rent the Philadelphia Academy of Music and read his railroad's annual stockholders' report to packed galleries. "In that era of gaudy, hideous display," writes George R. Leighton, "Gowen moved like a stage financier. . . . He was in life the novelist's idea of the Gilded Age; in him nature improved even upon art."[18] Gowen even left the scene mysteriously, dying by his own hand in a locked hotel room in 1889 at the age of fifty-three. Since he left no suicide note, seemed to be in good spirits, and was prospering in his law practice, some suspected he had been murdered, perhaps by the Mollies.

After he left school, Gowen had moved to the booming town of Pottsville to try his hand in the coal business. His firm went bankrupt, however, so at the age of twenty-three he switched to a new career, the law. This profession was perfectly suited to his talents—particularly his oratorical skills, which he polished to a fine finish in his addresses before the Pottsville Literary Society, an organization he and his brother had helped to found. After reading for one winter in a Pottsville lawyer's office, he was admitted to the Schuylkill County bar in 1860. Three years later—at age twenty-six—he won election as county district attorney.[19]

These were years of rising violence in the region, of alleged Molly Maguirism, but young Gowen, an aspiring Democratic politician in an area where the party depended upon the Irish vote, was notably inactive in pursuing crimes blamed on the Irish. He gained enough of a reputation, however, to become a counsel for the Reading Company after he left office. Following an important legal victory over the Pennsylvania Railroad, he gained the presidency of the Reading, the dominant company in the southern coalfields.

In this period the anthracite-carrying railroads were extending their control over the entire industry. In the northern fields the big companies already owned much of the coal-bearing lands and mining companies. The Reading, however, though it had pooling agreements with the Schuylkill Canal and smaller feeder railroads, did not yet own substantial coal lands. Gowen convinced the Reading's English bankers that domination also meant land ownership, and they generously supported his initiative in acquiring it. Between 1871 and 1875 the Reading purchased more than 100,000 acres at a cost of $40 million.[20]

While expanding the Reading's holdings in the southern field, Gowen also moved to consolidate the railroad companies' control. In 1873 he met secretly with the heads of the major anthracite roads and hammered out a trust agreement fixing the price of coal at five dollars a ton and carving up the market among themselves. It was a measure of Gowen's persuasiveness and the Reading's power that he obtained 28 percent of the total. Even in a day when such collusion was not illegal, these methods, when they became known, raised a public outcry. Gowen took a verbal pounding in the state legislature, but as he would do time and again, he simply climbed into his private railway car, traveled to Harrisburg, and convinced the politicians that his ways were sound and public-spirited.

Control over the industry, however, also required control over labor. Gowen knew that he had to crush the miners' unions. And he set out to do so. A keystone of his strategy was the battle for public opinion. He played upon public sentiment by castigating union leaders as anarchistic foreigners under the sway of the socialist First International, tyrannizing poor working men "who had to crouch like whipped spaniels before the lash." While he worked to win support, he moved against the union with concentrated determination.[21]

In 1871 miners in the Wyoming-Lackawanna field struck for the third straight year over the issue of wage cuts. This time they were joined by their brethren in the Schuylkill field. Their united front helped despite enormous deprivations suffered by the miners and their families. The smaller operators were ready to capitulate. Gowen, however, forced them into line by abruptly raising freight rates from two dollars to four dollars per ton, making it impossible for them to ship coal profitably. He then went to the northern shippers and persuaded them to do the same. Cries of protest went up in the legislature, and an investigative committee was formed, but Gowen was ready. He turned attention away from the conditions of the workers themselves by making sensational charges that the WBA was controlled by a secret society called the Molly Maguires that was conducting a campaign of industrial sabotage and killing in the region. Siney attempted to rebut the charges, but public opinion fixed on random acts committed against mine officials and strikebreakers. The WBA was forced into arbitration that resulted in rulings that lowered minimum wages and forbade employers to hire only union men.[22]

Inserting the issue of criminality into a labor dispute was a stroke of genius on Gowen's part. Since, under American law, property was a vested interest (a worker's job was not), owners had the legal right to protect their property. If attacks occurred against property, strikebreakers, or the police assigned to protect them, the strikers would be acting illegally. As a result virtually any method could be used against the striking miners. And Gowen, true to his nature, resorted to any tactic that worked. Unsatisfied with the defeat rendered to the WBA in the 1871 strike, he became determined to crush unionism once and for all. Systematically he set about preparing for the showdown.

First he strengthened the Coal and Iron Police, a private security force designed to protect coal properties and enforce law and order wherever the owners held sway. Then he hired Allan Pinkerton, head of one of the first private detective agencies in America, paying him $100,000 to infiltrate agents into the AOH and the alleged secret society known as the Molly Maguires. The agents' task was twofold: to gather evidence on the inner workings of the so-called Mollies and to provoke strikes, killings, and other violence against mine officials and miners, especially the English,

Welsh, and Germans. Gowen knew the blame would fall directly on the Irish strikers and sabotage would also sow chaos in the coalfields, forcing smaller operators to sell their holdings to the Reading at lowered prices. Gowen had the further advantage of a severe and prolonged national depression that began in 1873. Although the crisis did not seriously affect a sizable company like the Reading, it brought a number of smaller mine companies to the brink of bankruptcy.

Gowen then moved to force unity among the small operators. He established the Schuylkill Coal Exchange, which bound owners in the southern field served by the Reading, and accelerated production in order to meet public demands in the event of a long strike. Finally, when all was ready, wages for contract miners were cut 20 percent and those of laborers 10 percent.[23]

The miners had no choice. The Long Strike of 1875, which lasted more than five months, resembled a war more than a labor dispute. The miners did not seek the strike. For months their union had voiced increasing concern over the owners' preparations, and Siney had expressed the hope that outstanding grievances could be settled through arbitration. Even the *Miners' Journal*, a paper sympathetic to the owners, noted that the issue was not wages but the continued existence of the union.

Gowen's tactics were ruthlessly effective. Strikebreakers, protected by the security forces, were recruited and brought in by the trainload. Pinkerton agents and armed thugs attacked strikers and terrorized coal communities. Edward Coyle, a union leader and AOH head, was killed, as was another union activist when a mine boss fired without warning into a crowd of strikers, a crime for which he was later acquitted (he acted in "self-defense"). The union, infiltrated at the highest levels by spies, had its every move anticipated. It was unable to prevent provocations that resulted in violence and harsh reprisals against strikers. It was also unable to forge a united front of miners in all three fields, as miners in the Wyoming-Lackawanna field refused to support the strike.

As weeks and then months went by, the violence intensified. The miners struck back as best they could. Strikebreakers were beaten and murdered, police were hunted down, bosses harassed and intimidated; miners who even mentioned returning to work were sent death warnings. The miners derailed trains, sabotaged machinery, burned colliery buildings and a telegraph office, and dumped coal from laden cars.

On June 3, in the sixth month of the strike, more than 600 miners briefly occupied Shenandoah, then marched on the West Shenandoah Colliery to force "scabs" to close down production. They were met by a group of agents armed with rifles. James McParlan, one of Pinkerton's spies, tried to provoke an incident, but the miners, who had no better weapons than hickory staves, withdrew. They then moved on Mahanoy City and closed down several collieries. They joined with a group from

An illustration from Leslie's Popular Monthly *for March 1871, showing scabs, or blacklegs, being taunted by a crowd of miners and their wives. Mahanoy City, Pennsylvania, 1871.* Courtesy of the Library of Congress.

Hazleton which also was shutting down mines, and the combined strikers marched on the Little Drift Colliery. There they came up against parts of the state militia that had been sent to the region by the governor. Only the presence of the heavily armed troops prevented widespread bloodshed.[24]

The terrorism and destruction of property provoked heated outcries from the press, the churches, and other institutions of "respectable" society. The Irish church hierarchy, long the preachers of obedience and submission, openly condemned the Mollies and excommunicated members of the AOH. The methods of Gowen and the operators were defended as just and necessary in the face of illegal actions by the strikers.

During the Long Strike, hundreds of miners' families subsisted on little more than bread and water. Men, women, and children went into the woods to dig for roots and edible plants in order to survive. Yet the public reports that appeared were often distorted. A cartoon that ran in a New York daily showed a woman putting her last loaf of bread in the oven while a group of drunken men rollicked in the background.

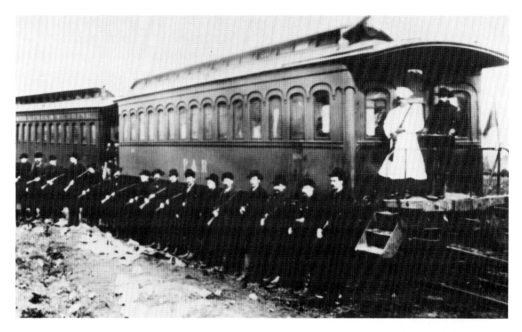

Philadelphia and Reading Coal and Iron Police patrolled the region in railroad cars protecting management's property and profits.   Courtesy of the George Bretz Collection, Albin O. Kuhn Library, University of Maryland, Baltimore County.

With their material resources gone, and faced by the overwhelming power of the owners and the state, the miners finally conceded. The union made a last appeal to Gowen for compromise, but he adamantly refused. By mid-June the strike was over, and those miners not blacklisted were allowed to return to work with 20 percent wage cuts in the nonunion mines.

"After the Long Strike," a miner's ballad, summed up the feelings of workers throughout the region:

> Well, we've been beaten, beaten all to smash
> And now, sir, we've begun to feel the lash,
> As wielded by a gigantic corporation,
> Which ran the commonwealth and ruins the nation.[25]

Gowen boasted that he had spent $4 million to break the strike and the union. Yet peace did not return to the anthracite fields. Undaunted, the miners reorganized within the AOH and carried out reprisals. Killings, assaults, and burnings continued throughout 1875. But these convulsive, last-ditch efforts by desperate men only hardened the determination of the operators.[26]

The Coal and Iron Police were kept intact and for a generation afterward remained the chief law enforcement agency in the region. Foremen and other mine officials were armed; hired thugs hunted down and killed militant miners. Charles O'Connell, one militant, was murdered along with a boarder in the presence of his family when a group of men broke into his house in the middle of the night. Now it was not the union that was under attack but the Molly Maguires, who were blamed indiscriminately for every act of terrorism. Gowen admitted that labeling a man a Molly was enough to hang him. Public opinion, outside the Irish communities, ran strongly against the Mollies and the AOH. But what Gowen really wanted was to crush organized labor in the region. This was the larger aim of his campaign against the Mollies.

The crackdown on the so-called Mollies began in September 1875 when two men from Tamaqua, a town not far from Shenandoah, were apprehended for the murder of a mine boss. At their trial the defense's every move was anticipated, and it became clear that someone was providing the prosecution with inside information. Suspicion fell upon James McParlan (alias "Jack McKenna"), one of the most active Mollies in the Shenandoah area. John "Black Jack" Kehoe, a leader of the Mollies, ordered his assassination, but before it could be carried out McParlan disappeared. Soon afterward, a Captain Alderson of the Coal and Iron Police walked into a telegraph office and sent a simple message—"Spring the trap!" Scores of suspected Mollies were immediately rounded up in an operation that had been planned in the Philadelphia office of the Reading months before.

In January 1876 the first trial of the Mollies opened in Mauch Chunk, but the second trial, which began on May 4 in Pottsville, set the tone for subsequent proceedings. In that trial five men were accused of the murder of policeman Benjamin Yost the previous year. The courtroom was jammed with miners and their families; militia with unsheathed bayonets patrolled the corridors. On the bench were a presiding judge and two associates. In the jury box sat Pennsylvania Dutchmen known for their hostility to the Irish.

Almost the entire case against the five accused men was made by one key prosecution witness, James McParlan. McParlan's testimony was based upon two and a half years of undercover work he had done as a Pinkerton agent. He had successfully infiltrated the inner circles of the Mollies, had ingratiated himself with the leaders, and had won recognition as one of the most active members in the Schuylkill field. Though his full role remains shrouded in mystery and embroiled in controversy, secret reports he sent back to the detective agency and the Reading provided accounts of his activities as well as substantial information on the personalities and workings of the secret society.[27]

A native of northern Ireland, McParlan came to the United States in the late 1860s and worked in a series of laboring jobs before turning to the new trade of industrial espionage—at twelve dollars per week. He had been selected personally by Pinkerton for the dangerous assignment in the coalfields, not only for his intelligence, but also because he seemed perfectly cast for the job, almost a stereotype of the Irishman of the time. He was a powerfully built man with red hair, a fine tenor voice, a wide repertoire of songs and jigs, a gregarious manner and glib tongue, unusual skill with his fists, and an inordinate capacity for rotgut whiskey. Furthermore, he was a Roman Catholic, and only Catholics were admitted to the Ancient Order of Hibernians. Perhaps most important, there was no indication that McParlan might develop any sympathy for those he had to inform on. He had little loyalty to the cause of Irish labor. Nor did he see the Mollies as a working man's organization. He regarded his job as one of investigating a criminal conspiracy.

Pinkerton had McParlan investigate the workings of secret societies in Ireland before sending him on to Philadelphia, where he was fully briefed on all known facts about the AOH by Benjamin Franklin, the detective agency's chief in that city. Together they worked out McParlan's "cover," as well as a system of communication. The agent's identity was so well disguised that only Pinkerton, Franklin, and one other agency head knew of his true identity; not even Gowen was informed—reports from McParlan to the railroad only bore the agent's initials.

James McParlan, alias James McKenna, in a picture probably taken after the Molly Maguire trials. Courtesy of the Historical Society of Schuylkill County, Pottsville, Pa.

Disguised as a tramp, McParlan left Philadelphia for the coal region on October 27, 1873. After a brief stopover in Port Clinton, he went on to Schuylkill Haven and made a swing through a number of mining towns in the Schuylkill field's western reaches. In its bars and "shebeens"—illegal, private drinking establishments—he quickly made acquaintances by his free-spending ways and learned something of the Mollies. He found out that their main strength apparently was centered on Pottsville, Shenandoah, Mahanoy City, and surrounding patches.

A chance remark sent the detective on to Pottsville. There, on a fine fall day, he lurched in feigned drunkenness through the doors of the Sheridan House, a saloon of considerable reputation owned by a gigantic Irishman—and reputed Molly leader—Patrick Dormer. While the regulars looked on suspiciously, McParlan broke into a sprightly jig to the accompaniment of a fiddler who was playing away in a corner. The skillful heel-and-toe routine did the trick; he was quickly set up with a shot of whiskey. He then touched the hearts of the good fellows with a lilting ballad from County Donegal—the ballad of Molly Maguire.

McParlan was then invited by Dormer to be his partner in a game of cards in the back room. The pair began to lose steadily, but the reason soon became obvious. McParlan grabbed the hand of one of his opponents, catching him using six cards instead of five. The cheater challenged the detective to a fist fight. The barroom was cleared; in five rounds McParlan soundly beat him. He then stood everybody to a round of drinks. The charmed Dormer sat the stranger down at a side table to find out more about him. His name was "James McKenna," and he was not a tramp at all but a fugitive on the run for a killing in Buffalo, New York. His money came in part from a pension fraudulently obtained for service in the U.S. Navy during the Civil War but mostly from counterfeiting—"passing the cheat." He also implied that he had been a member of the AOH in Ireland and New York state but suggested that any inquiries might expose his whereabouts to the law. Dormer evidently believed the whole story.

The free-spending McParlan became a popular regular at the Sheridan House, a gathering place for local Mollies. His alleged background as a criminal served him well; Mollies guilty of crimes were not afraid to talk to such a fellow once their tongues had been loosened by whiskey. Within a short time the detective had identified and become friendly with several leading "bodymasters," or top leaders of the society. One of them was John Kehoe, a tavern keeper from Girardsville and local politician who was later named by the press as the "King of the Mollies."

From Pottsville McParlan made a series of trips through the Schuylkill field to gather more information. He described Mahanoy City, literally divided into an armed camp between the Welsh and Irish, as the most "Godforsaken" place he had ever seen and reported that Tamaqua was filled, during that time of idle mines, with "excited men and exciting whiskey." "Law and order" was a meaningless phrase in these rough, ethnically divided mountain towns. Most men carried pistols or at least brass knuckles and knives; scores were settled personally or through the vigilante action of the secret societies. Every ethnic group had its own organization: the Welsh and Germans the "Modocs," the skilled Kilkenny miners the "Chain Gang," and of course the Mollies. These groups not only preyed on each other but also were ridden by murderous factional rivalries. When violence occurred it was virtually impossible to uncover the real motive. But McParlan was looking for only one kind of violence—Molly-inspired. To get information he needed to be inside the organization, if, in fact, such an organization existed.

In April 1874 he achieved his goal: he was initiated into the Shenandoah lodge of the Ancient Order of Hibernians in a secret ceremony by local bodymaster Michael "Muff" Lawler. The detective took an oath on his knees, paid a three-dollar initiation fee, and received the secret signs and passwords. (The sign of recognition was the right hand to the right hip and, as a reply, the forefinger and thumb of the left hand on the left ear.) Within only a few months he had been able to establish his reputation and to ingratiate himself with the top leadership, a fact of which he was justly proud. "A final triumph," he called it.

McParlan now began his work in earnest. In a series of meeting which he attended as a member in good standing (held in crowded taverns to avoid suspicion), he learned that active members usually used the names Molly Maguire and AOH synonymously. The AOH, of course, was a national beneficial organization, with state, county, and local affiliates. In the coal region, however, McParlan reported that its real purpose was to protect and avenge its members. Those individuals charged by the inner circle of the AOH with discriminating against Irish laboring men were usually first sent "coffin notices," crudely rendered drawings of themselves in an open coffin, with a "notice" of the charge against them. "Any blackleg that takes a union man's job while he is standing for his rights," one typical coffin notice read, "will have a hard road to travel and if he dont he will have to suffer the consequences." If this warning failed, the accused man "suffered the consequences." One bartender, William Williams, was killed, presumably because his brother, a mill foreman, fired three Mollies; Henry Yiengst, a boss carpenter, had his skull beat in and his tongue pulled out because he refused to hire Irishmen. Charles Green, a schoolteacher in Centralia, made critical remarks about the Mollies and had his ears cut off. After marking a man for murder or mutilation, the Mollies ended their secret meeting with a prayer.

When clandestine activities had to be carried out—whether they involved labor sabotage or the killing of a mine boss—only bodymasters were informed and charged

A crudely drawn coffin notice.   *Courtesy of the Historical*
Society of Schuylkill County, Pottsville, Pa.

with responsibility. They, in turn, appointed men, usually from a lodge in another town, to do the job. Elaborate alibis were fabricated to protect the avengers, and only a few men at the top, who were sworn to secrecy at pain of death, knew all the details. The general membership knew little or nothing; or if they suspected anything, they knew enough to keep their mouths shut.

The real Mollies were, then, a small group of leaders that formed a secret inner circle within the AOH. Yet according to McParlan, their influence was pervasive. Though they were not bound together into a tightly knit conspiratorial organization, the leaders of the largely autonomous lodges could, through their network of contacts, wield effective power. In McParlan's words, they were held "in such terror that all the office holders and politicians are on their side and they can always command both money and influence."

According to McParlan's reports and trial testimony, he was a trusted member of the inner circle in the Schuylkill area and took part in deliberations and planning but never was actually involved in any terrorist activities. Indeed, he explained at length how he maintained a precarious balance between talking and acting, sometimes developing elaborate excuses to avoid the latter and on several occasions managing to abort planned actions. Whether or not he was being completely honest is another matter.

As subsequent evidence revealed, McParlan certainly was aware in advance of several crimes committed by the Mollies. These included a near-fatal assault on a Welsh tough, "Bully Bill" Thomas, in Mahanoy City; the murder of Tamaqua policeman Benjamin Yost and Gomer James, another Welsh bully; and the assassinations of mine bosses Thomas Sanger and John Jones and miner William Uren. Later, during the Molly trials, he claimed that he did not act to prevent these crimes, either because he was unable to do so, or because he would have risked his life had he given the intended victims advance warning. In addition his reports indicate knowledge of other murders—for a total of seven—committed during June–September 1875, a period of reprisals following the Long Strike. He also provided the names of fourteen Mollies who, he charged, were either murderers or accessories.

The extent of McParlan's activities as an agent provocateur remains unclear. Certainly his leading role in the Shenandoah protest is known. Also not established is his knowledge of vigilante action against the Mollies, such as the murders of Charles O'Donnell and Ellen McAllister, who were killed in their homes in Wiggins Patch on December 10, 1875. McParlan claimed to have been deeply upset by the Wiggins Patch massacre, yet in the turmoil and violence after the Long Strike, vigilante groups were active and were even encouraged by Allan Pinkerton. That their activities remained unknown to McParlan is doubtful.

In mid-September 1875 McParlan traveled to New York and Philadelphia, where he met with Pinkerton agency chiefs George Bangs and Benjamin Franklin. He provided them with a carefully detailed list of all the known Mollies in the five anthracite counties, including addresses, occupations, and posts held in the AOH. Interestingly, there were only 347 names on the list, not many for such a supposedly powerful organization. Furthermore, there was no mention of crimes committed. The list, however, provided information for the printing of a handbill, marked "strictly confidential" and distributed for the consideration of the "Vigilance Committee of the Anthracite Region" by, apparently, the Pinkerton agency. It not only contained a list of murders committed between June and September 1875 but also named the alleged murderers, their hometowns, and their membership in the Molly Maguires. Charles O'Donnell's name was on the list.

In that same month three important Mollies, all well known to McParlan, were arrested for the murder of mine boss John Jones. The three had been arrested on scant evidence, but AOH badges had been found in their pockets, and in the heated atmosphere of the time the district attorney believed that he had a case. And the first Molly trial of one of the three, Michael Boyle, in January 1876, did indeed result in a conviction. As it turned out, the murder of Jones had been an "exchange killing" among different Mollies; the other victim was policeman Benjamin Yost.

McParlan's testimony was not needed in the first Molly trial, and he continued his undercover work into 1876. But his position became increasingly precarious. The Mollies were thrown on the defensive by a rapidly unfolding series of events: the Wiggins Patch massacre, Boyle's conviction, the turning of state's evidence by James Kerrigan, another well-informed defendant, and rumors sweeping the region about secret documents held by the authorities. As other arrests occurred, based upon Kerrigan's information, panic spread through their ranks. Then Father O'Connor, a Pottsville priest sympathetic to the AOH who had apparently investigated McParlan in Philadelphia, voiced suspicions about the detective. When a railroad conductor told John Kehoe that McParlan was a spy, McParlan's execution was ordered.

That McParlan escaped was the result of sheer incompetence on the part of the Mollies, astonishing bravado by the detective, and the decisive help of Frank McAndrew, one of Kehoe's rivals. McAndrew warned McParlan of the plot against him, convinced that he was not a spy. McParlan then went to Kehoe and demanded a "trial," claiming he could vindicate himself. This assertion did not convince Kehoe, but since there was so much uncertainty about McParlan, he had no choice but to call a "jury" of all local bodymasters. Yet Kehoe did manage to prevent the actual trial. On the night in question McParlan arrived at the appointed location—to find several Molly toughs waiting for him. The quick-thinking McAndrew spirited McParlan away in a wild, night sleigh ride, McAndrew driving and McParlan clutching his pistols. Two Molly avengers followed in another sleigh, but McParlan's would-be assassins were either too fearful or too drunk to carry out the job. On March 7, 1876, the Pinkerton detective, prudence now having gotten the best of bravery, dropped from sight.

The final demise of the Mollies began in the Schuylkill County courthouse in Pottsville on May 4, 1876. Five men—James Carroll, James Boyle, Hugh McGeehan, Thomas Duffy, and James Roarity—went on trial for the murder of policeman Yost. The evidence against them had apparently been provided by the Molly turned informer James Kerrigan. Public attention was riveted on the trial. For months the case had been widely debated in the press. What was purported to be Kerrigan's verbatim "confession" was printed in the *Bethlehem Times*. According to the *Philadelphia Inquirer*, Kerrigan had admitted that the twin purposes of the Mollies were murder and arson. The *New York Times* hinted at a vast conspiracy underwritten by the AOH. From Shenandoah, however, the *Herald* retorted that Kerrigan's information was fraudulent, only given to save his neck.

The debate raged, and the AOH as an organization was drawn in. There was widespread speculation about its motives and aims. Many viewed it as dangerous to the very security of the republic. The Bethlehem Steel Company went so far as to threaten to fire any employee who was a member. Priests began to deny the sacraments to the families of members. In the AOH's defense, the *Irish World* of New York City claimed that the organization had received the approval of the Vatican after careful study. Yet it became clear by trial time that more was at stake than the judgment of five men for a single murder.

On trial day the courtroom was filled with relatives and friends of the accused; many had journeyed since before dawn to be present. When the defendants were brought in, wives, fathers, mothers, sisters, brothers, and children rushed forward to touch and embrace them. The court allowed the unusual procedure of seating the wives next to the prisoners. Hugh McGeehan's young bride sat in an uncomprehending daze, and James Carroll's son climbed onto his father's lap.

District Attorney George Kaercher was assisted by the distinguished attorneys General Charles Albright, Frank W. Hughes, and Guy Farquhar. The defense had an equally impressive legal team: Congressman John B. Reilly of Pennsylvania, Len Bartholomew, and Daniel Kalbfus as well as local attorney Martin L'Velle. There was a bitter fight over the selection of the jury. The prosecution sought to impanel as many Pennsylvania Dutch as possible because of their well-known antagonism to the Irish. One would-be juror admitted that he knew little English and would not be able to understand the witnesses, while another admitted that he had been a member of a vigilante group. The judge nevertheless allowed them to be seated. It became clear that the proceedings were stacked against the Mollies.

In a trial filled with sensations, perhaps the greatest was provided by Franklin B. Gowen, who made an appearance on the second day as, incredibly enough, chief counsel for the Commonwealth. Dressed in formal evening clothes, the special prosecutor henceforth dominated the proceedings, the lead actor in a spectacular drama of his own creation. The following day the prosecution electrified the courtroom when it announced that James McParlan would appear as its chief witness. Almost at the same moment the news spread throughout the courtroom that eleven more Mollies, including Bodymasters John Kehoe, "Muff" Lawler, and Pat Butler, were being led into the courthouse in chains, victims of yet another sweep. Gowen had orchestrated this arrest to demoralize the defendants. The brilliant tactic worked.

For four days, under the careful questioning of Gowen, McParlan held the stand, providing a detailed account of his thirty months among the Mollies, a performance that he was to repeat at later trials. His feet resting on the rail before him, the detective revealed all that he supposedly knew about the killing of Yost, including the information that all of the defendants had confessed their crimes to him personally. This was probably sufficient evidence for conviction, but Gowen was not satisfied, and on the second day of McParlan's testimony D. A. Kaercher revealed the real motive of the trial, telling the jury that the detective had been sent into Schuylkill County "to become familiar with the workings of a secret association known generally in the locality as 'Molly Maguires' but the real name of which is the Ancient Order of Hibernians . . . [and] that it was a practice for the members to aid and assist each other in the commission of crimes, and in defeating detection and punishment."[28] This made it clear that it was not merely the defendants who were on trial but an entire organization. The heated objections of the defense to this blanket indictment were overruled.

The second key prosecution witness was James Kerrigan, the four-foot eleven-inch tough, hero of the Civil War, father of fourteen children, and participant in at least two murders. Again under the guidance of Gowen, Kerrigan gave damaging testimony, at the same time playing down his own role in the crimes he described. His wife, called as a defense witness, repudiated his testimony, charging that he was the one responsible for Yost's death and publicly calling him "a little rat." But Gowen skillfully made her admit that she was really angry at her husband not for his alleged crime but because he had turned informer, an offense worse than murder in the Irish community.

Kerrigan later composed a fifteen-stanza poem about his role that went in part:

Gentlemen, I'm that squealer they talk so much about,
You all know the reason of that I have no doubt;
If not, I will tell you as near as I can,
For I'm a bold American, and my name is Kerrigan.[29]

McParlan stood up well under defense questioning, which attempted to implicate the detective as an inciter of much of the violence attributed to the Mollies. Yet all that McParlan would admit was that he knew of three planned murders in advance but had not warned the intended victims because he feared for his own life. Whatever McParlan's actual role, the defense could not directly pin anything on him.

James Kerrigan, the Molly who turned informer.
Courtesy of the Historical Society of Schuylkill County,
Pottsville, Pa.

The defense brought forward a series of witnesses who of course contradicted McParlan's and Kerrigan's testimony. When John Mulhearn, one such witness, was undergoing cross-examination, Gowen suddenly demanded that he be arrested for perjury on the basis of what Gowen knew from McParlan's reports. The court was thrown into an uproar, and Gowen admitted that he had the wrong Mulhearn—either an honest mistake or a deliberate ploy. But the fact was established that witnesses could be charged with perjury, something that might have come as a surprise to people who normally took perjury for granted where the Mollies were concerned.

The point was further driven home during the cross-examination of another defense witness, when Gowen launched into a legally questionable diatribe. "Enough has been proved in this case, in the Court, in the last ten days to convict of murder in the first degree every member of that organization in the county, for every murder that has been committed in it. Every member of that organization is . . . in the eyes of the law guilty of every murder as an accessory before the fact and liable to be convicted and hanged by the neck until he is dead." That image must have made an impact upon the numerous Mollies present in the audience. When the jury returned its verdict, few observers were surprised. All the defendants were convicted. There were other Molly trials, but the Yost case was the decisive one. Gowen achieved his purpose. In stacked trials the Mollies were destroyed.

Perhaps the real meaning of the Molly trials came out during the judgment of Thomas Munley, accused of the murder of mine boss Thomas Sanger. When a witness was asked to identify Munley, he said, "That is not the man I recognize at all!" Munley's lawyer jumped to his feet and pleaded to the jury: "For God's sake give labor an equal chance. Do not crush it. Let it not perish under the imperial mandates of capital in a free country!" Munley was convicted and hanged anyway.[30]

The entire episode had some curious twists. Some prominent Mollies, such as Frank McHugh and Muff Lawler, turned state's evidence and managed to survive

Thomas Munley, alleged Molly Maguire, on June 20, 1877, the day before he was hanged for murder.
Courtesy of the George Bretz Collection, Albin O. Kuhn Library, University of Maryland, Baltimore County.

retribution. Others of those subsequently arrested and tried had ample opportunities to escape beforehand. A number of the most notorious did escape. Their number included Tom Hurley of Shenandoah, implicated in the audacious daylight picnic murder of Gomer James, and William Love, the alleged killer of Girardsville justice of the peace Thomas Gwyther.

As the day of the first hangings approached, it was thought that Mollies who were still at large would organize an effort to rescue their colleagues from jail. Rumors flew about a planned night raid on the Mauch Chunk jail and a massive takeover of the Pottsville prison. Prepared for the worst, officials took elaborate precautions. Heavily armed militia were stationed in the area. Telegraph lines were held open so that posses and militiamen could be dispatched to any location quickly. On the days before and after the hangings, saloons were closed in Mauch Chunk and Pottsville, and Gowen threatened any man not on his job with firing.

The rumors were unfounded, the precautions unnecessary. The night before their deaths the convicted Mollies were provided with candles for their cells. At 4:30 A.M. they were awakened for coffee, and at 6:00 A.M. their wives, children, and friends paid their last farewells. At 7:00 all attended mass. John Donohue even had a shave and jokingly asked what the barber would charge to cut his throat. After receiving the sacraments, the handcuffed men were led to the scaffold. Their thighs were bound with leather straps, and white hoods put over their heads. When all were ready, at 10:54 A.M., the hangman sprang the trapdoor. Later that day in Pottsville, a composed Jim Boyle, the first of the Mollies to be hanged in the jailyard of the fortresslike stone prison, stood on the gallows, spat, and shouted, "I ain't a bit sorry to die." That kind of bravado—and arrogance—made the Mollies legendary in the region long after the last Molly had been hanged in 1879 in Sunbury.

The bodies of the first group of Mollies who were hanged were delivered to relatives by the Coal and Iron Police, and armed detachments attended the funerals, which attracted huge crowds. True to form, large wakes were held. The widow of Alexander Campbell purchased sixteen pounds of tobacco and thirty dollars' worth of whiskey.[31] Though only a handful of the most important Mollies escaped imprisonment or the rope, peace did not return to the coalfields. In 1877 a wave of railroad riots and violence swept the region, especially in the Wyoming-Lackawanna field (William Scranton, superintendent of the Lackawanna Coal and Iron Company, attributed them to Mollies who fled north, but his charges lacked foundation). Labor was not crushed.[32] As new people from eastern and southern Europe poured into the region, many of them expressly recruited by management to divide ethnically a labor movement dominated by the Irish, the Irish found unexpected allies in their battle against capital. And the cry of Thomas Munley's defense lawyer became, in the 1890s, the fighting slogan for a final, united miners' struggle for a union.

6. Solidarity: The Slavic Community in Anthracite

THEY WERE SOMETHING OF A MYSTERY TO NATIVE-BORN AMERICANS WHEN THEY first appeared in the anthracite fields. They looked different, acted strangely, and kept to themselves. Newcomers were not very unfamiliar in hard coal country, but these people truly were puzzling. They came from places few mining people had ever heard of, lands with odd-sounding, almost unpronounceable names. Few could read or write even their own language. And they did not seem terribly interested in learning about their new land. When the first few arrived in the 1860s they aroused only passing curiosity. But as more and more poured into the coal towns in the following decades they stirred deeper emotions. Those emotions were described in a single word: "Hunky."

They were called Slavs by the English-speaking and American-born, these people from the plains and mountains and marches of eastern Europe and the Balkans. They were Poles, Ukrainians, Czechs, Slovaks, Serbians, Croatians, and people of more than a dozen other nationalities, mostly from the empires of Czarist Russia and Austria-Hungary. There were non-Slavic peoples like Lithuanians and Hungarians, and Italians, too, among them, but they were all lumped together as "foreigners." A few arrived as early as the 1860s, but beginning in the 1880s they came in a great flood. Most were peasants, simple tillers of the soil, unskilled, unlettered, and unspeakably poor. Most were also Roman Catholic or Greek Orthodox and they spoke a babel of incomprehensible languages. To the Americans they seemed a race apart, entirely strange, and wherever they went they encountered suspicion and undisguised discrimination.

They had been uprooted from their home soil by a complex set of factors. If they had been asked, some would have found it difficult to describe exactly why they had come. But one thing they knew—it had to do with survival. The unequal distribution of land, especially in Russia and Austria-Hungary, had a damaging effect on agricultural productivity. Vast expanses of land were owned—and often poorly used—by a landed aristocracy; the parcels held by small farmers and peasants were increasingly overworked and ill utilized by primitive farming methods which further depleted the soil. Mechanization and scientific agriculture were virtually unknown and beyond the economic means of the small landowners of Eastern Europe. Farm production was unable to keep up with rapidly rising birth rates. The population of what is now modern Poland doubled to 25 million in the last half of the nineteenth century. By 1900, 50,000 people starved to death annually in Galicia, and Russian Poland had to resort to importing large amounts of foreign grain.[1]

But economic conditions were not the sole reason for the exodus. Many of the

Overleaf: A Slavic worker returns to his old village for his son's first communion.
Donald L. Miller, family collection.

The Slavic family pictured here had not yet emigrated to America.
Donald L. Miller, family collection.

peasants were held in a condition resembling slavery by powerful feudal overlords; many of the able-bodied men left to escape conscription into the army; and some were escaping political or religious repression. They did not all leave their homelands because they wanted a better job, but once in America, it was the first thing they tried to find. The search lured them to the anthracite region. The coal operators made every effort to encourage them to settle there. For the coal companies the immigrants were "cheap men, and it was in their interests to employ cheap men. . . . They were willing to work longer hours than the English-speaking miners, do heavier and more dangerous work, and put up with conditions that the English-speaking miners no longer tolerated. They had a lower standard of living, and produced their labor at less cost and sold it at a lower rate."[2] Many of the immigrants were expressly recruited by big companies such as the Reading because of the labor troubles they were having with their English-speaking miners. Companies contracted with labor agents in Europe, who could entice an unskilled Pole earning twenty-four cents a day with the promise of a dollar and more a day for work as a laborer in the hard coal fields. For many, the offer was irresistible, though leaving was emotionally painful.

Many men who had gone to America earlier and returned to their villages for visits excited the imagination of those who had stayed behind. The immigrant writer Louis Adamic remembers what an impression such a "successful" man of the world made on the young men of his Slovenian village. "A man had quietly left the village for the United States," he writes, "a poor peasant clad in homespun, with a mustache under his nose and a bundle on his back; now, a clean-shaven *Amerikanec*, he sported a blue-serge suit, button shoes very large in the toes with india-rubber heels, a black derby, a shiny celluloid collar, and a loud necktie made even louder by a dazzling horseshoe pin, which, rumor had it, was made of gold, while his two suitcases of imitation leather, tied with straps, bulged with gifts from America for his relatives and friends in the village. . . . Indeed, to say that he thrilled my boyish fancy is putting it mildly."[3]

These visitors boasted of their new skills and achievements and the wages they earned in places called Carbondale and Mount Carmel. They claimed that in America everything was possible, that a common man could even shake hands with the president. They showed photographs, postcards, and newspaper clippings of coal towns, places peopled by fellow Slovenians who worked for good wages in the mines. You could go there and speak your own languages and be understood; you could practice your own faith in a church built and run by your own people. What a country this was—different, far better than any other on the face of the earth.[4]

So the exodus began—the journey to America. Like the Irish before them, these late arrivals traveled in steerage but now in iron-clad ships. When Louis Adamic came to America he sailed from Le Havre, France, on the *Niagara*, an old and small ship that carried mostly immigrants. The steerage passengers were mostly Poles, Slovaks, Czechs, Croatians, Slovenians, and Bosnians. It was 1913, and the immigrants were young and middle-aged men and women and children of all ages. Most wore their colorful national dress. At New York's Ellis Island they were subjected to a confusing round of bureaucratic procedures, including examination by a stern and sour official who sat behind a desk on a high platform beneath the American flag and a portrait of George Washington. Eventually those who were not rejected because of ill health or for other reasons were waved through to the ferryboat bound for Manhattan.[5]

The steamship companies and railroads often arranged for the movement of the immigrants to the anthracite region. Those bound for Shenandoah, Scranton, and other coal towns were packed onto trains and were sent on their way bearing large identification tags addressed to a local shipping agent. The windows of some of the trains were blacked out so that the immigrants would not be tempted to get off before they entered the region. At their destinations they were herded together on the station platforms to await the shipping agent, who was usually of the same nationality. He took them to his house, often large enough to accommodate boarders, or distributed them in the boardinghouses of others of the same nationality. The next day the men marched off to work with bright new coveralls, caps, miners' carbide lamps, and new picks. Fresh from the farms of far-off Europe, they were mine workers now, about to enter a world where daylight had been abolished. They were in America, but they were not yet a free people. In many cases their jobs had been "bought" from mine foremen by the shipping agent. On payday the agent received all their wages— and perhaps a commission from the coal company—and deducted the amount due for room and board. Any money left over was deposited in the "bank," often a strong box owned by the agent.[6]

The first Slavs in the region were curiosities to the Americans. A Slavic immigrant who arrived in Coaldale around 1885 found employment digging ditches near a colliery. Because he spoke no English he was the object of considerable local interest. Men, women, and children would gather where he was working and listen to

It was unusual for Slavic men as old as this to emigrate.   Donald L. Miller, family collection.

him talk. Almost everyone had a different idea about his origins. Some thought that he was Chinese or Indian, while others were sure that he was African. All agreed, however, that he and others like him had come to take their jobs. The coal companies had seen to that. In Gilberton, every time a train arrived and a foreigner descended, word spread and the boys would pick up stones and sticks and run down to the station to "welcome" him. Such welcoming was reenacted in countless patch towns.[7]

The very first arrivals were usually young men and adult males, aged fifteen to forty-five, who came without their families. Rarely did their women accompany them. Most intended to work for a time, save their money, and either send for their families or return to the old country and buy good farming land. A large number of Slavs actually did return to the Old World, perhaps as many as four out of every ten who emigrated to America before World War I. But the majority remained, painfully accumulated their savings, and sent for their families, brought over brides through arranged marriages, or eventually married the widows and daughters of other Slavs. Many of the immigrants married before they left for America, following a practice prevalent among Slovaks. The long absences of husbands sometimes had unintended results. The Slovak-American press was filled with stories about husbands who learned of their wives' infidelities, returned to their villages to beat their spouses and beat or even kill their lovers, and sailed again for America. One steamship company agent boasted in his advertisements that he had gotten one such husband to the old country and back in three weeks, minimizing his loss of wages.[8]

The very first Slavic and Italian immigrants endured abominable conditions. They were simply dropped off at the railroad sidings of towns and left to fend for themselves. Some of them, as George Korson writes, "lived in mine breaches like the ancient cave-dwellers because no provision had been made for their accommodation. . . . They were reduced to the level of animals foraging for food in the woods. When barks and herbs failed to satisfy the hunger of the children they sent their women into the mine patches to beg for food. Unable to speak English, the women made their pathetic pleas by gesticulations."[9]

The Americans often refused to take in these immigrants as boarders. Since housing was scarce, the foreigners were forced to live in old stables and shanties— any dry, sheltered place they could find. Barns were converted to dormitories where bunk space, sometimes no more than a pile of straw on the ground, was provided for as many as forty or fifty men, with rent of a dollar a month. One immigrant reported that he and others "slept on planks, having no pillows or bedding of any kind. There were double decks of bins, where a man couldn't even straighten out, and slept doubled up all night."[10] English-speaking landlords willing to take in the foreigners jammed them together in wretched-smelling boardinghouses, a dozen people living in a one-room cellar or as many as six men packed together in a windowless, nine-by-sixteen-foot room.[11]

A Slavic immigrant neighborhood in Shenandoah, 1891.
Courtesy of the Historical Society of Schuylkill County, Pottsville, Pa.

Eventually a group of single men might jointly build a shanty made of scrap lumber and any other materials they could scrounge. They slept on the bare ground and shared the necessary chores. In many of the patches, after the immigrants started moving in, the coal companies assigned them to the shacks and shanties where the Irish had previously lived. A contemporary observer described them as "a settlement of the queerest structures, some of them not much larger than dog kennels. There is no sewage system, and the alley is the dumping ground for all offal. At every few steps of this winding, reeking way are little openings leading into other passageways, not much wider than will permit a man to walk through."[12] When the Slavs began arriving in large numbers some of the coal companies built houses for them, but they were small and poorly constructed. They might have four rooms, two on the first floor and two on the second, while others were merely two-room shacks. The houses were constructed of the poorest grade of lumber; wind and rain came in through cracks in the walls and roofs. Many had neither ceilings nor floors. Sanitary facilities did not exist. There was no running water or drainage. Inside the only fur-

Slavic miners and their families in front of their new American homes.
Courtesy of the Burg Collection, MG-273, Pennsylvania State Archives.

niture was a table and a few chairs and beds. The children and some of the boarders were often compelled to sleep on the floor in the crowded rooms.[13]

The scarcity of housing, the need to accommodate large numbers of single males, and the Slavs' frugality brought into existence the so-called boardinghouse system. Married immigrants who had decided to remain in America saved enough to bring their families over and set up housekeeping. They usually took in boarders, generally men of their own nationality. As many as twenty or thirty boarders would crowd into a four-room house along with the landlord and his wife and family. A lean-to would serve as the kitchen and living room, while the other rooms were used as bedrooms. The family slept in one room, while the boarders slept in the others, though not infrequently boarders slept in the same room with the family. Occasionally one group of boarders occupied the beds during the day, while another group slept in them at night if there were two shifts working in the mines. The wife of the owner, aided only by her small children, did the cooking, laundering, and all the other household chores—down to the traditional scrubbing of the boarders' backs. The boarders bought their own food and paid the housewife for cooking it. Rent for a room averaged one dollar a month; in 1890 in the region the average boarder could subsist on ten dollars a month. In the crowded conditions of the boardinghouses privacy did not exist; they were raucous, noisy places overrun with adults, children, and the chickens and ducks that wandered in from the yard.[14]

A typical back yard in one of the fast-growing towns of the anthracite region.
Courtesy of the Wyoming Historical and Geological Society, Wilkes-Barre, Pa.

Slavic immigrants outside a boarding house. As many as thirty boarders sometimes crowded
into a four-room house.   Courtesy of the Balch Institute for Ethnic Studies, Applegate Collection.

The settlements of the first generation of Slavs were decidedly unpleasant in appearance. Historian Victor Greene writes that "most of the structures, standing 10 feet high and 25 feet square, were huddled together on small plots. The grey scrap wood was unpainted, as was the ever-present outhouse a short distance away. The peasants were no architects, and the conglomeration looked like a huge dump rather than a settlement."[15] They also smelled like dumps because of the mounds of garbage and offal lying everywhere. Until well into the second decade of the twentieth century, few towns in the region had either regular garbage collections or paved streets.

The immigrants tolerated these conditions because they regarded them as temporary. Soon they would have a farm back in the homeland or their own home in the new land. For this goal they would have to save; expenses would have to be kept to a bare minimum. And save they did. Per capita expenditures for Slavs in a store in Schuylkill County in the 1890s averaged $2.86 per month, while those of the English speakers averaged $5.48. The Slavs had minimum furnishings in their homes and ate a diet of cereals, starches, cabbage, cheap pork, and oily fish. Their women

Sanitary facilities were primitive or nonexistent in many late nineteenth-century coal towns.
Courtesy of the Wyoming Historical and Geological Society, Wilkes-Barre, Pa.

and children worked like slaves. They cultivated every available space around the dwellings for vegetables and spent tedious hours scrounging for coal on the culm banks.[16]

For the immigrants who remained in the region the purchase of a house became an all-absorbing ideal. Observers often commented upon the high proportion of Slavs who owned their own homes. Many were able to do so after only five or six years of careful saving on income earned by family members, including children, and money brought in by boarders. Though the new houses might not be well built or much larger than the company-owned houses, they were the Slavs' own, and they provided a sense of security and place, superimportant considerations for the former peasants.

According to the Slavic settlement pattern that evolved, several males or perhaps a couple of families of a particular nationality established themselves in a patch or town. They were followed by others of the same nationality. Or the coal companies settled a group in one area of a company town. Eventually, when there was a sufficient number of families, a parish was formed. Later a small store or saloon or other business appeared. The result was a patchwork of various ethnic groups scattered over the region in almost self-contained communities, clinging together for security and mutual support and holding fast to their own languages and customs. While the Slavs became part of the region, they also remained apart from it in significant ways.

The Slavic immigration dramatically altered the ethnic composition of the anthracite fields. In 1880 English-speaking peoples made up more than 90 percent of the foreign born, but only twenty years later, English speakers were less than 52 percent. In the same period the number of Slavs grew from 2 percent to more than 40 percent. By 1900 there were more than 100,000 Slavs in the region, 38,000 of them of Polish origin.[17] In the same year the number of foreign born, mostly Slavs, comprised about one-fourth of the populations of the cities of Wilkes-Barre and Scranton. And Slavic workers of course changed the ethnic composition of the anthracite work force. In 1880 less than 5 percent of mine employees were Slavs. By the turn of the century this figure had risen to about 50 percent, or approximately 34,000 adult workers.[18]

As the Slavs moved into the region they gradually displaced the older English-speaking groups, who either left mining or moved away from the area. The smaller towns, like Mount Carmel in the Schuylkill field, took on more and more of an Eastern European cast and character. Nanticoke, in the Wyoming-Lackawanna field, became the most "Polish" town in the state and perhaps in the nation. The small city of Shenandoah was populated by a jumble of nationalities; within its one square mile lived not only English-speaking people and Germans but also Slavs from a half-

Shenandoah, a center of late nineteenth-century immigration into coal country and one of the most Slavic towns of the region.   Courtesy of the Historical Society of Schuylkill County, Pottsville, Pa.

dozen European countries. At first, most of these groups did not get along together at all. People lived in places popularly known as Paddy's Land, Dutch Hollow, Little Italy, Hunky Hill, and Polack Street. The Slavs brought with them from the Old World the villager's suspicion of strangers and outsiders and a village clannishness. Unable to speak English, they seemed unusually dour and stiff. In the presence of strangers the Slavs were formal and obsequious; toward people in positions of authority they were distrustful but deferential. They were not at all outgoing and talkative like the Irish. But they did drink like the Irish, eliciting the disapproval of many of the stricter Protestant sects. "You don't think they have souls, do you?" one Protestant woman wondered aloud after observing a three-day-long Slavic wedding feast. "No, they are beasts, and in their lust they'll perish!"

In the popular press Slavs were widely described as lawless, slovenly, fatalistic, and stupid. The daughter of a Slovak immigrant described the kind of behavior that often arose from these attitudes. "My mother used to tell me that [back in the 1880s] when it was time to go to work the men would start gathering on the porch to go to work in a group. Because they were afraid they would be attacked by someone. But when they traveled in a group they felt protected. And my father was a big strong man, and he was given a team of four mules and he was to develop the ground around the breaker. And he was paid $1.60 because it was hard work. And they all stayed there because they thought he was a big strong man and they would be protected. In 1888 there was still trouble. The people didn't want the new immigrants coming in and taking their jobs. And it soon became a sport to hurt these people."[19]

Slavic religious practices contributed to the intolerance. Protestants were made increasingly uncomfortable by the appearance of more and more Catholic and Orthodox churches, many with strange-looking, bulb-shaped domes, and the Sunday spectacle of hundreds of Catholics marching in procession in the streets behind a priest carrying a seven-foot iron cross. Many of the governments of mining towns began to outlaw Catholic religious processions on public streets. The abstemious English and Welsh Methodists were especially offended by other Slavic Sunday habits, which included drinking, card playing, and dancing. One old Baptist deacon who visited a Slavic ward in Mahanoy City on a Sunday afternoon exclaimed, "It was terrible; saloons full blast; singing and dancing and drinking everywhere; it was Sodom and Gomorrah revived; the judgment of God, Sir, will fall upon us."[20]

The English-speaking miners saw the Slavs as competitors for scarce work who had been brought in by the mining companies to break the unity of the workers. They worked alongside the Slavs only because they had no choice. The Slavs, who began as laborers, were often prevented by one means or another from earning the status of skilled miners; in some cases state-required examinations were rigged against them. Although a separate wage scale for miners and laborers had been set in 1869, it was frequently violated. Skilled miners who hired Slavic laborers sometimes paid them what they liked or squandered their wages without bothering to pay them at all. The wife of a Polish miner remembers the difficulties her husband had, for he was unable to speak English:

> My husband knew a little bit about German and there was a guy there that knew German good and he knew Polish too . . . , but he would never let on that he knew anything about Poland. . . . But Irish people were very terrible to the Polish people. I'm not condemning them. I was working for Irish people and they were very nice to me but here they were rotten. They were the sick ones I guess. . . . They used to take their lunches in pails. The pail was tin, and they used to go to the bars and get 10¢ worth of beer, and sometimes they would take ladies in and sometimes I would go. But they would get their pails filled with beer and then sometimes the Irish or somebody else would come over and spit in the beer.[21]

In the mines the skilled English-speaking miners sometimes made signs to their Slavic laborers to use the shovel or load the coal car or repeated the names of things frequently until they were learned. But young English-speaking miners often taught the Slavs only cuss words, so that when the foreigners were spoken to they answered with a curse—and received a swift and unexpected punch in return.

In the face of these conditions, the Slavs developed an intense communalism. To survive—to obtain work, housing, and an understanding of American ways—immigrants had to cooperate, to band together against a hostile or, at best, indifferent world. This ethnic communalism was something new; it was not typically found in eastern Europe. There the peasant identified with the village or region. Rarely did he come to America with a national identification, the sense of being a Slovak or Pole. Even in America such peoples as Serbs and Croatians were divided at first by Old World village loyalties. Only when these and other Slavic groups recognized that they shared common problems and enemies did they unite along national lines or as a common Slavic people. Despite their dissimilarities, Poles, Slovaks, Ukrainians, and people of other nationalities eventually realized that they had more in common with each other than they did with the older, established "American" ethnic groups. Thus as the Slavic people settled themselves firmly in the region—and no matter how many diverse nationalities there were—they formed united communities with a strong ethnic consciousness. The resulting national pride and cooperation helped them to survive the uncertainties of life in the new world.

To understand the Slavic communities we must understand the immigrants' attitude toward work, for they had come to America, above all, to work. To many Slavic men life was work—almost their whole life. It was something they learned in the villages of the Old World, where wealth and material goods were limited and in short supply and where mere survival depended upon persistent, unending toil. But while they believed in the importance of hard work, among the Slavs there was little expectation of economic advancement; that was something generally beyond their reach. What they sought, most of all, was some security in a world over which they knew they had little control.

As John Bodnar points out, for first-generation Slavs in particular, economic mobility and advancement were the antithesis of the two values they prized most—order and continuity. Furthermore, they did not expect satisfaction in work, nor did they expect to make a fortune. Work was simply something that had to be done. They worked to survive and to save for their children, most of whom they expected to be workers or the wives of workers. What Slavic workers valued was finding a good job, working hard at it, saving money, and owning a house.

The Slavic work ethic differed profoundly from the prevailing American Protestant work ethic, which stressed mobility, economic advancement, and the acquisition of wealth. For the peasants, however, who for countless centuries had not seen work pay off in terms of advancement, work meant security. Upward mobility seemed

*A Polish miner and his son, circa 1900.   Courtesy of the
Burg Collection, MG-273, Pennsylvania State Archives.*

almost impossible. A whole tradition told them so. Since they possessed few sophisticated industrial skills, economic advancement seemed a distant dream, even in
America.

Emphasis upon individual advancement was also seen as destructive of community solidarity. To progress in business, for example, a person might have to take
action that cost his neighbors, or he might have to leave the community altogether.
When Slavic immigrants changed jobs they did so more often because of economic
dislocation (strikes, mine closings, and so forth) than from a desire for social advancement. Second-generation Slavs typically shared these attitudes. Even during
economic hard times when they were forced to leave the community temporarily and
sometimes found better jobs elsewhere, they usually returned. They preferred to
live among their own people, in their own neighborhoods. So while the lack of economic opportunity to advance often curbed Slavic workers' economic aspirations, a
reluctance to sever family and community ties did so as well.[22]

The overwhelming majority of Slavic immigrant workers arrived in the region without any industrial or trade skills; yet because of these deficiencies they were prized as workers by the coal operators. Peter Roberts, writing at the turn of the century, understood the reason. "The Sclav [*sic*] is a good machine in the hands of competent directors. He is obedient and amenable to discipline, courageous and willing to work, prodigal of his physical strength and capable of great physical endurance. . . . His confidence in competent leadership is absolute, and both in work and in society he is quick to copy others."[23] Roberts added that Slavs were fatalistic and stoic in the face of suffering and calamity, attributes which served them well in the mines.

The Slavs went into mining for the simple reason that wages in that industry were among the highest for unskilled workers in America. And since miners were paid by the amount of coal produced, hard work, something for which Slavs were known, seemed to pay off. By the end of the first decade of the twentieth century, 50 percent of the total anthracite work force was Eastern European. In 1910 the majority of Slovak males in America worked in the mines, as did 90 percent of all Polish workers in the anthracite region.

For the first-generation immigrants, untutored in the ways of a dangerous industry, the normal hazards of mining were increased. They were often assigned to the most difficult and dangerous tasks, or in their eagerness to prove themselves they took risks that more experienced men would not. They eventually earned a reputation as courageous workers, especially when accidents occurred, when they were often the first to volunteer for extremely risky rescue operations; for this bravery they paid a heavy price in deaths and injuries. Of the 12,032 men killed in the anthracite fields between 1900 and 1920, 3,177 were Poles, a number that exceeded the figures for every other nationality.[24]

As important as work was for them, Slavic men did not make it their life. They gave their most precious hours to family, faith, and friends. The church, not the mine site, was the soul and center of the ethnic community. Only with the formation of a parish did an active community come into existence. In fact, the words "settlement" and "parish" in Polish, Slovak, and Lithuanian are identical. Even physically, the parish church was the center of the community. The people lavished great wealth, love, and attention upon their churches, many of which were built by volunteer labor. In the towns and cities of the region, impressive red-brick edifices with towering steeples, their interiors adorned with marble altars, exquisite stained-glass windows and lamps, silver and gold candelabra, stand as monuments to strong faith and devotion. Around these houses of worship in the larger towns, and often in sharp contrast to their magnificence, clustered the parochial schools, clubs, bars, stores, and miners' homes. For those immigrants, almost everything was here in the enclave. Only on a few occasions did they need to venture beyond the perimeters of the settlement.

The priests, many of whom came from the Old World to serve their parishioners, held a highly respected, sometimes revered place in the community. Their counsel and guidance on spiritual matters went virtually unquestioned. Since they usually spoke English as well as the Slavic national language, they served as an important link with the wider community and dealt with an array of questions and problems beyond the purely religious. They served as moral authorities, arbiters of family and social matters, interpreters, teachers—and even bankers. Many an old widow, ignorant of English and distrustful of banks, placed her hard-won savings in the hands of the parish priest for safekeeping.

Just as the church was more than a religious institution, the priests became more than religious leaders. Through citizenship classes and English lessons held in the church basement, priests helped the immigrants adapt to their new world. Priests were among the very few in the community who could read and write, so they were asked to write letters to the home country or to speak in court in defense of a parishioner. Through the religious feast days and festivals they organized, the priests ensured the observation of national customs. In the parochial schools they taught national histories and religious traditions as well as the national languages. Until well into the twentieth century they said masses more often in the national languages than in English and frequently delivered the same sermon in both languages. They published parish newsletters or diocesan newspapers in Slavic languages, keeping the community in touch with local developments as well as with those in the old country. All of the Slavic church-related institutions stressed spiritual values and strongly reinforced the immigrants' intense suspicions of purely materialistic goals. The "Dollar God" of American culture was continuously and robustly criticized. "Those who measure success by the material things acquired are lost in the fog of life," a typical Slavic paper editorialized.[25]

Generally the dominant Irish Catholic hierarchy fostered and promoted distinct ethnic parishes. The Irish bishops clearly understood the desires of Slavs for their own national churches with specific cultural loyalties. Rather than viewing this need as a threat to Catholicism, the bishops regarded it as a positive factor in an ethnically diverse but universal church. Yet conflicts did occur, both within the church as a whole and within national groups. Slavic laymen, for example, who helped organize their parishes and financed the building of the churches, assumed, according to the custom of their homeland, that they exercised certain rights. These included control over financial matters and the appointment or dismissal of pastors, practices which differed with church policies in America. They also supervised the collection of annual family parish dues, another departure from the Irish habit of

Sunday collections. Such control over church treasuries gave the laymen an unusually high degree of independence, which they often demonstrated in the extreme, despite their usual respect for the clergy. One Slovak pastor in Hazleton had
an ongoing quarrel with his flock, which found his nationalist sentiments too weak.
When he attempted to fire the popular church organist, some parishioners bombed
the rectory. Naturally, the priest departed. In another case, when a bishop appointed
a priest against the wishes of the parishioners, a hundred of the parish women
marched on the rectory, broke down the door, chased the unfortunate reverend into
the attic, and ransacked the house. The Slovak paper *Jednota* deplored the action
but called upon the bishop to "be more responsive to the needs of the people."[26]

The heightened ethnic consciousness and nationalism that resulted from the
churches' singular role also brought about internal splits. When Polish workers in
south Scranton in 1897 began to agitate for a greater voice in church affairs, they
were flatly refused by the local Irish bishop. The workers then established their
own independent church, with Polish instead of Latin services, and found a young
priest to serve them. This action started the Polish National Catholic Church movement, which spread to more than fifty congregations in America and even to Poland
itself.[27]

Such conflicts, however, were rare, and generally the Slavs in the region accom-
modated themselves to the structures of American Catholicism as long as their parishes were able to maintain their national identities. But what they did have to
endure jointly was the continuing antipathy toward Catholics by the Protestants.
Though the Irish had made Catholicism at least familiar in the anthracite region,
the socially and economically dominant Protestants continued to view the faith with
distrust and suspicion. The ethnocentricity of the Slavic churches, as centers of separate communities, contributed to this ill feeling. The declining Protestant population in the region merely intensified the antagonism.

The Slavs met religious intolerance in characteristic fashion. They simply would
not be deterred from the active practice of their faith, which gave them unity and
consciousness ("Polishness and Catholicism are one"). In Nanticoke in the mid-
1870s Poles who worshiped at a temporary church were harassed by catcalls and
stone throwing on their way to mass. One Sunday the parish fraternal organization,
made up entirely of tough mine workers, paraded through the streets before mass in
full regalia with drawn swords. Whether or not the demonstration was intended to
intimidate the hecklers, it did so. There were no more abuses.[28]

The parish fraternal organization was another important part of Slavic life. Virtually every parish had its lodge or society for both male and female parishioners.
These sometimes developed to raise money for constructing churches and schools;
from building and finance committees they evolved into permanent organizations of

lay members. More frequently they came into existence to fill both spiritual and so-cial functions. They ensured attendance at mass and other religious ceremonies—especially of male parishioners. They organized dances, picnics, dramatic presenta-tions, festivals, and athletic events. Though these groups were voluntary, parishion-ers were expected to join. And almost every parishioner belonged to one or another church fraternal group. Women who sewed vestments for the priests, prepared the church for religious holidays, and cooked and served on social occasions found useful roles and fellowship outside family and home. A man who was required to attend an unpopular lodge member's funeral could feel secure that, no matter what kind of life he led, he would be guaranteed a well-attended send-off.

Like the Irish, the Slavs had national fraternal and beneficial societies, many of which had their roots in craft guilds and religious brotherhoods in the Old World. If the society had a religious orientation, it was a source of support and devotion for the faith. Often, however, like the more secular societies, it gave financial aid to needy members, sometimes providing extremely generous help over a long period. A major function was the provision of insurance for members at low premiums. The elaborate and extended funerals beloved by the Slavs placed a heavy burden on lim-ited family resources; insurance guaranteed a proper burial. Sometimes the funds provided for an improvement in the family's standard of living. A Polish miner's daughter remembers that, after her father's death and the funeral, $400 remained.

> My mother said to my oldest brother, I want you to go looking for a house. And my mother said to be sure it had a garden. He hunted and he found a house that had eight rooms. Imagine six children moving into an eight-room house, we had a bedroom of our own, imagine! So I thought she did very well for an illiterate woman. . . . We lived there until the family grew up and moved away.[29]

Among the Poles, at least, national fraternal and benevolent associations had little success in the region in the early days. As one observer remarked, "The Polish peasant's distrust of outside organizations, even Polish ones, had to be broken down before he consented to part with his hard-earned dollar to invest it in an insurance policy." Not only did the immigrant fear being cheated; he also suspected that his children might hasten his death in order to reap the benefits. Only after such suspi-cions had been allayed did organizations like the Polish National Alliance and the Polish Women's Alliance gain widespread membership in the region.[30]

Eventually the national societies won a prominent place in the American Slavic world. Through their publications, meetings, and local affiliates they contributed to ethnic consciousness and unity and served as forums where important issues were discussed. Some of them, like the churches, split over nationalist and religious questions—the Slovak Catholic Union (*Sokol*) formed in 1905 after members disagreed with the growing anticlericalism of the Slovak Gymnastic Union Falcon, for example. But whatever their orientation, they became an important focus of Slavic communal life.

On Sundays and church or national holidays the lodges gathered families—the boarders, too—for fellowship and celebration. The people feasted around tables groaning beneath the weight of ethnic foods washed down with hefty drafts of beer from a substantial keg. Afterward there were card games for the older men and wrestling or feats of strength for the younger. While teenagers danced folk dances to the accompaniment of accordian or violin, gossiping mothers kept an eye on possible spouses for their children of marriageable age. As evening came, the men gathered together to talk politics, wage scales in the mines, grievances against bosses. Later the people reminisced about home, about life in the old country—what had been gained and what had been lost. Then in the morning the shrill blast of the mine whistle returned everyone to the daily round of toil.

A Slavic fraternal hall.
Courtesy of the Burg Collection, MG-273, Pennsylvania State Archives.

The amateur theatrical group of a Ruthenian fraternal society, Lansford, 1915.
Courtesy of the Burg Collection, MG-273, Pennsylvania State Archives.

The family formed the heart of the Slavic community. The immigrants transferred family structures intact from the Old World. The family was, above all, a survival mechanism, especially important in the first years of adjustment. The typical
family was hierarchical, with the father and older males cast in authority roles, and
generally close-knit. The family might also be extended as well; certainly the proximity of relatives in the neighborhood made it seem so.

The patriarchal nature of the family allowed little place for equality among its
various members. Though there might be discussions between husband and wife,
the man had final say. With children, usually little physical discipline was needed.
They learned early to submit to parental authority, though the youngest children
generally had more latitude than the older ones. Even in small matters of discipline
the father's authority was extreme. Age was no factor—all children living under the
same roof were ultimately subject to his discipline.

Children were not only subject to greater discipline in the immigrant family;
they stayed at home longer, especially if they were males. Some Southern Slavs
practiced a system called the *zadruga*, a communal family structure based upon the
supremacy of the oldest male member and the belief that male progeny should not
leave their parents' home. Instead, after they were married, they were expected to
bring their wives back to their parents' home and work to support the *zadruga*. The

The Riccis of Mahanoy City, a family of Italian coal miners, circa 1906.
Courtesy of the Balch Institute of Ethnic Studies, Ricci Collection.

sense of family interdependency was instilled early in Slavic children. They, like the children of Italian immigrants, were often pressured to leave school early in order to contribute to the household. In Scranton, in 1911, Polish children contributed as much as 35 percent of the family income, working as breaker boys, mule drivers, and door boys or doing other lowly jobs in the mines.[31]

The male child was doubly preferred over the female. He could carry on the family name and could contribute more money to the family purse. He would also help his father about the house. The Slavic preference for males showed up in obvious ways; sons usually received the lion's share of any inheritance or property. One elderly Lithuanian woman worked without pay in the soda factory her son inherited from her husband until her death at eighty-four. At the same time she lived with a daughter and her family for many years and did not pay a cent for room and board.[32]

Despite the father's authority, at the center of family life was the wife, and her word carried real weight in matters strictly connected with the home. She often controlled the family's finances (with proper allowance for her husband's drinking, smoking, and gambling habits), had responsibility for the rearing of the children, and performed work that was endless and tedious but necessary. And in a hard world, she was often the sole source of warmth, affection, and close parental love.

What was valued in the Slavic woman were the same qualities most prized in a man: strength and endurance. In a society in which the greatest compliment that could be paid to a man was "He's a good worker," the same held true for the woman. What she gave was hard-won help in circumstances of constant struggle. The woman had to be an adroit manager of always scarce funds; family needs had to be met regardless of strikes, layoffs, and the other irregularities of mine employment. She made up the difference as best she could by keeping a garden, by shepherding the wages of children and income from boarders, or even by doing outside work. If necessary, she found employment in the silk mills and tobacco factories that came into the region to take advantage of the abundance of cheap female labor. She sent her young daughters into the homes of affluent families to work as servants at $1.50 per week. She watched with pain but stoic understanding on the day her husband took their nine-year-old son off to the breakers for the first time.

Her days began early and ended late. Up before dawn to stoke the coal stove, she packed lunches for the miners' pails and prepared breakfasts of coffee, soup, and

For the women, doing the laundry was an all-day job.
Courtesy of the Pennsylvania Canal Society Collection, Canal Museum, Easton, Pa.

black bread. With no electricity or gas for refrigeration, and ice a random luxury, she had to shop almost daily for the cheap cuts of pork, the occasional fresh vegetables, and the potatoes and cabbage that composed the family's fare. One or two days a week she made bread, a dozen or more loaves at a time, perhaps baked in an outside community oven. Mondays traditionally were wash days; buckets of water drawn from an outside pump were brought in to heat on the stove. The laundry was boiled on the stove top, scrubbed by hand with coarse soap on tin washboards until fingers were red and raw, then wrung out by hand and tossed over fences or spread upon the grass to dry. Soapy water was carried outside and emptied in the yard or ditch along the road, and more water was brought in and heated for rinsing. If the clothes were badly soiled, as they often were, the process had to be repeated, outside in the warm months and in the kitchen in winter. Ironing was done on the table brought close to the hot stove where the two or three heavy irons were heated.

There were no indoor toilets, so slop buckets from the previous night had to be emptied and cleansed. Floors were scrubbed on hands and knees, the carpets made of old rags washed or dusted with heavy sticks, and cast iron stove tops scoured with rough-edged bricks. Clothes were patched and mended by hand or, later, on treadle-

Slavic women and children.   *Courtesy of the Historical Society of Schuylkill County, Pottsville, Pa.*

operated sewing machines. In summer the garden needed tending, vegetables had to be canned, fruits preserved, and sauerkraut made and stored for use through the winter. Chickens, ducks, and sometimes a cow or pig had to be fed and watered, coops swept out, and, for holidays, the fowl killed and plucked.

Women participated with men in the slaughter of pigs. The son of a Lithuanian immigrant recalled:

> There was no refrigeration, and in the Fall most of them would buy a good-size pig . . . , about 300 pounds. . . . well, everybody in the street, all your neighbors would come over and help slaughter the pig. And all the women and all the men would clean it up and cut it up and in the back yard there was always sheds. . . . they were smoke houses. Certain kinds of wood— apple, apple trees were the best. We would smoke the hams and make all the base in them and stuff. . . . nothing was wasted. . . . and then next week you went to the next house and helped them.[33]

There were other tasks: the tending of small children, care of the sick and injured, cleaning and polishing of the kerosene lamps, a trip to the culm bank to scrounge for coal. In the afternoons water was heated for the men's baths, a bucket of beer sent for, preparation of the evening meal begun. Day after day the round went on, in cramped quarters, with few labor-saving appliances and only some help from the younger children.

A Slavic husband saw his wife's most important role as the bearing and rearing of children. In Eastern Europe peasant families were large, the result of both Catholic influence and the economic necessity for labor, and this tradition carried over to America. The women usually married young, soon after reaching marriageable age, and bore a large number of children. Eight or nine was not uncommon, though seldom did all of them survive. A physician with considerable experience among the Slavs commented that "among these women it's a birth every year." He may have exaggerated, but the birth rate of 70 per 1,000 population among the Slavs in the region at the turn of the century, a figure considerably higher than among native-born Americans, testifies to the fecundity of Slavic women. One observer noted that the streets of Slavic neighborhoods always seemed to be filled with children.[34]

Both childbearing and child rearing were fraught with danger. Physicians were not always available or affordable, and women, as in Europe, turned to midwives for help with birth in the home. With poor diets and sanitary conditions prevailing, infant mortality was appallingly high. In some mining towns 40 percent of the children died before they reached maturity, 70 percent of them within the first five years of life.[35] They were carried off by a multitude of diseases ranging from measles to typhoid, for none of which were there adequate antidotes. Photographs of family members surrounding a small pine coffin containing the white-clothed body of a child were often seen in Slavic homes.

Childbirth, however, gave the woman little reprieve from work. She was expected to be up and about her chores within a few days at most. One woman was seen milking her cow on the third day after the birth of her child; another was picking coal on a culm bank and wading home through an icy stream within a week after giving birth.[36] The women received little understanding from their husbands, as the following note from a 1915 report on Johnstown, a city outside the anthracite region, indicates:

> Mother aged 35 years; 6 births in 12 years; 4 live births and 2 still births. All live born died in first year . . . Says she had worked too hard keeping boarders in this country and cutting wood and carrying it on her back in the old country. . . . Father furious because all babies die; wore red necktie to funeral of last to show his disrespect for wife who can only produce children that die.[37]

The conditions in which women lived in the coalfields produced predictable results. They were worn from work and childbirth long before middle age and appeared much older than they actually were. The tragedy of burying children contributed to a deep sense of fatalism and resignation among them and reinforced the peasant perception of the world as a place of limited good.

Photographs of family members surrounding a small pine coffin containing the white-clothed body of a child were often seen in Slavic homes.
Courtesy of the Burg Collection, MG-273, Pennsylvania State Archives.

Childhood ended early in anthracite country.   Courtesy of the Lewis Hine Collection,
Albin O. Kuhn Library, University of Maryland, Baltimore County.

There was no such thing as adolescence in the coalfields. Childhood gave way to adulthood. The children might play for a time with homemade rag dolls and crude wooden toys, but by age five or six they were helping with chores around the house or were looking out for younger children. The boys learned early that they would follow their fathers into the mines; often they looked forward to starting in the breakers, for it meant some money and a certain independence—the reward for entering the world of working men. The girls stayed home longer, learning the routine of the house and sometimes running the entire household if the mother was sick or had died. Play was often an adjunct of work: herding ducks and geese in the fields, running errands to fetch beer or a needed staple, throwing lumber beneath the wheels of moving mine cars to jar out and steal lumps of coal. The highlight of the day might be nothing more than meeting the men as they came up from below; it was customary for the miners to save a bit of lunch for the children.

In the streets of the mining towns, lessons were hard and came early. The children learned to fend for themselves, to develop a tough independence free of otherwise occupied adults. Games were invented and were played with imagination and roughness and with the barest of castoff or handmade materials. Baseball required no more than a broomstick, a hard rubber ball, and flat rocks for bases.

The noon recreation hour, Kingston coal company.
Courtesy of the Wyoming Historical and Geological Society, Wilkes-Barre, Pa.

In the larger towns girls of nine or ten frequently found employment in the homes of prosperous families. The work was hard, the pay low, and the hours long, but there were often compensations. A Lithuanian grandmother looked back with a certain fondness on the years she had spent, beginning at age eight, working in the home of a Welsh insurance agent in the early twentieth century. The woman of the house had taught her to cook, launder, and do the other household chores necessary for her later married life. She had corrected and improved the girl's poor English and had taught her "respectable" manners. When the girl fell ill with pneumonia, the woman took her in and nursed her back to health because she did not believe that the girl would receive proper care in her own home. Always there was some leftover food from the weekend to take home to the family and occasionally a castoff piece of clothing that had some wear left in it. Even the Saturday polishing of silver for the traditional Sunday roast beef dinner had some appeal, for one could at least sit and rub at the kitchen table beside the warm coal stove.[38]

After the turn of the century, adolescent girls as young as twelve frequently went to work in the silk mills that sprang up in the region. The mills were massive brick structures four or more stories tall and half a block long, with many rows of windows—to catch all available light. They were ill heated and drafty, stifling in summer, damp and cold in winter. The mechanical looms made a horrendous racket, and the air was filled with dust and particles of silk. The silk racing through the machinery required undeviating concentration and attention, especially if it was from a bad lot and tore easily. Cuts on the fingers from the fine silk were an ignored commonplace. The girls stood at their machines for ten hours a day, worked five and a half days a week, and undoubtedly dreamed of early marriage as a means of escape.

The mining towns provided limited entertainment for young people. There were occasional dances and other social activities sponsored by the churches and fraternal groups, usually under the watchful eyes of priests and adults. For adolescent boys and young men, who had or took more freedom, there were more questionable diversions. In the roughhouse towns all kinds of gambling, especially on the favored slot machines and cock fights, were pervasive, and priests and ministers deplored the tendency of the young to squander their money on such activities. Few towns worth the name were without a brothel, tolerated and even protected by the authorities, and many young men went there for their first sexual experience. Drinking was learned early, and the time from fetching a pail of beer for "the old man" to taking a first nip at the bar was short.

Despite the constant cautioning of parents and priests against premarital sex, there was apparently a lot of it. Peter Roberts was appalled by the "licentiousness" and "bastardy" he claimed to see everywhere. It was not unusual, he noted, to see young girls parading on summer evenings on lonely paths or admitted to saloons for purposes of "trafficking." One of the girls, he wrote, when asked if she were not afraid of the consequences, replied, "Not as long as the drug store is handy." A Protestant pastor Roberts knew once told him that, "In most of my weddings I marry three and not two." Roberts ascribed these conditions to the lack of moral and religious training and the "want of moral sensitiveness" in the homes. But he added that irregular employment in the mines and the lack of industrial training for other trades contributed.[39]

Every town had its juvenile gangs. The competition and hostility between the various ethnic groups was learned early, and the youth of a particular nationality and neighborhood soon discovered that protection lay in numbers. Often imitating the behavior of their elders, they organized themselves for sportive forays against other gangs. Criminal activities, from the setting of random fires to robbery and assault, were common. Fractured families resulting from the deaths of parents or abandonment by husbands and fathers cast many children loose to fend for themselves. By the turn of the century numerous institutions with names like "Home of the Friendless" and "St. Patrick's Orphanage Asylum" had been founded by the churches and public authorities to deal with homeless, dependent, and delinquent children, who were frequently thrown together without discrimination.[40]

Most children, however, though gaining the hard experiences necessary to their survival, held fast to the traditions and values learned in their communities. Their childhoods may have been short and mean, and their prospects limited, but they gained independence, pride, and above all, the required sense of life as an incessant struggle.

Toward education, Slavic immigrants had a peculiar attitude: they valued it and they feared it, so naturally they sought to control it. Virtually every ethnic community of sufficient size to support one had its parochial school staffed by a few overworked but determined nuns. Though it might have few instructional materials and woefully unqualified teachers, it was preferred to the better-funded public schools because parents could be assured that their children received instruction in the values and traditions they themselves honored.

For many Slavic parents, the public schools were the great enemy. These immigrants did not accept the common notion that education opened the way for fast advancement in the larger world. In school you learned the skills essential to survive in society, and when you learned them, you left. But it was not how long public education lasted but what was taught that bothered them most. Public schools were condemned for their "antireligious" teachings and emphasis upon materialism and assimilation to "American" ways. They were seen as places which turned children against their parents and their ethnic heritage. The Slovak writer, J. T. Porincak, wrote:

> With a public school education they [children] go forth into the world, lost completely to the Slovaks. Their idea of life is a breezy and snappy novel, a blood-curdling movie and lots of money.
>
> But our duty to our people commands us to save our youth from the moral catastrophe that is confronting them.[41]

School children in an anthracite town, probably in the 1880s.   Courtesy of the George Bretz
Collection, Albin O. Kuhn Library, University of Maryland, Baltimore County.

The parish school stressed other and older values. There the principal subject
was catechism, often taught in the national language. There children prayed in
Latin before they saluted the flag.

Slavic attitudes toward education show up in school attendance figures. A 1911
national study by the U.S. Immigration Commission revealed that the percentage of
Slavic children in schools beyond the sixth grade was lower than the rate for recent
Irish and Jewish immigrants' children and Negroes. The numbers in high schools
also were exceedingly low. Even the figures for parochial schools reveal low attendance in the higher grades. In Scranton, in 1910, 99 percent of Polish immigrant
children were in the first five grades only, and in Shenandoah, where 32 percent of
the children of native-born Catholics went beyond fourth grade, no Polish children
advanced that far despite the presence of Poles in the region for at least a decade.[42]

Girardville school children dressed up for payday, circa 1891.
Courtesy of the Historical Society of Schuylkill County, Pottsville, Pa.

For many Slavs education beyond the rudimentary requirements of learning some simple reading, writing, and arithmetic wasn't considered important. Among first generation Slavs at least, education was not considered a tool in social advancement. Was a high school diploma really necessary if they were to spend their lives in mines and mills or as housewives? Many children also became discouraged because they did not speak English well. Frequently attending school was their first real exposure to the language. In addition, since economic necessity required most children to begin working at age ten or twelve, even the brightest and most ambitious children usually had their formal education cut off early.

An essential part of a Slavic child's education was his education in the customs and ceremonies of his nationality. Slavic ceremonies, nearly all of which had religious as well as national meaning, followed the natural cycle of a person's life. Baptism was an introduction to the church and the community. After the birth of a child, relatives and friends were invited to the house for a feast. The friends, called the

"Kum," were now considered bound to the family by special ties of friendship. Apart from the godparents, who stood for the child at the baptism ceremony, they had an informal paternal relationship to the child that implied spiritual guidance and material protection. On later occasions, such as first communion, confirmation, and marriage, they assumed personal interest and symbolic roles emphasizing their relationship to the individual and family.

Slavs were heartily criticized for their ceremonies, which were not understood by outsiders, who often considered them demonstrations of a barbarous and corrupt culture. Since many of the ceremonies involved drinking and dancing, they were eyed with particular suspicion by conservative Protestants. One wide-eyed reporter for a national publication, who witnessed a Hungarian baptism celebration, wrote about it with a mixture of wonderment and displeasure. After leaving the church, he reported, the party returned to the house, where the host had filled a huge vat with beer laced with two jugs of whiskey and a handful of hot peppers. While the mixture—called "polinki"—was stirred, the Hungarians sang and danced in a circle around it, "like Apaches," first on one foot, then the other. During the course of the celebration, as things heated up, the newly baptized infant was deposited in the outhouse safe from harm.[43]

Courtship was an important and serious business, especially in the early years when there was a scarcity of eligible women. "Matchmaking" filled the leisure hours of many fathers who had left their families behind in Europe and longed to have their wives and children with them in America. Saving sufficient funds to bring the family from the Old World and establishing a home required much saving and sacrifice; the mine worker who had a daughter of marriageable age, on the other hand, recognized that she was an asset which could be used toward that end.

The father of such a young woman usually looked for a young, unmarried worker with a reputation for thrift and good habits. He then became friendly with the potential son-in-law and was soon talking about his daughter. A tintype of her was a valuable aid; in its absence he simply described her physical charms, sound traits of character, and capacity for companionship. Invariably he stressed his daughter's fitness for marriage, her health, strength, and family training. Frequently the young man, faced with the scarcity of women and the social barriers surrounding those of other nationalities, agreed to forward money for her passage. The father of the bride then pledged her troth and agreed to live with the newlyweds and contribute to the maintenance of the new home until he could bring the remainder of his family and establish a home of his own.

This kind of matchmaking in the region resulted in the arrival of hundreds of young women, to meet and marry husbands they had never seen. Almost imme-

diately, the couple's new home became a boardinghouse for others of their nationality. As an observer noted:

> Inborn thrift and the will to labor laid the foundation for a competence which,
> once accumulated, later meant a private home and the rearing and education
> of a family in the newer, higher standard American way of living.[44]

Courtship, of course, was not only the responsibility of fathers. Young people in
the region took matters into their own hands. A singular custom among Russians
was for a group of young women to surround a group of young men on certain days
and shout and yell until the boys responded by chasing after them. The men caught
the girls of their choice and had the right to spend the remainder of the evening with
them. On Easter Monday, young Slavic women had the privilege of throwing water
on the young men of their choice, which was both a sign of partiality and a wish of
good luck. On Easter Tuesday the men responded. The custom grew out of the habit
of bringing some extra happiness to friends after the long Lenten season; the Slavic
nobility in the Old World expressed this sentiment with a delicate spray of perfume on
the coats and dresses of friends; the peasants, unable to buy perfume, used water.[45]

When marriage partners were selected, elaborate preparations began for one of
the momentous events in the lives of the Slavs. Though their marriage ceremonies
differed, depending upon the ethnic group, they always involved sizable numbers of
the community in joyous celebration. Prior to the engagement, the groom took his
best friend along to the home of his potential bride and asked her parents for their
formal consent to the marriage. The girl's parents then visited the boy's parents, and
the whole matter was settled. The boy and girl obtained a marriage license; a public
announcement was made before the ceremony. There were also several visits to the
priest for instruction and announcement of the banns in church. The bride-to-be at
this time gave her future husband a hand-picked bouquet of roses to wear in his hat
until the day of the wedding, when she presented him with another one. In the
weeks before the marriage the bride's mother cooked and baked, receiving help from
relatives, friends, and neighbors, while the father built up a generous supply of beer
and whiskey. In some groups the bridegroom purchased the wedding garment for
the bride and contributed money for the wedding feast.[46]

Among Lithuanians, the wedding usually lasted three days. It began the day
before the ceremony, when a bridal party, consisting of five to eight couples besides
the bride and groom, was selected. The men were selected first and they, in turn,
picked their partners for the following day. A party was held, at which the men gave
flowers and candies to their partners before the dancing and singing began. On the
following day, before departure for the church, the bridal party sat at the wedding
table, and the bride and groom were given a cross to kiss. A song of farewell was

A Slovak bride and groom, both newly arrived in America.
Donald L. Miller, family collection.

sung. As the orchestra played a march, the bridal party walked around the table for luck and out of the house. Following the mass when the bridal party returned to the house, the bride and groom were given wine, bread, and salt to eat and were serenaded by the orchestra. When the newlyweds sat for the wedding feast, they were toasted by all present, and songs were sung in their honor.

Dancing, singing, and game playing followed through the afternoon. Tables were set for all who desired to eat and drink. After the evening meal came the "donations" for the bride and groom. The parents and relatives of the newlyweds came first. As the orchestra played, the married couple were congratulated, the donations were given, and the donor tried to break a plate, usually with a silver dollar. After the bride's veil had been removed and her hair let down by other married women to signify her new status, the bride danced with all the guests, who were required to deposit money in her apron for the privilege. Mock bidding might also be held for the veil, which the bridegroom was expected to purchase. The money collected by the bride and groom helped them to set up housekeeping.

Following donations for the bride, money was solicited for the musicians, who were not paid in any other way. A comically dressed couple entertained the guests with jokes and stories to encourage their generosity. On the evening of the third day donations were given to the cooks, who then gave the donors a piece of the wedding cake and the right to a drink. The cake and drinks were usually provided by the best man. At the conclusion of these donations the final dinner was served, and dancing and singing followed again until the guests departed in the early evening.

Late in the evening of the wedding day, after she had danced with the guests, the bride danced one final time with her husband, who then rushed her out toward the house where they were to spend their wedding night, accompanied on their way by much shouted encouragement and advice. The following morning the couple were awakened by a member of the household, who presented them with a wash basin and water. The person who awakened them was given something in return.[47]

The Slavic bride often received a new pair of boots on her wedding day. She seldom put them on again for fear of wearing them out, but she would carry them to church and festive occasions over her shoulder—to show that she had a pair. Many women saved their boots to be buried in.[48]

Weddings were clearly important in the immigrant community, but the funeral perhaps best epitomized the communal, village tradition of the ethnic settlements. After the death of a parishioner—let us say a respected worker who had helped build the immigrant colony—the church bells tolled three times a day, at dawn, noon, and evening. The tolling continued every day until the deceased was buried and the "Eternal Memory" had been sung. The viewing took place in the home of the deceased. Lodge members and friends would gather in the coal cellar, after the priest had led the rosary, to drink and celebrate a life lived in commitment and strength. When the viewers had left, and late night approached, they would, one after another, lead an all-night vigil by the side of the coffin. In rural settlements lodge or parish members would dig the grave on the morning of the burial. On the day of the burial a procession formed after the mass. First came the priest and altar boys, followed by men from the neighborhood carrying church banners, the pallbearers, the family, and other mourners. After the burial all attended a feast prepared by the family, relatives, and neighbors. For weeks, sometimes months afterward, lodge members and ladies from the church visited the widow regularly to help provide for her material and emotional needs. Here was the immigrant community at its best—a world and a tradition a thousand years in the making—communal, compassionate, intensely religious, calling itself together in one final celebration for a son who had given himself in equal measure to family, lodge, church, and community.

Religious feast days also provided ceremony and celebration, both for the community as a whole and within individual families. What annoyed the English-speaking miners and inhabitants of the region, however, was the number of feast days. The Greek Catholics had twenty-nine and the Roman Catholics twenty-six, nearly all of which were observed. To the despair of the coal operators and the disgust of miners who wanted to work, many mines were frequently idled because half the force was absent.

The most important religious holy days were, of course, Easter and Christmas. On Easter large crucifixes were laid in the churches near the altars and close to votive candles, and after the mandatory confession of sins during the Lenten season, parishioners came forward, sometimes on their knees from the rear of the church, to kiss the feet of the crucified Christ. They then lit a candle and prayed for souls in purgatory. Tombs were often constructed over the site, and male members of the church's religious organization stood guard for a period equal to that in which Christ remained in the tomb. Good Friday was observed with a great deal of ceremony;

A Slovak graveside ceremony.   Donald L. Miller, family collection.

many people stayed in the church and prayed during the hours when Christ hung on the cross. On Good Saturday baskets of food were brought to the church and were left near the altar, where they were blessed by the priest. Following divine liturgy on Easter Sunday morning the consecrated food was eaten by the family.

A Ukrainian priest, Monsignor Stephen Hrynuch of Saints Cyril and Methodius Church in Olyphant, remembers Easter during his youth:

> Easter was the time when we rejoiced in the resurrection of the Christ. Before Easter all the children wait for the priest to come bless them, and their Easter basket, and usually he would come to each house . . . and give the cross to the kids. . . . Easter day was a solemn day also, and then we would go to church and ring the bells all day long. . . . the boys and girls would dance.[49]

Christmas was a gala time for the gathering of family and friends, the consumption of ethnic foods, and the most intensive observance of Old World customs. In Polish families, for example, the Christmas season was ushered in with the traditional Christmas Eve supper—*wilja*—at which every member of the family gath-

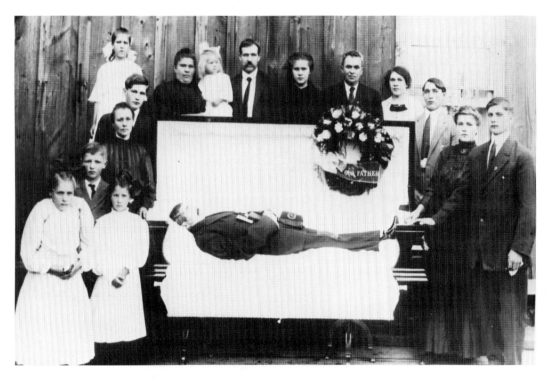

A miner's funeral, Minersville, Pennsylvania.
Courtesy of the Historical Society of Schuylkill County, Pottsville, Pa.

ered in the home of the parents or grandparents. For the dead and for the living who were unable to be present a place was set at the table. Straw or pine boughs to represent the manger were placed on the table, which was covered with a white cloth. Meatless dishes, as many as ten or more, were served. During the supper the age-old custom, the breaking of the communion wafer—*oplatek*—blessed by the church, took place. Everyone ate a bite of the wafer and wished all people present good health, wealth, and happiness as well as forgiveness for all misunderstandings. After supper the candles on the tree were lit and gifts presented to the children. That was followed by the group singing of Christmas carols—*kolendy*—and midnight mass—*pasterka*. After mass there were visits with neighbors for the exchange of greetings.[50]

Holidays, especially Christmas, were occasions for the preparation of special foods. The son of a Slavic immigrant remembered:

> the things that they had [at Christmas] they had to work hard for. . . . And some of the special things were homemade butter. They didn't have any churners, and you had a two-quart bottle and you would roll that bottle until the butter started to appear. . . . *Pierog* was good, and *collachie*, which was poppie seed rolls, and crescent rolls. But it was a festive occasion when they had meat. The Christmas Eve supper we had *collat*, which was a wafer and they would come out on a platter. . . . they used honey and a little smear of garlic, and they would eat that before they sat down to eat. But they ate that to be reminded of how sweet life can be.[51]

One of the most picturesque Christmas customs among the Slavs was the traveling narrative. Several men, dressed in costumes, went from house to house, telling of the birth of Christ, in a performance of considerable dignity but also much fun. There were three "Brothers of the Church" representing the wise men from the East. One carried a miniature house on the end of a pole to represent the church. His two companions walked at his side and with songs told the story of the Nativity. The group was accompanied by grotesque figures dressed to represent the devil, heathens, and nonbelievers, and they danced and indulged in ludicrous performances to furnish the fun. The "Brothers" tried to persuade the nonbelievers to worship, efforts which were rewarded by money or cakes. The money was turned over to the church.

The week between Christmas and New Year's Day was a time of merrymaking. During the week, instead of exchanging presents, friends distributed *piroge*, small cakes containing either fruits or vegetables. Each family made an enormous pie, about thirty inches in diameter and several inches thick, containing seventeen different ingredients, from which each member of the family had to eat. Barley mixed with honey was also a dainty made during this period. When it was first made, the head of the house threw a spoonful against the ceiling. If it stuck, it was a sign of prosperity and happiness in the new year. If it failed to stick, it was a sign of bad luck and all fun-making in the house ended.

On New Year's Eve members of the community marched to the house of the wealthiest among them and threw handfuls of wheat, corn, or rye upon him because they wished it to grow upon good ground and ensure continued prosperity. In return, the recipient was expected to furnish drinks and cakes to his well-wishers.[52]

In addition to the family and church with their ceremonies and celebrations, members of the community came together in various informal ways. A favorite diversion among women in winter was the gathering to make articles used in the home. During the cold months people often slept under feather covers, which were continually refurbished and in some cases were passed down from generation to generation. Whenever possible the people kept chickens, ducks, and geese, and after they had been slaughtered for food the feathers were gathered, put in bags, and stored until they were dried. When several bags had been collected, a number of women or girls were invited to help tear and peel the feathers. This was regarded as a social occasion that gave the ladies an opportunity to exchange stories, jokes, and gossip. At the conclusion of the peeling, a big dinner was served or a party held for the members of the group. The feathers were then used to make pillows or feather covers; very few people bought readymade pillows. Quilting also provided social evenings. It was common to find several women sitting around quilting frames while others prepared dinner.[53]

The social institution that most frequently brought the men together was the saloon. Slavs were famous for their hard drinking—but probably no more so than miners of other nationalities—a fact that earned for them a considerable and not necessarily upstanding reputation among certain native-born Americans. But for the Slavs the saloon was more than a place for carousing with friends and neighbors. In the early days it was a center of information and services: a place where the immigrant might find temporary lodging, exchange news, find an interpreter or translator or have a letter written, notarize papers, purchase a money order to send home, obtain credit, and even deposit savings—the so-called "immigrant bank." Perhaps the saloons' most important function was that of hiring hall, where mine foremen knew that they could find readily available labor. Since the saloons opened early and remained open until late, they offered convenient hours for the transaction of business.[54]

It was customary, even mandatory, for the miners to have their drink at the end of a shift. Part of the folklore of the region was that a "shot and a beer"—the classic and still-favored setup—helped to clear the body of coal dust. So at certain hours of the day the saloons would be filled with men with lunch pails, miner's hats, and

*Saloons in the anthracite region were a major institution.   Courtesy of the Historical Society of
Schuylkill County, Pottsville, Pa.*

mud-encrusted boots, seeking relaxation after the rigors of a workday underground
and regaling their fellows with stories, insults, and jokes.

The saloons could be anything from a simple shack with a bar made of rough
planks resting on several overturned barrels to an establishment with polished ma-
hogany bar, brass spittoons and bar rail, and large mirrors. In the larger saloons
there would be tables, sometimes set up in a back room, for card playing or "lady
guests." (Women, except those of a certain type, were frequently prohibited from entering the bar area itself.) On paydays miners often paid off their laborers in the
saloons, and on Sundays, despite local ordinances against opening on the Sabbath,
the men would flock to the saloons after mass. Many saloonkeepers on such days
would offer free lunches as an additional enticement. On election day the saloons
sometimes served as polling places.

The most common beverages were beer, ale, and porter, made in the breweries
established in the region by Germans. Whiskey was also favored, substantial shots
being drawn from large barrels. The origin of much of the whiskey was questionable; the designation of the common "five cents a drink" type as "rotgut" is sugges-
tive. Yet the miners consumed it in vast quantities, while frequently complaining
about its vile taste and doubtful qualities. Despite the pervasiveness of drinking in

the region, alcoholism did not appear to be a greater problem than in other industrial centers. Roberts estimated that the average miner spent from four to six dollars a month on alcohol—not an excessive amount.[55]

Established saloonkeepers held a place of considerable influence in their communities, often serving as representatives or mediators for their particular ethnic group. Opening a saloon, even the simplest, required some capital and more risk, and those who did so usually had a flair for enterprise. A few of them went on to invest in other businesses and became men of substantial wealth and local standing. Since the Slavs were the best frequenters of saloons, it was not surprising that many of the saloons in the region ended up in their hands, purchased from the original German owners. Then they became true ethnic community centers.

*   *   *

By the final decade of the nineteenth century the Slavs had become firmly established in the region. Those who had decided to remain in the hard coal fields—and they were the majority—had set down roots, started families, built parishes, founded organizations, and begun the process of becoming Americans even as they held on to what they had been. They were tough people, most of them, but their toughness was tempered by their strong attachments to family, church, lodge, and neighborhood. And from their families and communities they drew the strength and steel-hard perseverance that helped them in their enormous struggles to better their lives and working conditions.

7. Lattimer

THE SLAVIC IMMIGRANTS ARRIVED IN ANTHRACITE COUNTRY DURING TIMES OF profound trouble for the industry and its people. Gowen had crushed the Mollies, but his dream of a sprawling anthracite empire turned into a nightmare. The year the first group of Mollies were hanged, the country slipped into a severe economic depression that had a devastating impact on the coal industry. The large anthracite railroads, successful in their battles against the canals and independent operators, turned on each other in cutthroat competition. Their efforts to combine and limit shipments failed amid mutual suspicion and greed. Several of the carriers fell on hard times. The powerful Reading, financially overextended by its purchase of coal lands, careened toward the brink of bankruptcy. Gowen became the victim of his own ambition. In the meantime the mine workers suffered as wages were cut sharply. In 1877 the monthly income of Pennsylvania Coal Company employees averaged thirty dollars, and a contract miner in Taylorsville reported that he received only sixty-three cents per carload of coal.[1] The men fought back as best they could. In July they joined railroad workers who were striking the anthracite carriers. It was the first of a series of violent, uncoordinated strikes that swept the region in the following years.

Public and corporate officials, alarmed over the spreading labor turbulence, organized vigilante committees and special police squads comprised of "respectable" middle-class citizens. Fearing a resurgence of Molly Maguirism and determined that their communities would not fall victim to the kind of labor riots that had recently shaken Pittsburgh, they dealt with the workers in ruthless and often murderous fashion. When vandals looted the Philadelphia and Reading Railroad's Shamokin station on July 25, a vigilante group fired into the mob, killing one and wounding several others. On August 1 in Scranton a special police force organized and armed by the Lackawanna Coal and Iron Company, and led by the company's general superintendent, W. W. Scranton, who ordered his men "to shoot low, and to shoot to kill if they shot at all," killed six and wounded fifty-four marching strikers. Following this incident, 5,000 Pennsylvania National Guardsmen were rushed into the region. Despite the protests of the mine workers, the troops remained as an occupying force for the duration of the strike. There was little doubt as to whose interests they served. At one point heavily armed detachments surrounded the strike-ridden town of Plymouth and arrested everyone in sight.[2]

The strike spread and had some initial success despite the menacing presence of the troops. In August the entire Lehigh field shut down. By September independent

Overleaf: Philadelphia and Reading Coal and Iron Company Guards, circa 1880. This private police force was responsible for keeping labor peace in the anthracite fields.
Courtesy of the George Bretz Collection, Albin O. Kuhn Library, University of Maryland, Baltimore County.

coal operators in the Wilkes-Barre and Hazleton areas agreed to terms, offering a restoration of previous wage rates. The workers of the large corporations, now believing that they could bargain from a position of strength, sent committees to New York to negotiate with the presidents of the big coal and railroad companies. But the companies held firm, arguing that the depression did not permit them to meet the workers' demands.

The strategy of the corporations was devastatingly simple: starve the workers into submission. And it worked. Hardship intensified among the hundreds of families of striking mine workers despite the efforts of nonstriking miners in the Lehigh and Schuylkill fields to provide relief. The scope of necessary support was too great for the miners' limited resources. By October, for example, the Pittston relief committee was issuing a weekly ration of only fourteen ounces of flour, a half bushel of potatoes, and four pounds of fish per family. As hunger became alarmingly widespread, the mine workers capitulated.[3]

The strikes of 1877 taught the mine workers a hard lesson. Concessions might be wrung from the smaller independent operators, but the large coal companies dominated the industry and had to be challenged and brought to terms. This feat could be accomplished only by a strong union capable of organizing and unifying workers in all three fields for concerted action. But organizing such a union was exceedingly difficult in the decade after 1877, a time of vigorous nationwide anti-union sentiment. That the anthracite workers finally managed to put together two unions which achieved a measure of cooperation in the late 1880s was testimony to their stubborn persistence in the face of adversity.[4]

The first of the two unions to have some organizational success was the Knights of Labor. Agents of this secret national union had been active in the anthracite fields since 1871, but not until 1876 were they able to form a local assembly in Scranton. The Knights provided some leadership during the strikes of the following year, but not until after the strikes did the union succeed in organizing assemblies throughout the region. Their efforts, however, encountered considerable opposition. Local parish priests, with memories of the Mollies fresh in their minds, denounced the Knights, despite their bishop's approval of the union. When the Reading's workers struck for back pay against the company, Gowen once again raised the issue of terrorism. Seeking to avert the spread of a strike, which could be disastrous for his financially troubled company, he sent an open letter to the *Weekly Miners' Journal* exposing the names of the officers and membership of the Knight's assemblies. He also implied that there was a "gang" within the union, similar to the Mollies, whose task was to sabotage coal company property. The Knights fought back by challenging the Schuylkill County judicial authorities to arrest the alleged terrorists; since Gowen's charges were unsubstantiated, the matter was dropped.[5]

The incident, reported along with a regional newspaper's account of the Knights' constitution and internal organization, helped to allay the public's fears about the union. When the Reading paid back wages to its employees, and workers in Shamokin successfully struck another coal company, the Knights took full credit. In July 1879, buoyed by its gains, the union renounced its policy of secrecy and held a public meeting at Shenandoah attended by thousands.

But progress toward a single union embracing all anthracite workers was hampered by two factors. First, the Knights of Labor was a national organization that sought to enlist all craft workers under its banner. Many mine workers, however, wanted a union of their own. Second, the Knights' membership in the hard coal fields was predominantly Irish; tension between them and English, Welsh, and German miners continued to cause difficulties. As a result, efforts went on among non-Knights of Labor mine workers to organize a separate union. In 1879 Lehigh miners formed the Workingmen's Protective Association, and the following year veterans of the Workingmen's Benevolent Association attempted to revive that organization. Though neither endeavor succeeded, the two groups did keep interest in a union alive and laid the basis for an industrywide union several years later.

In 1883 the Amalgamated Association of Miners of the United States, comprised of workers in several bituminous-producing states, sent an organizer into the anthracite fields. By 1885 considerable success had been achieved among the English, Welsh, and German miners in the Lehigh and Schuylkill fields. The new union, the Miners' and Laborers' Amalgamated Association, put aside ethnic hostilities and formed a joint coordinating committee with the Knights. Another dramatic confrontation between organized labor and the coal operators was in the making.[6]

In August 1887 the Amalgamated called for a 15 percent increase in base wages. When the large corporations and the major independents in the Lehigh field rejected this demand, 20,000 miners struck. Despite the impressive show of strength, the unions failed to persuade all anthracite workers to walk out. The now-bankrupt Reading reached an agreement with its miners that resulted in a temporary 8 percent wage hike, and the Schuylkill independent operators went along. Workers in the less well organized Wyoming-Lackawanna field failed to heed the strike call.

In the Lehigh field management reacted to the strike with characteristic toughness. The spokesman for the independents there, Hazleton operator Ario Pardee, Sr., summed up their attitude perfectly. "Our position," he said, "always had been and is now that we are unwilling to treat with anyone outside our employ, who knows nothing of our business and who is in no way connected with us, and we are just as firm in that position as we ever have been."[7]

At first the operators kept the mines open, expecting to entice the new Slavic and Italian immigrants back to work. But to the operators' surprise, the immigrants not only supported the strike but also reacted violently against scabs, even those of their own nationality. In one incident, Hungarian strikers at a colliery near Hazleton attacked Hungarian "black legs." When the operators failed to break labor's united front, they recruited workers from outside the region. Calvin Pardee brought in Italian workers, and rumors spread that Belgian miners would soon be imported. Such reports caused widespread public protest; Congressman Charles Brunn supported his striking constituents by pressuring the president to enforce the Immigration Act of 1885. A dozen Belgian miners were eventually detained by customs officials in Philadelphia, and the threat ended.

Failing in their attempts to use nonunion labor, the operators resorted to other methods. In November a rise in the price of coal resulted in an automatic increase in wages. The miners were guaranteed the increase if they returned to work, but the operators refused to recognize their union. The miners rejected what they considered to be a bribe. When management began the eviction of families from company houses, the miners obtained a temporary restraining order. But the operators had other weapons in their arsenal. Company stores denied credit; strike leaders were fired; due wages were withheld by operators' refusal to pay in cash or by deduction of rents in advance; and pressure was put on other employees not to hire strikers. Still, the mine workers held firm. They wrote a song about their intentions:

In looking o'er the papers now,
   A funny thing appears,
Where Eckly Coxe and Pardee say
   They'll stand for twenty years,
If God should call us miners off,
   We'll have children then alive,
Who will follow in our footsteps
   Keep the strike for thirty-five.[8]

The miners were able to hold out for a number of reasons. Several hundred found employment in the Schuylkill and Wyoming-Lackawanna fields. Others temporarily moved out of the region to find work in Reading, Pittsburgh, and other cities or in the bituminous fields of western Pennsylvania. Immigrants with sufficient funds returned to their homelands for the duration of the strike. Workers in the other fields also gave considerable support. The Schuylkill miners contributed 5 percent of their pay, and railroad employees in Reading gave a day's wages. Organized labor also responded generously to the appeal for relief funds made by the Knights' executive board.

Of major importance was the support provided by the local business community. Merchants in the anthracite towns and cities served as financial advisers on strike committees, contributed to relief funds, made their stores food distribution centers, and encouraged other individuals in their communities, including the clergy, to work on the strikers' behalf. Their efforts were based upon resentment that had developed over the years because of the domination of the economy by the independent operators. Families such as the Markles and the Pardees competed directly with local merchants through their ownership of company stores. They also exercised tremendous influence and power by their control of banks, other industries and businesses, and extensive real estate holdings. The independents' high-handed treatment of their workers also earned the latter genuine sympathy among nonmining sectors of the population. One newspaper called the independents "petty nabobs" and compared their "antics" to those of the despotic Russian aristocracy. The *Pottsville Daily Republican*, defending the striking miners, declared that the issue was one of might versus right. "The defiant stand taken by the operators against what is only fair and just, has awakened the American people to the fact that a few millionaires have combined to gather to defeat the mining class of people in their endeavors to get a fair compensation for a fair day's labor."[9]

The Lehigh miners might have been able to hold out if they had had full cooperation from workers in the other fields. But a turn of events in the Schuylkill in December 1887 suddenly reduced their prospects of carrying on the strike. The Reading's earlier conciliatory agreement with its mine workers had assured continued production. But as the strike in the Lehigh continued, suspicions arose that the company was filling the Lehigh operators' contracts. The Reading also was now on sounder financial footing and appeared to be preparing for an all-out battle with labor. When the company hesitated about extending the temporary agreement it had reached with its workers, a confrontation appeared likely.

It came first on the railroad operation, when members of the Knights of Labor who refused to move a shipment were fired and blacklisted. The company announced that it would operate the trains even if a regiment of troops had to be called in to do it. Austin Corbin, the Reading's president, then rejected an extension of the temporary wage agreement. Early in January 1888 the company's mine workers walked out. When the miners of independent operators refused to dig coal shipped by the Reading, the Schuylkill field shut down.

Unlike their co-workers in the Lehigh field, however, the Schuylkill miners failed to enlist full community support. Local businessmen refused to back the strike. The Reading did not operate company stores, and its domination of the field kept the independent operators in line. Business in the Schuylkill viewed the company as a protector against the "autocratic domination" of the "petty coal kings." The merchants believed that their prosperity was tied to the fortunes of the large corporation, with its ability to regulate production and influence markets, and gave them a free hand locally. When the Reading's president rejected all efforts at concil- iation, and the miners held firm in their demands, the businessmen turned against labor.[10]

The strikers sought redress at the judicial and legislative levels. They peti- tioned the state to enforce the Pennsylvania constitution of 1874, which prohibited transportation companies from owning coal lands. The Reading, organized earlier, however, had ex post facto protection. The miners then turned to the U.S. House of Representatives, requesting an investigation of the coal operators. An investigating committee subsequently did discover that the operators had formed a pool to regu- late production and prices and were engaged in a conspiracy against organized labor. The committee recommended legislation to separate the railroads from min- ing, but in the pro–big business atmosphere of the Congress nothing came of the recommendation.[11]

The increasingly desperate miners continued their strike. They showed their defiance of Corbin and the Reading in "The Knights of Labor Strike" song, composed during the struggle:

> Here's to the Knights of Labor,
>   That brave and gallant band,
> That Corbin and old Swigard
>   Is trying to disband.
> But stick and hang brave union men;
>   We'll make them rue the day
> They thought to break of K. of L.
>   In free Americ-a.[12]

Bravado and determination, however, were not enough. Hunger once again settled the issue. Organized labor could not provide sufficient relief; and with man- agement forging a united front, operators in Wyoming-Lackawanna began firing strikers from the other fields who found employment there. When a colliery near Shenandoah announced its reopening in February, and started working despite a minor riot, labor's solidarity crumbled. By mid-March both unions had capitulated.

The bitter strike of 1887–1888 impressed upon labor as never before the need for a single union to embrace anthracite workers in all three fields. The years im- mediately following the strike, however, were not auspicious for union building. Demoralized and dispirited, the mine workers abandoned the Knights and Amalga- mated in large numbers. Efforts by the national leadership of both unions to revive them by dispatching teams of organizers into the fields yielded few results. The only miners' associations that continued to have any viability existed on the local level, and these proved themselves singularly ineffective in improving wages and working conditions.

Management also took advantage of labor's weakness. Earlier hard-won gains such as the semimonthly wage guideline were ignored. Wages were cut, and by June 1888 workers were receiving 10 percent less than they had the previous June. The independent operators also instituted the so-called "dockage confession," a waiver signed by the miners declaring that they would not take action against illegal weighing practices. Finally mine foremen were instructed to fire militants.

As the operators' counteroffensive intensified in the early 1890s, the mine workers once again sought to build an effective union. The presence of numerous local associations provided a base; what was needed was an organization which could bring them together. The opportunity was provided by the formation of the United Mine Workers Union (UMW), by an 1890 merger between the Miners' National Trade Assembly 135 of the Knights of Labor and the American Miners' Federation, successor to the Amalgamated Association of Miners. The first United Mine Workers local was formed in Shamokin in 1892; during the next two and a half years sixty-two more locals were organized, largely through the efforts of the talented George Harris of the former Miners and Laborers' Amalgamated Association.[13]

Unfortunately, the UMW had some of the same weaknesses as its predecessors. It was strong only in the Schuylkill field; attempts to make headway in the other two fields were largely unsuccessful. And like the earlier unions, it failed to attract the Eastern and Southern European immigrants who now comprised a significant proportion of the anthracite labor force. Too weak to force management to deal with it, the UMW turned to political action. It attempted to have semimonthly wage law violators prosecuted; fought against a bill allowing the deduction of taxes from miners' pay; and lobbied for legislation outlawing company stores—all with little success. The union did, however, secure passage of one important law. It was to have an enormous, although unforeseen, impact on the future course of the union movement in the region.[14]

John Fahy, the UMW organizer, believed that the principal impediment to the union's expansion in the anthracite fields was the new immigrants' reluctance to join any labor association. Along with most English, German, Welsh, and Irish miners, he looked upon the Slavs and Italians as wage-cheapening laborers easily controlled by management. With the solid backing of his membership, he pressed for passage of the Campbell Act, an anti-immigrant law which taxed employers 3 cents per day for every adult immigrant they employed. The coal operators naturally opposed this legislation; and when the state legislature made it law, they began to deduct the tax from the miners' wages, confident that they would have no trouble with their immigrant workers. It was a grievous miscalculation.[15]

Like most other major historical happenings, the terrible events of September 1897 began with a single, seemingly unimportant incident. Gomer Jones, a recently appointed forty-two-year-old Welsh district superintendent for the Lehigh and Wilkes-Barre Coal Company, was thinking of ways to save money for his employers. Jones already had a reputation as a hard-nosed boss. He had been sent to the company's Honey Brook operations near McAdoo, outside Hazleton, to restore labor discipline. And he had done so with a vengeance, demanding a full ten hours' work for ten hours' pay and driving his workers furiously. As he told a newspaper reporter: "When I came here a year ago, I came to restore discipline in the mines and to operate them in such a manner that the company could continue in business." Some workers considered him "the worst slave-driver who ever set foot in the coal region." But this reputation did not bother Jones. His job was to make money for the company, and after thirty-five years' experience in the mines, starting at age seven, he was convined he knew how to do it. "The [former] . . . superintendents associated with the men," he said, "mixed with them, drank with them. . . . Now I cannot do that. I'm not a drinking man, and I've never made it a practice to hobnob with the men. . . . When I give orders I expect them to be obeyed. . . . I dismissed a good many men—about 80 I think." He knew what he could get out of the miners, even the "slow-moving" Slavs, for whom he expressed open contempt.[16]

In August 1897 Jones's efforts to cut costs focused on the first jobs that the immigrants usually had: as weighers, air boys, mule drivers, and breaker boys. He hit upon the idea of setting up a centrally located stable for the mules, which would house all the animals from the surrounding mines. This would provide savings in care, feeding, pasturage, facilities, and labor crews. The drivers, of course, would have to arrive an hour earlier and work an hour later in order to take the mules back and forth, but the extra hours did not matter, because they were paid only for the time their animals were at the mine.

On August 12 Jones announced his new procedure. The drivers protested, demanding extra pay for the extra time, but Jones ignored them. So on August 14, as translations of Jones's order spread among the drivers, a group of them went on strike at the Honey Brook colliery. The next day they set up a picket line to prevent anyone from working. Jones, armed with a crowbar, approached the line of thirty-five strikers, singled out a young boy named John Bodan, and attacked him. Bodan grabbed the crowbar in self-defense while the other drivers leaped to his aid. Jones was thrown to the ground and pounded. He might have been killed had he not been saved by a local foreman, who took him away from the angry drivers. Within minutes the victorious strikers raced to the whistle tower and sounded the signal for a work stoppage. As news of the incident spread, 800 workers marched off their jobs. The following Monday John Bodan entered a complaint against Jones and named witnesses. Jones was arrested. While he awaited trial, free on bond of $500, the Slavic workers' protest continued. It looked like the beginning of something big.[17]

On Sunday, August 15, the Catholic holy day of the Assumption, the ethnic patches around Hazleton buzzed with news of the incident at Honey Brook. The immigrants were tired of being pushed around, and this time they decided to do something about it. Jones's intemperate act had come in the wake of a series of setbacks for immigrant mine workers. The coal market was depressed, and most miners were working only half time. The companies, ignoring the half-month wage rule, were paying the workers at the end of the month, causing them to go into debt, and were then deducting sizable amounts for rents and bills at the company stores—a particularly onerous burden for the frugal Slavs. Finally, there was the discriminatory tax on wages, which fell on the immigrants.

On Monday morning, August 16, more than 350 angry mine workers marched to each of the Lehigh and Wilkes-Barre collieries and systematically shut them down. Their methods were persuasive. Miners armed with guns and clubs convinced their reluctant colleagues to quit working; the recalcitrant were dealt with roughly. By the end of the day more than 3,000 workers had walked off the job. The company responded by firing administrative employees sympathetic to the strikers and by calling for two squads of Coal and Iron Police, who made a round of the patches armed with Winchester rifles.

In the late afternoon hundreds of excited strikers crowded into Michalchik's Hall in McAdoo to decide what to do next. At the end of a tumultous meeting, with speeches in several languages, a temporary committee was elected to represent the workers. It was headed by a Slovak and an Italian. The "American" miners did not participate. Reporters covering the meeting were shocked by the militancy and determination of the foreigners. The *Hazleton Evening Standard* observed that "the Strike now in progress on the South Side has furnished an object lesson that it will be well for the operators in this section to make note of. The day of the slave driver is past and the once ignorant foreigner will no longer tolerate it."[18]

The strike committee made two demands: an increase in wages, and the removal of Gomer Jones. The next day the committee met with Elmer H. Lawall, the company's general superintendent, who claimed that he did not have the authority to make a decision. The committee, now expanded to include two representatives of English-speaking miners, some of whom had begun to support the strike, then traveled to New York to meet with high company officials. There they received a promise that the demands would be considered following an investigation but only if the miners returned to work. The strikers refused the offer. Finally, on Friday, August 20, the company gave in. Superintendent Lawall agreed to a 10 cent wage increase and told the committee that Jones's behavior would be investigated. The English-speaking workers urged acceptance; the immigrants remained uncertain. But as individual workers began to return to the mines, unity collapsed and the strike ended. Meanwhile, the immigrants awaited the resolution of the Jones issue. It would be the determining factor in their future actions.

While the strike committee met in New York with company officials, the UMW's John Fahy came up from Harrisburg. He was not sure how he would be received because of his support of the Campbell Act, but the first serious strike in the region since 1887 presented him with an opportunity he could not let pass. He need not have worried, because he was greeted warmly by the strikers. They invited him to speak before a crowd of more than 1,000 at McAdoo. The men apparently blamed the companies, not the union, for the tax.

Fahy, speaking slowly so that his remarks could be translated, urged the strikers to refrain from violence, for they could not possibly win such a confrontation. Better, he said, to join an association representing the entire anthracite labor force. Only such a union, with a strong national base, could deal successfully with the mining companies at the bargaining table, not on the picket line. Fahy made it clear that he opposed strikes, except as a last resort.

He did not convince everyone in the aroused audience, but the strikers did vote to affiliate with the UMW. Fahy immediately began organizing local chapters. He decided to place each ethnic group in a separate chapter because of the somewhat different interests of each nationality and because of the prevailing settlement patterns in the mining patches. At the end of Thursday, August 19, Fahy had in one day formed six chapters representing six different ethnic groups, with a total of more than 800 members. It was a major breakthrough for the UMW in the region.[19]

With the Honey Brook strike settled and the mine workers busy organizing their new union, calm temporarily returned to the Hazleton area. But on Saturday, August 21, the first pay envelopes with the deductions for the immigrant tax were distributed. Anger and resentment festered until August 26, when slate pickers at Coleraine walked off their jobs. Within the next few days the ranks of the strikers swelled to more than 2,000 as the mine workers marched from colliery to colliery, shutting them down. When, after ten days, the Lehigh and Wilkes-Barre Company took no action regarding Jones, its workers joined the walkout.

Once again, the immigrants took the lead. One astounded Irishman remarked, "Holy Mother, is it miself that's quittin fer the shallow faced spalpeens?" The *Wilkes-Barre Times* reported that the Hungarians and Italians were "masters of the situation."[20] The grievances, however, concerned all daily wage workers. In addition to the protest over the immigrant tax, the workers announced several demands: a 15 percent wage increase; an end to the company stores; and the right to pick and pay their own physicians. The immigrants also inserted their own special demand: the same pay scales as the "Americans."

By the end of August the coal operators had come to realize the seriousness of the situation. Negotiations had gone on with the strikers but had produced no results. Furthermore, the presence of the Coal and Iron Police had not intimidated the workers. But the operators were in no mood for major concessions, certainly not with the depressed coal market and the presence of so much surplus labor.

What the major Hazleton independents such as the Coxes, Markles, Pardees, and Van Wickles feared most of all was the possible sabotage and destruction of valuable mining properties. They were also concerned about the growing willingness of the English-speaking miners to align with the immigrants. They had used the Slavs and Italians against the English-speaking miners in the past; the growing solidarity of the various ethnic groups was an ominous development in terms of the operators' future relations with labor. So the operators met secretly in Hazleton on August 31 to decide on a course of action. Reporters discovered on the same day that 500 Winchesters had arrived in the Coxe Company offices and that 300 more were on their way to A. Pardee and Company.[21]

The operators had plenty of force upon which they could call if necessary. The structure of state government in Pennsylvania gave the counties primary responsibility for the maintenance of law and order, and the chief law officer in each county was the sheriff. In Luzerne County the sheriff was the amiable James L. Martin, a man who had worked in the mines long enough to know above all else that he did not want to return to them. Martin also knew whom he had to please if he wanted to remain sheriff. He agreed to put 1,000 men, if necessary, at the disposal of the operators. And they were reliable men because they, like Sheriff Martin, owed their livelihood to the coal barons.[22]

A handful of powerful families dominated the Lehigh field. Clans such as the Markles, Coxes, Pardees, Van Wickles, and Fells owned not only mining companies but also railroads, land trusts, banks, lumber companies, powder and flour mills, ironworks, and retail establishments. They interlocked their holdings through memberships on boards of directors and convenient marriages, and they invested in each other's ventures. They built stately mansions and churches on Hazleton's highest hill, with a fine view of their surrounding collieries and mine patches. Politicians and local businessmen were in their debt; the clergy and teachers upheld their values. Thousands depended upon the soundness of their decisions for their livelihoods. They were lords of a small fiefdom they had made through their own enterprise.

The first among equals of the Hazleton coal barons was Ariovistus Pardee. He set a standard of success others would seek to match. The son of a farmer in New York state, he left home in 1830 at the age of twenty to work for a family friend who was a surveyor for canals and railroads. Three years later he had attained enough knowledge of the trade to direct an entire survey project for a railroad connecting the mines with the Lehigh Canal at Mauch Chunk. On finishing the job he set out for Hazleton, where he worked for a time as a supervisor for the Hazleton Railroad and Coal Company. In 1840 he opened his own business as an independent coal operator. Rumor has it that he began buying coal lands quietly after observing a deer uncover the black rock while pawing the earth on a hillside. Whatever the truth of the story, Pardee eventually established, in association with J. Gillingham Fell, the A. Pardee and Company, which became the single largest anthracite shipper in Pennsylvania. By 1863 Pardee was one of the richest men in America, with a personal annual income of more than $1 million; at the time of his death in 1892 his far-flung empire in coal, iron, lumber, and other enterprises extended into eight states and Canada.[23]

Like other pioneers of American industrialization, Pardee, "the silent man," as many called him, possessed both vision and organizational genius. He was a strong supporter of technical innovations, especially those which enhanced hard coal's value as a fuel. His major contribution to the infant coal industry, however, was in transportation. He pioneered in the development of short-haul feeder railroads that delivered coal from the mines to inland canal ports for trans-shipment to major markets. At a time when the railroad was revolutionizing transportation in America, he understood its crucial role, not only for anthracite, but in linking together distant and distinct but related industries such as coal, iron, and timber.

Pardee's achievements did not come easily. He lost several fortunes and at times the fate of his entire empire was uncertain. But what carried him through were the qualities noted in his obituary in the *Hazleton Plain Speaker*: "He was a master mind that could grasp easily every detail of even the greatest plans. His force of character was such that energetic action followed upon his planning as day follows night. And he worked as giants worked. Back of all was an iron will that brooked no contradiction. The secret of his success was the concentration of purpose, he swerved not a hair's breadth from the direct line of his business interests."[24]

Like many of the entrepreneurs of his era Pardee was a complex man who held his own counsel, took no one into his confidence, and practiced a strong self-reliance. Various accounts describe him as cool, strong, brooding, and introspective. He was a dreamer who realized his dreams.

Closely associated with the Pardees were the Markles. The founder of this family dynasty was George Markle, a man of humble means who had risen to become general superintendent of the Pardee collieries before being backed by Ario Pardee, J. G. Fell, and other individuals in opening his own operations at Jeddo and Highland near Hazleton. Like the Pardees, and often in association with them, he extended his business interests into banking, railroads, land, and iron.

George Markle was a mechanical genius. He invented the famous Markle pump for use in the mines, and it, together with his many other inventions, added to his substantial wealth. His most important technical contribution to the industry was the design of an efficient coal breaker, which greatly speeded the processing of coal for shipment.

George Markle's son, John, took over full control of the family business following his father's death in 1888. John had been sent by his father to study mining engineering at Lafayette College, an institution which enjoyed the generous financial support of several generations of Pardees, Markles, and other coal barons. During summer vacations John worked on the railroads and at nearly every occupation in the mines. Upon graduation in 1880 he became general superintendent of G. B. Markle and Company. After his father's death he consolidated and expanded the company's holdings by buying out the Asa Packer estate interests and purchasing additional mining lands. These included the flooded Harleigh and Ebervale mines, a venture which involved considerable risk. Despite the skepticism of many in the industry, John Markle set out to drain the valuable abandoned mines. He invested a million dollars in a three-year project which he personally supervised. He had his men drill two underground drainage tunnels toward each other over a considerable distance. When the teams of workers finally met, the floors of their respective tunnels varied less than an inch. This remarkable engineering feat did more than establish his reputation; it kept his mines free of water during subsequent strikes, when pump men walked off the job.[25]

The Pardees, Markles, and Van Wickles were secure in the world they had made and were convinced of the superiority of their ways. This caused them to develop a certain attitude, in practice more autocratic than paternalistic, toward people under their influence or control. As John Markle put it, they believed that their power and wealth made them "trustees" for their fellow men, with responsibility "for the proper use of them."[26]

As undisputed leaders of the independent coal operators, the Pardees and Markles set the pattern for labor relations; they naturally preferred to deal with their employees directly rather than through autonomous unions, and they forcefully resisted all attempts by the mine workers to organize. George Markle had hired Pinkertons to use against the Mollies; and Calvin Pardee, Ario's son and successor, had brought immigrants into the anthracite fields to divide and weaken the labor force further. When, in August 1897, their workers, led by these immigrants, turned against them, the coal barons were gravely challenged. They failed to understand— or refused to understand—the determination of the individuals over whom they exercised their proclaimed trusteeship.

By early September, it became clear to the coal operators that the strike would have to be crushed by force. The Van Wickle Company miners from Coleraine, reinforced by men from the Lehigh and Wilkes-Barre collieries, had closed down the local Lehigh Coal and Navigation Company operations and five other collieries, swelling the number of strikers to 5,000. On September 1 the managements of the

Breaker at Beaver Meadow burned by strikers, 1897.
Courtesy of the Burg Collection, MG-273, Pennsylvania State Archives.

Lehigh and Wilkes-Barre and the Van Wickle companies increased wages and made other concessions intended to appease the immigrants. The Lehigh and Wilkes-Barre increases, however, did not match those of the Van Wickle Company, so the strikers voted to stay out. On September 3 they organized a march of more than 1,000 men from McAdoo to Hazleton for the purpose of closing down mines that were still working.

The march began almost spontaneously after the Lehigh and Wilkes-Barre officials delayed in responding to another appeal by the company's workers. The strike committee urged the men to wait for a message from the company, but most of the miners were in a mood for action. A burly Italian started things going when he cried out, "Whata da good of eighta da men to do'a the job? Too'a man'a!" He then drew a huge carving knife and, waving it wildly, shouted, "Vendetta! . . . We getta do move on, and closa up the district." Over a thousand men, brandishing pokers, fence pickets, and clubs then formed a column behind a sole marcher with an American flag and set off through the streets of McAdoo to the cheers of their women and children. Squads were dispatched to round up the reluctant: one nervous Hungarian who took refuge in his cellar was assisted into the column of marchers by several well-placed blows; his distraught wife fainted and had to be assisted by neighbors. Similar scenes were repeated along the line of march. In Jeansville the strikers descended upon a working breaker. Warned by the whistle of the approaching danger, some of its work crew rushed to join the demonstrators while others took off at full speed over the nearby culm banks. The Italians then fastened a plank to the whistle, leaving it blowing to announce their victory. As the column approached the outskirts of Hazleton it hesitated. Rumors flew through the ranks that the U.S. Army and the entire state militia were defending the city. Then a messenger arrived to warn that the city's police were awaiting the marchers. The Italian leader thought for a moment, then taking his naturalization papers from his pocket and waving them aloft, shouted: "I gotta the right! I am an American citizen. I have my papers. They cannot stoppa us. Forward!"

A roar of "On to Hazleton!" went up as the marchers set off again. Down the last hill they came toward the city, 3,000 of them, prepared to confront the force of three policemen led by a bewhiskered captain. As the column approached, the police captain, his star glistening on his breast in the bright sun, stepped forward: "Why come ye here? Disperse ye agitators of the peace!" he announced stiffly. "Getta outa de way. We noa stop," came the response. But the captain held firm: "Disperse or I'll run ye in!" The marchers' leader, waving his papers under the captain's nose, laughed scornfully, "Ha, ha. I am an American citizen. I a defia you. We a goa through your a city." The captain then suggested a compromise: his men would accompany the marchers so that they would not become lost in the confusing streets of the city. The offer was accepted and the strikers moved forward again. After they passed through the city, the column halted before the Hazle breaker and prepared for an assault. The forewarned employees abandoned the works in a few seconds. Similar victories followed at Cranberry and Hazle Brook. Even the local press was impressed. "'Twas a grand stroke to march 11 miles and close up four breakers," the *Wilkes-Barre Times* declared. "Napoleon's greatest achievements were overshadowed. And as the setting sun cast its last ray over the distant mountain the grand army of striking Huns, Italians and Slavs marched to their homes to enjoy the calm and quiet peace after a day of war."[27]

The coal operators were not amused; they believed they had a war on their hands. As marches and demonstrations continued over the long Labor Day weekend, company superintendents met on September 6 to plan a quick course of action. They decided to make no further concessions to the strikers. While Superintendent Lawall of the Lehigh and Wilkes-Barre Company made a public display of seeking negotiations by exchanging telegrams with the strike committee, he and the other company officials secretly authorized Sheriff Martin of Wilkes-Barre to go to Hazleton and organize a posse. The message Martin received was clear: the owners wanted the strike broken and they did not care how it was done.

Martin knew he was on touchy legal ground. To form a posse he had to declare a state of disorder, which constituted a riot or threat to life or property. Since the strike was centered in McAdoo, just across the county line and outside his jurisdiction, he had to persuade the Schuylkill County sheriff to make a similar declaration. Yet the operators had called upon him to break the strike because most holdings were in Luzerne County, and he was responsible to them because they had put him in office and kept him there.

Sheriff Martin met with the sheriffs of Schuylkill County and neighboring Carbon County and persuaded them to follow his lead in declaring public order disturbed. He then set about organizing a posse, not a difficult task, for advance word had already reached influential men in Hazleton. By the evening of September 6 Sheriff Martin had eighty-seven volunteers, mostly professional men with English, Irish, and German names—sound, churchgoing citizens whose careers were intimately bound up with the fortunes of the coal operators. Among them were Calvin Pardee, Jr., and Ario Pardee Platt, whose family-owned mines at Lattimer, just north of Hazleton, remained open. Sheriff Martin swore in his deputies and distributed new rifles and three-inch, metal-piercing bullets as well as buckshot loads.

At the same time the sheriffs of Schuylkill and Carbon counties were organizing their posses. Soon the operators had several hundred deputies, 300 Pinkerton detectives, and a large number of armed company guards at their disposal.[28]

On the Tuesday and Wednesday after Labor Day the strikers, undaunted by the size of the forces arrayed against them, resumed their marches on working collieries. This time, however, the sheriff's men managed to disperse several demonstrations. It was a herculean task to deal with 10,000 strikers spread over a wide area. Sheriff Martin's deputies were especially hard-pressed. They were mostly men in their forties and fifties with comfortable office jobs, not used to strenuous physical effort. As the day wore on their resentment toward the strikers reached a fever pitch. The *Pottsville Republican* reported that they used "tantalizing, dictatorial, domineering, unnecessary, brutal language" in describing the demonstrators.[29]

On the evening of Thursday, September 9, while members of the new UMW local at the Pardee operations at Harwood were meeting, a group from Lattimer arrived to request their assistance. The Lattimer miners said that they wanted to join the strike and asked that a group from Harwood march over the following day in support. Since the Lattimer mines were also Pardee-owned, closing them would shut down all the company's operations. The Harwood strikers knew that they could wring no concessions from Pardee unless they all stood as one. Going to the aid of their Lattimer brothers would also be a demonstration of solidarity on the part of the UMW local.

On the morning of Friday, September 10, some 300 men assembled at Harwood for the march to Lattimer. None of them had yet confronted any deputies, but they were aware of Sheriff Martin's proclamation and had listened carefully to the advice of UMW organizer John Fahy, given the evening before, to be extremely cautious. The leaders were determined to remain nonviolent; they went up and down the line of march, forcing the men to throw away even their walking sticks. When all was ready, the marchers set off four abreast with two American flags at their lead. Their six-mile route would take them through Hazleton and on to Lattimer, just northeast of the city. Along the way they hoped to pick up additional supporters from collieries they passed.

News of the march reached Sheriff Martin, who immediately mobilized his deputies. This time he was determined to stop the strikers. As his men rushed to head off the column before it reached Hazleton, they broke through the ranks of marchers, pushing and striking several of them. Then Sheriff Martin, his pistol pointing at the head of a striker, ordered the marchers to disperse. The defiant miners refused. Suddenly, when a worker bent toward a rock to strike a match for his pipe, an edgy deputy struck him with a rifle butt. A fight broke out and Ario Par-

Strikers on their way to Lattimer mines, near Hazleton on September 10, 1897, the day of the massacre. Courtesy of the Burg Collection, MG-273, Pennsylvania State Archives.

dee Platt rushed forward and tore one of the American flags from the hands of its bearer and ripped it to pieces. Further violence was averted only when the Hazleton police chief intervened. He insisted to Sheriff Martin that the strikers had the right to march peacefully and that they could continue if they agreed to march around the city rather than through it. The leaders agreed and the column started off again. Furious, Sheriff Martin and his men boarded trolleys for Lattimer. One of the deputies was overheard saying, "I bet I drop six of them when I get over there."[30]

The first bloody encounter with the strikers had aroused the deputies. They expected a showdown. Passengers on the trolleys to Lattimer later reported that all the talk was of shooting. A reporter for the *Wilkes-Barre Times* sent a dispatch to his paper stating that serious trouble was anticipated. In Lattimer women hurried their children from the village school and locked themselves in their houses. Colliery

Children of Italian miners on "Dago" street in Lattimer.
Courtesy of the Burg Collection, Pennsylvania State Archives.

whistles announced a shutdown. Company police and other deputies arriving from
nearby Drifton prepared for action. By the time Sheriff Martin arrived he had almost 150 armed men at his disposal.

A more inauspicious place for a major confrontation between capital and labor
could hardly be imagined. In 1897 the mine patch, tucked into a hillside, consisted of
two dusty streets which led beyond to two breakers and other smaller patches. The
village had been laid out by the Pardee company in 1869; its first residents were
mostly Welsh, and they or their descendants as well as some Germans and Irish occupied the larger, better-kept houses on the upper street, called Quality Row. They
were the skilled miners or mine bosses. On Main Street, the lower road, lived the
latest arrivals, mostly Italians, in a jumble of shanties of odd shapes and sizes put
together from scrap lumber and tar paper and surrounded by vegetable gardens. At
the end of Main Street was the company store and various colliery buildings and
workshops. Lattimer resembled scores of other company towns, both in physical
layout and social composition.

The road from Hazleton curved over a rise and forked to form the two streets
just at the approach to the village. There stood a large, stately tree (still standing
today, it is known as the "massacre tree"); and there in its shade Sheriff Martin
waited after positioning his men in an enfilading position along the road so that
they could cover the entire line of marchers. On the other side of the road from the

deputies was a raised trolley track embankment. The marchers would be trapped between the embankment and the deputies, some of whom, nearer the village, would be no more than fifteen yards away. The sheriff informed his lieutenants that he would first find out what the marchers intended to do; he suggested that he might even allow them to pass.[31]

The strikers soon came into view, marching in orderly fashion behind the flag bearer, secure in their knowledge that they were acting as peaceful citizens within the law. After they had come two-thirds of the way past the deputies, Sheriff Martin stepped forward, pistol drawn, to deal with the situation alone. He held up his hand and said firmly, "You must stop marching and disperse. This is contrary to the law and you are creating a disturbance. You must go back. I won't let you go to the colliery." The front ranks of the marchers stopped, but those farther back, unable to either hear or see the sheriff, pressed forward. Someone yelled, "Go ahead!" Martin reached for the flag, but the bearer pulled it away. Furious, the sheriff, unable to identify the leaders, grabbed a man in the second row and pulled him aside. Several marchers came to his aid and a scuffle broke out alongside of the road. The sheriff, panicking as the column continued past him, aimed his pistol at one of the men sur-

The site of the shooting, Lattimer Mines. The "massacre tree" is on the left.
Courtesy of the Burg Collection, MG-273, Pennsylvania State Archives.

rounding him and pulled the trigger, but the weapon did not fire. Then someone—
two of the marchers claimed it was Martin—shouted "Fire!" and "Give two or three
shots!" At that moment, a full volley rang out. Steve Jurich, the Slovak flag bearer,
was the first man hit, a bullet shattering his skull. As he went down he yelled, "O
Joj! Joj! Joj"—the Slovak appeal to God. Some of the marchers were cut down in
their tracks; others were shot in the back as they fled. Several of the deputies broke
ranks and followed the fleeing men, taking beads on them from as far away as 300
yards. A number of the sixteen-cartridge Winchester magazines were completely
emptied. A witness claimed that at least 150 shots were fired. Deputies were heard
shouting, "Shoot the sons of bitches!"

There are no exact casualty figures, but at least nineteen men were killed and
thirty-two wounded—twenty-six Poles, twenty Slovaks, and five Lithuanians. It
was a terrible scene of carnage. The steel bullets literally tore the bodies to pieces
and even those who had taken limb shots were horribly wounded. One nineteen-
year-old boy, his knees shattered, lay in the road in agony, begging for help. The
townspeople and even some of the deputies rushed to the aid of the wounded and
dying as soon as the shooting stopped, but a few of the deputies walked among the
fallen men, kicking them savagely. One deputy answered a wounded man's plea for
water with: "We'll give you hell, not water, hunkies!" As the deputies boarded their
trolleys they were heard laughing and joking about how many men they had hit.
The first words Sheriff Martin uttered after the shooting were, "I am not well."

The news of the massacre spread quickly throughout the Hazleton area. Wagons were soon on the road to Lattimer, and trolleys were sent to bring in the wounded.
Families of the miners began to rush into the city from the outlying towns, many
already praying aloud and wailing in the tradition of Slavic peasants. The hospital
was soon filled with the wounded and milling crowds; physicians, their aprons covered with gore, worked steadily through the evening and long night. Journalists reported that the floors of the surgery rooms were "running" with blood. The bodies of
the dead were laid side by side in the cellars of undertakers, fluids still seeping from
the gaping wounds. Panic spread among the "Anglo Saxons," who feared retaliation
by the immigrants, especially after word came that the home of Gomer Jones in Audenried had been ransacked by an angry mob. Many of the deputies, sobered and
made fearful by what they had done, fled the city. Ario Pardee, Jr., and several
others went into hiding under assumed names at the Traymore Hotel in Atlantic
City. The shaken Sheriff Martin quickly left for Wilkes-Barre, where he was seques-
tered in a hotel by his attorney. City leaders gathered in an emergency meeting and
sent an urgent request to the governor for protection. By Saturday, September 11,
the mobilized Third Brigade of the state militia had arrived from Wilkes-Barre, to
the great relief of the English-speaking people in the area.

Yet except for the attack on Jones's house, the immigrants carried out no major reprisals. Instead they poured out their grief and sorrow in massive funeral demonstrations. On Sunday, members of the St. Joseph's National Slovak Society, the Italian St. Peter and Paul's Society, and the Polish Socrasa Fondata, dressed in colorful uniforms, and some men bearing drawn sabers, marched behind a brass band as they led more than 3,000 mourners through the mine towns to St. Joseph's Slovak Church in Hazleton. There they heard a fiery sermon by Father Richard Aust of the city's Polish St. Stanislaus Church, a priest who had worked feverishly consoling the wounded and dying and the grieving families in the hours after the shooting. From the pulpit in the tiny, stifling church Father Aust exhorted his listeners to trust in God's wisdom and in His ultimate justice. Some of those present thought that they heard the priest say that God would punish the deputies. From this statement came the legend that the individuals responsible were under a terrible curse and that they all died horrible and painful deaths. On Monday another great funeral procession formed, this time numbering 8,000, the largest ever seen in the region. The mourners marched to St. Stanislaus Church, where Father Aust, assisted by five priests, celebrated a solemn high requiem mass. On the following days two members of the United Mine Workers were buried, accompanied to their graves by long lines of silent union members wearing across their chests the impressive, multicolored sashes of their fraternal organizations.

Lattimer brought together the immigrant communities in the anthracite region as never before. As shock turned to outrage over the indiscriminate killings, the immigrants expressed their indignation in meetings and demonstrations in all the major towns and cities. Their newspapers condemned what they regarded as murder and demanded justice. *Straz*, the newspaper of the Polish National Catholic Church, called for the formation of a new working man's party. On the national level, the Lithuanian Alliance, the Polish National Alliance, and other Slavic organizations expressed outrage and sympathy, and contributed, along with members of other ethnic communities throughout the country, thousands of dollars for the relief of the victims' families. The event became an international incident when the ambassador from Austria-Hungary demanded, but without success, compensation from the U.S. government. He did, however, aid Father Aust in forming a committee that brought formal charges of murder against Sheriff Martin and his deputies.[32]

In the days following the massacre and funerals the strike continued to spread. On the twelfth, 1,500 workers at Lattimer walked out and joined the UMW en masse. They formed a committee consisting of a Pole, a Slovak, and an Italian to present their demands to Pardee. By the fourteenth, 11,000 men were off the job and fifteen mines belonging to all the major operators had closed down. In the face of the massive shutdown all of the owners except the Coxe Brothers made wage adjustments and granted concessions. With the militia now guarding the collieries and their religious leaders urging moderation and restraint in order to avoid another disaster, the immigrants began to return to work on the sixteenth.

The back-to-work movement, however, encountered an unexpected difficulty. A group of angry Slavic women, described in the press as the "amazons," resisted the efforts of their men to return to work. The leader was "Big Mary" Septak, an outspoken, powerfully built woman who ran a boardinghouse for Eastern Europeans in Lattimer. Like many Slavic women, Big Mary ran her household with a dictatorial hand, ordering around her husband and boarders alike as if they were children. Though she loved her husband of thirty years dearly ("When I away from my man I cry all the time, and when he 'way from me he cry all the time"),[33] she scorned the docility and deference in the face of authority she had seen in so many Slavic men. When the strike broke out she became excited. At last the men were going to fight for their rights. Then, after Lattimer, no longer able to rein in her anger, she organized her "band" of like-minded women. When the miners began to return to work, she turned on them. Big Mary and her contingent of 150 women, armed with rolling

Pennsylvania National Guard Camp, Hazleton, after the Lattimer Massacre.
Courtesy of the Burg Collection, MG-273, Pennsylvania State Archives.

General John Gobin and staff of the Pennsylvania National Guard, Third Brigade, in Hazleton, 1897.   Courtesy of the Burg Collection, MG-273, Pennsylvania State Archives.

pins, pokers, and clubs, with children in tow and babies on hips, set off to intimidate workers in the collieries. At Lattimer they swept over the workings before being driven off by a squad of militia cavalry. The following day they marched ten miles south to McAdoo, disrupted work at a washery, and inflicted some injuries on the workers. Sheriff Scott of Schuylkill County rushed to the scene from Pottsville, but by the time he arrived pandemonium had broken out. On September 16 the amazons raided at least five more collieries and the strike threatened to erupt all over again. When the English-speaking miners joined the immigrants, Sheriff Scott called upon the militia.

When the women struck again at McAdoo on the seventeenth, they encountered the mounted troopers. But Big Mary sent part of her band up a culm bank to shout insults and throw coal at the cavalrymen; her second contingent remained hidden. After the troopers left, they all went on to close down collieries at Bunker Hill and Honey Brook. The militia officers did not know what to do; they complained that the women were harder to handle than the men. "I thought we had come to Hazleton to fight men,"[34] General Gobin, their commander, declared at one point. Finally, on

September 18 at Lattimer, a skirmish line of militia with fixed bayonets was sent against the women as they attempted to prevent several hundred men from returning to work. Big Mary, armed with a wooden sword and cheered on by miners on nearby culm banks, led a charge right up to the line of bayonets. But such bravery was not enough. The strike initiative had passed, and by the twenty-eighth the mines were working again.[35]

The massacre at Lattimer was the worst disaster yet to befall American labor, and the injury to labor was compounded during the subsequent trial of Sheriff Martin and his men. The district attorney's office was persuaded to present an indictment that singled out only one victim while at the same time naming all eight-seven deputies as a collective defendant, thus constraining the prosecution and freeing the defense. The district attorney was badly prepared; translations of witnesses' testimony were muddled and delayed; the jury was antagonistic; Sheriff Martin obviously perjured himself. In his final summation for the defense, former attorney general Henry W. Palmer, scion of an old aristocractic family from the region, delivered a scorching attack on "the barbarian horde" of anarchistic foreigners who were threatening the fragile foundations of the republic. John Fahy, he stormed, is "like all the other foul birds of prey called labor agitators, low brow beating villains who are crawling over the country." Palmer then demonstrated that it was impossible to determine exactly who had killed Mike Cheslak, the single victim named in the indictment. He played upon all the fears and prejudices of the jurors by explaining that the deputies, through their courageous action in the face of such menace, had prevented a bloody civil war from breaking out in the region. In the words of the *Wilkes-Barre Times*, "The peroration was a brilliant effort on the rights of American citizenship, and the danger threatened by the lawless Slav."[36]

The jury returned a verdict of not guilty. When the former deputies returned from Wilkes-Barre to Hazleton following the trial, they went directly to the Old Hazle Brewery on the city's south side to celebrate. Word got out, and from that moment on Hazle Beer became known as "Deputies Beer." The brewery went bankrupt within six months.

The massacre at Lattimer, however, did not go unanswered. Shocked by the shooting, miners throughout the anthracite fields expressed their solidarity with the martyrs by joining the United Mine Workers. It would take several more major strikes and further organizing efforts before the UMW became the single powerful representative of 150,000 anthracite workers, but the bloodshed at Lattimer ensured the union a solid future in the region. And the heroic efforts of the despised Slav and Italian immigrants made it possible.

The strike of 1897 established the "new immigrants" as a force among the anthracite workers.[37] Lattimer shattered popular notions about their docility, their lack of unity, militancy, and discipline. Ironically, the quality for which the immigrants had been most criticized by leaders of organized labor gave them cohesiveness and strength. Some people called it clannishness; they called it, in their native languages, community, solidarity. Their collective action grew from this source. They would be heard from again.

8. The Great Strike

I N THE FALL OF 1899 JOHN MITCHELL, THE NEW TWENTY-NINE-YEAR-OLD PRESIDENT of the United Mine Workers, entered the anthracite country with a group of union organizers. He and his men went there, according to Mitchell, "in order to arouse from their lethargy the thoroughly subdued workers . . . , to revive their hopes and rekindle in their hearts the spirit of resistance which we feared would be put to the severest test before the close of the year 1900."[1] Mitchell's union was preparing for a full-scale labor war, a titanic struggle that would set the country's largest labor union against the mightiest financial combination of American capitalism. Such a fight only an aroused and united labor union could win. The issue was the right of the anthracite miners to organize. And the economic powers that controlled the region were firmly determined, at almost any cost, to prevent their workers from forming a union.

Mitchell had no illusions of quick victory. Even some of his field organizers told him that he was confronting overwhelming odds. At Lattimer the coal owners had shown their resolve. That unarmed and peacefully marching men could be shot down in the streets and their murderers escape punishment convinced many individuals that further struggle was futile. The English-speaking miners were especially discouraged. For them the Lattimer Massacre was the fateful culmination of a punishing series of defeats stretching back over decades. One union drive after another had failed. Labor's efforts had changed nothing. Wages had not improved in twenty years. Annual earnings for miners ranged from $210 to $616, with a mean of about $375—not enough to support a family. As a result women and children were forced to seek work of some kind just so that their families could subsist. Work for miners was still sporadic and scarce. Erratic market conditions and overproduction had cut working days to 190 yearly.[2]

Nor had labor's efforts in any way changed the prevailing system of company servitude. Tens of thousands of people in the anthracite area still lived in company-owned housing with day-to-day leases, constantly in debt to "pluck me" stores and forced to pay for medical services they rarely received. Even outside the company towns the influence of the operators was immense. They were the biggest employers in the region—in many towns, the only employers. They often provided community services such as water or contributed heavily to churches and local charities. They influenced the selection of candidates for public office; retained the best lawyers; and became, in fact, the real government in the region. Through their private Coal and Iron Police they enforced law and order—their law and their order. Little of economic, political, or social significance occurred without their notice or approval.

But it was the workers whom they controlled most directly. More than one writer who toured the area in these years compared the lot of anthracite miners with that of medieval serfs. "In the anthracite region," Elsie Gluck reported, "dockage charges are more unjust, the cost of supplies more exorbitant, hours longer, work more uncertain, favoritism more unjust, child labor more cruelly widespread, and the death and accident toll much higher than in the worst period of soft coal industry." Gluck added that such conditions made the men not more militant, just more "hopelessly despairing."[3]

The mood of the men was just one of the several problems John Mitchell's union faced. It was preparing to confront the most powerful industrial combination in the country. Since the 1870s the railroad companies that shipped anthracite had begun to buy coal lands and to organize coal companies. Though early efforts by the railroads to regulate the coal trade were unsuccessful, they did establish a community of interest among themselves. Gradually most of the smaller independent operators were absorbed or forced out of business. Following the depression of 1893–1897, the J. P. Morgan interests made a final drive to control the industry. The bankrupt Philadelphia and Reading Company, along with its mining operations, was reorganized through the Reading, a holding company. The Reading then purchased the Central Railroad of New Jersey, which also carried coal and owned coal lands. When all of the paper transactions had been completed, the Reading controlled companies that transported one-third of all anthracite mined in Pennsylvania. At the same time another major anthracite shipper, the Erie Railroad, also gained control over several carriers and mining enterprises. Then the five leading carriers jointly acquired the Lehigh Valley Railroad and organized interlocking directorates in order to coordinate their activities. By 1902 more than 96 percent of all anthracite coal lands were controlled by the railroads, with 91 percent of deposits owned outright. The major independents like the Markles and Pardees were locked into the combination by the so-called 65 percent, seven-year contract, by which the transportation companies agreed to purchase all production and to pay the independents 65 percent of the sale price of coal at tidewater over a seven-year period. As a result of the combination, the railroad companies were able to fix the price of coal, determine production levels, and establish tonnage quotas. The entire anthracite region became, in effect, an economic colony of the powerful financial interests located in New York and Philadelphia. Both coal and profits flowed out of the region to immensely wealthy absentee owners.[4]

While this consolidation drive was going forward, the big companies made a final effort to bring the anthracite workers totally under their control. The arrival of large numbers of Eastern and Southern European peasants in the region gave them their opportunity. These simple people were willing to do hard work for almost any wage; and before Lattimer, at least, the owners, like the unions, thought that new immigrants were docile and clannish and hence unlikely to join other workers in a united union. Their entrance into the anthracite industry would also further divide the workers along ethnic and religious lines. The coal operators made a deliberate effort to encourage ethnic divisions and tensions by reserving the skilled mining positions for the English-speaking men, leaving the jobs that paid less well to the new immigrants. The nature of the coal mining itself, they knew, would further divide the workers. Miners paid their helpers and supervised their work, so grievances by the immigrants were more often than not directed against the skilled miners rather than against the companies. The very structure of the industry pitted worker against worker.

The geological differences between the three anthracite fields also worked to the companies' advantage in controlling labor. Wage rates varied widely, depending upon the configurations of the coal seams. As one contemporary observer noted: "In different regions [anthracite miners] are paid on a different scale; and in the same colliery will be found miners working on contract at so much per car, others by the week; rockmen working by the yard, and prices varying according to the kind of passage driven and whether it is timbered or not; inside laborers getting one price, outside laborers another, while breaker boys received still another rate."[5] All these factors made united action by the miners terribly difficult, some felt impossible.

Despite the overwhelming array of obstacles before them, Mitchell and the UMW leadership began their organizing drive with stubborn confidence. The union had already made significant headway in the soft coal fields. In 1898, following the bituminous workers' strike of the previous year, it had signed an agreement with bituminous operators in Illinois, Indiana, Ohio, and western Pennsylvania that increased wages and reduced working hours. Organizing efforts were under way in West Virginia and Kentucky. If the anthracite fields remained unorganized, their production could conceivably be used to undermine the new unity of the soft coal miners. The union leadership believed that the survival and ultimate success of the UMW depended upon bringing the more than 140,000 hard coal workers into the organization. For that reason it had responded to the resolution of Benjamin James, one of the anthracite locals' few delegates at the UMW convention in 1899, which called for an organizing drive in the region.

The key question was how to organize. UMW pioneers in the fields, such as John Fahy and Miles Dougherty, thought they had an answer. They sensed a change occurring in the mines. The brutal conditions under which all miners worked were breaking down the barriers of ethnic hostility, suspicion, and jealousy and were making the men realize that they had a common cause. Cave-ins and "rotten gas" did not distinguish between Welshmen, Irishmen, and Slavs. Bodies brought to the surface in the iron cages bore names like O'Connor and Butscavage; the women who rushed to the pit heads at the shrill blast of the alarm whistle grieved together despite the different languages they spoke and the different churches they attended. When little Bratt Michalochik was killed near Shenandoah, his fellow breaker boys of all nationalities marched silently together behind the coffin. The English and Irish mothers, who had witnessed the scene many times before, crowded together around the mourning mother to offer comfort. In the common experience of death everything was forgotten except perhaps the unspoken desire for revenge.[6]

In the aftermath of Lattimer, John Fahy had kept the union idea going. Buoyed by his success in organizing locals in the Lehigh field, he turned his attention in early 1898 to Wyoming-Lackawanna. The very size of its work force made this area crucial to organizing the entire region. At first, the better-off English-speaking miners were reluctant to commit themselves yet again, but the immigrants welcomed the union. Fahy capitalized on their enthusiasm by naming Slavs and Italians to top positions in the locals. By the summer of 1898, fifteen new locals had been formed and five others reorganized. Slavic militance showed itself during the five-month strike against the Susquehanna Coal Company near Nanticoke in the second half of that year. Club-wielding strikers, aided by their women, kept the company's collieries closed and the weak-willed in line. The strike ended in victory for the workers.[7] As Peter Roberts, one eyewitness, noted, "The men won their case because of the unyielding stand of the Sclavs [sic]."[8]

Experienced anthracite organizers like Fahy knew that not all immigrants were "hopelessly despairing." They were still abused by the press, harassed by public officials, cheated of wages by their employers, and mocked in the streets for their poor English and their strange ways. But these hard-willed people had held on. And they had begun to probe "the system" in an effort to make it work for them. They met manipulative lawyers on their own ground and acquired citizenship. They learned English and began to get their mining papers. They formed political clubs and bargained their votes for candidates who would support them. In many towns they elected their own people. By 1902 in Shenandoah, which was two-thirds Slavic, five Eastern Europeans were on the city council and a Pole was the burgess. These immigrants, as one writer put it, "quarreled with no institution; they simply observed the institution carefully and then proceeded to absorb it, corruption and all."[9] By the end of the century the foreigners had something to fight for.

In mid-1899 Fahy had returned to the Schuylkill field, the scene of the first UMW organizing in 1894 and 1895. He chose as his assistant one of the first native Polish-Americans, Paul Pulaski of Mount Carmel, whose work proved invaluable. "He speaks," Fahy said, "five different foreign languages . . . , makes a good stagger at two more . . . , and speaks good English. . . . I do not know of a man better fitted for the work." [10] Using men like Pulaski with influence in the immigrant enclaves, Fahy made considerable headway. By mid-1900 he had established fifty-five affiliates and a new union district in the Schuylkill. [11]

The answer to the question of how to organize the hard coal fields, then, was to concentrate on the immigrants. The English-speaking miners would not be ignored, but the head effort would be among those who were immediately willing to fight for improved working conditions. With the ground thus prepared in advance by Fahy and his new allies, Mitchell and his organizers came into the anthracite fields in the final year of the century.

*   *   *

In later years, when he had passed into the realm of legend, John Mitchell would be remembered by old miners with reverence and affection. They would forget the stories of his embittered years after he had left them, the rumors of personal gain at the workers' expense, the charges that he was a "sellout," a "traitor" to the working men. The anthracite workers remembered him only as their beloved "Johnny," "Johnny d'Mitch," "Father." They would repeat what a delegation of Slavic workers had once told him: "Blessed be the day . . . when you came amongst us." [12] For years after he left the region, Mitchell's photograph hung in many miners' homes alongside an icon or a picture of the Sacred Heart. These people would remember him as the only president they really knew or cared about.

Mitchell was born the son of a soft coal miner in Braidwood, Illinois, in 1870. Both of his parents were dead by the time he was six, leaving him only poverty and a heavy old soldier's coat under which he and a half brother snuggled during cold winter nights. [13] He was raised by a stern Presbyterian stepmother who earned the family's living by taking in washing, work with which the boy had to help. The steady round of tasks at home kept him from attending school regularly, and he could not keep up. "The humiliation and shame of lagging behind . . . [the other students] caused me to lose interest in my studies," he said later. [14] His stepmother remarried when John was ten, and soon afterward he left home. He wandered the countryside, working for keep and a dollar a week as a water boy to farmhands. Eventually he returned to Braidwood and, like thousands of other boys in the nation's coalfields, entered the mines. He was twelve years old.

Young John Mitchell was a loner, quiet and withdrawn. He rarely took part in the raucous, brawling activities of the mining town, nor did he drink. Yet—and perhaps his seriousness recommended him—he rose quickly in the mines, from doorboy to miner's helper. Though slight of body, he soon developed the miner's necessary toughness. And no one doubted his courage. After a mine disaster in nearby Brace-

John Mitchell, "boy president" of the United Mine
Workers of America, 1903.
Courtesy of the Library of Congress.

ville in the winter of 1883, he helped in the rescue operations. Another miner remembered seeing a trail of blood on the ice left by Mitchell's cut bare feet.[15]

Like other hopeful mine workers, he joined the local chapter of the Knights of
Labor when he was sixteen. When hopes were dashed in the Knights' collapse, he
headed west to work in the mining camps of Colorado, bumming his way on the rails
as did thousands of other unemployed workers. He stayed for a while in the house of
Dan McLaughlin, an old labor activitist from his hometown, who talked to him
about unions and the need for interstate agreements between management and labor in the bituminous industry. By 1888 Mitchell was back in Spring Valley, Illinois,
where he participated in losing labor struggles at the end of the decade, learning
firsthand the bitter taste of defeat and company blacklisting. But he also met two
men who changed the direction of his life, who converted him to a new cause. Father
Power, a Roman Catholic priest long active in the miners' cause, encouraged him to
read the reform literature of the day and helped to form his social consciousness. He
also taught Mitchell the potential value of the clergy in the workers' struggles, a

lesson that proved to be useful in later days. From William Ryan, one of the UMW's top organizers, Mitchell learned about union work and the need for solidarity and militance.[16]

Encouraged by Power and Ryan, Mitchell began to take an active role in local public and union affairs. He studied law on his own for a time, was elected while in his early twenties to the Spring Valley board of education and, in 1894, under Ryan's guidance, worked in UMW organizing. The union was still weak and it needed men who were willing to work without salary, trudge about the state addressing nightly meetings, and face all the hazards of company opposition and the daily grind of life on the road. Mitchell was a tireless and effective organizer, and he rose quickly to a position of power with the union. By 1896 he was secretary-treasurer of his Illinois subdistrict and a legislative representative of the miners in Springfield, where he gained recognition by helping secure an amendment to an antitrust law that gave miners and operators the right to fix a scale of prices jointly. In 1897, the following year, he was named to the state executive board of the UMW.[17]

In the summer of 1897, 150,000 miners, half of the labor force in the bituminous industry, walked out. Mitchell distinguished himself during that strike, which his union won, gaining the first interstate joint agreement between the operators and UMW. He worked among the recalcitrant southern Illinois miners whose support for the strike was crucial, whipping them into line. For his success he was rewarded with the vice-presidency of the UMW in 1898.[18]

The signing of the interstate agreement, which raised wages and reduced working hours, was only the opening phase of the struggle. Many of the operators in southern Illinois refused to honor the agreement on wages and hoped to undercut the equality of competition that it had established. The result: more local strikes and violence. Mitchell was once again dispatched to the area, where he succeeded in the type of work he did best: calmly arbitrating differences between the workers and operators and enforcing discipline and unity on the miners. In the heated atmosphere of this struggle, his temperament made him the ideal conciliator. UMW president Michael Ratchford spotted in this young organizer qualities that the union would need in the coming era of board-room negotiations and contractual obligations. Mitchell, in the words of one author, "could offer . . . coolness of judgment, rational behavior even in the most-tension-filled situations, and an ability to persuade and strike a compromise."[19] When Ratchford moved on to a political appointment in 1898, he circumvented the UMW's constitution and named Mitchel acting president.

The following year Mitchell, guided by Ryan and supported by Ratchford, won election to the UMW presidency in his own right at a raucous national convention. He overcame more experienced and better-known contenders such as Tom Lewis, leader of the Ohio miners, because of his clean political record and because his rapid

rise in the union was the result of work in the field, where he had not become embroiled in factional battles. His youth and relative inexperience in union politics at
the national level actually worked to his advantage. The union leadership, which
saw him as a compromise candidate, was willing to give him a chance, and his lack
of identification with any one faction made him a man the leaders could trust.[20]

Mitchell knew, of course, that his long-term success depended upon building a
solid base in the fields. He left the details of administration to a competent associate
and traveled widely, meeting with local leaders and the rank and file. He patiently
listened to everyone, took down suggestions and ideas, and conveyed an impression
of self-confidence. He disarmed his union opponents by naming them to important
organizing positions; to the enflamed and emotional he counseled reason, the necessity for compromise, and the sanctity of contracts. He soon won the trust and respect
of the workers. The writer Lincoln Steffens shrewdly observed:

> The hardest fight of a conservative labor leader is always within the union,
> and Mitchell's finest work has been done there. The passions and the igno-
> rance of the men . . . , the vanity and envy of the orators, and the cunning
> politics of his associates in the councils of the organization . . . , these try the
> soul of the leader. But Mitchell keeps still, meets plot with openness, passion
> with reason, eloquence with dry statements of hard facts, and against im-
> pulse he plants a patience which is wonderful to see. "A little at a time," he
> says, "Anything is better than nothing. And the big thing is the main thing—
> honor. That is all a union has."[21]

The miners in the anthracite country took an immediate liking to Mitchell. He
was especially popular among the immigrants, most of all because he listened to
them and seemed directly interested in their welfare. And he was forthright, as honest and trustworthy, they believed, as one of their parish priests. He even looked like
a young priest, with his long, western miner's coat buttoned up to a straight collar.
Steffens reports that in 1901 when news spread throughout the anthracite region
that the president had been shot, crowds of immigrants gathered crying, "Who shot
our President!" But they dispersed when they learned that President Mitchell had
not been shot but only President McKinley.[22]

John Mitchell had a straightforward strategy for organizing the anthracite
workers, summed up in the phrase that he converted into a litany: "The coal you dig
isn't Slavish or Polish or Irish coal, it's coal." Unity was his single theme; the need
for one strong union, reaching across all three fields, embracing every worker regardless of faith, nationality, or skill level. This message he carried everywhere as
he made his way through the region, by train and horse-drawn carriage, identifying
local leaders, appointing them to work with their own language groups, encourag-

ing their efforts. He spoke before small and large crowds, in town halls and open fields, in private homes and at pit heads, even from the pulpits of churches. He overlooked no one. He especially sought out the clergy and the editors of the foreign-language newspapers, for they had great influence in the ethnic enclaves. Working from his one-room headquarters in a shabby hotel in Hazleton, selected so that miners would feel comfortable when they came to visit, Mitchell laid the groundwork for the union. After months of exhausting work, he and his small staff of UMW organizers had enrolled about 9,000 in a total anthracite work force of almost 150,000. Mitchell told the UMW convention in January 1900 that this represented "almost phenomenal" growth. He was not exaggerating.[23]

Most of the UMW's membership was in the Wyoming-Lackawanna field, where by mid-1900 some 65 percent of the workers were enrolled in the union. This was the new UMW District 1, headed by the radical Thomas D. Nicholls, and from him came pressure for a strike during the late winter and spring of that year. Mitchell resisted, however, because organizing was going much slower in the lower fields: 25 percent of the workers were union members in the Schuylkill field, and only 15 percent in the Lehigh.[24] John Fahy, now president of the Schuylkill District 9, also opposed the strike movement owing to the weakness of the union. But when it was learned that bituminous workers had received a 20 percent wage increase, clamor for a convention of the three districts (the Lehigh field comprised District 7) to consider action became irresistible. Mitchell reluctantly agreed to an anthracite convention in Hazleton in mid-August.

The convention delegates sent an invitation to the operators to meet with them in a joint conference to discuss wages and grievances. The delegates noted that living costs had risen 20 to 50 percent over recent years without a corresponding increase in wages. They also compared the condition of anthracite workers with those in bituminous: the soft coal miners had received wage increases of 40 percent and a reduction in the work day to eight hours. The delegates then listed a series of demands, the most important of which were a wage increase of 20 percent, pay on a piecework basis of the 2,240-pound "short" ton rather than the more-than-3,000-pound "long" ton, and relief from the dockage system, whereby miners arbitrarily lost as much as 25 percent of their wages because of impurities.[25] Other demands included reduction in the cost of powder, an end to compulsory buying in company stores, semimonthly pay according to the law, and the elimination of favoritism. When the operators failed to respond to either the invitation to meet or the demands, the delegates petitioned the national executive board of the union for permission to strike.

The executive board, which knew that the union did not have the resources to provide sustained aid in the event of a long strike, instructed Mitchell to seek a compromise agreement with the operators personally. At the same time Senator Marcus A. Hanna of Ohio, chairman of the Republican National Committee, brought pressure to bear on the operators. Hanna, who had long been associated with the UMW's leadership, was concerned about the impact on public opinion of a strike in the midst of the campaign to reelect President McKinley. Terence Powderly, former head of the Knights of Labor and now U.S. commissioner of labor, sought the influence of James Cardinal Gibbons, archbishop of Baltimore, in averting a strike.[26] Thus the anthracite workers suddenly found their plight gaining attention on the national level. The behind-the-scenes maneuvering represented a new stage in their struggle that had important implications for the future and marked a new departure in labor-management relations.

The operators, however, stood firm. They refused to meet with Mitchell and rejected all attempts to effect a compromise. The operators felt secure in their position. They regarded Mitchell as a western upstart who needed to be taught a hard lesson. They had seen big capital crush railroad and steel strikes in the recent past, and they were confident that they could do the same. They even refused to recognize Mitchell as the spokesman for the hard coal workers. For them the union simply did not exist.

On September 17 the UMW issued a strike call. The decision was reached reluctantly because of the weakness of the union and the uncertainty as to how many men would actually walk out. But the union leadership understood that there was no other choice. To wait until a majority of anthracite workers were enrolled in the UMW was impossible. The only other alternative was to withdraw from the fields entirely.

To the surprise of both union officials and operators, the vast majority of the anthracite work force struck. Within a week 125,000 men were idle, and by the end of September all but 8,000 or 9,000 workers were off their jobs. The Wyoming-Lackawanna field was completely shut down; by early October the Reading reported all of its collieries closed.[27] In the forefront of the strike in the Lehigh and Schuylkill fields were the Slavs, whose strong community solidarity, once again, kept them united and organizationally focused. Very few Eastern Europeans dared to risk the wrath of their countrymen by staying on the job.[28]

During the early weeks of the strike the mine workers followed their usual practice of marching from colliery to colliery in order to shut them down. One of the most effective organizers of these "raids" was the colorful Mary Harris "Mother" Jones, widow of a miner and long-time labor militant. A veteran of the Pittsburgh labor riots of 1877, the Chicago Haymarket massacre of 1886, and the American Railway Union strike of 1894 in Birmingham, Mother Jones had "a talent for vigorous and moving speech, characterized by a picturesque vocabulary, a sharp and

Mother Jones during the anthracite strike of 1902.
Courtesy of the Historical Society of Schuylkill County,
Pottsville, Pa.

ready wit, and a strong sense of drama." Dressed like an old matron, with a dark, baggy dress and a flowered hat on her head, and armed with a black umbrella, she marched at the head of her recruits—miners, their wives, and their children. She became so effective that the operators had the police threaten to use force to stop her. Only a direct personal appeal by Mitchell finally persuaded her to stop the marching.[29]

From the outset of the strike the UMW made a strong plea to the strikers to avoid acts of violence, even if they were provoked. Incidents did occur, however. Men who continued working were stoned; a guard at the Coxe Brothers operation was killed by gunfire; and a riot against scabs involving the Slavs in Shenandoah re- sulted in one death and the calling out of the state militia. But compared with previous strikes, this one was singularly peaceful. Despite the intimidating presence of Coal and Iron Police and troops, the region remained relatively calm during the six-week strike. Newspaper accounts emphasized the grievances of the strikers rather than the random acts of violence, described the horrible conditions in the fields, and commented favorably upon the union's willingness to have differences arbitrated. Public opinion soon began to swing decisively behind the workers.[30]

The union skillfully played upon public sentiment during the strike. This was an era of widespread and mounting opposition to economic monopolies. The Democratic candidacy of the populist William Jennings Bryan in 1900 was symptomatic of this anti-big business feeling. Early in the strike the UMW issued a public letter pointing out that the real opponents of the miners were the coal-carrying railroads. The railroads, the union admitted, made small profits in actual coal mining, but they charged exorbitant freight rates for moving anthracite to market, rates as much as 300 percent higher than those prevailing in the bituminous industry. Even while attacking the operators, the union maintained a conciliatory stance by holding open the offer of arbitration. It also declared its willingness to hold a joint conference with the operators for negotiation of differences, similar to the arrangement existing in the soft coal fields. Finally, in the face of the operators' resistance to recognition of the miners' organization, the UMW requested that the individual companies meet with representatives of their employees but with the condition that the talks be held simultaneously so that the companies could not claim that competition prevented them from increasing wages.[31]

While establishing an image of moderation and agreeableness, the UMW moved to enforce an iron unity on the workers. The biggest obstacle to unity was the actions of the independent operators in the Lehigh field, notably the Markle family. Following the strike of 1888, the Markles had reached an agreement with their employees that all grievances would be arbitrated and that as a condition of employment the employees would not strike or join any outside labor organization for the purpose of settling differences. Mitchell personally met this challenge by meeting with the Markle workers and telling them that permanent improvement in wages and working conditions was dependent upon collective action, not local and individual efforts, and that arbitration would not work unless it included the railroad companies. In a public debate with the Reverend Edward Phillips of Hazleton, a respected and influential Catholic priest, Mitchell not only won over the workers to the strike cause but also persuaded the priest of the validity of his argument. Soon afterward the Markle employees walked out.[32]

The union also showed considerable political astuteness during the strike. Mitchell knew that big business feared that a long strike might trigger a depression which would make a mockery of McKinley's campaign promise of "A Full Dinner

Pail." An economic downslide might even throw the election to William Jennings Bryan. Opponents of the union charged that the strike was politically motivated from the outset, a charge that Mitchell had to refute constantly. Mitchell nevertheless knew that the McKinley administration would be forced to intervene or face possible defeat at the polls. And on one occasion he did admit that the timing of the strike was not entirely accidental. "We cared nothing for one party or the other but we did take advantage of their trouble to try to secure something for our people."[33]

Mitchell's calculation turned out to be correct. By early October Mark Hanna was putting intense pressure on the operators to work out a compromise by threatening them with the specter of a Bryan victory and the spread of the strike to the bituminous fields. The companies still refused to negotiate with the union, though many of them, including the Reading, did post notices of a 10 percent wage hike. The workers responded by staying off the job. They insisted that the wage increase had to continue into the following year, that the sliding wage scale prevalent in the Lehigh and Schuylkill fields had to be discontinued, and that the operators had to meet with committees of their employees to discuss grievances. After Hanna went over the heads of the railroad presidents to J. P. Morgan, the coal companies in mid-October began posting notices agreeing with the demands. The union ordered the men back to work on October 29.

The strike of 1900 did not gain the UMW the official recognition it sought as representative of the anthracite workers. Nor did it force the operators into direct negotiations. Yet the union had won de facto recognition. Though the miners' gains were limited, the union had won the most successful strike in the history of the industry. It made the anthracite workers a powerful, united force that could no longer be ignored or easily crushed by the giant companies. Through the recruitment of 125,000 members, the anthracite workers now had an equal weight with the bituminous miners in the UMW. Most important, the victory gave the rank-and-file workers an injection of confidence. For Mitchell, the strike "stood out in bold relief as the most remarkable contest between labor and capital in the industrial history of our nation."[34] The strike also gave the labor leader national prominence. He brought to labor-management relations a cool, rational, "modern" style. He preferred talking to shouting and was willing to compromise. Some of the cooler heads in the coal trust saw him as a man they could reason with.

To the mine workers he became an authentic hero; they voted October 29 a holiday and named it Mitchell Day. The workers called him their savior, their Lincoln, and lavished gifts and memorials upon him. The breaker boys were especially touching in their appreciation. When contract miners had attempted to keep the breaker boys away from union meetings, Mitchell had insisted upon their right to attend because they worked hard and long hours and were exploited even more shamelessly than the men. Mitchell had said of them: "They have the bodies and faces of boys but they came to meetings where I spoke and stood as still as the men and listened for every word. I was shocked and amazed . . . as I saw those eager eyes peering at me from eager little faces; the fight had a new meaning for me; I felt that I was fighting for the boys, fighting a battle for innocent childhood." Before he left the region, 20,000 breaker boys paraded before him in an unprecedented show of gratitude. They presented him with a gold medallion. He responded by telling them that their terrible lot had made his work in the anthracite fields a crusade.[35]

                              *   *   *

The union had won the first skirmish, but management never doubted it would win the war. The operators regarded their concessions, even in the planning stage, as no more than a tactical retreat; next time they would not be caught by surprise. The workers sensed this attitude and settled down to wait for the next confrontation. The coal companies began building stockades around the collieries, stockpiling coal, and hiring extra guards. All the while the UMW continued to increase its membership. Both sides were preparing for a final fight.

The operators honored the new wage scale, but there they drew the line. They refused to meet with the miners' committees, declaring that they did not represent the employees. Other promises of improvements were ignored. The violations spread discontent among the workers, who demanded action from the union. Mitchell wrote to Hanna in March 1901 explaining the workers' dissatisfaction and complaining about the operators' "unwarranted opposition."[36] But the political leader could do nothing; the operators would not be moved. They resented the political pressure that had been brought to bear on them, and they were determined to stand firm.

The UMW convention that met in early March 1901 authorized a strike if the operators did not recognize the union and negotiate on the settlement of grievances. Mitchell found himself in a difficult position. The conservative labor leader was opposed to strikes except as a last resort. He much preferred conciliation and compromise. Mitchell had become a member of the National Civic Federation (NCF), an organization founded in 1900 to bring together top leaders in labor and business for the purpose of dealing with the great problems of the day outside the influences of the Congress and state legislatures. Since the most critical issue of the time was the question of relations between capital and labor, the NCF focused most of its attention on this issue. During its first national conference in 1901, the NCF formulated the trade agreement as the best solution to avoid labor conflicts, a position supported by Mitchell, Dan Keefe, president of the International Longshoremen's Association, Martin Fox, president of the Iron Moulders Union, Samuel Gompers of the American Federation of Labor, and other individuals. These conservative labor lead-

ers, who were loudly criticized by many of their labor brothers for their easy willingness to collaborate with capital, pledged to establish "harmonious" relations and
cooperation between labor and capital, to avoid strikes at almost any cost. Through
the good offices of the NCF, trade agreements would be made between the heads of
labor organizations and the representatives of industry groups.[37]

Mitchell was committed to the NCF position, but others in the UMW leadership
were not. They were suspicious of the NCF's motives and feared that its probusiness
attitudes would lead to a sellout of the workers' interests. After the strike call,
Mitchell was therefore forced to mobilize all of his conservative support within the
union. The best he could do was to delay action while he personally sought an agreement with the operators. Once again he wrote to Hanna, warning of the consequences of the operators' intransigence and setting forth his philosophy: "I believe
you know that I am in favor of peace and the establishment of harmonious business
relations with the employers of labor, to the end that strikes and lockouts may become unnecessary." Mitchell also wrote to the presidents of the anthracite carriers
urging recognition of the union because "the miners' organization is a responsible
institution, conducted on conservative business lines."[38]

Mitchell's initiatives throughout the remainder of 1901 came to nothing. At
Morgan's behest, George Baer, the Reading's president, met with the labor leader
and agreed to continue the wage scale but committed himself to nothing else. A
meeting between Mitchell and Morgan ended inconclusively. President J. P. Thomas
of the Erie Railroad refused even to see Mitchell and a union delegation. Requests
made by the UMW and the Civic Federation that the operators agree to a conference
were rejected. Only after the UMW's convention in March 1902, when another strike
call was issued, did the operators finally agree to meet with Mitchell. But they used
the occasion to attack the UMW roundly, several of the presidents defiantly declaring that they would go bankrupt before they recognized the union. When Mitchell
privately agreed to lower the wage demand to 5 percent rather than 20 percent, the
coal owners took it as a sign of weakness and flatly rejected the offer. Mitchell could
hold off no longer. The miners were disgusted by the stalling and were growing disil-
lusioned with the union leadership. Finally, they forced Mitchell's hand. He agreed
to a "temporary suspension" of work on May 12, 1902, expressing his apprehension
in a letter to Mother Jones:

> I have every reason to believe that the strike will be made general and per-
> manent. I am of the opinion that this will be the fiercest struggle in which
> we have yet engaged. It will be a fight to the end, and our organization will
> either achieve a great triumph or it will be completely annihilated. Person-
> ally I am not quite satisfied with the outlook, as the movement for a strike is

strongly antagonized by the officers of the lower District, and of course the success of the strike depends entirely upon all working in harmony and unison.[39]

Three days later at the anthracite miners' convention in Hazleton, the delegates voted overwhelmingly to continue the strike despite a last-ditch appeal from Mitchell for still more time. Dragging their reluctant union leaders along, more than 147,000 anthracite workers walked off their jobs in one of the greatest strikes in American labor history. As they walked they sang a parody of one of the day's popular tunes, "Just Break the News to Mother":

> Just break the news to Morgan that great official organ,
> And tell him that we want ten percent of increase in our pay,
> Just say we are united and that our wrongs must be righted,
> And with those unjust company stores of course we'll do away.[40]

Bravado buoyed morale but the mine workers needed more than drive and inspiration, for they were up against the stupendously powerful empire of New York's J. P. Morgan. In 1902 the spokesman for the Morgan interests in the region was George F. Baer, president of the Reading Company and a man who some said resembled Morgan more than any other of the financier's associates. A dark, bearded veteran of the Civil War who styled himself a classical scholar and who enjoyed giving long-winded speeches on the sacred themes of democracy, Baer had first come to the Reading as counsel under Franklin B. Gowen before being appointed president of the reorganized company by Morgan. He was, as one writer said, "an intense and ruthless reactionary."[41] And as expected, from the very outset of the strike he took an uncompromising stand. "We will give no consideration," he announced in June, "to any plan of arbitration or mediation or to any interference on the part of any outside party."[42] He regarded the strike as a private affair that did not concern the public, and he refused outright the union's offer of arbitration. In his mind, arbitration directly interfered with the company's rights to manage its own affairs, its own property. He considered it his constituted duty to protect persons and property in his industry from what he regarded as the "mob rule" of labor radicals. On this fundamental issue, he had the undeviating support of the coal operators.

The intransigent attitude of the operators was demonstrated by their reaction to the anthracite workers' executive committee's instructions regarding mine maintenance workers. The committee had excluded the engineers, firemen, and pump men from the strike order because they were necessary to keep the mines from flooding. The committee was willing to allow them to keep working if the operators

A young mine worker at the time of the anthracite strike of
1902. Roughly one-sixth of the anthracite work force was
under legal age (twelve years old for surface workers
and fourteen for underground workers).   Courtesy of
the Lewis Hine Collection, Albin O. Kuhn Library,
University of Maryland, Baltimore County.

would agree to grant them an eight-hour day with no reduction in pay. Mitchell argued that this demand was only just, because maintenance workers usually had twelve-hour shifts and a twenty-four-hour shift on alternate Sundays. The operators responded by charging that Mitchell was seeking revenge by desiring to see the mines flooded, and they announced that they would replace any maintenance worker who left his job. When the June 2 deadline passed, most of the firemen walked out, along with substantial numbers of engineers and pump men. The operators kept most of the mines clear by using the workers who remained and by hiring others, many of whom had to live like prisoners within the protected colliery stockades. It was clear that the operators were willing to engage in all-out warfare against the union, even if it meant damage to their valuable properties.[43]

The mine workers struck in 1902 for basically the same reason they had struck two years earlier. They were still well behind the bituminous workers in pay. In the mines working conditions were abominable. Minimal mine safety regulations were all but ignored; state-appointed mine inspectors made their rounds accompanied by foremen, with the result, as one miner said, that "if the boss was along with him I would sooner be still" than voice a complaint. In 1901 alone, 111 mine workers were killed in the anthracite fields, and hundreds more were injured or permanently disabled from breathing coal dust.

Wage scales varied widely, which meant that men working side by side in the same mine often received different pay, depressing all wages to the lowest level ("mining the miners," it was called). Another grievance was the so-called dockage system. Miners had to produce between 2,600 and 3,200 pounds before being credited with a ton. Arbitrary deductions for impurities were made by the docking bosses above ground, so that the miner did not know whether he was being credited honestly for his work. The pay that he did receive was often not enough to cover expenses in the company stores, which charged excessively high prices. Many mine workers found themselves permanently in debt to the companies.[44] A miner's wife described what happened to her husband's pay envelope for two weeks' work:

> People comes in and wants money so quick we haven't time to have it in our hands, hardly. I can't count it up: sure not. . . . I throw it to his feet sometimes, when there is nothing in it. . . . Eight dollars was not so bad, or ten or twelve, but when he brings home only three or four, or two dollars, I had to cry.[45]

Mrs. Kate Burns went to work scrubbing floors and taking in wash in order to support her children, the youngest a boy of eight, after her husband had been killed while employed by the G. B. Markle Company. When her boy reached fourteen he went to work in a breaker but after a month's work brought home only a due bill for $396—the amount of accumulated rent on the two-room shack in which the family had lived since the father's death. Mrs. Burns, her son, and another younger son worked twelve years to pay off the debt.[46]

The mine workers walked out in 1902 to protest conditions such as these. But this time it was not just another strike, for it had an air of finality about it. It was

Breaker boys, Plymouth Coal Company, 1900.
Courtesy of the Wyoming Historical and Geological Society, Wilkes-Barre, Pa.

not only a work stoppage for current demands—a wage increase of 20 percent and a minimum scale, an eight-hour day, the weighing of coal using the legal ton—but a rebellion against the pernicious past: the lost strikes and broken unions, the dead and maimed, the shattered dreams. This time the hard lessons of the past had finally taken hold, and the miners knew that they had to stand firm for however long it took. They understood that the great companies would grant concessions only if they were forced to do so, if they were convinced that the solidarity of the workers would not break. Behind the miners' resolve was their conviction that their only hope for an improved existence was a union recognized by the companies.

The strike had an immediate and far-reaching impact upon the region. The wages of more than 140,000 men and boys, which averaged a total of $3½ million monthly, disappeared from the economy. Wholesalers and retailers cut back drastically on their orders; for many merchants business simply dried up. Banks reported deposits down sharply; hotels where commercial travelers stayed lost more than 50 percent of their trade. Society in the region divided into two sharply antagonistic camps. The 5,000 mine superintendents, foremen, and clerks were on the side of the operators, while the overwhelming majority of the rank and file sided with the union. Most professional men, many of whom had ties to the companies, discreetly kept their probusiness sympathies to themselves. Merchants prudently avoided taking sides. The clergy, with only a few exceptions, remained cautious and attempted to keep the factious struggle out of their churches, sometimes without success. Most of them simply prayed for peace. A few became staunch allies of Mitchell.

Most miners and their families settled in for a long siege, but many left the region, fearing that they would be unable to ride out the strike. Of the 30,000 Slav bachelors in the region, hundreds packed their trunks and cheap suitcases and began the long trek back to their homelands. Thousands of others, bachelors and mar-

Breaker boys at work under close supervision. At the time of the strike of 1902 60 percent of these boys were foreign born, and they were involved in a disproportionately high number of industrial accidents.   Courtesy of the National Archives.

ried men alike, left the region to seek work in the bituminous fields or the industrial cities of the east and mid-west. Crowds daily jammed the railway depots to see off their friends and loved ones. Merchants and tax collectors were also there, and many a debtor who attempted to slip away suddenly found his possessions attached. An observer noted that the "only persons kept busy for the first month of the strike were ticket agents, constables and justices of the peace." One of the latter remarked, "Business is good; I've taken in over five dollars a day for the last month." [47]

The strike was especially hard on young men and women. When family incomes vanished, the older children often had to leave so that the youngest could survive. Boys jumped freight trains—dubbed "Johnny Mitchell excursion specials"—bound for New York and Philadelphia. In the cities surrounding the region they glutted the market for cheap labor as they tramped about looking for work and begging for food. One boy who found work in Philadelphia regularly sent money back to his mother. She insisted that he visit home so that she could see how he looked. He delayed returning, however, until he had gained at least fifteen of the thirty pounds he had lost

*Hazleton, 1902. Thousands of mine workers and their families left
the region during the Great Strike of 1902.*
Courtesy of the Library of Congress.

while looking for a job. Girls as young as sixteen also joined the exodus. One seventeen-year-old, who could afford only a one-way fare, arrived in the city with little more than the clothes on her back. She found work for $3.50 a week and returned to her family after a month, hungry and dressed in rags.[48]

Though the English-speaking miners did not leave in large groups like the Slavs, few of their families went unaffected. In addition to the older children who left, many families simply packed up and joined the migration of the English-speaking from the region that already was two decades old. They left behind, in towns like Shenandoah and Hazleton, houses with "for rent" signs on every street. The outmigration made many of the smaller towns and patches ghost towns, inhabited only by old men, women, and children.

Many reporters who came to observe the strike were surprised at how peaceful the region seemed. The novelist Frank Norris wrote:

> The streets in the mining districts of the suburbs wore simply a Sunday aspect. I saw miners by the thousands—as a matter of fact all the men upon the streets of Parsons, South Wilkes-Barre, Miners' Mills, Stanton and East End were miners. But they seemed to be doing nothing more terrible than taking a day off. Very naturally each corner saloon had its group of loafers, sitting, for the most part, on the steps smoking, ruminating, their elbows on their knees. They were inert, voiceless, and from within the swinging doors of the saloon itself there came no sounds of vehemence; no "oaths and outcries," no crash of fists banging upon the bar, no reverberations of angry discussions. The men simply talked and lounged and smoked.[49]

The writer Alice Fallows, who was warned beforehand that she was entering dangerous territory, attended a rally of 7,000 workers and their families for John Mitchell in Dickson City. She wrote that the Italians, Greeks, Slavs, Hungarians, and other individuals listened attentively to their leader, who impressed upon them the necessity for maintaining law and order. The crowd showed real enthusiasm only when Mitchell announced that the strike would not be ended without their consent. That promise brought them to their feet.[50]

The relative tranquillity that prevailed in the region was due largely to the work of Mitchell and other UMW officials, who constantly urged the strikers to refrain from violence. Mitchell traveled from town to town and delivered speech after speech in which he explained to the workers the meaning of the strike and what he was doing to bring about its successful end. He urged the people to stand firm. His passage through the region took on the aspect of a triumphal march. In Shenandoah he rode with "Big John" Fahy in an open barouche pulled by black horses with cockades on their bridles, escorted by a guard of honor of well-scrubbed breaker boys and led by a brass band. Overhead, stretched across Main Street, was a huge banner: "Welcome to Our National Pres., Jno. Mitchell." Another banner read, "We are slaves now but Mitchell will set us free." The greeting for the beloved "Jonny d'Mitch" was emotional, even hysterical. For the mine workers and their families, who hung reverently on his every word, "This pale-faced man belonged to them; they worked for a living at the mines, and this being descended from heaven, this man so close that they could touch him, had been a miner also; he was theirs!"[51]

After Mitchell had gone and the enthusiasm had subsided, the hard part began. The days of idleness stretched into weeks, then months. Expenses were cut to a minimum, but soon paltry savings were used up. The summer gardens provided their last produce. Relief came from the bituminous miners and from nationwide contributions—$1.5 million during the strike—but it had to stretch far to sustain 750,000 men, women, and children, and ultimately it was not enough. Hunger, that terrible and historic weapon of the coal operators, once more threatened to kill the workers' resolve.

As the strike dragged on, families in the region had trouble getting fuel. It was

John Mitchell visits Shenandoah, during the Great Strike of 1902.
Courtesy of the Library of Congress.

John Mitchell arrives in Shenandoah in an open four-horse carriage during the Great Strike of 1902. Courtesy of the Library of Congress.

customary for the companies to provide coal to their employees at a reduced price. But when the strike began, this practice stopped. The companies also prohibited coal picking on the culm banks and used their armed guards to enforce it. Despite the ban, women and children went scrounging for coal anyway. Sometimes parties of children were organized to go to distant culm banks. They scurried over the wastes on their hands and knees, quickly filling their coal scuttles, alert for the approach of the guards and running like frightened deer when the men were sighted. One young mother, surprised by a reporter while stealing coal with her seven-year-old daughter—as her infant rolled on a shawl nearby—promised to throw back the coal from her half-filled scuttle if only she were let go. "We haven't got no money to pay fines with. We'll have to go to jail," she pleaded. When the reporter asked why the com-

*Miners' wives scavenging for coal on a culm bank in Hazleton during the
strike of 1902.   Courtesy of the Historical Society of Schuylkill County, Pottsville, Pa.*

pany guarded so carefully what it considered waste, the woman replied: "All the
people round here is striking. So, of course, the company wants them to starve, and
if they can't get coal to cook their food with, they will starve faster."[52]

In desperation some men returned to work. They slipped quietly from their
houses into the closely guarded confines of the collieries where they were, for the
moment, safe. But few of them escaped for long the wrath of their striking fellow
workers. Testimony taken by the Anthracite Strike Commission tells what happened to scabs:

> I went to bed about seven o'clock after I came home . . . I laid down with my
> clothes on . . . and I fell asleep and I didn't hear nothing until I heard a noise
> outside . . . and I looked out the window and I seen them all coming inside
> the yard.

QUESTION: About how many were in the crowd?

ANSWER: I should judge about 50 or 60. Saw them come in the yard and all start to throw stones at the house through the windows. I looked out and they seen me, of course, and Macguire was the ringleader, I asked him was he the leader. He says "Yes, come down and talk to me like a man." I says, "I won't go to work no more." He says, "Come down and talk to me like a man." I says, "Put that crowd outside of the gate and I will come down and talk to you." He invited them to go outside of the gate. As I was going down the stairs my wife called me back and says, "Here they are all coming in again." As soon as I got down and opened the door they rushed in on me. I went back up again and I told them to go out or I wouldn't come down. He asked them outside of the gate back, and as I was coming down my wife called me back and I put my head out of the window and says, "Boys, I won't come down now." "Go up and shoot the son of a bitch, all hands load up." When I heard that I thought the best thing I could do was to get out, it was me they were after. So I went up in the garret and broke a board off and crawled through there and went down through the neighbor's side.[53]

Miners' homes directly adjacent to colliery and culm bank.   *Courtesy of the Library of Congress.*

268 THE KINGDOM OF COAL

A fireman named John Williams explains an incident that occurred as he returned home from work:

> I must have gone about an eighth of a mile before I saw a person, and they were waiting for me! They could see me from a distance on the next street, coming out of the place. As soon as I got up to near where they were, one of the men ran out with a club, and he said to me, "You are a scab." Then I saw the crowd, and he ran after me and said, "Son of a bitch scab! I kill you!" He was a Hungarian. I saw the crowd and ran a ways, and the one that ran at me first struck me with a club over the right arm and disabled me. . . . And I ran down towards the breaker and had my back turned towards the men, and got hit in the back with a cobble. That knocked me down, but did not knock me down bad enough to hurt me, but it hurt me enough. Then I received another blow from a cobble on the hip . . . and was going in the swamp when a man hit me across the temple with a large club and knocked me down senseless.[54]

A father who attempted to rescue his miner son from a mob was also attacked. His son reported:

> They were hollering "give it to the son of a bitch of a scab, kill him! he is no good." I had a revolver in my pocket. They tore my coat and tore my shirt, rubbed my coat off my back, and took everything I had out of my pockets. They took my revolver and pipe and by that time they almost had me on their shoulders when they seen my father coming across the street and Squire McElvey hollered, he stood away from the crowd a few steps and hollered, "look out, here comes the old son of a bitch, give it to him. Take the gun off him!" At that time, no sooner had he said that than Cooper Ocheski turned around and threw a stone.

> QUESTION: At whom?

> ANSWER: My father. It hit him on the side of the head and then he jumped on him. I tried to assist him and McElvey grabbed me and said, "you son of a bitch I will take care of you." Every time I made an attempt to get to my father they would pull me back. . . . They were punching us, kicking us, jumping on us and doing everything they could.

William Bardner, a mine docking boss, told the commission that a tombstone bearing his name and the words "scab docking boss" was placed in front of a hotel on the main street of his town. He said that pressure was put on the local milkman and grocery store owner to keep them from dealing with him.[55]

Dynamite, a weapon of miners, was used with devastating effect. Porches of houses belonging to the hated scabs were blown away as a dire warning. But public censure could be just as convincing. In Lansford when a Lutheran minister attempted to conduct burial services for one of his foreign-born parishioners he was greeted by an aroused strike committee—which demanded that he not bury the man because he was a scab. When no one would enter the house to carry out the corpse, the minister searched the streets until he found four reluctant pallbearers. When the body was carried toward the cemetery, hostile crowds followed, yelling, "Let that dog lie! Bury somebody else! It's a shame to bury a scab!"[56]

Mrs. Krupa was on her knees one morning praying for the success of the strike in Shenandoah when she looked out her window and saw two men stealthily walking past. Though her men were out on the picket line, she rushed from the house, screaming "scab" at the top of her voice and calling for the nonexistent crowd in her house to come deal with the traitors. The two men took one look at the formidable Mrs. Krupa, another at the house, and fled; the devout lady returned to her prayers. Mrs. McCann, who feared that her husband might weaken and attempt to work, kept his clothes permanently in the washtub so that he would not yield to temptation.[57]

The strike, like a civil war, sometimes divided families. Two brothers left their homeland together, lived together, and shared their earnings equally but became bitter lifelong enemies when one went on strike and the other stayed on the job. The striking brother forever after simply referred to his brother as "the scab." Social ostracism, a most formidable instrument of persuasion among the communal Slavs, fell heavily upon the wives and children of scabs, whose lives were made miserable by their neighbors. The family of a working miner after being constantly insulted and threatened moved to another part of town, the wife complaining, "I couldn't stand it no longer; those women [her neighbors] were terrible." The family's landlord professed to be "glad they're gone. I don't want dynamite here because of scabs." Women from Lackawanna County whose husbands had slipped quietly away to the Schuylkill field to work finally could stand no more. They went in pursuit of their husbands and threatened to remain, either in the collieries or until the men returned home with them. The children of scabs were also subjected to abuse, and sometimes brutal beatings, by other children. Even the youngest children were affected. One youngster, banned from playing with a group of children of striking fathers, pleaded, "I'll be Johnny Mitchell man, only let me play."[58]

The older boys, the slate pickers, door tenders, and mule drivers, learned early that the worst crime was to be a scab, and that the largest honor of all was to be a "union man." Specially favored and encouraged by Mitchell, the child workers set up their own "junior locals," complete with elected officers, for all boys under the age of sixteen. They met weekly and in secret, usually in the evening, and paid dues of ten to twenty-five cents monthly, depending upon wages. The boys conducted their business entirely by themselves; a local UMW representative attended only to provide instruction and guidance. During the strike the boys were quite as militant as their fathers and older brothers. One slate picker from near Hazleton was overheard explaining the process by which a certain scab might be blown up with dynamite.[59]

The boys' strong loyalty to the union showed in their attitudes at school. Though most of the older boys had already given up on formal education, some of them took advantage of the strike to attend school for a few months. In the rural and small-town school districts of the region, directed by local boards of education consisting almost entirely of miners, prounion sympathies were mandatory for teachers. Those with family members or sweethearts friendly to scabs, however, were subjected to harassment; there were even instances when the entire school went out on strike. In one incident, a breaker boy member of a junior local called his classmates together during recess, told them about the teacher's relationship with scabs, and informed the students, "We must all hang together now if we wish to assert our manhood." During afternoon classes, when the teacher's back was turned, the students marched out of the school together. In Plymouth a school strike occurred when students refused to sit in a building heated by steam from the boilers of a nearby colliery. The pupils announced that they "wouldn't sit in no room what was heated by scab steam." But school strikes seldom lasted very long because the ringleaders were usually expelled. A ten-year-old breaker boy at McAdoo who could neither read nor write nevertheless managed to organize a strike at a local school before he was expelled. The boy, tobacco juice ringing his mouth, lamented that the younger children simply could not get properly organized. He added, "This school will never amount to nothing until it is organized."[60]

The powerful emotions that built up during the strike finally could not be contained, despite all the efforts of John Mitchell. On July 30 in Shenandoah a deputy sheriff who was escorting two nonunion men was attacked by 5,000 strikers and was forced to seek refuge in the Reading Railroad depot. When the sheriff's brother tried to smuggle arms into the building he was beaten to death. Somehow the sheriff managed to escape and send word to Governor Stone. Two regiments of National Guard and a cavalry troop under the command of General John Gobin were sent into the city. Eventually the entire Pennsylvania National Guard was assigned to the region. In August General Gobin ordered his unit commanders to "shoot to kill" if they were attacked in any way by the strikers.[61]

Fortunately Gobin's order was never carried out; the troops killed no one. But their presence in the region, along with the heavily reinforced 3,000 Coal and Iron Police—which, rumor had it, recruited its newest members from among the lowest members of Philadelphia society—intensified resentment among the populace. One

Coal and Iron policeman guarding company property during the strike of 1902. Courtesy of the Historical Society of Schuylkill County, Pottsville, Pa.

of the members of the cavalry unit stationed in Shenandoah reported that the soldiers considered themselves to be in enemy territory. They took all of the normal military precautions of an occupation force, but they acted with restraint. As a result they were less hated than the Coal and Iron Police and the 1,000 private detectives stationed in the region. Still, the cavalryman did note that one day a gray-haired Irish woman cried out after him as he rode by in full uniform: "God bless ye, and may ye die of the hunger." [62]

When the governor called out the Eighth Regiment of the Pennsylvania Guard on July 30, the loyalties of many union men who also were members of the Guard were severely tested. One man told his mother that he would run away rather than serve. His mother pleaded with him to respond to the call, reminding him that his brother had recently been killed in the Philippines: "Fred, no; Will, your brother, was no coward." Yet most strikers regarded union men who now wore the Guard uniform as turncoats and traitors. Crowds gathered around the armories as the companies formed and shouted "scab, scab" at their friends and neighbors. The sudden transformation from striker to soldier left many men shaken. Some believed that they would be expelled from the union; others vowed to leave the Guard as soon as the strike ended. "To think of shooting down my fellow-workmen is terrible," one miner commented. "No more for me as soon as this is over." [63]

The operators had other ways of driving the workers into line. In the immediate aftermath of this strike, John Markle summarily evicted thirteen of his employees by canceling the fifteen-and-one-half-cent day-to-day leases on their company houses. One man had worked for Markle and his father for thirty-one years. He was able to conclude only that he had been discharged because his son, also a miner, had worked on a relief committee that distributed food to the families of needy workers.

Testimony taken by the Anthracite Strike Commission tells what happened to some of Markle's employees:

QUESTION: Are you a miner?

ANSWER: Yes sir.

Q: Did you hold any office in the union?

A: I was treasurer of the local.

Q: Were you arrested, charged with any crime?

A: No sir, I was never arrested in my life.

Q: Are you working now?

A: No sir.

Q: Did you make an effort to get back your work at Jeddo?

A: No sir, I did not.

Q: Why?

A: Because after I got the notice to leave the house I went along with another brother member who was notified at the same time to see what was the trouble, and all the satisfaction we could get was that we would never work for that company again. I had that from Mr. Markle himself. This is the reason I did not apply for my work.

Q: How much of a family have you?

A: Eleven in all.

Q: How many children?

A: Seven children, myself and my wife's father and mother.

Q: How many rooms are in the house you lived in?

A: Four rooms.

Q: And the eleven of you lived there?

A: Yes sir, we had to.

Q: What time of the day was it when you were evicted?

A: It was between eight and nine o'clock . . . , a very damp morning. . . .

Q: Was the Sheriff present when you were evicted?

A: Yes sir.

Q: What did he say?

A: I met him on the street and I said, "This is very sudden, ain't it?" He said, "Yes, it is kind of sudden." I says, "I am in a pretty bad fix, both of the old people are sick, have been ailing for three or four days, and the old gentleman in particular, he is in bed; I would like if you could give me until tomorrow morning. I am ready to go to Hazleton now and will try all in my power to get a house". . . . He says, "That is a pretty fair proposition, I will see about it." He left me and went down towards the store . . . and before I had time to get back to the house the Sheriff came up and said, "Paul, you will have to get out in five minutes." I says, "If I have, you will have to do the putting out; I have to try to find some place to get in."

Q: What did he do with your things?

A: Pile them out on the street.

Q: What became of the old people?

A: My next door neighbor was a very fine old lady and before she would see them exposed to any unnecessary hardships she came in and asked them in there next door, and then the old lady was able to go down town among some of the other neighbors, and the old gentleman stayed there until the following day.

Q: How many of them are there in the family of the lady who took the old people in?

A: Seven, I believe. . . .

Q: You heard the lease that was read here on Saturday, did you sign one of these leases?

A: All that I ever signed to my knowledge under G. B. Markle and Com-

An eviction during the strike of 1902.
Courtesy of the Burg Collection, MG-273, Pennsylvania State Archives.

pany was the lease to my house. . . .

Q: What effects do these leases have on the miner, making it at the will and pleasure of Mr. Markle? . . .

A: There is one effect. He has to take any kind of a place that he gives him, if he is not in a position to move. . . .

Q: Supposing that a very hard place is given to him and he is told to work it. If he does not work there what effect has that on him with reference to his house?

A: He has to get out of the house.[64]

Another miner told the following story:

QUESTION: How long have you worked at Markle's?

ANSWER: It will be 19 years next June.

Q: How long have you been a miner?

A: I am a miner about 29 years. . . .

Q: Who was there in your family at the time you were turned out?

A: My wife and my mother-in-law and two adopted children, and a son of mine. . . .

Q: How old is your mother-in-law?

A: I had no record of her age but by her appearance and what people say she must be over 100 years of age.

Q: Was she sick at the time?

A: Always sick, and blind besides . . .

Q: Have you ever been hurt in the mines?

A: Of course I was hurt in the mines. . . . I haven't a safe bone in my body, only my neck. My back was hurt too, and I have a leg no better than a wooden leg, my ribs are broke, I have only one eye, and my skull is fractured. . . .

Q: How old are you?

A: Fifty-seven years old . . .

Q: How many hours a day do you think a man ought to work in the mines?

A: I think if I had justice since the time I began to work first I ought to have a pension instead of working an hour at all.

Q: What do you think about eight hours; is that as long as a man can stand it?

A: I think eight hours is too much for a man to work, if he is contending with powder smoke and bad air from morning to night. I have worked in the mines in powder smoke and bad air where the first two hours was enough to kill me, let alone the rest. . . .

Q: Were you ever able to save any money on your wages?

A: Save money? How could I save money and raise a family on two days a week sometimes and sometimes three days and keep a house and pay house rent and pay for coal?

Q: Did you ever have a bank account?

A: Yes. Once my woman got about $60. at one time and put it in the bank, but the very next pay day she would get nothing at all and would have to take $5. out of it, and maybe in a year or two she would get $10. she could spare and she might put that in the bank, and then maybe I would get hurt or something and she would have to draw it all out again, and so I never got a hundred dollars in a bank account in my life.

Q: Did you ever get any money in any way for any of the times you were hurt?

A: Yes sir. Mr. Superintendent Smith and the employees of the G. B. Markle and Company gave me something at the time I came out of the hospital and was on crutches. My woman was in poor circumstances then and she was into the store and my fellow-workmen went to work and made a contribution among themselves . . . and when they went into the office Mr. Markle was asked if he would give something. He told them—this is what I was told by the men who made the collection—that he would do his part hereafter; but Mr. Smith, the superintendent he had there, gave me $50. for my sore leg afterwards. That is the money I received.

Q: Do you know whether that was out of Mr. Smith's own pocket?

A: I do not know, I could not tell, but it was Mr. Smith who done it. He was the superintendent of the store, $50. to give me. Frank Walk told me, "This is a present Mr. Smith has given you for your leg." I was on crutches at the time, after my fellow-workmen contributed one hundred and sixty and some odd dollars, and that money was kept in the company store for rent and for what kept my woman and for keeping the house during this time I was in the hospital and idle, and it was all kept there except $25. that I had after I came home.[65]

Clarence Darrow, the attorney who represented the miners, commented to the Anthracite Strike Commission on Markle's actions:

Gentlemen of the commission, you may roll together all the cruelty and all the violence and all the misery that all of these irresponsible Goths and vandals have committed in the anthracite region; you may pack them in one, and they cannot equal the fiendish cruelty of John Markle when the cause was gone, and he turned these helpless people into the street simply to satisfy his hellish hate.[66]

The strike dragged on despite threats, arrests, court action, and planted rumors that other trade unions were abandoning the miners. Yet by the fourth month, the resolve of the workers began to weaken. Mitchell wondered how much longer the men and their families could hold out. "I am fully convinced that the strike would have collapsed had the operators at this time opened their mines and invited the strikers to return," he remembered thinking in early August.[67] But the companies remained obstinate, even in the face of mounting political pressure from Hanna and the Civic Federation.

In August, just as the workers' morale was beginning to wilt, the spokesman for the companies committed an enormous blunder. Never known for his restraint, George Baer wrote a revealing letter to a Wilkes-Barre clergyman sympathetic to the strikers' cause. The letter was made public, and it soon made history. Baer wrote:

> I see that you are a religious man; but you are evidently biased in favor of the right of the workingman to control a business in which he has no other interest than to secure fair wages for the work he does. I beg of you not to be discouraged. The rights and interests of the laboring man will be protected and cared for—not by the labor agitators, but by the Christian men of property to whom God has given control of the property rights of the country, and upon the successful management of which so much depends.[68]

The nationwide publication of the letter had an electrifying effect. Even the conservative newspapers challenged the arrogance of Baer. "A good many people think they superintend the earth, but not many have the egregious vanity to describe themselves as its managing directors," the *New York Times* noted.[69] The *Chicago Tribune* added, "It is impudent, it is insulting, it is audacious, of the coal presidents to speak of 'lawlessness' in the coal regions when they themselves are the greatest offenders of the law. They are the real anarchists, the real revolutionists, the real subverters of law and order." While the majority of the press attacked Baer's "Divine Right" philosophy, Clarence Darrow merely referred to him as "George the Last."[70] Baer's letter swung public opinion decisively to the side of the strikers. It gave them new determination to stand firm.

As autumn approached and the widespread fear of fuel shortages in the eastern cities took hold, pressure intensified for a settlement of the strike. President Theodore Roosevelt, who had been closely following the strike, instructed Attorney General Philander Chase Knox to look into the possibility of federal intervention, including prosecution of the coal companies for violation of the Sherman Antitrust Act for restraint of trade. In September the New York State Democratic Convention, attended by 10,000 people, called for government ownership of the anthracite mines. From Massachusetts, Senator Henry Cabot Lodge sent a message to Roosevelt noting that hard coal prices in New York had risen from six dollars to twenty-six dollars a ton and warning of the consequences for the Republican party in the upcoming congressional elections. Roosevelt himself expressed his fears to Robert Bacon of J. P. Morgan and Company: "There will be fuel riots of as bad a type as any bread riots we have ever seen."[71]

Actually, Roosevelt's fears had little basis in reality. Bituminous coal continued to reach eastern cities throughout the strike, and in New York soft coal with a heating value comparable to that of anthracite was selling for five dollars a ton. Had the anthracite shippers chosen to transport bituminous from western Pennsylvania rather than allow their trains to remain idle, all market demands could have been met. Furthermore, Mitchell had already ruled out a sympathy strike of soft coal miners. The fuel crisis that did occur in the East was largely made by panicky public officials and speculating retailers. As rumors spread and everyone from mayors to the president talked about a coal shortage, retailers raised prices and caused more confusion and fear that coal would soon disappear.[72]

As alarm grew among the public and politicians, another development occurred with potentially far graver consequences, especially for business interests and the UMW. The strike had attracted scores of "radical" agitators and organizers to the anthracite fields. Mother Jones reappeared in the region, calling the operators "sewer rats," and the Pennsylvania section of the Socialist party established locals at what was called a "phenomenal" rate. One Socialist organizer proclaimed, "The Coal Strike has done more for the cause of Socialism than all the events that ever happened in the United States before. There is nothing like an object lesson for instructing the people." The successes of the Socialists and even the anarchist-oriented Industrial Workers of the World ("Wobblies") in recruiting anthracite workers caused considerable concern in the leadership circles of both the Civic Federation and the United Mine Workers. The head of the Civic Federation wrote to Morgan associate George W. Perkins, warning that the "radical element" would "open the floodgates to all kinds of hostile legislation, political moves, etc." Mitchell, who feared the impact upon his union—and leadership—informed Hanna that the Socialists were holding "immense meetings in every mining town" and added that "there is a great and growing independent political sentiment in the coalfields."[73] Mitchell had ample cause for concern because the length of the strike and the increasing radicalization of the miners was undermining his moderate position. Dissatisfaction already existed among anthracite UMW leaders because of his role in warding off an attempt by the union's anthracite districts to persuade the bituminous workers to join in a nationwide general strike of all coal miners.

By September President Roosevelt was coming under intense pressure to intervene. There were growing demands, even from conservative congressmen, that he seize the mines under the law of eminent domain. The noted journalist Jacob A. Riis wrote to the president that "a remedy must be found or the arrogance of the money power will bring a revolution"; while Senator Lodge warned him that the operators' "attitude is a menace to all property in the country and is breeding Socialism at a rate which is hard to contemplate." Roosevelt himself later told a Boston newspaperman that at the time he was convinced that if the strike lasted one more month there would be an outbreak of the "most awful riots which this country has ever seen."[74]

The president finally decided to act. He sent telegrams to the heads of the railroad companies and to Mitchell, calling them to a conference in Washington on October 3. When the participants gathered, the atmosphere in the meeting room was not even coolly cordial. The company presidents sat stiffly at one end of the room; Mitchell, looking more like a coal company lawyer than a union leader, sat at the other end with the heads of the three anthracite districts. In between were Attorney General Knox, Roosevelt's secretary, George Cortelyou, and the commissioner of labor, Carroll Wright. The president, on entering the room, made a direct plea for peace. "With all the earnestness there is in me, I ask that there be an immediate resumption of operations . . . in some such way as will, without a day's unnecessary delay, meet the crying needs of the people." He appealed to both sides' patriotism and asked that they make sacrifices for the national good. Mitchell said he agreed wholeheartedly, and he asked Roosevelt to appoint an investigative commission to look into the issue, promising that the miners would accept the findings even if they went against their claims.

Baer spoke for the railroad companies, once again demonstrating his light touch:

> We represent the owners of coal mines in Pennsylvania. There are from 15 to 20 thousand men at work mining and preparing coal. They are abused, assaulted, injured and maltreated by the United Mine Workers. Thousands of other working-men are deterred from working by intimidation, violence, and crimes, inaugurated by the United Mine Workers, over whom John Mitchell, whom you have invited to meet us, is chief.[75]

Then John Markle, representing the independent operators, asked Roosevelt if he expected the companies to deal with a "set of outlaws." Markle went on to lecture the president on his responsibilities: "I now ask you to perform the duties invested in you as President of the United States, to at once squelch the anarchistic conditions of affairs existing in the anthracite coal regions by the strong arm of the military at your command."

Teddy Roosevelt, gritting his big teeth, just managed to hold his temper. Later, he reportedly said of Baer: "If it wasn't for the high office I hold, I would have taken him by the breeches and the nape of the neck and chucked him out of the window."

The president claimed that Mitchell was the only man in the room (besides himself, he probably thought) who comported himself like a gentleman. In fact, Mitchell's behavior, and that of the operators, gave Roosevelt the feeling, for the first time, that perhaps the miners were right.[76]

The conference failed to end the strike. Roosevelt did propose to Mitchell that the miners return to work, after which the president would appoint a commission to investigate the issues. The operators, however, would not commit themselves to abide by the commission's findings, nor would they agree to arbitration. Furthermore, there was no assurance that the union would be recognized. When the anthracite workers met on October 8 in mass meetings and voted overwhelmingly to stay out until their demands were met, Mitchell had no choice but to reject the president's proposal.

The blame for the failure of the conference, however, fell squarely upon the operators, especially after word of their behavior and attitude got out. Public indignation against them mounted. When the White House leaked the news that the president was seriously considering sending in the army to take over and operate the mines, even the great house of Morgan finally paid attention. On October 11 Secretary of War Elihu Root met with the financier in New York and worked out a memorandum requesting that Roosevelt appoint an arbitration commission. Morgan recognized that the position of the operators was no longer tenable, and within twenty-four hours he secured their agreement, as well as their promise, to accept the recommendation of the commission.[77]

Despite their agreement to the commission, the operators did not completely surrender. They specified the kinds of individuals that they wanted appointed to the commission, making sure that there were no representatives of organized labor. This stipulation created an impasse, because Roosevelt had assured Mitchell that at least one prolabor man would be appointed. The president and Mitchell also believed that a high-ranking Catholic prelate should serve, since most of the miners were Catholic. The operators could not very well refuse the appointment of the prelate, but they stood firm in their opposition to a labor representative. A crisis was finally averted on the evening of October 15 while Roosevelt was with two of Morgan's partners in Washington. The president suddenly realized that appearance rather than substance stood in the way of a resolution of the problem. It occurred to him "that the mighty brains of these captains of industry would rather have anarchy than tweedle-dum, but that if I would use the word tweedle-dee they would hail it as meaning peace."[78] The operators had suggested that an "eminent sociologist" be appointed to the commission; since Roosevelt believed that a sociologist was one who had studied social problems and had a practical knowledge of them, he found a way out. He proposed that E. E. Clark, grand chief of the Order of Railway Conductors, be named to the commission, not as a representative of labor, but as an "eminent sociologist." To everyone's relief, the operators agreed.

Roosevelt skillfully selected the other members of the commission, striking a balance that satisfied both sides. Clark and Bishop John Lancaster Spalding of Illinois were members with prolabor leanings; Edward Parker, editor of the *Engineering and Mining Record*, and former mine owner Thomas H. Watkins, had promanagement attitudes; and U.S. Circuit Court Judge George Gray and Brigadier General John M. Wilson, former army chief of engineers, were considered neutral. Labor Commissioner Wright was appointed by the president as recorder; the other commission members elected him a full member. Following an inspection tour of the mines, the Anthracite Coal Strike Commission opened its hearings in Scranton on November 14. Meanwhile, the anthracite workers had met in convention on October 21 and voted to return to work.[79]

The hearings held in Scranton and Philadelphia lasted for more than three months. The number of witnesses who testified totaled 558: 240 for the United Mine Workers, 153 for nonunion workers, 154 for the operators, and 11 called by the commission. The testimony filled fifty-six volumes. Both sides were represented by some of the best legal talent in the country: Clarence Darrow, the famous "attorney for the damned," led the miners' team; former U.S. attorney general Wayne MacVeagh, the operators' group. With the attention of the public riveted on the hearings, both sides played for maximum effect.

As his first witness, Darrow called John Mitchell. The somber, nearly exhausted union leader, speaking in a calm, level tone, reviewed the miners' case. Without the union, he said, any improvements in wages and working conditions that the workers might gain would gradually be eroded, and there would be no spokesman to defend them. Recognition of the union, therefore, was imperative to the workers. He added that only the union could bring about labor peace. He then explained at length each of the union's demands. Following the friendly questioning of Darrow, Mitchell was cross-examined by MacVeagh and other operators' attorneys for more than four days. The questioning was hostile and provocative, but Mitchell never lost his composure. He even displayed occasional flashes of unexpected wit. On the matter of calling strikebreakers scabs, MacVeagh asked: "Having designated one as a scab, what else would you do?" Mitchell smiled and replied: "That is all." MacVeagh then asked Mitchell about a "poor, suffering" miner who had accumulated $40,000 worth of property. Mitchell responded that the miner "must have been one of those who mined the miners." During questioning as to how the operators were expected to raise wages when profits were low without passing the increase along to consumers, the following exchange occurred:

MACVEAGH: . . . If you demand an increase and they have no profits, where are they going to place it except on the bowed backs of the poor?

MITCHELL: They might take it out of their profits and so put it on the bowed backs of the rich.[80]

In the days and weeks that followed, Darrow brought 239 more witnesses before the commission. They were workers, wives, children, widows, mothers—a pitiful procession of humanity. There were crippled men who had never received a penny of compensation, one of whom testified that a miner was not considered injured unless he lost an eye or a leg; widows of miners who had been killed and who continued to be charged rent for company houses; a twelve-year-old child whose pay of forty cents a day was credited against the debt of his dead father; a man who had worked for seventeen and a half years at a stretch without ever having drawn a cent in ready cash; another boy of eight, who looked five and earned sixty-two cents a week in a breaker. They were men, women, and children of all nationalities and mine workers of every skill and occupation. And along with them appeared priests and ministers to verify their testimony. So moving was their testimony, that the commission finally asked that the so-called spectacle of horrors be stopped.[81]

The final summations for both sides were presented by Darrow and George Baer. As one writer noted: "American history rarely presents such an opportunity to study within a narrow compass the contrast between two utterly opposed philosophies of the social order. Baer . . . spoke for the glories of the half century just passed, when capitalism was unrestricted and capitalists answered only to their stockholders. Darrow . . . spoke for the century just beginning, which would assert the rights of the individual workingman and his union, and would bring an end to the world George Baer had known."[82] Baer spoke of the rights of management to manage as it pleased; he condemned the lawlessness and crimes of the strikers; claimed that if a man was willing to work for so much a day, that it was "a bargain as good and as sacred in the eyes of the law as any bargain could be"; he quoted Seneca, Cervantes, and the Roman law to support his arguments. Darrow, on the other hand, with his dramatic flair and florid phrases sought to win his audience by reaching their hearts. "Gentlemen," he directly addressed Baer and company, "this was an industrial war. . . . you on your side were fighting 147,000 men with their wives and children, and the weapons you used were hunger and want. You thought to bring them to terms by the most cruel, deadly weapon that any oppressor has ever used to bring men to his terms, hunger and want. . . .These gentlemen," he turned to the commission, "precipitated the greatest conflict between capital and labor which the world has ever seen, the most gigantic strike in history, because in their

minds it was a question of mastery—nothing else; because they felt and they believed that upon this contest depended the question of whether they should be the
masters or whether the men should be the masters. . . . This strike from its inception and before was brought about for one purpose and only one, to crush out this
union which had brought to these downcast, suffering men, women and children the
first ray of light and hope and inspiration that had ever come into the darkness of
their lives."[83] Baer had read his meticulously prepared statement; Darrow spoke for
a total of eight hours without using a single note. At the conclusion of Darrow's summation, the overflow crowd in the Philadelphia courtroom gave him a standing ova-
tion that lasted for more than five minutes.

On March 22, 1903, the commission announced its findings. It awarded the
miners a 10 percent pay increase, a sliding wage scale which Baer had suggested, an
eight-hour day for several categories of work, and weighing men to be paid by the
miners. The United Mine Workers did not receive recognition, but a conciliation
board on which representatives of miners' organizations were to sit was established.
The purpose of the board was to adjudicate all disputes arising between the miners
and their employers. The commission also prohibited discrimination against union
workers and criticized the employment of children.

Because recognition of the union, the major objective of the strike, had not been
achieved, many in the labor movement believed that the strike had been lost. But
the anthracite workers had gained enough to convince themselves that the battle
had been won—formal recognition of their union was only a matter of time. Mitchell
felt that the workers had won a stirring victory. Most important for the union movement in the United States, the federal government had intervened in a labor dispute
for the first time in the country's history, not to break a strike, but to bring about a
peaceful settlement.

Though the Great Strike of 1902 permanently established the United Mine
Workers in the anthracite fields, it cost both the union and Mitchell personally. The
decision to organize the anthracite fields instead of West Virginia's soft coal fields
resulted, in 1904, in Mitchell's being forced to accept a two-year wage reduction in
bituminous because of West Virginia nonunion competition. Two years later other
defections weakened the joint conference agreements in soft coal. Dissatisfaction resulted in Mitchell's being voted out of office in 1908, despite the high regard in which
he was held by the public and by the anthracite workers. He found desultory employment for a time with the National Civic Federation and in a minor political
office, but when he died at age forty-nine rumors of questionable financial specula-
tions and alcohol abuse followed him to the grave.

J. P. Morgan personally benefited from the strike. He emerged as a man who
was willing to use his immense power responsibly and for the public good, at least in

the eyes of the press. The coal companies, for their part, came to understand that it was in their interest to do business with the conservative UMW, and that the costs of wage increases could be passed on to the public. But the companies did not get off scot-free; their actions during the strike and the indignation they aroused among the public resulted in a series of antitrust suits.[84]

Roosevelt, perhaps, benefited most of all. As historian Robert H. Wiebe writes: "Roosevelt contributed materially to the welfare of a union and an industry he did not understand; enlarged the power and prestige of the executive by misinterpreting both the immediate issues of the strike and the motives of those who participated in its settlement; and helped to create a public panic which helped him to end the strike." Two years later Roosevelt won election in his own right to the presidency as the man who had given the people "a square deal."[85]

"It was generally conceded," in Clarence Darrow's words, "that labor gained greatly by this arbitration."[86] But in his riveting final speech before the Anthracite Coal Strike Commission, Attorney Darrow described better than anyone what the anthracite miners had really won in their Great Strike of 1902. In his mind it was primarily a spiritual victory.

> The blunders are theirs, and the victories have been ours. The blunders are theirs because, in this old, old strife, they are fighting for slavery, while we are fighting for freedom. They are fighting for the rule of man over man, for despotism, for darkness, for the past. We are striving to build up man. We are working for democracy, for humanity, for the future, for the day that will come too late for us to see it or know it or receive its benefits, but which will come, and will remember our struggles, our triumphs, our defeats, and the words which we spake.[87]

9. Decline

L ABOR PEACE FINALLY CAME TO THE COALFIELDS IN THE WAKE OF THE GREAT Strike of 1902. The mine workers had their union, and if it did not get them all that they wanted, at least it gave them an organizational unity that they had lacked before. In John Mitchell they found a champion; they gave him their personal loyalty, a loyalty stronger than their allegiance to the union he led. For many anthracite workers he was the UMW. Though he had stood for compromise and conciliation in 1902 when many of his constituents demanded greater militancy, he did win them unofficial recognition. The union was now a major force in the region, as even the most recalcitrant operators knew. The operators certainly did not like it, but they saw that the union was a power with which they had to contend and one with which they might even work to their own advantage.

The benefits of cooperation between management and the disciplined UMW workers soon became apparent. In 1901, on the eve of the Great Strike, production stood at 67 million tons. Through the following years it rose steadily to the historic high of nearly 100 million tons in 1917. Wartime demands spurred extra output, but it came from a mature and stabilized industry.

The mighty coal combination put together by J. P. Morgan and his associates after 1890 was decisive in imposing order upon the industry. Seven big railroad companies linked together by interlocking boards of directors and tied by joint stock ownership to large New York and Philadelphia banking interests controlled anthracite. The handful of mining companies that were subsidiaries of the railroads accounted for 70 percent of production. The monopoly had a captive market in millions of households and institutions throughout the Northeast, New England, and parts of the Midwest. It limited production and set prices high enough to assure substantial and constant profits.

The organized mine workers shared in the benefits of a controlled industry. Production stability brought greater regularity of employment. Wages improved. The supply of cheap labor was reduced as immigration slowed during World War I and afterward. As a result of worker opposition, the most flagrant abuses of company stores and company housing ended. In the largely urbanized anthracite region, where most people lived in towns of more than 2,500 people, the majority of workers owned or rented their homes. And in the tiny, isolated patch towns, prosperity brought new services such as electricity, municipal water, and public schools. As the Irish, Slavs, and Italians elbowed their way into local public offices, they confidently used their new-found political power to improve their communities. The rising standard of living helped reduce ethnic conflict and social discrimination. The miners' long struggles for a living wage and the right to raise their families decently appeared finally to pay off. Many of them undoubtedly believed that they were on the verge of realizing the hopes that had first brought them to America.[1]

Yet even as the industry enjoyed prosperity and labor peace its foundations were eroding. By the end of the first decade of the twentieth century, bituminous coal and coke, its by-product, had largely replaced anthracite as the nation's industrial fuel. During World War I hard coal production could not keep pace with demand, and many users shifted permanently to other fuels. During these years shippers in the unregulated coal industry continued to raise prices. Outraged consumers protested without effect. Government investigating committees exposed the monopolistic character of anthracite but failed to bring about effective legislative action. The public was left with the impression that neither the operators nor the union cared at all about consumers.

Following the war a series of developments occurred that steadily undermined anthracite's supremacy as a heating fuel. Technological improvements allowed for the increasing use of oil and later of natural and manufactured gas. Though the initial costs of heating plants were high, the safety, convenience, and cleanliness of these fuels, touted in high-pressure advertising campaigns, appealed to affluent families. The new heating substitutes made their greatest inroads in the densely populated, urbanized Northeast, where anthracite had its biggest market. Even bituminous, long scorned as dirty and inefficient by anthracite users, successfully challenged hard coal. Better firing and heating equipment made soft coal attractive in distant markets like New England and the Midwest, where transportation costs pushed the price of anthracite even higher. By the mid-1920s the cost differential between the two coals in these areas was often as much as seven dollars per ton. As coke was adapted for home heating it also cut into anthracite markets.[2]

Oil, gas, coke, and electricity for domestic use were the products of technological change, of an advanced industrial economy that anthracite originally helped create. From the 1920s on, the increasing adoption of these new fuels brought about anthracite's decline. And that decline was amazingly rapid for an industry that had seemed so solidly established.

But the shift to other fuels, though perhaps inevitable, was also due in part to decisions made by the hard coal industry itself. The stubbornly conservative operators, comfortable with profits earned in a limited but controlled market, did not seek innovation or expansion. They made no great effort to search for alternate uses for anthracite in industry, nor did they reduce shipping costs to the point where their fuel was competitive in distant markets. They did not move decisively to counter growing adverse publicity about their monopolistic practices or to match the aggressive advertising and promotional efforts of oil competitors. Their actions, in fact, alienated the public. In dealing with their workers during the 1920s they absolutely refused to make concessions; the prolonged strikes that resulted undercut production and, eventually, profits. For the absentee financial interests that controlled anthracite, the industry was simply one component in a vast conglomeration of capital. In a rapidly expanding economy there were larger and more attractive opportunities. A national market had been created and now, in the aftermath of war, an international one as well. Anthracite was and would remain a regional fuel. If it still gave good returns, the wise invested them elsewhere.

A renewed outbreak of labor strife in the 1920s hastened anthracite's demise. Every work stoppage that interrupted the supply of coal compelled more and more consumers to switch to alternate fuels. Those who invested in oil heating did not go back. The strikes further tarnished the industry's image. When confronted by the confusing charges and countercharges made by the operators and union, public opinion damned both their houses, holding management and labor equally responsible for unfeeling disregard of those dependent upon hard coal. Some public figures even called for federal regulation, echoing cries heard during the strike of 1902. To a consuming public disgusted by the high prices of a monopolized industry, strikes were further proof of unreliability. Though the immediate impact of labor strife on subsequent consumption is open to dispute, the statistics tell a chilling tale. Production dropped from 84 million tons in 1926 to 69 million in 1930. The number of collieries operating fell from 185 in 1923 to 163 in 1929. While much of the nation enjoyed the prosperity of the Roaring Twenties, the anthracite region began its long decline.[3]

The labor troubles of the 1920s had their origin in the structural crisis that beset the industry after World War I. Throughout the war prices had remained high. But when the depression of 1920–1921 broke upon the country, production fell dramatically. In 1922 it was down some 40 percent from the previous year. At the same time other fuels began to make inroads in hard coal markets. Operators seeking to maintain profit levels moved immediately to cut costs, blaming labor for high prices. When contract negotiations opened in March 1922, the operators demanded a 21½ percent wage reduction. Their claim was that the low profits of the coal companies justified it. What they did not reveal was that the mining companies operated with low profits because the money was made on freight charges. The anthracite railroads bought coal from their own mining subsidiaries at low prices and carried it at high cost. The *New York World* of May 26, 1922, hit close to the truth when it observed that "the price of anthracite is certainly high, but labor is only one item in the cost to the purchaser. . . . The profits in mining, handling, transportation and retailing hard coal have been carefully obscured."[4]

In demanding wage cuts the anthracite operators merely followed the lead of others. The economic depression and shifts to fuel-efficient technology by the railroads and the iron and steel industry resulted in a sharp decline in bituminous production. Soft coal operators took advantage of the situation by eliminating marginal operations and insisting on wage adjustments and, finally, by moving strongly against the UMW. The soft coal fields were only partially unionized, and especially in southern states such as West Virginia and Kentucky, operators increasingly used nonunion labor. The UMW simply did not have the power to respond effectively, and membership began to drop. Though almost all anthracite workers were union members, the operators sensed that the growing weakness of the UMW elsewhere made it vulnerable in the hard coal fields. So in addition to the wage cuts, they challenged collective bargaining itself; the very thing that the union had battled and spilled blood for in the Great Strike of 1902. The operators asked for a four-year contract with annual negotiations on wages. If a joint labor-management committee could not agree on wages each year, the issue would automatically go to arbitration. The operators knew full well that the UMW would never agree on arbitration as a substitute for collective bargaining. A 1919 decision rendered during the Wilson administration had been badly received by the mine workers and resulted in a rash of wildcat strikes. It was unlikely that favorable arbitration decisions could be expected from a conservative, probusiness Republican administration.

Finally, the operators refused a request of the UMW leadership for a union dues checkoff plan. Dues checkoff from the organized anthracite fields was badly needed by the union because of declining membership elsewhere. It would cost the operators nothing and might even work to their benefit, for union dues would be sent directly to the national, thereby undercutting the independence of the anthracite locals, whose members were generally more militant than the leaders of the national. By refusing cooperation with the union on such a minor issue the operators displayed an astounding lack of vision. The union was the dreaded enemy; it had to be eliminated or radically weakened. But these operators, deep into a battle for survival with other fuel-producing industries, failed to understand that yet another labor war would damage them as greatly as the union. In such a conflict there could be no winner.[5]

The UMW countered by demanding a 20 percent wage increase, a moderate increase, its leaders claimed, for labor costs accounted for only a small part of the retail price of coal. Even if the union accepted the operators' wage cut, consumers would save only twenty-seven and one-half cents per ton, or about 2 percent of the retail price in New York City. To the men in the UMW, the real problem was profiteering by the industry. From the time the coal left the breaker until it reached the consumer, costs were added through excessive freight charges, royalties to coal land owners, and disguised handling transactions by sales companies. Wages could be increased and retail prices cut dramatically if exorbitant profit levels were reduced. On this issue, the union was absolutely adamant. The miners' welfare would not be sacrificed to uphold the unwarranted gains of the anthracite monopoly, its vice-president, Philip Murray, declared.[6] The UMW demanded a full-scale investigation of production and labor costs by the Federal Trade Commission and the Interstate Commerce Commission, refusing even to discuss arbitration until the operators agreed to such an inquiry.

With both sides standing firm on their positions the inevitable strike occurred. On April 1, 1922, the anthracite miners walked out, joining bituminous workers in the first nationwide coal strike in history. American Federation of Labor President Samuel Gompers, who threw the full support of organized labor behind the 600,000 mine workers, claimed that the struggle concerned justice for the many as opposed to profit for the few. "The men who go down in the earth to dig the coal that fires the furnaces of the nation and warms its homes shall not be crucified on the altar of greed! The whole strength of our great humanitarian movement is mobilized against that brutal project."[7]

When the mines fell idle an unusual quiet descended on the region. In this strike, unlike all previous ones, there was no violence. The Pennsylvania State Miners' Certificate Law of 1897, which required the mining of anthracite only by experienced, licensed miners, effectively ruled out the use of strikebreakers by the operators. Since the 40,000 to 50,000 licensed miners stood strongly behind their union, the other 100,000 mine workers who labored under their supervision could not work. Not that they would have tried. The strike demonstrated the absolute unity of all anthracite workers in their struggle for a higher standard of living.[8] The one disturbance that occurred at a colliery near Wilkes-Barre over maintenance workers was quickly resolved. The peace in the organized anthracite region contrasted sharply with the violence in the largely unorganized bituminous fields during the strike.

The main battle was fought out elsewhere. As coal supplies dwindled during the spring and early summer the public clamored for an agreement. Stories circulated about rich and poor people alike standing for hours in lines with bags and bushels waiting to buy coal at twenty dollars per ton. Progressive Republican senators such as William Borah of Idaho warned the industry to regulate itself or face the possibility of public ownership. Even conservative newspapers such as the *Washington Post* took up the call for federal intervention. More ominous for the industry was the suggestion by public officials that consumers turn to alternate fuels. New York Governor Nathan Miller proposed that "oil, gas and electricity should be substituted for anthracite whenever possible and people should equip themselves with the facilities to use them."[9] As pressure mounted, President Harding finally moved to bring the union and operators together. Harding was no Theodore Roosevelt. Yet while he refused to apply more than "moral" pressure for a settlement, his action opened the way for a compromise agreement eventually worked out by Senators Reed and Pepper of Pennsylvania. The 163-day anthracite strike ended on September 2.

UMW President John L. Lewis claimed an enormous victory for the mine workers. In reality, everyone had lost. Wages were not reduced, but neither were they increased. The old contract was continued, and the arbitration issue was temporarily suspended along with the dues checkoff. The mine workers could be thankful for work during the coming winter, but hard coal consumers faced the prospect of a severe fuel shortage because no coal had been mined for five and a half months. The shift to other fuels accelerated, now with the encouragement of a federal fuel distributor set up to deal with the crisis. Meanwhile the problems of high industry profits and high coal prices remained. The only positive development was the establishment of a U.S. Coal Commission charged with investigating the industry. But the commission's recommendations for disclosure of operators' financial reports and licensing of interstate coal carriers, when finally made more than a year later, were ignored by Congress.[10] In the end the operators, who thought they could continue to gouge consumers with impunity, believed that they had lost nothing. The mine workers, desperately clinging to wage levels in a threatened industry, believed that they had won everything. A disgusted public, not knowing what to believe, simply turned its back on anthracite.

Neither the anthracite operators nor the leadership of the UMW faced up to the problems threatening the industry. Though there were men in the companies and the union who correctly read the ominous signs concerning the future of coal, their voices were silent. In 1923, when the patchwork contract of the previous year again came up for negotiations, both sides put forward the same old demands. A replay of the costly 1922 strike was narrowly averted only by the last-minute intervention of President Coolidge, Governor Pinchot of Pennsylvania, and the U.S. Coal Commission. It was not a sense of disinterested concern that moved the politicians to seek a settlement. They feared the impact of another strike on the approaching November elections. The miners won a 10 percent wage increase, but nothing else was settled. Two more years of the uneasy status quo were bought.

By 1925 the situation had changed for the worse. But it did not change the policy of the coal companies. Other fuels began to cut deeply into anthracite markets. The operators finally recognized that they had to cut prices in order to meet the competition. In their view the only way to do it was to reduce labor costs, which, they said, comprised 70 percent of the cost of producing a ton of coal. The operators wanted either a wage reduction or binding arbitration that could be used to lower wages later. They were prepared to break the union if necessary in order to restore the competitive position of the industry.

The UMW by now faced a severe problem of its own. The 1922 strike had nearly bankrupted the union. In the economically prostrate bituminous fields union membership declined precipitously. Nonunion soft coal was supplying much of the nation's needs. Soft coal operators violated contracts with impunity, secure in the general antilabor atmosphere of the mid-1920s. President Lewis, charged with mismanagement of the 1922 strike by union dissidents, spent much of his time putting down rebellions in bituminous districts and trying to hold the UMW together. By comparison with its situation three years earlier, the union was in a badly weakened position. Yet the 155,000 organized anthracite workers formed the one stable element in the UMW. The region was the union's only remaining stronghold outside Illinois. The votes of anthracite delegates meant the difference between victory and defeat for Lewis at union conventions. He simply could not ignore the hard coal miners' interests. Though he did not want a strike and was willing to extend the existing contract, he had to fight when challenged so directly by the operators. So when contract negotiations broke down in the summer of 1925, the nation was treated to the spectacle of a battle between two threatened and wounded giants— the operators and the UMW—who believed that their very survival was at stake.[11]

On September 1, 1925, the longest strike in the history of anthracite began. For 170 bitter days, through the fall and into the winter, both sides held unwaveringly to their original demands, until finally an aroused public demanded efforts to end the impasse.[12] While President Coolidge vacillated between complete inaction and threats of federal intervention, Governor Pinchot stepped in and offered a compromise. It included a five-year contract based on existing wages, a voluntary checkoff, and voluntary arbitration that could raise but not lower wages. The union immediately accepted the proposal, but the operators rejected it. They flatly refused to sign a contract that had no provision for reducing labor costs.[13]

The solidly formed army of anthracite workers, veterans of many such campaigns, resolved to fight to the finish. Lewis, who knew that he had the complete loyalty of the miners, bluntly told the operators that they could not break the strike. "The men may cuss their leaders . . . and the women become sorer than they are now, but there is nothing to indicate revolt or break," a federal informant reported.[14] This determination held in the face of considerable suffering. By February 1926 the region's principal industry had been shut down for more than five months. Scores of small businesses were closed and thousands of nonmining employees in other businesses and industries that depended upon the mine workers were out of work. As in previous strikes, many people left the region. For those who stayed, there were soup kitchens and relief provided by religious and charitable organizations. Appeals for help went out nationwide. American Federation of Labor President William Green implored the labor movement to aid the miners and their families: "Men, women and children in the anthracite field are hungry. The intense cold of mid-winter has added to their sad plight and intensified their suffering. Hungry children are calling upon us for help. Come to their rescue."[15]

Suddenly, in mid-February, a breakthrough occurred. On February 12 Lewis unexpectedly signed a pact with the operators. Exercising his flair for the dramatic, Lewis signaled the end of the strike by telegraphing a Tamaqua miner who wanted to marry on the day it ended: "Get married today!" The UMW president then called reporters to his room at Philadelphia's Bellevue-Stratford Hotel and showed them a huge basket of roses sent by the Anthracite Operators' Negotiating Committee and a copy of Carl Sandburg's *Life of Lincoln*, inscribed to "The Lincoln of Labor." It was Lewis's forty-sixth birthday, and with great relief he exclaimed, "Some birthday!"[16]

In the region, few concerned themselves with the terms of the contract. More important, the mines were working again. The regional press announced a new era of work, peace, and the return to prosperity. Lewis was hailed as a "savior" and great "labor statesman." The attitude of many of the mine workers was summed up by Anthony Swazik, president of UMW Local 898 of Nanticoke: "The men will stand back of President Lewis to the end. We have won a great victory."[17] At the miners' ratifying convention the contract passed with little debate. Amid the euphoria and self-congratulation the question of what had been gained and what had been lost did not come up.

John L. Lewis, Alvin Markle, and W. W. Inglis, head of the operators' committee, in Philadelphia at the announcement of the settlement of the coal strike of 1926.   Courtesy of the Library of Congress.

Again, neither side had "won," though the contract language was carefully constructed so that both the union and the operators could claim "victory." The existing contract with the same wage structure was extended for five years. A clause on reopening negotiations on wages at the request of either party was inserted, but it was virtually meaningless because it called for arbitration only by mutual consent. Since the UMW was firmly against arbitration, there was little chance it would be invoked. The checkoff issue was circumvented by a phrase about "reciprocal cooperation," which Lewis publicly claimed allowed for the checkoff but which he privately conceded meant nothing. What the longest strike in anthracite history gave the mine workers was the promise of five years of work at fixed wages. What it did to the industry was damage it even further. Markets lost during the strike were never recovered. In the four years after 1926, production declined by 25 percent. Anthracite became, in the words of the *Nation*, "a critically sick industry." [18]

John L. Lewis emerged from the conflict with his reputation intact among the anthracite workers. His method of reaching the settlement, however, foretold trouble between the UMW leadership and union members in the hard years ahead. The open hostility between Lewis and some of the operators had contributed to the prolongation of the strike. Progress in negotiations only became possible when Richard F. Grant, president of the Lehigh Coal Company, took the initiative to reach a private agreement with Lewis. Grant, who held the confidence of the operators, gained Lewis's trust in a series of private meetings. Both men agreed on a general approach to labor-management relations. Negotiations would occur in private, and divisive issues would not be discussed. Since it was in the interest of both sides to keep the mines working, and the circumstances of the industry prevented either side from "winning," contracts would be worked out that essentially continued the status quo. The union and the operators would cooperate toward that end. It was a way out of a difficult situation and made sense in the context of the strike. What it did, however, was establish a system of negotiating that excluded active participation in decision making by the rank-and-file members. [19]

That Lewis chose to circumvent normal procedures to strike a private deal with Grant was not surprising. The UMW president needed a settlement in anthracite, and he was certain that he could persuade the membership to go along. After a long and damaging strike, the men wanted most of all to return to work. As long as they believed that they did not lose anything they would stand behind him—or so Lewis thought. His principal concern was keeping the anthracite workers in the union and behind him. With membership declining in the overdeveloped bituminous fields, and the union under attack by the soft coal operators, Lewis had to preserve his strength in the region. But he did not push for more than he did in 1926 because he believed that the anthracite industry and the UMW needed to reach a truce. The industry had to be stabilized. This was not the time for militancy or aggressive action. A deeply practical man, schooled in the pragmatic ways of his mentor Samuel Gompers and something of an old-fashioned patriot, Lewis held to the view that American capitalism offered to workers more opportunities for advancement than any other economic system in the world. He merely sought to make the free enterprise system more orderly and humanly equitable and to convince big business that everyone gained by fair wages, improved working conditions, and cooperation between capital and labor. Lewis also recognized that if the coal industry was to become more efficient it would have to trim its work force. He accepted this idea as the "natural" working of economic laws. For a union leader, his was a dangerous position to hold. Lewis squared this view with his fight to maintain existing wage levels by arguing that reductions in pay merely allowed marginal and inefficient operators to hang on longer. As for the unemployed miners, they would find work in other sectors of a healthy and expanding capitalist economy.[20]

Lewis's dealings with Grant also revealed an important side of him. Starting in 1908 as a young district organizer in the Illinois fields, he had moved up rapidly through the faction-ridden bureaucracy of the UMW by making himself the available tool of more powerful leaders. Along the way he mastered the intricacies of political infighting at a time when fraudulent elections, corruption, intimidation, and violence were commonplace in the union. In his own rise to the top he was widely accused of opportunism, betrayal, questionable financial dealings with coal operators, even blackmail. But he was known as well as a man who got things done. Once he headed the union, Lewis richly enjoyed the power and privileges of his position as one of the nation's top labor leaders. He was on a first-name basis with higher-ups in both political parties and at ease in the company of well-heeled financiers such as the Harrimans of New York. Within the UMW he consolidated his hold by centralizing the organization's structure, disarming opposition by redbaiting, and by skillful use of the press, patronage, and other payoffs. By the mid-1920s, at the high point of his power and prestige, he was the most formidable labor leader in the country, with a powerful mind and a large-chested body to match it and a booming baritone voice that some said could raise the dead. At the bargaining table he could be an absolute terror; on issues he truly cared about he could not be budged. But he also saw himself as a realist. And so did Richard F. Grant of the Lehigh Company. Here was a man John L. Lewis felt he could deal with, but preferably in secret. For despite his notorious public theatrics, Lewis had always worked best behind the scenes.[21]

Until his final confirmation as president by a UMW convention in 1921 Lewis had never faced the rank and file in an election. Unlike John Mitchell, he had no close following among the membership. He was a machine-made labor politician who remained coolly distant not only from the workers but also from other union officials as well. Many sensed that he had no real understanding or feeling for the day-to-day problems of the miners even though he had come from mining country. Though his considerable talents enabled him to win and hold the leadership of the mine workers, they did not extend to finding a solution to the crisis that afflicted the miners in the late 1920s. Nor did his beliefs about cooperation between capital and labor do much good when the coal industry entered its long depression in the late 1920s. Many anthracite members found both him and their union barren of ideas, actual obstacles to dealing creatively with the problems they now faced.

The first trouble occurred in 1927. Sprawling District 1, encompassing the Wyoming-Lackawanna field and half of all anthracite workers, had always been difficult to govern. Its size and the fact that there were three large, separate mining centers around Wilkes-Barre, Pittston, and Scranton meant that there were always contending groups seeking influence and control of the district leadership. At the time the president of District 1 was Rinaldo Capellini, a former union insurgent and foe of Lewis who had made peace with the international president only after he, Capellini, had captured power. But Capellini's base was never secure. Many of the older, conservative miners resented the arbitrary methods of the fiery district president, and in 1927 a district convention blocked his bid to extend his term of office from two to four years. There were charges that Capellini had accepted payoffs from the operators and that he had ignored the welfare of the workers. These were a normal part of the political fighting between union "ins" and "outs" and in themselves were not very serious, but in the context of events during the following year they took on an ominous meaning.[22]

In January 1928 the 1,600 members of Pittston Local 1703 suddenly ousted their officers in an extraordinary meeting. The move was led by 400 miners laid off the previous month by the Pennsylvania Coal Company. The insurgents elected new leaders who immediately called a strike that completely shut down all of Pennsylvania Coal's operations. The men were protesting not only the layoffs but the contract system used by the company. Contract mining was particularly loathsome to the predominantly Italian Pittston miners because it reminded them of the exploitative "padrone" system under which they had worked at the turn of the century. Under the contract system the operators leased their mines to independent contractors who were paid by the companies according to the tonnage delivered. The contractors naturally drove the miners relentlessly to produce as much coal as possible while cutting corners on equipment costs and safety procedures. They also had a reputation for cheating on wages and were quick to fire workers who did not produce at the rate they expected. The miners had always opposed the contract system, and the union fought against it, but it had never been completely eliminated. It tended to disappear when times were good, but as the industry slid into depression the companies introduced it again in order to avoid investing additional capital.[23]

The Pittston miners were asking their district and international leaders to do something about their deteriorating economic situation. But Lewis and Capellini refused to recognize either the new local officers or the strike and ordered the men to return to work. When the strikers stayed away, violence broke out. Three of the top insurgents were murdered; in retaliation one of Capellini's close associates was gunned down. Pittston erupted in a wave of dynamitings and rioting. The town's desperate mayor appealed to Lewis to restore calm, but the president refused to intervene, claiming that the problem was caused by "the agents of the Communist party, who are now in Luzerne seeking to cause further confusion and disorder."[24]

Capellini became the victim of Lewis's indifference. The district president, ironically, had first made his reputation fighting against contract mining and for workers' rights. Now, however, he had no idea what to do. He became the target of both his old foes in the district and the many miners fed up with the union's inability or unwillingness to deal with the economic problem. As the strike continued, dissatisfaction spread. There was a call for a special convention to oust Capellini, and in June 1928 a majority of the 130 locals in the district sent representatives to do the job. Under the UMW constitution their action was legitimate, but Lewis refused to recognize either the convention or the new officers whom the delegates elected. Capellini naturally sided with Lewis. Assuming that he had Lewis's support, he expelled the insurgents from the union. But Lewis suddenly shifted direction. With the district in disarray and the miners' anger beginning to focus on Lewis for keeping the unpopular Capellini in office, the president decided on a compromise solution. He pressured Capellini to resign and installed in his place John Boylan, a popular, moderate district executive board member. The smooth and ambitious Boylan, who was Lewis's secret informant during the affair, managed to gain the recognition and confidence of the rebellious locals by the end of summer. He preached the necessity of unity and harmony during hard times while skillfully isolating the insurgent leaders politically. Like his predecessor in office, however, he had little to say to the growing numbers of unemployed miners.[25]

As collieries reverted to part-time operations or shut down completely, the UMW experienced difficulties in the other two anthracite districts. In hard-hit District 9, where the Shamokin American Legion opened soup kitchens for hungry children in May 1929, and miners protested conditions with wildcat strikes, District President James McAndrew offered his resignation because he could not deal with the situation. In writing to Lewis about "this unprecedented era of broken time," McAndrew stated that "there has been more trouble in our District for the past year than any year that I can recall."[26] In 1928 the District 7 leadership asked its members for contributions to support the unemployed. With so many men out of work, union membership fell to its lowest level since 1912. In these districts the clamor for the union to do something increased. Major trouble was avoided only because the officers at least gave the impression that they were listening to the rank and file. In mid-1928 the District 9 executive board passed a resolution demanded by its members and sent it on to the Board of Conciliation with a request for approval. Though the board refused to approve it, the resolution brought into the open the issue that became the major objective of the anthracite miners during the following decade: work equalization.[27]

The idea came from the miners themselves, not from their union leaders. It was their unique response to the depression that had struck the region several years before it hit the rest of the nation. Anthracite people wanted the available jobs to be shared. Their request grew out of the communal tradition of the region. When family and community proved inadequate to meet the needs of the hard-pressed people, it was natural that they should turn to the UMW in their search for economic security. For decades they had given their unstinting loyalty to the union; now, in desperate times, they expected it to respond to their needs.

Essentially, work equalization called for the distribution of mining and processing of coal among the various collieries of a company rather than in the few where the coal was close to the surface and cheaper to dig. In this way all collieries would work at least part time and would provide some employment for the largest number of men. It was a radical idea at the time because it challenged management's right to control production and to make decisions based upon profit considerations alone. It also forced a union accustomed to dealing with limited issues such as wages and working conditions into a new and unprecedented role.[28]

As expected, the operators opposed work equalization, insisting that they had the right to mine coal where labor and production costs were cheapest. The operators flatly rejected District 9's resolution; industry spokesmen argued forcefully against it. As for Lewis, he essentially ignored the question. It belonged to a group of "explosive" issues that he and Grant had agreed to avoid. The fact was that the UMW had no experience in the uncharted area of a miner's right to work and support his family. Equalization also went against Lewis's own orthodox economic views, which were actually closer to those of the operators than to those of the miners. Yet work equalization could not be ignored. As the depression struck with full fury, an angry and desperate people swept aside the objections of both operators and union leadership.

By 1930 regular work in the mines was becoming rare in many parts of the region. In some of the smaller coal towns as many as three of every four men were either unemployed or underemployed. The number of man days of available work fell more than 25 percent from the mid-1920s. For men who continued to work, conditions worsened. Contract mining continued to spread, and operators pushed fewer men to produce more. Since the principle of the "last hired, first fired" was not yet in effect, older, experienced miners with higher wages—and often with larger families—were the first to be laid off. With work scarce, payoffs to mine foremen and collusion between union officers and mine officials increased. John Sarnoski of Glen Lyon explained:

> There used to be a lot of payoffs to foremen for jobs. Some men wanted to get a decent chamber [with easily accessible coal] on a good gangway. They would meet foremen in beer gardens on payday and pay them, buy them drinks. If you got a better place in the mines you could make more money. But you couldn't do nothing about it. If a boss didn't like you you could lose your job. And the union leaders didn't fight it because they were friendly with the company. Union leaders and local officials would be given the best jobs in them days. If you a miner, president of a local, and have two laborers, you could put your bedroom slippers on in the morning and just go and see how your laborers work. And you just give them orders what they gonna do and you came home. And you would get more pay than two miners did.[29]

Against such practices the mine workers were virtually helpless. Each local had its grievance committee, but its members, eager to hold on to their jobs, often did nothing to upset the company. Romaine Stewart, a Wanamie miner, recalled, "In those days the president of the local union and the men on the grievance committee had the best jobs in the colliery. You would see them in the morning always talking with the mine foremen in the offices. If you wanted to get one of those committeemen on your side, all you had to do 'was sugar him up.'"[30] But the groups of desperate men hanging around mine offices waiting for a chance to work was enough to remind most working miners where they stood. "So when there was something that the boss would tell you to do in the mines, and you told him you wasn't going to do it," one miner explained, "well, then, he said, if you don't want to do it there's fifteen guys outside waiting for your job. This was their song all the time."[31]

Dissatisfaction mounted among the rank and file as employment declined, working conditions deteriorated, and union officers continued to look after themselves. At the anthracite tri-district convention in Hazleton in May 1930 angry delegates directly challenged Lewis, demanding that work equalization, contract mining, seniority rights, and job exploitation be considered in the upcoming contract negotiations. Only the adroit maneuvering of Lewis and the lack of organization among the dissenters prevented a major rupture. Lewis retained control because he prear-

Lansford during the Great Depression.   Courtesy of the Library of Congress.

ranged the convention's agenda and stacked the steering committee, which decided
what would be negotiated in the contract talks. With the nation in the midst of the
worst depression in its history, UMW membership down to 150,000, and collieries
closing almost daily, Lewis believed that he was in no position to deal with the membership's demands. He did not think that work equalization could be achieved
through collective bargaining or even that it could be successfully implemented.
Like many other American labor leaders in the early 1930s, Lewis was paralyzed by
the crisis afflicting the country. Against all the evidence that times had changed and
that imaginative new initiatives were required to save the working man, Lewis continued to cling to traditional workplace issues. Nor did his personal philosophy
change. He held to the belief that capitalism would correct itself and that prosperity,
in the words of his friend President Herbert Hoover, "was just around the corner."[32]

The widening gap between Lewis and the members was demonstrated by the 1930 contract. Following the 1926 precedent, Lewis privately negotiated the main points of the contract in advance with Grant. Even before the tri-district convention met, the UMW president knew what he would take to the formal contract talks that followed. Both Lewis and the operators got what they wanted, while the demands voiced by the delegates on the convention floor were ignored. The existing contract was simply extended for another six years. The operators agreed to a partial check-off of one dollar per pay period, which Lewis desperately needed to replenish the union's depleted treasury. Another joint committee of operators and miners' representatives was established to investigate problems arising from the contract. In return for the operators' agreement not to cut wages and in deference to their desire for "efficiency and the production of an improved car of coal," Lewis agreed to oppose wildcat strikes and shutdowns that violated the contract and in addition took strong action to reduce the powers of locals to act unilaterally. At a time when the membership most needed greater independence and autonomy in meeting diverse local situations, Lewis removed it.[33]

The regional press reported a "euphoric" public in the wake of the successful conclusion of the contract negotiations; the mine workers, however, were less than pleased. Despite Lewis's orders to union officials to instruct delegates to vote for the contract at the ratifying convention, and his ruling at the convention that the contract could only be discussed in its entirety, strong objections were voiced from the floor. "There isn't one demand, there isn't one resolution in the contract," Delegate Thomas Maloney of Wilkes-Barre rose to say, "that was formulated in the Tri-District Convention in Hazleton." Another delegate called Lewis on his claim that the contract represented a victory for the mine workers. "Where is the victory—where is it? Where are any of the demands that you asked for at the Tri-District Convention in Hazleton brought back? Not a one!" But Pat Shovelin best expressed the delegates' mood in his response to Thomas Kennedy's claim that the contract would bring peace and prosperity.

> I believe it was Mr. Kennedy who said in this place [in 1926], "You are going to have five years of substantial prosperity." Did we have it? Are we going to judge him as a prophet? I have lost my faith in him as an oracle of the mine workers any longer.[34]

Most of the opposition centered on the section of the contract that reduced the powers of local grievance committees and called for an "improved car of coal." The miners feared that the operators would use the clause to increase work for less pay while at the same time limiting their abilities to resist unjust demands. The miners also opposed the mandatory dues checkoff, which they felt would diminish the power of the locals. Such fears were eventually justified, as Nanticoke miner George Treski explained:

> Before, you had to go to the union hall to pay your dues and then you would see the other members. If there were any problems you would thrash it out right there. After the checkoff system the union got the money but the people didn't go to the meetings and the union was doing whatever they wanted with the bosses. . . . Before, if you had a grievance you would holler at the union officials. After the checkoff you hardly saw them.[35]

Another point of contention was that the operators were not compelled to sign the contract jointly. With a huge pool of unemployed and surplus labor already available in the region, the possibility arose that individual companies might be tempted to employ nonunion mine workers if they felt that they could not abide by the terms of the contract.

After three days of furious debate, Lewis finally brought to bear his prestige as international president and all of his considerable oratorical skills to effect a resolution. With tears filling his eyes and his voice alternately thundering and choking with emotion, Lewis pleaded for ratification. "My God, men," he exclaimed, "I don't mind fighting your adversaries, and your opponents and your enemies, but I do shrink from being placed in a position where, after fighting them to exhaustion, I have to come back here and you force me to fight you."[36] He went on to say that the union negotiators had bargained honorably, and that the contract was the best that could be secured under the circumstances. He gave a virtuoso performance—though not a completely candid one—and in the end the delegates ratified the contract. There was really nothing else they could do.

Lewis urgently hoped that the pressing issues such as work equalization would simply disappear as prosperity returned to the nation and the anthracite region.[37] In the meantime, as a stopgap measure, he advocated federal and state relief to alleviate suffering and assessed fifty cents to a dollar from mine workers' paychecks to help the unemployed. Though the call for governmental aid was a departure from the UMW's hands-off position of the 1920s, it was no solution for men who wanted work, not charity. Nor was the assessment particularly agreeable to men working two or three days a week. One miner with five children complained that he could not afford to contribute one dollar from a seven-dollar paycheck. A Plymouth miner, Chester Brozena, went right to the main issue: "We were assessed three dollars a month for a long period of time to help soft coal because they were down on their knees, and when we tried to get some help . . . , we were turned down by John L. Lewis."[38]

The delegates to the ratifying convention accepted the 1930 contract with resignation, but the opposition was not stilled. As more and more men were laid off, it proved unfeasible to honor the contract. Companies and locals began to make their own arrangements. Down-and-out miners willingly accepted cuts in pay in order to obtain work. Some companies even agreed to limited equalization schemes. In Glen Lyon the union local placed a limit on production at the Susquehanna Coal Company. "What we decided," Stanley Salva, president of the union local, said later, "was you couldn't load more than was required for a normal day's pay. In most of the places it was five cars a day. In some gangways it was four. . . . If you were over the limit you would pay a fine. We wanted everyone to have an equal load and pay."[39] Salva admitted that the bosses could be bribed and often played favorites in work assignments; but, he added, the system of limiting production succeeded because of the vigilance of the men. Such practices, in violation of the contract, came to the attention of district officers and Lewis, but the UMW wisely avoided a confrontation. In public the UMW insisted on the sanctity of the contract; privately it usually ignored what was happening.

The UMW's continuing refusal to fight for work equalization finally drove the impatient miners into open rebellion. The most serious trouble occurred in the Wyoming Valley area of District 1. In January 1931, only months after W. W. Inglis, the Glen Alden Company's president, had called upon Lewis to honor the 1930 contract by intervening to quell a wildcat strike, the company announced the closing of nine collieries. The move shocked the mine workers and the community, who believed that Glen Alden's action violated the spirit of cooperation between the operators and the union. When District President Boylan could not persuade Lewis to do anything, the Glen Alden General Grievance Committee took matters into its own hands. Led by Thomas Maloney, the committee called a strike against all of the company's operations. It demanded reopening, work equalization, and an end to wage reductions and other contract violations. When Inglis refused to consider the demands, 20,000 men walked out on March 19. Lewis promptly supported Inglis, calling the stoppage "illegal and unwarranted" and charging that the strikers brought "dishonor to the union."[40]

The strike ended after three weeks when Inglis agreed to meet with representatives of the workers. But nothing came of the talks. Instead of supporting the strikers, the District 1 leadership, with the agreement of Lewis, attempted to try Maloney and another strike leader for insubordination. This move surprised even Inglis, who was well aware of Maloney's popularity. The matter was eventually dropped, but the entire incident sent a clear signal to the mine workers. Lewis's alliance with the operators effectively prevented the union from defending its members' interests. The men of anthracite now had two foes to fight—the companies and their own union. Lewis's apparent indifference to the mine workers' plight set in motion a chain of events that nearly wrecked the UMW in the anthracite fields. His further efforts to drive the insurgent leaders from the union rather than attempt reconciliation contributed mightily to the violence and bloodshed that swept the Wyoming Valley in the following years.[41]

Thomas Maloney was an unlikely rebel. For twenty years he was a loyal member of the UMW who served in various union offices, including as president of a local. He also was a justice of the peace in Wilkes-Barre. A moderate, fair-minded man, he detested violence to the same degree that he respected the law. He was the perfect example of the outraged citizen who, in the face of injustice, finally says "enough is enough" and whose courage and candor draws others to his cause. In the wake of the Glen Alden strike, Maloney challenged Boylan for the presidency of District 1. When the challenge failed, amid charges of fraud and ballot tampering, Maloney took his fight to the district convention in July. Despite overwhelming support among the Wyoming Valley mine workers, his delegates were challenged and disqualified on technicalities. The proceedings degenerated into a riot that was quelled by state police using tear gas. Maloney's plea to the delegates that Boylan's electoral victory be overturned was ignored.[42]

But the failure did not stop Maloney or his supporters. The Glen Alden mine workers hit the company with wildcat strikes, withheld dues from the UMW, and threatened to form an independent union. Maloney called for a special district convention to deal with the issues of work equalization, contract mining, reopening, and wage cuts. When the UMW leadership responded by branding the dissidents' actions illegal, Maloney called a general strike in District 1 on March 12, 1932. It was supported by forty-four locals.[43]

The UMW's hard line inflamed emotions and deeply split the membership. Many miners were reluctant to break with the union. Others feared the loss of scarce jobs and company reprisals. Under the circumstances, violence was inevitable. Clashes broke out almost daily at collieries between miners attempting to work and strikers and the unemployed. Shootings and dynamitings of homes and automobiles were widely reported. The strike itself was not completely successful. The operators refused to give way as long as some collieries continued working. The lack of money and organization also hampered the strikers. With the operators standing firm, with the national union opposed to the strike, and with the state authorities threatening massive police intervention, Maloney called a halt on March 31. He blamed the lack of solidarity among the mine workers for the failure and bitterly announced that he would never lead another strike. Glen Alden and the UMW moved to assure exactly that. Maloney and other strikers were locked out of their jobs, and the union suspended Maloney for fifteen years.[44]

The failure in District 1 did not end the agitation for equalization elsewhere. In March 1932 delegates from forty-two locals representing 5,000 members in the Shamokin–Mahanoy City area overrode their district officers' objections and struck the Pennsylvania Iron and Coal Company. In August 1933 more than 15,000 men in the Panther Valley, backed by an equalization committee comprised of miners and local civic and business leaders, struck the Lehigh Coal and Navigation Company. The strikes, though unsuccessful, forced the Roosevelt administration's National Recovery Administration (NRA) to hold hearings in 1933 to establish a code for the anthracite industry. Insurgent miners' groups, regional business and civic leaders, and local equalization committees all voiced their demands in Washington for wider work distribution. Secretary of Labor Frances Perkins, a Roosevelt appointee, recommended it. The UMW reluctantly went along. In 1932 Lewis had abandoned the Republican party and had jumped on the Roosevelt bandwagon. After the election victory Roosevelt made Lewis a major power in determining the administration's labor policy by naming him to the new National Labor Board and the NRA. Lewis hoped that his new-found prestige as an associate of Roosevelt would eventually still the demands for equalization; in the meantime, he bowed to the pressure and gave equalization his lukewarm support. The Roosevelt administration's quest for a consensus failed, however, as operators adamantly opposed equalization. Inasmuch as no NRA code for anthracite was forthcoming, calls for an independent union were again heard in the region.[45]

In a sudden turnabout, Maloney reappeared in the summer of 1933 at the head of a grass-roots opposition movement. He was joined by none other than Rinaldo Capellini. These two unlikely allies held a series of mass rallies and meetings in District 1, loudly denouncing Lewis and the UMW leadership for corruption, dishonesty, and collusion with the operators. On August 7 delegates from fifty-five locals, representing 45 percent of all the locals in District 1, jammed into Regel Hall in Scranton and backed the call for a new union. The United Anthracite Miners of Pennsylvania (UAMP) came into existence with Maloney as president and Capellini as state chairman.[46]

Many of the delegates to the Scranton convention supported the new union for one reason only. "It was just a matter of everybody had enough of John L. Lewis at that time," as one delegate put it later.[47] Even local officers of the UMW joined the new union in disgust. Anthony Piscotty from Plymouth explained:

> They [the UMW] weren't doing nothing for us. They're taking our money, they're taking our checkoff out of our pay, and they weren't doing anything for us.[48]

Others joined the UAMP because of collusion between UMW officers and the companies. Leonard Wydotis, a Wanamie miner, charged, "The company and the union leaders went hand in hand. So if you didn't support them [the UMW] you wouldn't have no jobs. Hell, the boss would go around and tell you who to vote for when we elected union officers."[49]

Starting from a strong base of support among the miners of the region's two largest companies, the Glen Alden and Lehigh Valley Coal, Maloney launched a drive for recognition. He stressed the need to avoid confrontations and promised not to resort to strikes if the companies and the government recognized the UAMP as a legitimate union. But Maloney's hopes were dashed almost immediately. The companies were too comfortable with the conservative UMW and Lewis. They branded Maloney and other insurgent leaders as troublemakers and radicals. The Roosevelt administration, although professing its willingness to listen to the insurgents, actually worked against the UAMP from the outset. With Lewis an important member of Roosevelt's national recovery program and a vital part of the administration's strategy to court and control labor, Washington was not about to support a dual union that shattered labor unity. Lewis, of course, worked constantly behind the scenes to make sure that it did not.[50]

The followers of the UAMP, however, were desperate men. They believed that they had run out of alternatives. They counted on widespread dissatisfaction with Lewis and the district leadership to rally the mine workers and eventually the public to their cause, hoping that the groundswell of support would force government officials to deal fairly with them. As events showed, Maloney and the UAMP's leaders miscalculated badly, but the operators, UMW, and federal government contributed to the tragedy by their intransigence and deception.

Despite its desire to avoid a confrontation with the operators, the UAMP was soon forced into one when some of the larger companies began to fire insurgent supporters. Maloney felt that he had no choice but to call retaliatory strikes. By the fall of 1933 three of the largest companies in the district, including Glen Alden, had been hit. Maloney insisted on peaceful picketing, but he lost control of the situation when brawls broke out between strikers, police, and miners attempting to work. Pitched battles occurred at collieries throughout the Wyoming Valley. The violence

John L. Lewis and Thomas Kennedy of the United Mine Workers
with Father John J. Curran around a photograph of Theodore Roosevelt.
Courtesy of the Wyoming Historical and Geological Society, Wilkes-Barre, Pa.

soon spilled over to the mining towns. Beatings, shootings, bombings, and burnings became commonplace. A tenuous truce was called only after John J. Curran, a Wilkes-Barre priest and a long-time supporter of miners' causes, persuaded Maloney to suspend the strikes and seek a solution through the federal government. Curran argued that the UAMP would at least be given an objective hearing by an administration sympathetic to labor.

The National Labor Board did send a mediator to the region and did launch an investigation. Though the mediator and the investigating committee found substantial evidence for the UAMP's grievances, the pro-Lewis Labor Board merely called for another, more thorough probe. The insurgent leaders realized that a long drawn-out investigation was a stalling tactic that worked against their union, that the government would listen but not act. In mid-January 1934 Maloney responded by calling another general strike in District 1.[51]

The strike demonstrated the UAMP's widespread support. Production at every colliery was stopped or disrupted. Regional newspapers reported almost 14,000 men on strike. Other estimates put the number of strikers at 50 percent of the total mine work force. Despite UMW disclaimers that the rival union represented only a small minority of all mine workers, the UAMP's membership at this time reached between 10,000 and 12,000, or about one-third of the UMW's strength. The effectiveness of the strike was, of course, increased by the widespread violence that accompanied it. The intensity of the violence persuaded Maloney to listen once again to Father Curran, public authorities, and federal officials, who entreated him to take his case before the National Labor Board.[52]

Maloney suspended the strike in February after receiving assurances that the UAMP would get a fair hearing. Though the National Labor Board heard the grievances of the UAMP, a series of federal decisions dashed the hopes of the dissident union. The National Labor Relations Board in October 1934 recognized the UMW as the only legal union in the anthracite fields; refused, under pressure from Lewis, to allow a jurisdictional election; and ruled that operators were not required to reinstate workers fired during an illegal strike—or one not called by the UMW.[53]

Maloney and the insurgents now had their backs to the wall, as Maloney understood when he opposed the renewal of the general strike at the UAMP convention in October. Still, he vowed somehow to continue the struggle despite low morale and declining membership. At this point Maloney may have been willing to compromise in order to save the members' jobs. The operators, however, gave no reprieve. Backed by the NLRB rulings, they now began a ruthless policy of retribution. By January 1935 fighting had again become widespread when the companies locked UAMP members out of their mines.

In what was to be the climactic battle of the UAMP, Maloney ordered a strike against Glen Alden on February 2, 1935. It was his last hope of protecting jobs while attempting through court action to force the company to honor $25,000 in dues coupons that the UAMP had in its possession, money the union needed for survival. Glen Alden immediately obtained an injunction from Judge W. A. Valentine against the strike. When it was ignored, Maloney and other UAMP officers were jailed. The imprisonment, combined with the hiring of thousands of unemployed miners as strikebreakers by Glen Alden, ignited the worst explosion of rioting and violence in the history of the Wyoming Valley. After Judge Valentine's car had been blown up on March 26—an act Maloney strongly condemned—Luzerne County authorities declared limited martial law.[54]

The UAMP threw all of its remaining resources into the strike. Women and children, in line with the region's strong tradition of communal and family solidarity, played active roles in this, the new union's last desperate effort. Schoolchildren organized support activities; in Nanticoke several hundred high school students struck in sympathy with teachers who had relatives working for Glen Alden. The UAMP women's auxiliary was everywhere, soliciting help from local unemployed councils and recruiting speakers who could talk to mine workers in Slavic languages. Twelve of the ninety defendants charged with contempt of court for violating the strike injunction were women. In Hanover and Nanticoke, women were arrested by state police for stoning miners attempting to work. In Wilkes-Barre ten women attacked and beat three strikebreakers. One hapless miner was stripped of his clothes and was sent home naked to the women's taunts of "Scab!"[55] The intensity of feeling often resulted in deplorable acts. Stacia Treski of Nanticoke tells of "a young man . . . [who] had to work because he had two children and his wife was expecting another. He went to work—crossing the pickets—and was killed in an accident in the mines." Before the burial the dead miner's funeral procession was stoned and his open grave filled with tin cans. "The people were so mad that he went to work they wanted to dig him out," Treski recalls. "They had to get the police to keep him in his grave."[56]

Against the strikers the public authorities, UMW, and companies mounted a variety of tactics. Local police chiefs such as Vincent Znaniecki of Nanticoke greatly expanded their police forces and cooperated closely with state police, even to the extent of finding local housing for them. But as a community member, Znaniecki often dealt leniently with strikers; he once refused to arrest a woman who smashed a strikebreaker's car window because there wasn't a "decent" place to imprison her. The imported state police, however, acted with particular brutality. They were frequently called in by the companies to attack pickets at collieries and break up meetings.[57] Two hundred state police surprised and savagely beat a group of Maloney supporters when Maloney appeared before Judge Valentine at the Luzerne County courthouse in Wilkes-Barre. The UMW used less direct but equally effective intimidation. "Even when the insurgents had meetings they found out if you attended," a UAMP miner at Glen Lyon said later. "I remember one meeting at the Roosevelt School. One UMW official went through and anybody attending that meeting they would have no job. You keep your mouth shut and you had a job."[58]

The companies and the UMW worked together against the insurgents. Sometimes it was difficult to distinguish between union and management. William Everett, a tough Glen Alden mine superintendent, boasted that he ran the union at his collieries as well as the mines. Everett deployed everything from physical force to bribery against the insurgents. He transferred one UAMP militant to a colliery sixteen miles distant from his home with the warning, "If I ever hear why you were transferred from any source, you gonna be out of a job." He assigned an incompetent worker to UAMP leader Mike Savilich's gang, explaining, "You had to handle the people, manipulate them." At the Truesdale colliery Everett took a different approach with Victor Matusa, the local "brains" of the insurgent union:

> "Victor," [Everett] said, "what makes you a radical?" "Bill," he says, "my father worked for years at Truesdale and he got nothing. Father was in a 'Catholic place' at Truesdale [a place where they had to carry the coal out like Christ carried the cross]." So I [Everett] promised that I would get him [father] a better place to work. But I asked for one promise, "If you're having trouble of any kind, you sit down with me". . . . Matusa then trusted me and we got along.[59]

What finally ended the strike and years of violence in District 1 was the exhaustion of the adversaries. In the spring of 1935, after Governor Earle had failed to effect a settlement, President Inglis of Glen Alden—with the blessing of Lewis—persuaded Maloney to allow the Nanticoke Business and Professional Men's Association, a leading civic group, to mediate among all the parties. Inglis acted because he feared the impact of a war of attrition on his company, Maloney because he realized that he could not much longer sustain the UAMP. A settlement was reached whereby Maloney called off the strike in exchange for Inglis's pledge to hire back the strikers on an "as needed basis."[60] Furthermore, a secret deal was undoubtedly made between Maloney and the UMW. In July, Boylan suddenly resigned as president of District 1 and the district leadership was replaced. In the months that followed, Glen Alden hired back many of the strikers while the UMW encouraged the insurgents to reapply for membership. The UAMP quietly expired on October 23, 1935, after Judge Valentine ruled that the union was not entitled to the dues money from Glen Alden. Maloney's last act as president was a magnanimous call for unity behind the UMW in the upcoming industry negotiations.[61]

Lewis was naturally exuberant over the demise of the rival union. But Maloney, in defeat, had at least accomplished this—he had forced Lewis to fight as hard for the men of anthracite as he did for the bituminous miners. The 1936 contract negotiations brought not only an increase in wages but also a work equalization clause that committed the operators to employ as many of their mine workers as possible.[62]

Maloney did not live to see the acceptance of the principles for which he had fought. On Good Friday, 1936, he and his young son were killed when a package that was mailed to their home exploded. Other bombs were sent on the same day to members of the coal operators' executive board, several public officials, the county sheriff, union leaders, and a judge, but only the bomb targeted for Maloney and one other man (and he a case of mistaken identity) went off. A close friend of Maloney, a German miner named Fugman from the UAMP's executive board, was finally charged with the killings. Despite Fugman's protestations that he was the victim of a frame-up—and almost everyone believed him—he was sent to the electric chair. The question of who was responsible for Maloney's death is still controversial in the Wyoming Valley. Some claim it was the operators, others, the UMW.[63]

The years of bloodshed and turmoil taught the anthracite workers a bitter lesson. The union they had relied upon and to which they had long given their unreserved loyalty gave them nothing in time of crisis. The coal companies abandoned them as they would eventually abandon the region. Once again the workers had to fall back on their own resources, on their families, friends, and kinship networks.

The strikes, occurring during the worst depression in American history, placed enormous strains on families in the region. Yet the people responded with determination born of a deep-rooted solidarity. When government poor relief, public charity, and union aid proved inadequate to alleviate the widespread suffering, the people responded in various ways. In the late 1920s many simply left the region, beginning an exodus that continued through the 1960s, seeking jobs in the automobile factories of Detroit, the steel mills of Buffalo and Pittsburgh, or the industries of Philadelphia. But with the onset of the depression, there was no place else to go. The region's people had to rely once more on their tradition of communal self-help and their strong kinship bonds to get through. The established familial obligation of wage sharing was reinforced as women and children went into textile mills and shops to augment family earnings. Adolescents especially played a vital role in helping their parents and family members. For working-class children of the era, adulthood was viewed as an extension of their family culture rather than the beginning of independence. Families and communal groups stayed together, struggling against adversity collectively. Helen Hosey, a Nanticoke woman, summed up the common feeling: "You took care of one another. You never questioned it. In our family we never expected anything in return. It was an honor that we had. The trust—that's why we all felt so close to each other. There was no house divided here."[64]

Hard times brought people closer together, often breaking down long-standing ethnic divisions. English, Germans, and Slavs reached out to help each other. When a man needed work, employed mine workers came to his aid, interceding with foremen to try to find a place for him. If he was out of work for long, his neighbors brought his family food or clothing or simply attended the fires in the household stoves or took care of the younger children while he and his wife and his other children searched for work. Very few people had savings to fall back on. "They just made the best of what they had," Victor Znaniecki recalls, often sharing with others what little they could spare.[65]

The local hero in many neighborhoods was the small storekeeper. Everybody was "on the book" to him, charging for groceries and other supplies and squaring up on payday. He often carried families for long periods during strikes and layoffs even

A miner ready for work.   Courtesy of the Burg Collection, MG-273, Pennsylvania State Archives.

if he hurt himself financially. He trusted his customers and knew that they would pay him off sooner or later. The small storekeeper should have had a monument erected to him during the depression, a miner later claimed. "You didn't pay him until you started back to work. But if he had demanded his money when it was due, then you couldn't have survived."[66]

The sense of collective responsibility often extended to other small businessmen. Joseph Shergalis of the Heights section of Wilkes-Barre inherited a small soda manufacturing business from his Lithuanian immigrant father. When Prohibition ended and business at local saloons and clubs picked up, he did what he could to help. Homeless men looking for a meal were seldom turned away from the family house. His mother bought used clothes and cheap shoes from itinerant peddlars and distributed them to the needy. After he won election to local office, Shergalis used his political influence to obtain relief for miners' widows and public works jobs for the unemployed. A somewhat more doubtful practice was his distribution of fifty-cent pieces outside of polling places on election day; Shergalis always delivered a solid bloc of voters to the local political machine.[67]

The most important self-help was within families. As they always did, children living at home went to work at an early age and turned over most of their earnings to their parents. Older children frequently delayed plans for marriage or gave up a cherished hope for education because their families needed them. One woman recalled that she willingly left school because she could not concentrate on her work when her parents so desperately needed the little money she could earn in a tailor shop. Younger married couples often moved in with parents, either because it was cheaper or because the older people needed help. One sick miner who could not maintain his house sold it to his son-in-law for a dollar in return for keeping it in good repair.[68]

With miners working two or three days a week, the income from women's work in silk mills, six dollars' pay for a sixty-six-hour week, often made the difference in family survival. Sometimes desperation drove women far from their families and homes in search of work. During the thirties "hard working Polish maids" were greatly in demand in New York City. Many women found temporary employment there and, in a reversal of the usual pattern, sent money back to the region. Men, too, went far afield to find work and sent what they could back home.[69]

Everyone had to sacrifice, especially young women of ethnic families who, though they might have had other aspirations, were expected to stay home and help out. Helen Mack of Nanticoke remembers how it was for her:

> I always liked bookkeeping and numbers. I liked to figure, but I never could because I had to stay home and help raise the other children. The older ones like Bill, I, Stanley, Henry, Johnny, were the oldest and worked early. . . . I sacrificed. But I'm not sorry, because I helped them. . . . All had to give their pay to my parents. . . . Sometimes I wanted to get married and at times I didn't want to get married. Certain things were private, so I wouldn't say anything about them. I didn't have a chance to think about any other person because that's more or less on the outskirts, since we all lived together. Never got in anybody's way. Even the next-door neighbors would bake for each other.[70]

Tensions and difficulties naturally arose from such family and communal obligations. Children rebelled against the demands of their parents, sometimes to the extent of running away and cutting all ties. The incidence of alcoholism, an ever-present social danger in the coalfields, rose during the depression. Men who could not support their families sought refuge in drink and often took out their rage on wives and children. Others abandoned their families altogether and joined the thousands of homeless people roaming America. Depression and other mental illnesses filled state hospitals or incapacitated people who could not withstand the rigorous code of family responsibilities. The conflicts between rival unions often set families and groups against each other. Aberrant social behavior, broken homes, and embittered lives were sometimes consequences of family commitment during hard times.

For most families, however, it was a matter of getting by as best they could. Together and with others in the community they cooperated toward that end. The securing of food often became a collective project. Whole neighborhoods organized berry-picking and mushroom-gathering expeditions in the mountains. Several families' ducks and geese were herded together into flocks and were watched by younger children. Groups of men smoked sausage while women prepared sauerkraut and preserved fruits and vegetables. People exchanged foods for greater variety. Milk cows almost became community property. The family garden was more important than ever; children as young as five years old were taught how to grow vegetables. Some families made ingenious efforts to improve their food supply. A group of Swoyersville Italians used nearly inedible government-distributed canned "beef" to feed and raise ducks for their tables. Even obtaining housing became a collective activity. Single unemployed men, many of them former boarders with families that could no longer keep them, helped each other build shacks on unused land with whatever materials were available. They gave their dwellings names such as "Prosperity is just around the corner." And everybody picked coal on culm banks or raided coal trains to supplement fuel supplies.[71]

Shenandoah, 1938. Courtesy of the Library of Congress.

Miners on the way to the mines often walked past the silk mills where their daughters entered the world of work.   Courtesy of the Burg Collection, MG-273, Pennsylvania State Archives.

The drive for survival also produced collective social action. Many people re-mained uncritically committed through the depression to capitalism and country, but working-class militants fought to make the democratic system more responsive to the needy. The people of the region not only strongly supported the reformist pro-grams of the Roosevelt administration; in many cases their collective agitation caused pressure that helped bring into existence social welfare measures at local, state, and federal levels. One of the principal methods used by the region's people to influence public authorities was the unemployed council. Many of the grass-roots organizations developed throughout the region in the early and mid-1930s before the New Deal programs took hold. They responded to the inadequacy of public relief measures during the early years of the depression by mobilizing community action for everything from suspension of mortgage foreclosures to support for national un-employment insurance. Their effectiveness was implicitly recognized by old-line politicians who set up rival, "official" unemployed leagues that were more amenable to traditional control.

One of the first organizers of unemployed councils in the region was Steve Nelson. An immigrant from Croatia, Nelson [born Stjepan Mesaros] was a long-time

Communist party organizer who was sent into the anthracite fields by the party in late 1930 after years of activity among industrial workers in Pittsburgh and Detroit. He was a practical, experienced organizer who knew better than to simply preach the abstract doctrines of class warfare. He concentrated most of his efforts on organizing around immediate issues such as food for the needy and additional welfare relief funds. He worked primarily for the people, not the party, as he knew there was little chance of expanding the party's small membership in the region.

From his first days in the region Nelson's commitment, courage, and simple, down-to-earth style won adherents to the cause of the unemployed.[72] He and his wife Margaret—also a party organizer—had almost no resources of their own. They stayed with people like Stella and Tom Petrosky of Ashley, young Polish immigrants with eight children, in the Petrosky's three-room house (Stella later became a militant community activist). The first unemployed councils grew out of meetings with friends and neighborhoods in church halls, cellars, and living rooms. Nelson usually started such meetings with his "mule story":

> Coming into town, I saw the mules that pull the coal cars. What do the owners do with *them* when unemployment sets in? Well, they put the mules out to pasture. In fact they feed them well and fatten them until work starts up again. They feel a responsibility to those mules because they represent an investment, but they refuse to accept any responsibility for the miner and his family. What can we do? I say we must fight for unemployment insurance.[73]

Nelson would go on to explain what unemployment insurance was and how it could be obtained through legislation, concluding with an appeal to his audience to organize a council for that purpose but in the meantime to address local grievances, for example by reasoning with "some cold-blooded landlord [who] decides to kick a family out."

Nelson sometimes received help from unexpected sources. While organizing in Hazleton, he met a Greek professional gambler named Gus who claimed to be concerned with the plight of the unemployed. Nelson naturally was suspicious, but he took Gus along on an organizing tour through Mahanoy City, Mount Carmel, Shamokin, and other mining towns. The pair went into local pool halls where Gus was a familiar face. Gus would introduce Nelson and explain why he was there. Nelson would then step forward and give his "mule story" to the unemployed miners, who would squat down in the low-ceilinged pool room to hear what he had to say. These pool hall assemblies gave birth to several strong unemployed councils. In Mahanoy City the miners even organized a labor library in an empty store that became a popular place for the men to meet, to hold discussions on working-class literature and to listen to radical folk music. Eventually some of the miners joined the Communist party. As for Gus, he gave up gambling and went on to become a party activist and a union organizer for the United Electrical Workers in Schenectady, New York.[74]

Nelson and other activists were constantly redbaited in the press, and local police jailed them frequently to prevent them from holding meetings. Before the atmosphere began to change with the Roosevelt administration, they met constant opposition as "troublemakers" and "outside agitators." Despite the harassment the unemployed councils continued to grow in number and size. By mid-1931 they had a total membership of more than 20,000 throughout the hard coal fields. The anthracite councils were part of a national movement of the unemployed that struck deep roots in industrial regions and began to exert considerable pressure on the Roosevelt administration by 1933. In Pennsylvania the movement also mobilized for mass action at the state level. In the spring of 1934 movement leaders from throughout the state organized a hunger march on Harrisburg. Petitions were presented to the state legislature demanding relief in the form of food, provision of coal or other heating fuels, maintenance of electricity or gas for lighting and heating, postpone-

Salvaging coal from the slag heaps for ten cents per 100 lbs.
Courtesy of the Library of Congress.

ment of home and farm mortgage payments, the ending of sheriffs' sales of homes, and the cancellation of all mortgage auctions.[75]

The anthracite councils played a major role in the hunger march. Almost a thousand men and women journeyed to Harrisburg in cars and trucks loaned for the purpose by local merchants. They included a group of miners from the staunchly conservative, fundamentalist German community of Hegins, whom Nelson persuaded to go. When state police prevented the caravan from entering the state capital, the marchers camped overnight in the barns of a Pennsylvania Dutch farmer, who explained to his wife: "The Lord sent them here, and perhaps it's up to us to do something to help them."[76] The following day, as thousands descended on the city, Governor Pinchot wisely allowed them to parade through the streets to the state capitol. Attempts to limit the number of spokesmen for the marchers to one failed when three more speakers slid down ropes from the packed gallery of the capitol to the legislature floor. Soon others slid down the ropes to stand beside their representatives and ensure that they paid sufficient attention to what was said. The legislators eventually passed several motions the marchers sought, including the demand for relief and support of a national unemployment insurance bill. As a re-

Boys who salvage coal from slag heaps, Nanty Glo, 1937.
Courtesy of the Library of Congress.

sult of such pressure nationwide, the Roosevelt administration greatly expanded public employment projects through the Works Progress Administration. In 1935 the Social Security Act incorporated the goals of unemployment compensation and a pension system.[77]

By the mid-1930s the unemployed councils in the region were well established. The Luzerne County council was headquartered in a rented hall in Wilkes-Barre where meetings and other activities were regularly held. The council published the *Anthracite Unemployed Worker*, with a circulation of 5,000, which carried news of happenings in Congress, the state legislature, and the unions. News affecting the unemployed also was broadcast on the "Sunday Worker Radio Hour," a popular program sponsored by the Communist party.[78]

The unemployed councils were not, as some charged at the time, "fronts" for the Communist party. Though Communists such as Nelson devoted much of their time to the councils, they were sustained by thousands of people working together for survival. They were authentic popular organizations that developed to meet real and urgent needs. As Nelson said later, it was enough to plant the idea and suggest the direction; the people soon took over and acted on their own. Communists in the region saw themselves as part of a broader struggle for change. They attempted to balance party work with other activities, but often the latter won out. Nelson himself suggested that the Communist National Miners Union, which had several small pockets of membership in the region, change its policy of opposition to all rival unions and collaborate with people who were seeking to reform the UMW. Communists also overcame their biases by supporting miners engaged in "bootleg mining."

The proximity of thin coal seams to the surface, especially in the rugged Schuylkill field, provided a major temptation to unemployed miners. The seams were not substantial enough to be worked profitably by the big companies, but for a father and son and a few friends willing to sink a "dog hole" and operate with primitive equipment they represented bread on the table. The first bootleggers used the coal for their own fuel or bartered it for goods, but soon pickup trucks were delivering it to eastern Pennsylvania cities where it was sold door-to-door at discount prices. By 1933 an estimated 20,000 men were engaged in bootleg mining in an illegal industry worth $35 million. The coal companies naturally were enraged by the practice. They brought in state police, dynamited the illegal holes, began surface strip mining of the seams, and demanded that the authorities act against the bootleggers. Nothing worked. One company blasted shut more than 1,000 holes on its properties one year, only to see several thousand more opened the next. A stripping operator had his steam shovel blown up. A Coal and Iron policeman who threatened a group of bootleggers had his car burned. When he showed up the following day on a horse, the miners shot the horse. Local officials were obviously reluctant to tell a miner that he could not support his family. For their own protection, the bootleggers established the Bootleg Miners Union at the suggestion and with the help of Communist organizers. Nelson wrote the constitution of the union, which included articles for the regulation of the illegal industry. The Communists viewed bootleg mining as an affirmation of the concept that "human life comes first and private property second."[79]

Many people active in the unemployed councils supported the United Anthracite Miners of Pennsylvania. The organizations worked closely together during the insurgent union's existence. In District 1 the Luzerne County council distributed leaflets among the unemployed explaining the UAMP's position, and during strikes cooperated with the union to prevent scabbing. In 1934 the councils joined with UAMP leaders to organize the short-lived Luzerne County Labor party, which unsuccessfully ran candidates for sheriff and county commissioner. Since the UAMP was solidly established only in District 1, councils in the lower fields generally supported progressive UMW leaders like President Marty Brennan of District 9.[80]

The degree of social activism in the region's communities often depended upon the existence of militant groups that predated the depression or had a tradition of struggle. One such town was Minersville in the Schuylkill field, a center of Molly Maguire activity in the 1870s and the scene of a series of bitter, Socialist-led textile strikes before World War I. Minersville was inhabited by Lithuanians, Ukrainians, Russians, and Germans, all of whom had their own fraternal and social organizations. The Lithuanians, many of whom were Communists, were the best organized, but all of the groups possessed a high level of class consciousness. As Steve Nelson recalled, "It was almost as if a man was not a good Lithuanian or Russian unless he was also a militant union member."[81] During the 1930s Minersville contributed a large number of leaders to the popular movements in the anthracite fields and always raised more money and sent more people to rallies and marches than other, comparable communities.

The sustaining power of communal tradition and collective action helped anthracite people survive during the Great Depression, but they could not reverse the inexorable decline of the industry. By the end of the 1930s hard coal was finished as a major industry. In 1938 production was down to 46 million tons. There were still about 97,000 employees in the industry, but payrolls were 50 percent shorter than ten years earlier.[82] Prosperity never returned. The long painful dying continued during the following two decades as the nation completed its switch to alternate fuels. Mines closed and breakers shut down; the anthracite railroads began their slide toward bankruptcy. The old miners worked on as long as they could, but their sons, for the first time, did not follow their fathers into the mines. By the 1950s the sight of weary, dirt-encrusted middle-aged men straggling home after a shift in the few working deep mines was already a curiosity. They symbolized an era now past and seemed as utterly obsolete as the industry in which they labored.

Anthracite was a nearly dead industry, but it took a terrible crisis to awaken many of the region's people fully to this fact. On January 22, 1959, the flooding Susquehanna River broke through rock strata and poured into the workings of the Knox Coal Company adjacent to the River Slope mine in Jenkins Township, Luzerne County. Three men drowned immediately and thirty others were trapped by the water. To close the huge hole in the riverbed through which millions of gallons of water poured, the tracks of the nearby Lehigh Valley Railroad were diverted and 30 railroad gondola cars and 400 mine cars were pushed into the brink. Vast pumping operations were begun at once. Huge earthen coffer dams were constructed to divert the river, while underground work crews risked their lives to build bulkheads. Despite these efforts, rising waters forced the suspension of work in more than two dozen mines. Production dropped 94,000 tons per week as a result, and estimates placed the number of jobs lost at 7,500, with a payroll loss in excess of $32 million.[83]

A subsequent state investigation uncovered a pattern of negligence, incompetence, and disregard of safety procedures by the company, along with shady contractual arrangements that eventually led to convictions for income tax evasion.[84] The investigation revealed the condition the industry had reached, in which unscrupulous contractors sent poorly supervised men into old workings to "rob" supporting pillars of coal and mine seams clearly marked as dangerous on maps. The Knox mine disaster, which ended deep mining after almost 100 years in the Wyoming Valley, was a sad final comment on a great American industry.

The people of anthracite had been badly served by the men for whom they labored and by those to whom they gave their loyalties and their votes. The great coal and transportation companies, owned by outsiders and operated according to nineteenth-century principles of profit and sovereign property rights, abandoned their collieries and leased or sold their lands to the industry's scavengers: surface strippers and small-time operators. The companies did not believe they had any responsibility for the men who worked their mines. Their policy of excluding outside industry from the region through their control of local officials and chambers of commerce paid off for them in a captive labor market, but it left the towns they deserted helpless and impoverished. The UMW accepted work equalization when it was already too late and after too much blood had been shed. The union lingered on through the final years, watching its membership rolls drop steadily and shifting attention once again to the bituminous fields. There was not even a UMW hospital for miners suffering from debilitating asthma; in the soft coal fields there were ten. For many old miners the name John L. Lewis was a curse. Nor were distant politicians any more responsive to the needs of the people of the anthracite region. Both the state and federal governments declined to embark on the massive redevelopment program that was needed to save the region from economic disaster.

Inevitably, the disaster occurred. Statistics tell the story. Mine employment fell

A mine accident in anthracite country.
Courtesy of the Historical Society of Schuylkill County, Pottsville, Pa.

The Knox mine disaster, 1959.
Courtesy of the Wyoming Historical and Geological Society, Wilkes-Barre, Pa.

from 80,000 in the late 1940s to approximately 3,000 today. More than half of the 6 million tons presently produced annually comes from strip mining, which is done by giant shovels and few men. Underground mining accounts for only 6 percent of the total. The largest remaining company in the fields employs no more than 400 workers. Long ago the people, without work or the means of finding it, began leaving the region. In the decades after World War II the outmigration became a flood. The young left first, followed by heads of families. Eventually the middle-aged and some of the elderly went. The region lost a quarter of its people. Some mining towns lost 50 percent of their inhabitants; a few disappeared entirely. Unemployment never fell below 10 percent, even during the expansive 1950s; usually it was much higher. The region had—and has—the lowest per capita income in Pennsylvania and one of the lowest in the entire Northeast. Until the 1960s unemployment compensation provided the major source of income in the largest cities of Scranton and Wilkes-Barre. In smaller towns a large proportion of the people subsisted on social security and welfare checks or on money sent back home by family members working elsewhere. Towns in the southern fields became bedroom communities, their residents commuting daily more than 100 miles to steel mills in the Lehigh Valley and government jobs in Harrisburg.[85]

For the miners too old to make a new start, there was enforced idleness: long days rocking on front porches, a few dime beers in the corner saloon, walks along town streets lined with shuttered stores. Many could not come to terms with the waste of their lives. Stories abound of men who dressed every morning for descent into the mines, who, after an idle day at the fraternal hall, would return home claiming they had worked a full shift. Proud men who worked all their lives to support families watched wives and daughters go off to textile mills; for such men dependency came as a degrading shock. Some cracked under the strain. A Pittston miner, concluding that he was useless, sat on a keg of powder and ignited it with his pipe. Many slipped into apathy, waiting for death.

The legacy of anthracite's decline—economic and human devastation—included severe environmental damage. One-fourth of the region's 484 square miles was disturbed by mining operations. Culm banks remain from the days of underground mining. With the spread of strip mining after the 1920s, the region's mountains were blasted and ripped apart to reach the coal seams. Refuse from underground mines and stripping operations altered or destroyed the course of streams. After abandonment deep mines filled with water, and the acidic overflow polluted—and continues to pollute—surface waters in the region and beyond. Subsidence of the earth's surface, which follows from underground mining, twisted and damaged highways and roads, broke underground utilities, and cracked the foundations and walls of buildings. Houses, automobiles, and occasionally people have fallen into holes caused by subsidence. Fires in abandoned mines have spewed toxic fumes into the air and have

A retired miner and his grandchildren.
Courtesy of the Historical Society of Schuylkill County, Pottsville, Pa.

threatened communities. In 1983 the federal government agreed to relocate the entire population of the town of Centralia in Columbia County in order to save people from the poisonous fumes of an underground fire that has been burning out of control since 1962.

The kingdom of coal is gone. The black rock that broke America's dependency on foreign coal, fueled an industrial revolution, kept millions warm, created great wealth, and gave birth to a vibrant immigrant culture has served its time in history. Anthracite's final legacy is a warning to all Americans that human lives and natural resources are finite and precious, that they can no longer be sacrificed indiscriminately on the altar of private greed.

Epilogue

The marine corps honor guard in full dress uniform marched into the ballroom of the Gus Genetti Hotel carrying the American and Marine Corps flags. Behind them walked the seventy-four-year-old guest of honor. As he entered the hall the crowd of more than 500 people greeted him with a rousing rendition of "America the Beautiful." From the podium, speaker after speaker acclaimed him as "the greatest Congressman ever." The Wilkes-Barre Lion's Club honored him as their 1978 "Citizen of the Year."[1]

Later that year Daniel J. Flood, Democratic congressman from northeastern Pennsylvania's Eleventh Congressional District, was indicted twice by federal grand juries on charges of perjury, bribery, and conspiracy. On November 7 the voters responded to the allegations by reelecting him overwhelmingly to his sixteenth term. The mood in the district was perfectly expressed by Bill Cherkes, chairman of the March 16 Dan Flood Day: "We don't care what outsiders say. They're just trying to hurt a member of the family." As another of the Congressman's constituents put it: "Dan Flood is the next closest thing to God!"[2]

In keeping with their traditions, the people of anthracite rallied around one of their own. They were returning a favor. In thirty-two years in Congress Dan Flood did more than any other single individual to help revitalize the dying economy of anthracite country, using his political clout as a senior member of committees with influence over three-fourths of the federal budget to channel billions of dollars into northeastern Pennsylvania. He worked his will through persuasion, manipulation, horse-trading, arm-twisting, and ornate oratory of a kind rarely heard in the House of Representatives in this century. The government money he brought to the region attracted new businesses and industries that contributed to growth and diversification in the wake of anthracite's decline.

In the mid-1940s when Flood, a young lawyer, first took a seat in Congress, the region was declining badly. Veterans returning from World War II found decaying cities and towns, an aging population and deep demoralization. Annual coal produc-

Congressman Daniel J. Flood.   *Courtesy of Daniel J. Flood.*

tion dropped below 50 million tons and the mine labor force of 80,000 was less than half of what it had been two decades earlier and was still decreasing. By the early 1950s unemployment was 19 percent and the region's most notable export, in Flood's words, was "high school graduates." Pessimism about the region's future prevailed everywhere.

In his long career Dan Flood was accused of many things but pessimism was not one of them. After establishing his seat in Congress and earning seniority in the 1950s, he lost no opportunity in promoting the region's interests. He was convinced that federal money could lay the basis for rejuvenation. By using classic pork-barrel techniques, such as attaching riders to legislation of wider national significance, he had a large Veterans Administration hospital, a regional airport, and a major highway built. Flood used his influence to have Interstate 83 rerouted through the region as a condition for his vote in a transportation subcommittee. He used his position in the House Appropriations Committee in similar ways. The generals and admirals in the Pentagon could always depend upon Flood's support for a strong military; they in turn encouraged the building of Reserve installations and the distribution of defense contracts to manufacturers in the region. Primarily because of Flood, the remote Tobyhanna Army Base was converted from a little-used shooting range to a principal East Coast center for repairing military communications equipment.[3]

Nor did Flood neglect anthracite. In a move that outraged many of his congressional colleagues and even had the military men shaking their heads in disbelief, the congressman wrote into the permanent Department of Defense budget a requirement that all military installations in West Germany use either Pennsylvania anthracite or coke rather than the cheaper fuel oil. A later amendment prohibited the conversion of coal-fired furnaces to oil. The anthracite producers, who shipped their first million tons after enactment of the Flood amendment in 1962, agreed that the military order had saved the industry from complete collapse.[4]

Why did the army allow Flood to arrange a measure that cost the taxpayers more than $20 million a year? The congressman explained:

> They can't be blamed. After all, here's Flood, a nice fellow, and he's got a great reputation for being for defense appropriations—bang, bang, bang, and all that. Jesus Christ, suppose you were one of those goddamn generals or secretaries or deputy secretaries. What are you going to do? Jeopardize the Army materiel command with a son of a bitch like that for a couple of million dollars, for a couple of tons of coal? Bullshit.[5]

Flood also looked out for the men in his region who could no longer mine coal. He had the U.S. Congress enact special legislation providing disability payments for former miners crippled by black lung disease. Most congressmen had never heard of black lung. Some representing asbestos, textile, and steel workers, questioned why their constituents were not similarly protected. Yet in a masterful speech in the House—which Majority Leader Thomas "Tip" O'Neill, Jr., called one of "the most impressive speeches I've ever heard"—Flood overwhelmed the opposition and persuaded his colleagues to pass the measure. It gave 25,000 black lung victims in his district and many others in the coalfields payments of $165 a month. "You can't get away with that kind of speech very often," Flood recalled. "I went pretty far—a very stylized performance, in full costume. Oh yes, I pulled out all the stops."[6]

Though Flood showed a special talent for persuading defense contractors to locate in his district, his major efforts toward reducing unemployment and encouraging new businesses came through a series of federal regional redevelopment programs for which he can claim primary responsibility. The Flood-Douglas bill, which provided long-term, low-interest loans to enterprises in depressed areas, was later expanded in the Area Redevelopment Act signed by President John F. Kennedy in 1961. Flood convinced Robert Kennedy that the anthracite region should be included in the Appalachia redevelopment act to take advantage of President Kennedy's pledge to help that region. These initiatives culminated in the establishment of the Economic Development Administration under President Lyndon B. Johnson in 1965. Through Flood's efforts the EDA's regional headquarters for the eastern United States, Puerto

Rico, and the U.S. Virgin Islands was located in Wilkes-Barre. When the later model cities legislation, intended to further renewal of inner-city ghettos, was before Congress, Flood had it modified to include old industrial cities generally. Wilkes-Barre became the first city aided under that program.[7]

Flood's shrewd use of the legislative process during an era of direct federal commitment to economic growth and development produced sizable results. By the early 1970s unemployment in the region's major towns and cities had been reduced to approximately the level of the national average. In the healthy climate of revitalization, new businesses such as insurance, finance, real estate, hotels, food processing, textiles, building supplies, and electrical equipment contributed to economic diversification. If the region still lagged behind other Pennsylvania areas in overall per capita income, significant progress was nonetheless being made in lifting it out of its decades-long depression.

Flood, of course, was not alone in his efforts to restore the economic health of the region. Businessmen, professionals, religious, civic, and labor leaders rallied to the cause in the 1960s and 1970s. Groups comprised of prominent local citizens, like the

Jim Thorpe, Pennsylvania, formerly Mauch Chunk, is now a tourist center. The Asa Packer Mansion, a museum, overlooks the Carbon County Courthouse, the former headquarters of the Lehigh Coal and Navigation Company and Saint Mark's Episcopal Church, largely endowed by the Packer family. Photo by Rachel E. Haddad, Easton Express.

Committee of 100 in Wilkes-Barre, or the CAN DO organization in Hazleton, developed imaginative programs to spur investment and attract and hold new enterprises. They worked collectively to bring together disparate and sometimes conflicting interests in their communities for a common goal. These groups tapped into the deep reserve of loyalty the people had for their region and demonstrated once again the anthracite people's remarkable resilience in the face of adversity. The old pride of the "coal crackers" began to return.

A major setback to recovery occurred in June 1972 when Hurricane Agnes struck the region. By June 23 the Susquehanna River had risen more than forty feet above normal and had sent raging flood waters through Wilkes-Barre and a score of neighboring communities. More than 200,000 people were evacuated and property damage all along the river was estimated at $4 billion. It was the worst civil disaster in the nation's history. The hardest-hit area was the Wyoming Valley.

The drama unfolding on the Susquehanna perfectly suited the Wilkes-Barre congressman, who had been a popular stage actor in his younger days. "This is going to be one Flood against another," he announced at the opening moment of a performance that some claimed was his greatest. Immediately after being awakened in his Washington apartment in the early hours of June 24, Flood called Secretary of Defense Melvin Laird and said that he was taking the secretary's personal helicopter back to the region and was assuming command of all rescue operations. Flood added that he expected full cooperation from the military. "Yes, sir," the secretary of defense replied.

Flood was not authorized to act as he did. Nor is there any precedent for a congressman's decision to take charge of disaster relief efforts. But the irrepressible Flood brushed aside all legalities. Straightforward action had always been his trademark. Working for twenty-two-hour stretches from his Naval Reserve command post, Flood in the following days coordinated and directed rescue and relief missions. Forty military helicopters appeared like magic to evacuate people from rooftops and transport the injured; they saved at least a thousand lives. Other equipment and troops were dispatched by the Pentagon. Food, medical supplies, and personnel were sent by the General Services Administration and the Department of Agriculture. When fires broke out in flooded downtown Wilkes-Barre, Flood had a Coast Guard fireboat flown in by the Air Force to put them out. The amount of relief provided by the federal government was double what it would have been had Flood not orchestrated the operation.

Two days after his arrival in the region the sixty-eight-year-old Congressman capped his virtuoso performance by appearing on local television. Dressed in army fatigues, and standing on a hill above Wilkes-Barre, he dramatically told his audience: "This is Dan Flood. Today I have ordered the Army Corps of Engineers not to allow the Susquehanna to rise one more inch." Significantly, the flood waters stopped only two blocks from Flood's modest frame house in Wilkes-Barre.

Back in Washington, Flood called in the political IOUs he had carefully accumulated over the years. He had a reputation as a man of his word who had helped hundreds of his colleagues in both political parties. Now he needed their help. "Now look, goddamn it," he was overheard yelling at one reluctant congressman, "I've taken care of you before, now you get in line." Rules were bent and precedents set, but hundreds of millions of dollars for reconstruction entered the region. Flood's lobbying and the resulting federal monies laid the base for rebuilding downtown Wilkes-Barre and other towns in the Wyoming Valley.[8]

The flamboyant Dan Flood seemed an unlikely representative of the down-to-earth, working-class people of the Eleventh Congressional District. He brilliantined his hair, waxed his long, upturned moustache, wore Edwardian ice-cream-colored suits and a satin-lined cape, and carried an ebony sword stick. He looked every bit like a character out of an old vaudeville melodrama, not a coal cracker politician. His windy rhetoric, laced with Shakespearean expressions and allusions to classical literature, dazzled and bewildered many voters who had never seen the inside of a schoolroom. "Dapper Dan," who had wowed the girls as a matinee idol in the 1920s, stood out like a rosebush in full bloom on a culm bank.

Yet he could deal with the toughest of his mining town constituents. In 1946, as a freshman congressman, Flood appeared at a rowdy meeting of striking miners who were well fortified with booze. He had just come from a formal gathering and still wore a silk top hat, evening gloves, a white tie, and tails. A burly miner remarked, "Who is this pansy?" Flood carefully laid aside his walking stick, removed his gloves, and folded his cape over a chair. Then he leaped from the stage and nailed the offender with a solid right that sent him sprawling over several rows of chairs. Flood had been a champion boxer in college. "I used to get into a fight most every night," he recalled years later of his days as a little-known politician. "There was always some joker trying to start things. That was until they found out just who Dan Flood was."[9]

For the people of the anthracite region Dan Flood was, of course, many things—a combination, one reporter writes, of guardian angel, father, priest, ombudsman, employment bureau, entertainer, miraculous "fixer," and, finally, savior.[10] For that reason they stood by him when he was indicted for influence-peddling. (The government was unable to get a conviction, and Flood was later considered too old and sick for retrial. Some observers suspected jury tampering.)

Flood reflected a political tradition noteworthy for its "we take care of our own" attitude. Patronage, favoritism, influence-peddling, and outright corruption were a common, often accepted, part of the political process. They were the practices, as the old saying goes, "that greased the wheels" of public life. In that respect politics in the region was no different from politics in many other urban industrial areas in the late nineteenth and twentieth centuries. The ethnic political machines of the region had a pronounced local orientation. Local, not national or international, issues mattered most to people. Voters wanted to know what a candidate could do for them—for their family, for their town, for their region of the country. The politician who did not understand this concern simply did not get elected.

In the anthracite country politics was also closely intertwined with religion and ethnicity—and still is. The Irish who arrived in the mid-nineteenth century were excluded from the overwhelmingly Protestant Whig party and flocked to the Democratic party in great numbers, joining the Germans, another outsider group. Eventually they gained control of the Democratic party when German voters began to move back to the Republican party toward the turn of the century. Early in the twentieth century Slavic immigrants tended to gravitate toward the Republican party, in part to counter the power of the Irish Democrats and also because it was the party of John Mitchell and "Teddy" Roosevelt, heroes of the 1902 strike. During the Great Depression and afterward, Slavic voters continued to divide their vote, but in

Tamaqua in 1984.   Photo by Rachel E. Haddad, Easton Express.

1960 they joined the Irish in support of John F. Kennedy. The fact that he was Catholic was more important to them than that he was an Irish Democrat. After his death in 1963, many Slavic voters, the region's largest ethnic constituency, returned to the Republican party. So while today the region is one of the depressed areas in the state it has more registered Republicans than Democrats.[11]

Flood understood the voting habits of the people of his area—what they expected from the political process and why they voted as they did. In his district voter registration is almost equally divided between political parties. When he first ran for Congress in the mid-1940s, political power resided in several machines with strong bases in ethnic neighborhoods. He skillfully transcended their influence by appealing to voters of both parties. Though he was a Democrat of Irish origin in a district almost 57 percent Slavic, he acted independently to help both Democrats and Republicans. He identified himself with the welfare of all his constituents, regardless of political affiliation. And his character and behavior made him just different enough to stand out in the voters' minds.

Flood entered Congress when the old machines were losing their grip. The economic crisis in the region, the institution of merit and civil service procedures, and the increasing importance of federal and state programs all undermined the old system of patronage-based politics. Local bosses simply had less to offer. By the 1950s the future of the region depended to a large degree on decisions made elsewhere, especially in Washington. Influence and power there was what counted, as Flood realized. His genius lay in using them to full effect.

In a real sense Dan Flood represented the transition of the region from its coal-based economy and culture to its new diversified and socially varied present. Though a product of the old-style politics, he made them irrelevant through his use of modern techniques. He always had the support of organized labor, but he won the confidence of other interest groups, especially businessmen. He supported the initiatives of private enterprise yet effectively used the programs of an activist and interventionist federal government to promote the general welfare. Dan Flood understood the changing temper of the times. He remained rooted in the traditions of the region while also symbolizing and embodying its new spirit of revival.

*   *   *

Hard coal is not yet part of the region's economic recovery. Years ago the big companies sold or leased their lands to small operators. Some of them survived; many did not. Today little more than 1 percent of the region's work force is engaged in mining. The largest company in the fields employs no more than 400 people. It is primarily a stripping concern that uses mammoth shovels, or "drags," to tear the coal from the earth. That is the modern method of anthracite mining: it is more effi-

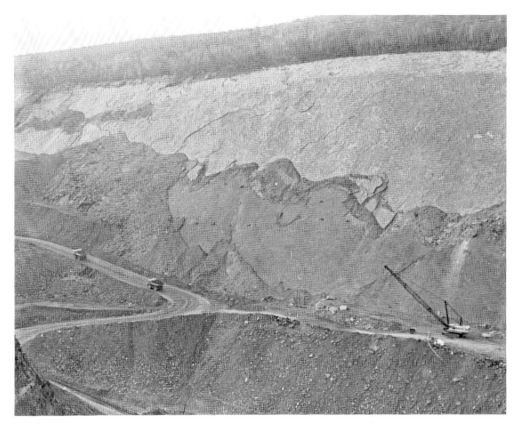

*The modern method of mining anthracite. Stripping operations in Bethlehem Steel's open pit
mine near Tamaqua.   Photo by Rachel E. Haddad,* Easton Express.

cient and less costly but capital intensive; few miners are needed. Here and there a
few deep mines continue to work, but their production is limited. Methods have been
developed for processing culm, but culm also provides low yields.

The future of anthracite is uncertain. Existing technology can extract 8 billion
tons that still lie in the ground. The 6 million or so tons that are shipped annually go
to domestic and industrial users in New England, Canada, Europe, and South Korea;
the market is otherwise limited. During the fuel crisis of the 1970s there were hopes
that anthracite would make a comeback, but so far the hopes have not been realized.

In 1977, in large part through Dan Flood's initiative, the Anthracite Task Force,
comprised of state and local officials, industrialists, and members of Congress, formed
in an effort to increase production and expand markets. It made a series of recommendations designed to revitalize hard coal. A few, such as an exemption of anthracite from the costly antipollution "scrubbing" process required of utility plants
that use soft coals, were implemented. Federal funding was also provided for more

*Gregory Lettich, a modern underground miner, works on in the old tradition,
Porter Tunnel, Tower City.   Photo by Rachel E. Haddad,* Easton Express.

than forty demonstration projects studying the problems of the industry or testing
new technology. But the federal Office of Anthracite, created to promote hard coal,
was subsequently abolished, and most of the task force's suggestions have not been
pursued.[12]

Operators claim that they are caught in a vicious circle. They say that they
could expand present production to 12 to 15 million tons annually but that doing so
would require a substantial capital investment. An uncertain market, however,
makes financing difficult to obtain for the relatively small businesses now mining.
They cannot increase production because of the limited market; but expanding the
market requires additional production. In addition there are other constraints, such
as prohibitive environmental restrictions, a decrepit rail transportation system, and
the shortage of adequate shipping facilities in East Coast ports.

Despite the clouded outlook, anthracite operators are optimistic. James Tedesco,
president of the region's largest producer, the Jeddo-Highland Coal Company of
West Pittston, believes that "there is going to be a fuller realization of the part that
anthracite coal can play in this energy situation our nation is facing." And Alfred J.

Pierce, vice-president and general manager of the Gilberton Coal Company, adds: "I guess as an American I'm confident that the only time we seem to do things is when we have our backs against the wall. I think we're going to come out of this, probably through our own efforts without much help from anybody else."[13]

The optimism of Tedesco and Pierce reflects the people's mood throughout the region. Theirs has been a history of hard times. And yet time and again the people have demonstrated a remarkable resiliency: they keep coming back. Though their future, like that of dethroned King Coal, is uncertain, they remain confident. The people of anthracite are, as they have always been, the region's richest resource.

Notes

INTRODUCTION

1. Harry M. Caudill, *Night Comes to the Cumberlands: A Biography of a Depressed Area* (Boston: Little, Brown, 1962), x.

1. ANTHRACITE PIONEERS

1. Alfred Mathews and Austin N. Hungerford, *History of the Counties of Lehigh and Carbon in the Commonwealth of Pennsylvania* (Philadelphia: Everts and Richards, 1884), 754–69.

2. *Hazard's Register of Pennsylvania* 1 (May 1828): 310.

3. Harold W. Aurand, *From the Molly Maguires to the United Mine Workers: The Social Ecology of an Industrial Union, 1869–1897* (Philadelphia: Temple University Press, 1971), 3–8; Delaware and Hudson Company, *The Story of Anthracite* (New York: Delaware and Hudson, 1932), 11.

4. William E. Edmunds and Edwin F. Koppe, *Coal in Pennsylvania* (Harrisburg: Topographic and Geologic Survey, Commonwealth of Pennsylvania, 1966), 1–12; A. Raistrick and C. E. Marshall, *The Nature and Origin of Coal* (London: English Universities Press, 1939).

5. Delaware and Hudson Company, *The Story of Anthracite*, 21.

6. Ibid., 24–25; H. Benjamin Powell, *Philadelphia's First Fuel Crisis: Jacob Cist and the Developing Market for Pennsylvania Anthracite* (University Park: Pennsylvania State University Press, 1978), 16.

7. George Korson, *Black Rock: Mining Folklore of the Pennsylvania Dutch* (Baltimore: Johns Hopkins University Press, 1960), 10.

8. Ibid., 9, 11–12.

9. Ibid., 14.

10. On Necho Allen, see Korson, 21–23; on John Charles, see *The Story of Anthracite*, 34–35.

11. On early uses of anthracite in Philadelphia, see Powell, *Philadelphia's First Fuel Crisis*, 63; "If the world should take fire" quoted from Korson, 34; on Colonel Shoemaker, see Korson, 35–36.

12. Quoted from Korson, 53.

13. Delaware and Hudson Company, *The Story of Anthracite*, 26–27.

14. Ibid., 38–40.

15. Powell, *Philadelphia's First Fuel Crisis*, 27–28.

16. For an outstanding study of Jacob Cist and his contribution to the development of the anthracite industry, see Powell, *Philadelphia's First Fuel Crisis*.

17. Ibid., 19.

18. Ibid., 28.

19. For a colorful account of the expedition to the Summit Hill mine, see Korson, 37–42; the quoted passage appears in Korson, 38–39; a description of the organiza-

tion of the enterprise may be found in Powell, *Philadelphia's First Fuel Crisis*, 29–36.

20. Powell, *Philadelphia's First Fuel Crisis*, 34–40.

21. Ibid., 33.

22. Ibid., 37–39.

23. For a detailed description of Cist's efforts to advertise and propagate the uses of anthracite, see Powell, *Philadelphia's First Fuel Crisis*, chap. 3, "Anthracite Advocate."

24. Quoted from Frederick Moore Binder, *Coal Age Empire: Pennsylvania Coal and Its Utilization to 1860* (Harrisburg: Pennsylvania Historical and Museum Commission, 1974), 6; Binder's is the best history of early anthracite use and promotion.

25. "Rules for Buying and Burning Anthracite Coal Done in Verse," reprinted in the *Miner's Journal*, February 1832. Also quoted in Binder, 18. For a fine bibliography, see H. Benjamin Powell, "The Pennsylvania Anthracite Industry, 1769–1976," *Pennsylvania History* 46 (1980): 3–27.

2. THE ANTHRACITE CANALS

1. Eleanor Morton, *Josiah White, Prince of Pioneers* (New York: Stephen Daye Press, 1946), 92–93. Historians differ regarding exact dates, the number of barges that arrived in Philadelphia, and even their landing place. The point is that White and Hazard did purchase the coal for use in their mill.

2. Josiah White, *Josiah White's History, Given by Himself* (Philadelphia, 1909), 69–70; Erskine Hazard, "History of the Introduction of Anthracite Coal into Philadelphia and a Letter from Jesse Fell, Esq., of Wilkes-Barre," *Memoirs of the Historical Society of Pennsylvania* 2: 155–64; Richard Richardson, *Memoir of Josiah White* (Philadelphia, 1873).

3. Quoted from Donald Sayenga, "The Untryed Business: An Appreciation of White and Hazard," in *Proceedings of the Canal History and Technology Symposium* (Easton, Pa.: Center for Canal History and Technology, 1983), 105.

4. Ibid., 106–7.

5. Korson, *Black Rock*, 43; Morton, 93.

6. Quoted from John P. Miller, *The Lehigh Canal: A Thumb Nail History, 1829–1931*, printed for the Sesquicentennial of the opening of the Lehigh Canal (Allentown, Pa.: Jiffy Printing, 1979), 6.

7. Ibid.

8. Josiah White, *Josiah White's History, Given by Himself* (Jim Thorpe, Pa.: Carbon County Board of Commissioners, 1979), 19. This shortened version was published in a numbered edition to commemorate the 150th anniversary of the opening of the Lehigh Canal and is hereafter cited as anniversary edition.

9. Ibid., 19–20.

10. Sayenga, 111.

11. Chester Lloyd Jones, *The Economic History of the Anthracite-Tidewater Canals* (Philadelphia, 1908), 11–12. Although it is dated, this is the best general history of the canals.

12. Sayenga, 112.

13. Anniversary edition, 29.

14. Ibid., 28.

15. Ibid., 37.

16. Jones, 10–11.

17. Alfred D. Chandler, Jr., "Anthracite Coal and the Beginnings of the Industrial Revolution in the United States," *Harvard Business History Review* 46, no. 22 (Summer 1972): 141–81.

18. Sayenga, 113; see also H. Benjamin Powell, "Establishing the Anthracite Boom Town of Mauch Chunk, 1814–1825: Selected Documents," *Pennsylvania History* 41, no. 3 (1974): 248–62.

19. Sayenga, 113.

20. Jones, 13.

21. Sayenga, 114.

22. Miller, 14.

23. Sayenga, 114.

24. Miller, 15–16.

25. Quoted in Miller, 16–17.

26. Ibid., 17.

27. Ibid., 18.

28. Jones, 29.

29. Quoted in Jones, 19.

30. Ibid.

31. Sayenga, 117.

32. Quoted from Morton, 163.

33. Sayenga, 117–18.

34. John N. Hoffman, *Anthracite in the Lehigh Region of Pennsylvania, 1820–45* (Washington, D.C.: Smithsonian Institution Press, 1968), 104.

35. Ibid., 106–8.

36. Jones, 22–23; Miller, 20–21; Sayenga, 119.

37. Jones, 53.

38. Quote from Morton, 163.

39. Quote from Miller, 23.

40. Jones, 126; George Korson, *Black Rock: Mining Folklore of the Pennsylvania Dutch*, 110.

41. Korson, 111–12.

42. Ibid., 111.

43. Jones, 130, 132; Korson, 112.

44. Jones, 131.

45. Ibid., 133; Korson, 110.

46. Sayenga, 123–24.

47. Jones, 76; see also Delaware and Hudson Company, *A Century of Progress: History of the Delaware and Hudson Company* (Albany, N.Y.: J. B. Lyon, 1925).

48. Jones, 77–78.

49. Vernon Leslie, *Honesdale and the Stourbridge Lion* (Honesdale, Pa.: Stourbridge Lion Sesquicentennial, 1979), 32, 33; see also Edwin D. LeRoy, *The Delaware and Hudson Canal and Its Gravity Railroads: A History* (Honesdale, Pa.: Wayne County Historical Society, 1980).

50. For discussions of the economic impact of the canals, see Ronald L. Filippelli, "The Schuylkill Navigation Company and Its Role in the Development of the Anthracite Coal Trade and Schuylkill County, 1815–1845" (M.A. thesis, Pennsylvania State University, 1966); and Charles Waltman, "The Influence of the Lehigh Canal on the Industrial and Urban Development of the Lehigh Valley," in *Proceedings of the Canal History and Technology Symposium* (Easton, Pa.: Center for Canal History and Technology, 1983).

51. Ethel M. Springer and Thomas F. Hahn, *Canal Boat Children* (Shepherdstown, W.V.: American Canal and Transportation Center, 1981), 21–23.

52. Korson, 116.

53. Willis M. Rivinus, *A Wayfarer's Guide to the Delaware Canal* (W. M. Rivinus, 1978), 7.

54. Springer and Hahn, 23.

55. For accounts of canal life, see James Lee, *Tales the Boatmen Told* (Easton, Pa.: Canal Press, 1977); and C. P. "Bill" Yoder, *Delaware Canal Journal* (Bethlehem, Pa.: Canal Press, 1972).

56. Quoted from Lee, 15–16.

57. Ibid., 23.

58. Ibid., 239–40.

59. Ibid., 8.

60. Korson, 115.

61. Ibid., 117–18.

62. Quoted from Lee, 213–15.

63. *History of Schuylkill County, Pennsylvania, with Illustrations and Biographical Sketches of Some of Its Prominent Men and Pioneers* (New York: W. W. Munsell, 1881), 263–64.

64. Ibid., 377.

65. All quoted statements appear in Clifton K. Yearly, Jr., *Enterprise and Anthracite: Economics and Democracy in Schuylkill County, 1820–1875* (Baltimore: Johns Hopkins University Press, 1961), 30–31.

66. Ibid.

67. Ibid., 40–41.

68. Quoted from ibid., 62.

69. Ibid., 65–66; see also Ronald L. Fillippelli, "Pottsville: Boom Town," *Historical Review of Berks County* 35 (Autumn 1970): 126–29, 155–57.

70. Yearly, 42.

71. John N. Hoffman, *Girard Estate Coal Lands in Pennsylvania, 1801–1884* (Washington, D.C.: Smithsonian Institution, 1972), 19.

72. Ibid., 60.

3. ANTHRACITE IGNITES AN INDUSTRIAL REVOLUTION

1. George Korson, *Black Rock: Mining Folklore of the Pennsylvania Dutch* (Baltimore: Johns Hopkins University Press, 1960), 123.

2. Ibid., 122, 134.

3. Jules I. Bogen, *The Anthracite Railroads: A Study in American Railroad Enterprise* (New York: Ronald Press, 1927), 12–13. Although this study is dated, it is by far the best on the anthracite railroads and their origins and development. See also Korson, 123.

4. Quoted from Dee Brown, *Hear That Lonesome Whistle Blow: Railroads in the West* (New York: Holt, Rinehart and Winston, 1977), 21. See also John F. Stover, *American Railroads* (Chicago: University of Chicago Press, 1961). On transportation in the early railroad era, see George P. Taylor, *The Transportation Revolution, 1815–1860* (New York: Holt, Rinehart and Winston, 1962).

5. Quoted from Brown, 21–22.

6. Quoted from ibid., 26.

7. Bogen, 11–13; Korson, 124.

8. Korson, 124–25; Hanns G. Altner, "Frederick List, 1789–1846," *Historical Review of Berks County* 1 (October 1935): 6–11.

9. Bogen, 20–22.

10. Ibid., 19.

11. Ibid., 23–26.

12. Ibid., 24–27; Korson, 130.

13. Bogen, 26–27.

14. Quoted from Korson, 132.

15. Chester Jones, *The Economic History of Anthracite Tide-Water Canals* (Philadelphia: University Publishers, 1908), 137.

16. Spiro G. Patton, "Charles Ellet, Jr., and the Canal Versus Railroad Controversy," in *Proceedings of the Canal History and Technology Symposium*, vol. 2 (Easton, Pa.: Center for Canal History and Technology, 1983), 14–15; Spiro G. Patten, "Railroad versus Canal in the Southern Schuylkill Anthracite Trade," in *Proceedings of the Canal History and Technology Symposium*, vol. 2 (Easton, Pa.: Center for Canal History and Technology, 1983).

17. Jones, 144; Robert F. Archer, *A History of the Lehigh Valley Railroad* (Berkeley: Howell-North, 1977); Robert J. Casy and W. A. S. Douglas, *The Lackawanna Story: The First Hundred Years of the Delaware, Lackawanna Railroad* (New York: McGraw-Hill, 1951); Robert M. Vogel, *Roebling's Delaware and Hudson Canal Aqueducts* (Washington, D.C.: Smithsonian Institution Press, 1971).

18. Technically speaking, the first furnace to smelt iron using anthracite, with Thomas's advice, was the Pioneer Furnace in Pottsville. See Craig Bartholomew, "Anthracite Iron Making and Industrial Growth in the Lehigh Valley," *Proceedings, Lehigh County Historical Society* 32 (1978): 129–83. On early iron making, see Arthur Cecil Bining, *Pennsylvania Iron Manufacture in the Eighteenth Century*, 2d ed. (Harrisburg: Pennsylvania Historical and Museum Commission, 1973); Joseph E. Walker, *Hopewell Village: A Social and Economic History of an Iron-making Community* (Philadelphia: University of Pennsylvania Press, 1966); on

iron making also see James M. Swank, *The Manufacturing Iron in All Ages* (Philadelphia, 1892); W. Ross Yates, "Discovery of the Process of Making Anthracite Iron," *Pennsylvania Magazine of History and Biography* 98, no. 2 (April 1974); Peter Temin, *Iron and Steel in Nineteenth Century America* (Cambridge, Mass.: MIT Press, 1970).

19. Bartholomew, 137–39.

20. Burton W. Folsom, Jr., *Urban Capitalists: Entrepreneurs and City Growth in Pennsylvania's Lackawanna and Lehigh Regions, 1800–1920* (Baltimore: Johns Hopkins University Press, 1981), 25–26. An important study of the Philadelphia economic region is Diane Lindstrom, *Economic Development in the Philadelphia Region, 1810–1850* (New York: Columbia University Press, 1978); also see Roberta B. Miller, *City and Hinterland: A Case Study of Urban Growth and Regional Development* (Westport, Conn.: Greenwood Press, 1976).

21. Folsom, 27–28.

22. Ibid., 28.

23. Quoted from ibid., 32.

24. Quoted from Alfred D. Chandler, Jr., "Anthracite Coal and the Beginnings of the Industrial Revolution in the United States," *Business History Review* 46 (Summer 1972): 159. The preceding statistics come from Chandler; see also Thomas C. Cochran, *Frontiers of Change: Early Industrialism in America* (New York: Oxford University Press, 1981).

25. James M. Swank, *History of the Manufacture of Iron in All Ages* (Franklin, N.Y.: Burt, 1892), 362.

26. Chandler, 163.

27. Ibid., 166, 169.

28. Ibid., 173.

29. Bartholomew, 140–41.

30. Karyl Hall and Peter Hall, *Lehigh Valley: An Illustrated History* (Woodland Hills, Calif.: Windsor Publications, 1982), 62–65. Also see William J. Heller, *History of Northampton County, Pennsylvania, and the Grand Valley of the Lehigh*, 3 vols. (Boston, 1920); and Anthony J. Brzyski, "The Lehigh Canal and Its Effects on the Economic Development of The Region through which It Passed, 1818–1873" (Ph.D. diss., New York University, 1957); on the Lehigh Valley also see Gillian L. Gollin, *Moravians in Two Worlds: A Study of Changing Communities* (New York: Columbia University Press, 1967); Raymond Walters, *Bethlehem Long Ago and Today* (Bethlehem, Pa.: 1923); W. Ross Yates, *Bethlehem of Pennsylvania: The Golden Years, 1845–1920* (Bethlehem, Pa.: Bethlehem Book, 1976); M. S. Henry, *History of the Lehigh Valley* (Easton: Bixler and Corwin, 1860).

31. Folsom, 34–35. Also see chaps. 3 and 4, for Scranton's growth. Also see the Scranton Papers in the Edmund T. Lukens Collection, Eleutherian Mills National Library, Wilmington, Delaware, and in the Lackawanna Historical Society, Scranton, Pennsylvania. Other valuable studies include John P. Gallagher, "Scranton: Industry and Politics, 1835–1885," Ph.D. diss., Catholic University, 1964); Benjamin H. Troop, *A Half-Century in Scranton* (Scranton, 1895); Frederick L. Hitchcock, *A History of Scranton and Its People*, 2 vols. (New York, 1914); on the Scrantons' efforts in coal and iron, see W. David Lewis, "The Early History of the Lackawanna Iron and Coal Company: A Study in Technological Adaptation," *Pennsylvania Magazine of History and Biography* 96 (October 1972): 424–68.

32. Information on Packer appears in Milton C. Stuart, *Asa Packer, 1805–1879: Captain of Industry; Educator; Citizen* (Princeton: Princeton University Press, 1938).

33. Folsom, 120; also see Bogen, chap. 5 on the Lehigh Valley Railroad.

34. Folsom, 121.

35. Ibid., 126–27; also see Brzyski for

the early nineteenth-century economic development of the Lehigh Valley.

36. Folsom, 126–31.

37. Ibid., 133; Hall and Hall, 61–62.

38. Edward J. Davies, "The Urbanizing Region: Leadership and Urban Growth in the Anthracite Coal Regions, 1830–1885" (Ph.D. diss., University of Pittsburgh, 1977), 85; Folsom, 72.

39. Davies, 87–89; for early histories of the Wyoming Valley, see Charles Miner, *History of Wyoming* (Philadelphia, 1845); Horace Hayden, Alfred Hand, and John W. Jordan, *Genealogical and Family History of the Wyoming and Lackawanna Valleys, Pennsylvania* (New York: 1906); and W. W. Munsell and Company, *History of Luzerne, Lackawanna, and Wyoming Counties* (New York, 1880).

40. Folsom, 71.

41. Davies, 89, 90–95.

42. Ibid., 105, 116, 122, 138.

43. Ibid., 156–57.

44. Folsom, 79.

45. Bogen, 206–10; D. F. Shafer, *A Quantitative Description and Analysis of the Growth of Pennsylvania Anthracite Coal Industry, 1820–1865* (New York: Arno Press, 1977).

4. WORKING IN THE BLACK HELL

1. Lewis Mumford, *Technics and Civilization* (New York, 1933), 67.

2. John S. Carroll, interview with Chester Siock, July 13, 1939, in "A Long Wall Miner," Federal Writers' Project, Works Progress Administration, Scranton, Pa. In the 1930s the Federal Writers' Project of the WPA collected material through field research and interviews for a "Pennsylvania Anthracite Book." The book was never published, but typed interviews and reports from the field remain. They currently are located in the Bureau of Archives and History, Pennsylvania Historical and Museum Commission, Harrisburg, Pa. The authors have relied heavily upon these sources, especially in this chapter. Though no common citation was used when the sources were collected, the authors identify them hereafter as Pennsylvania or Federal Writers' Project, WPA.

3. Quoted from Stephen Crane, "In the Depths of a Coal Mine," in Paul B. Beers, ed., *The Pennsylvania Sampler* (Harrisburg: Stackpole Books, 1970), 100.

4. Ibid.; see also Louis Poliniak, *When Coal Was King* (Lebanon, Pa.: Applied Arts Publishers, 1977), 6. For early coal mining techniques, see Samuel H. Daddow and Benjamin Bannan, *Coal, Iron and Oil* (Pottsville: Bannan, 1866); for late nineteenth-century methods, see Henry Martin Chance, *Report on the Mining Methods and Appliances Used in the Anthracite Coal Fields* (Commonwealth of Pennsylvania, Harrisburg: Second Geological Survey, 1883).

5. William Joseph Showalter, "Coal—Ally of American Industry," *National Geographic* 34 (November 1918): 415.

6. Interview with William Whyne, former mine foreman, Ashland Pioneer Tunnel, Ashland, Pa., March 28, 1982. A transcript of the complete interview is in the authors' files.

7. John S. Carroll and John Bexon, Sr., interview with Robert L. Reid, in "Drove Headings for Thirty Years," Job 54, Pennsylvania Writers' Project, WPA.

8. John S. Carroll, interview with Dominick Just, in "Shifting Jobs," Field Notes 716, WPA Writers' Project.

9. Interview with William Whyne.

10. Ibid.

11. John S. Carroll, interview with Chester Siock.

12. Rossamond D. Rhone, "Anthracite Coal Mines and Mining," *Review of Reviews* 16 (1902): 60.

13. James J. McMullen, "History of Anthracite," WPA Writers' Project, 70–71.

14. John S. Carroll and John Bexon, interview with Robert Reid.

15. Ibid.

16. Crane, 103.

17. George Korson, *Minstrels of the Mine Patch* (Hatboro, Pa.: Folklore Associates, 1964), 100–102.

18. Ibid.

19. John S. Carroll, interview with Chester Siock.

20. John S. Carroll, interview with Joseph Mataconis, in "Nipper," Pennsylvania Anthracite Book, WPA Writers' Project.

21. Carter Goodrich, *The Miner's Freedom* (Boston: Marshall Jones, 1925), 56.

22. Showalter, 409.

23. Anthony F. C. Wallace, *The Social Context of Innovation: Bureaucrats, Families, and Heroes in the Early Industrial Revolution, as Foreseen in Bacon's "New Atlantis"* (Princeton: Princeton University Press, 1982), chap. 3.

24. Ibid., 409–10; see also Rhone.

25. Harry M. Caudill, *Night Comes to the Cumberlands* (Boston: Little, Brown, 1962), 118; on dangerous gases, see Homer Greene, *Coal and the Coal Mines* (New York: Houghton, Mifflin, 1889), chap. 12.

26. Rhone, 58; Anthony F. C. Wallace has noted that, when the safety lamp was introduced in England by Sir Humphry Davy and Michael Faraday, there was a *rise* in the number of fatalities from gas explosions in the mines. "Operators were encouraged to send miners into workings previously considered too dangerous to enter; and miners, impatient with the lamp's poor light, too often used a naked candle instead, testing for fire-damp by observing the length of the flame" (Wallace, 114–15).

27. The statistics come from the *Washington Post*, June 26, 1983. For an account of efforts to deal with accidents through mine safety see Harold W. Aurand, "Mine Safety and Social Control in the Anthracite Regions," a paper delivered at the 1984 Annual Meeting of the Organization of American Historians.

28. Rhone, 58.

29. Caudill, 120–21.

30. Ibid., 119–20.

31. Ibid., 119.

32. Quoted from Thomas W. Knox, *Underground Life below the Surface* (Hartford: J. B. Burr, 1876), 586.

33. Mary Siegel Tyson, *The Miners* (Pine Grove, Pa.: Sweet Arrow Lake Press, 1977), 136–37.

34. Greene, 157.

35. Tyson, 140.

36. McMullen, "History of Anthracite," 69, 70.

37. John S. Carroll, interview with Dominick Just.

38. Crane, 101.

39. For a lively account of breaker boys, see Perry K. Blatz, "The All-Too-Youthful Proletarians," *Pennsylvania Heritage*, Winter 1981, pp. 13–17; see also Korson, *Minstrels*, 98.

40. The quoted statement appears in Blatz, 15.

41. Job 54, Pennsylvania Anthracite Book, WPA Writers' Project.

42. McMullen, "History of Anthracite."

43. Job 54, Pennsylvania Anthracite Book, WPA Writers' Project.

44. Goodrich, 99ff.

45. Quoted from Alvin W. Gouldner, *Patterns of Industrial Bureaucracy* (Glencoe, Ill.: Free Press, 1954), 108. Although quoted about gypsum miners, the attitude clearly expresses the feelings of all miners.

46. Ibid.

47. George Korson, *Black Rock: Mining Folklore of the Pennsylvania Dutch* (Baltimore: Johns Hopkins University Press, 1960), 320.

48. Gouldner, 111.

49. Korson, *Black Rock*, 349.

50. Gouldner, 110.

51. Ibid.

52. Ibid.

53. Quoted from ibid., 115.

54. Quoted from ibid., 116.

55. Korson, *Black Rock*, 322–23.

56. Gouldner, 120–21.

57. Ibid., 119.

58. Korson, *Black Rock*, 310.

59. Ibid., 311.

60. Gouldner, 129.

61. Quoted from ibid., 135.

5. THE MOLLY MAGUIRES

1. Sidney Lens, *The Labor Wars: From the Mollie Maguires to the Sitdowns* (Garden City, N.Y.: Anchor, Doubleday, 1974), 11–13.

2. For a review of the various interpretations of the Mollies, see Harold Aurand and William Gudelunas, "The Mythical Qualities of the Molly Maguires," *Pennsylvania History* 49 (1982).

3. For background on the Irish in Ireland and America, see William D. Griffin, *A Portrait of the Irish in America* (New York: Charles Scribner's Sons, 1981); Carl Wittke, *The Irish in America* (Baton Rouge, La.: Louisiana State University Press, 1956); T. W. Moody and F. X. Martin, *The Course of Irish History* (New York: Weybright and Talley, 1967); J. C. Beckett, *A Short History of Ireland* (New York: Hutchinson University Library, 1966); Lawrence J. McCaffrey, *The Irish Diaspora in America* (Bloomington: Indiana University Press, 1976). The best account of Irish emigration is R. D. Edwards and T. D. Williams, eds., *The Great Famine* (New York: New York University Press, 1957).

4. Quoted in Andrew M. Greeley, *That Most Distressful Nation: The Taming of the American Irish* (Chicago: Quadrangle Books, 1972), 28.

5. William F. Shannon, *The American Irish* (New York: Macmillan, 1963), 18.

6. Quoted in Giovanni Costigan, *A History of Modern Ireland* (New York: Pegasus, 1970), 185–87; Greeley, 36.

7. Shannon, 41–43.

8. Peter Roberts, *Anthracite Coal Communities* (New York: Macmillan, 1904), 89.

9. An excellent description of conditions in the mining towns is found in Roberts, chap. 4.

10. Quoted from George Korson, *Minstrels of the Mine Patch* (Hatboro, Pa.: Folklore Associates, 1964), 13.

11. John S. Carroll, "Folklore and Customs," WPA Writers' Project, Bureau of Archives and History, Pennsylvania Historical and Museum Commission, Harrisburg, Pa.

12. Korson, 13.

13. Carroll, "Folklore and Customs," 13, 9–10.

14. Lens, 18–19.

15. Wayne G. Broehl, Jr., *The Molly Maguires* (Cambridge, Mass.: Chelsea House–Vintage, 1964), 85–86. The best study of the Irish in politics in this era in the region is William A. Gudelunas and William G. Shade, *Before the Molly Maguires: The Emergence of the Ethno-Religious Factor in the Politics of the Lower Anthracite Region* (New York: Arno Press, 1976).

16. Broehl, 90–95.

17. Lens, 19–22.

18. George R. Leighton, "Shenandoah, Pa.: The Story of an Anthracite Town," *Harper's* 174 (1937): 131ff.

19. For a biography of Gowen, see Marvin W. Schlegel, *Ruler of the Reading: The Life of Franklin B. Gowen, 1836–1889* (Harrisburg: Archives Publishing, 1947).

20. Lens, 24–25.

21. Ibid., 27.

22. Ibid.

23. Broehl, 184–85; Lens, 28.

24. Ibid., 205–6.

25. Quoted from Lens, 32.

26. Ibid., 33.

27. Of the numerous accounts of the Mollies, perhaps the most balanced and informative is Broehl, *The Molly Maguires*, on which we have relied; see especially parts 3 and 4.

28. Quoted from Broehl, 297.

29. Quoted in Paul B. Beers, "The Mollie Maguires," *American History Illustrated* 1, no. 5 (1966): 19.

30. Lens, 35.

31. For a colorful account of the events surrounding the hangings, see Beers, "The Mollie Maguires."

32. The Pennsylvania state legislature blamed the violence in Scranton in 1877 on Molly Maguires who had fled Schuylkill County. See Commonwealth of Pennsylvania, Legislature, *Riot Commission Investigation*, Legislative Documents, 1878, vol. 5, Docs. 29, 30.

6. SOLIDARITY: THE SLAVIC COMMUNITY IN ANTHRACITE

1. Victor R. Greene, *The Slavic Community on Strike: Immigrant Labor in Pennsylvania Anthracite* (Notre Dame: University of Notre Dame Press, 1968), 25–26; see M. Mark Stolarik, *Slovak Migration from Europe to North America, 1870–1918* (Cleveland: Slovak Institute, 1980); William I. Thomas and Florian Znaniecki, *The Polish Peasant in Europe and America*, 5 vols. (Boston: 1918–20).

2. Frank Julian Warne, *The Slav Invasion and the Mine Workers* (Philadelphia: J. B. Lippincott, 1904); the quoted statement appears on p. 77. The best novel of the Slavic experience in America is Thomas Bell, *Out of This Furnace* (Pittsburgh: University of Pittsburgh Press, 1976); M. Mark Stolarik, "From Field to Factory: The Historiography of Slovak Immigration to the United States," *International Migration Review* 10 (1976): 81–102.

3. Louis Adamic, *Dynamite: The Story of Class Violence in America* (1930; reprint, New York: Chelsea House Publishers, 1980), 3.

4. Ibid., 15–16.

5. Ibid., 39, 43–45.

6. For this citation, see Job 54, Field Notes 277, WPA Writers' Project.

7. Job 54, Folder 27, WPA Writers' Project; on the government's attitude toward the impact of Slavic labor in the anthracite region, see U.S., Industrial Commission, *Report of the Industrial Commission*, vol. 12: *The Relations and Conditions of Capital and Labor Employed in the Mining Industry* (Washington, D.C.: U.S. Government Printing Office, 1901).

8. Stolarik, 35.

9. Quoted from George Korson, *Minstrels of the Mine Patch* (Philadelphia: University of Pennsylvania Press, 1938), 125.

10. Job 54, Field Notes 93, WPA Writers' Project.

11. Greene, 41.

12. Quoted from Jay Hambridge, "An Artist's Impressions of the Colliery Region," in Harold W. Aurand, ed., *Coal Towns: A Contemporary Perspective, 1899–1923* (Lexington, Mass.: Ginn Custom Publishing, 1980), 12.

13. Job 54, Folder 27, WPA Writers' Project; Mary Buell Sayles, "Housing and Social Conditions in a Slavic Neighborhood," *Charities* 13 (1904): 257–61.

14. Annie Marion MacLean, "Life in the Pennsylvania Coal Fields with Particular Reference to Women," in Aurand, *Coal Towns*, 31; Greene, 46.

15. Greene, 42.

16. Peter Roberts, *Anthracite Coal Communities* (New York: Macmillan, 1904), 106.

17. Greene, 34–35.

18. Roberts, 20.

19. "You don't think they have souls ..." quoted from Herbert G. Gutman, *Work, Culture and Society in Industrializing America* (New York, Vintage, 1977), 25; Protestant women quoted from Roberts, 49–56, 219, 236, 291, 294–95; Scranton Oral History Project, Bodnar-Vauter interview, tape 11, side 2, June 19, 1973. The tapes and transcripts of the project are located in the Pennsylvania Historical and Museum Commission, Harrisburg.

20. Quoted from Roberts, 53; see also Rowland Berthoff, "The Social Order of the Anthracite Region, 1825–1902," *Pennsylvania Magazine of History and Biography* 89 (July 1965): 261–91.

21. Scranton Oral History Project, Pacholee-Vauter Interview, tape 8, sides 1 and 2, July 13, 1973.

22. John Bodnar, "Immigration and Modernization: The Case of Slavic Peasants in Industrial America," in Milton Cantor, ed., *American Working Class Culture: Explorations in American Labor and Social History* (Westport, Conn.: Greenwood Press, 1979), 341–46; see also John Bodnar, "The Formation of Ethnic Consciousness: Slavic Immigrants in Steelton," in *The Ethnic Experience in Pennsylvania* (Lewisburg, Pa.: Bucknell University Press, 1973), 309–30. On the village outlook of Poles, see Caroline Golab, "The Polish Communities of Philadelphia, 1870–1920: Immigrant Distribution and Adaptation in Urban America" (Ph.D. diss., University of Pennsylvania, 1971); Josef J. Barton, *Peasants and Strangers: Italians, Rumanians, and Slovaks in an American City* (Cambridge, Mass.: MIT Press, 1975).

23. Roberts, 36.

24. *Report of the Department of Mines of Pennsylvania, Part 1. Anthracite 1919–1920* (Harrisburg, Commonwealth of Pennsylvania, 1921), 50–51.

25. Quoted from Bodnar in Cantor, *American Working Class Culture*, 337.

26. Quoted from Stolarik, 53.

27. Bodnar in Cantor, 340–41; Victor L. Greene, "For God and Country: The Origins of Slavic Catholic Self-Consciousness in America," *Church History* 35 (December 1966).

28. Sister M. Accursia, Bern., "Polish Miners in Luzerne County, Pennsylvania," *Polish American Studies* 5 (1948):8; Timothy Smith, "Lay Initiative in the Religious Life of American Immigrants, 1880–1950," in Tamara K. Hareven, ed., *Anonymous Americans* (Englewood Cliffs, N.J.: Prentice-Hall, 1971).

29. Scranton Oral History Project, Serafim interview, tape 11, side 1.

30. Sister M. Accursia, 9.

31. Bodnar in Cantor, 335.

32. Interview with Margaret Fasulka, Wilkes-Barre, July 3, 1983, authors' files; Bodnar, "Immigration," 335–36.

33. Scranton Oral History Project, Earl-Aukscunas interview, tape 4, side 2.

34. Roberts, 69, 70.

35. Ibid., 72, 79; MacLean, "Life in the Pennsylvania Coal Fields," 29–43; on the boardinghouse system, see John Modell and Tamara K. Hareven, "Urbanization and the Malleable Household: An Examination of Boarding and Lodging in American Families," *Journal of Marriage and the Family* (August 1973): 467–78; Bessie Pehotsky, *The Slavic Immigrant Woman* (Cincinnati, 1925); Peter Roberts, "The Employment of Girls in Textile Industries of Pennsylvania," *Annals of the American Academy of Political and Social Sciences* 23 (1904): 435–37; Pennsylvania Department of La-

bor and Industry, Bureau of Women and Children, *A History of Child Labor Legislation in Pennsylvania* (1928), no. 27; on Slavic family budgets, see Margaret Byington, *Homestead: The Households of a Mill Town* (New York, 1910).

36. Roberts, 71.

37. Bodnar in Cantor, 348.

38. Interview, Margaret Fasulka, Wilkes-Barre, July 3, 1983, in the authors' files.

39. Roberts, 291; U.S., Congress, Senate, *Report on Conditions of Women and Children Wage Earners in the United States*, vol. 4: *The Silk Industry*, 61st Cong., 2d sess., S. doc. 645, 1911.

40. Roberts, 289.

41. Bodnar in Cantor, 337.

42. Ibid.; see John Bodnar, "Maternalism and Morality: Slavic-American Immigrants and Education, 1890–1940," *Journal of Ethnic Studies* 3, no. 4 (Winger, 1976): 1–18.

43. Henry Edward Rood, "A Pennsylvania Colliery Village," in Aurand, *Coal Towns*, 7.

44. Job 54, Field Notes, Luzerne County, WPA Writers' Project.

45. Job 54, Field Notes 148, WPA Writers' Project.

46. Job 54, Field Notes 36, WPA Writers' Project.

47. Job 54, Folder 28, WPA Writers' Project.

48. Job 54, Field Notes 148, WPA Writers' Project.

49. Scranton Oral History Project, Hrynuck interview, tape 9, side 1.

50. Job 54, Folder 27, WPA Writers' Project.

51. Scranton Oral History Project, tape 14, side 1.

52. Job 54, Field Notes 148, WPA Writers' Project.

53. Job 54, Field Notes 148, WPA Writ-

ers' Project. See also M. Mark Stolarik, "Slovaks," in Stephen Thernstrom, ed., *Harvard Encyclopedia of American Ethnic Groups* (Cambridge: Harvard University, 1980).

54. Greene, 47–48.

55. Roberts, 222–43; the authors are indebted to several pioneering studies on the relationship between culture and work: Herbert G. Gutman, *Work, Culture, and Society in Industrializing America* (New York: Vintage, 1977); E. P. Thompson, *Making of the English Labor Class* (London: Vintage, 1963); and Lewis Mumford, *Technics and Civilization* (New York: Harcourt, Brace, 1934).

7. LATTIMER

1. Harold W. Aurand, *From the Molly Maguires to the United Mine Workers: The Social Ecology of an Industrial Union, 1869–1897* (Philadelphia: Temple University Press, 1971), 110. This is the best study available on early unionization efforts in the anthracite fields.

2. Ibid., 112.

3. Ibid., 113.

4. Pennsylvania Secretary of Internal Affairs, *Report, 1884*, pt. 3: *Industrial Statistics* (Harrisburg: Commonwealth of Pennsylvania, 1884), 7.

5. Aurand, *From the Molly Maguires*, 115–16.

6. Victor R. Greene, *The Slavic Community on Strike: Immigrant Labor in Pennsylvania* (Notre Dame: University of Notre Dame Press, 1968), chap. 5; also see Aurand, 120–30.

7. Quoted from Harold W. Aurand, "The Anthracite Strike of 1887–1888," *Pennsylvania History* 35 (1968): 175.

8. Ibid., 177.

9. *Pottsville Daily Republican*, December 6, 1887; also quoted in Aurand, "The Anthracite Strike," 178.

10. Aurand, "The Anthracite Strike," 179–84.

11. Ibid., 180–81.

12. Quoted from George Korson, *Minstrels of the Mine Patch: Songs and Stories of the Anthracite Industry* (Philadelphia: University of Pennsylvania Press, 1938), 230.

13. Aurand, *From the Molly Maguires*, 133–36; see also Andrew Roy, *A History of the Coal Miners of the United States: From the Development of the Mines to the Close of the Anthracite Strike of 1902* (Columbus: J. P. Tauger, 1907).

14. Aurand, *From the Molly Maguires*, 136–37.

15. Greene, 127.

16. *Wilkes-Barre Record*, September 15, 1897; *Hazleton Daily Standard*, August 17, 1897; also quoted from Michael Novak, *The Guns of Lattimer: The True Story of a Massacre and a Trial, August 1897–March 1898* (New York: Basic Books, 1978), 17; see also Victor R. Greene, "A Study in Slavs, Strikes, and Unions: The Anthracite Strike of 1897," *Pennsylvania History* 21 (1964): 204; [Samuel Gompers], "Lattimer Tragedy—Wilkes-Barre Farce," *American Federationist* 5 (1898): 11–14.

17. Novak, 18–20.

18. Quoted from Aurand, *From the Molly Maguires*, 138; Novak, 26.

19. Novak, 54–56.

20. Quoted from Aurand, *From the Molly Maguires*, 138; Novak, 64–65.

21. Novak, 68–69.

22. Ibid., 31–34.

23. For a history of the Pardee family business interests, see C. Pardee Foulke and William C. Foulke, *Calvin Pardee—1841–1923: His Family and His Enterprises* (Philadelphia: Drake Press, 1979); also see Novak, 36–43; and Robert J. Spense, *John Markle, Representative American* (New York, 1929).

24. Quoted in Novak, 37; for more on the Pardees, see S. J. Coffin, *The Men of Lafayette* (New York: Scribner Press, 1891).

25. Novak, 40.

26. Ibid., 42.

27. The account is taken from the *Wilkes-Barre Times*, September 4, 1897; see also Novak, 78–80.

28. Greene, "A Study in Slavs, Strikes, and Unions," 206.

29. Quoted in Novak, 104.

30. Quoted in Novak, 122.

31. The authors have relied upon the account of the events surrounding Lattimer found in Novak, 123–64. All quoted statements appear in his book. See also Greene, *The Slavic Community on Strike*, 137–42; Harry B. Schooley III, "The Lattimer Massacre and Trial," *Slovakia* 27 (1977): 62–79; and especially George A. Turner, "The Lattimer Massacre and Its Sources," *Slovakia* 27 (1977): 9–43; for the major events of the strike we have relied on some of the region's leading newspapers—the *Hazleton Daily Standard*, *Wilkes-Barre Record*, *Wilkes-Barre Evening Leader*, and *Pottsville Republican*.

32. Greene, "A Study in Slavs, Strikes, and Unions," 209–10.

33. Novak, 174.

34. Ibid., 177.

35. For an account of the women's efforts, see Novak, 47–48; 174–77; see also Greene, *The Slavic Community on Strike*, 143–44.

36. A summary of the trial is found in Novak, 199–237; the quoted statement appears on p. 234.

37. Greene, "A Study in Slavs, Strikes, and Unions," 214–15.

8. THE GREAT STRIKE

1. John Mitchell, "The Miner's Life and Aims," *Cosmopolitan* 31 (October 1901):

624; McAlister Coleman, *Men and Coal* (New York: Arno Press, New York Times, 1969).

2. Philip S. Foner, *History of the Labor Movement in the United States*, vol. 3 (New York: International Publishers, 1964), 87.

3. Quoted from Elsie Gluck, *John Mitchell, Miner* (New York: John Day, 1929), 67–68. For further information on John Mitchell, see the John Mitchell Papers at Catholic University, Washington, D.C.

4. For an account of the combination see Eliot Jones, *The Anthracite Coal Combination in the United States* (Cambridge, Mass.: Harvard University, 1914), especially chaps. 2 and 3.

5. Quoted from Bruno Ramirez, *When Workers Fight: The Politics of Industrial Relations in the Progressive Era, 1898–1916* (Westport, Conn.: Greenwood Press, 1978), 35; Peter Roberts, *The Anthracite Coal Industry* (New York: Macmillan, 1901); Scott Nearing, *Anthracite: An Instance of a Natural Resource Monopoly* (Philadelphia: John C. Winston, 1915).

6. George R. Leighton, "Shenandoah, Pennsylvania: The Story of an Anthracite Town," *Harper's Monthly Magazine*, January 1937, p. 140. Victor R. Greene, *The Slavic Community on Strike: Immigrant Labor in Pennsylvania* (Notre Dame: University of Notre Dame Press, 1968).

7. Greene, 154–56.

8. Quoted in ibid., 158.

9. Leighton, 138–40.

10. Quoted from Greene, 158.

11. Ibid., 159.

12. Quoted from Leighton, 140.

13. Gluck, 4–5.

14. Quoted from ibid., 5.

15. Ibid., 8–9.

16. Ramirez, 50–51.

17. Ibid., 51; Gluck, 27.

18. Gluck, 29–30; Ramirez, 51.

19. Quoted from Ramirez, 53.

20. Ibid., 53; Gluck, 57.

21. Lincoln Steffens, "A Labor Leader of Today: John Mitchell and What He Stands For," *McClure's Magazine* 19 (1902):356.

22. Ibid., 355.

23. Robert J. Cornell, *The Anthracite Coal Strike of 1902* (Washington, D.C.: Catholic University Press, 1957), 39–40. This is the best and most detailed history of the strike; see also Gluck, 72–74.

24. Cornell, 39.

25. Gluck, 75; Cornell, 42.

26. Cornell, 44.

27. Ibid., 47.

28. Michael Barendese, "Slavic Immigrants in the Pennsylvania Anthracite Fields, 1880–1902" (Ph.D. diss., Ball State University, 1976), 122.

29. Cornell, 47–48; quoted in Cornell from the *Dictionary of American Biography*.

30. Cornell, 48–50.

31. Ibid., 50–51.

32. Gluck, 77–78.

33. Quoted from Cornell, 53.

34. Quoted from Gluck, 83.

35. Gluck, 83–84; quoted from Robert L. Reynolds, "The Coal Kings Come to Judgment," *American Heritage* 11, no. 3 (April 1960):61.

36. Quoted from Foner, 88.

37. Ramirez, 66–67; Marguerite Green, *The National Civic Federation and the American Labor Movement, 1900–1925* (Washington, D.C.: Catholic University Press, 1956).

38. Quoted from Foner, 88.

39. Quoted from Cornell, 91.

40. Quoted from Foner, 92.

41. Leighton, 141.

42. *Dictionary of American Biography*, s.v. "George Frederick Baer."

43. Cornell, 98–99; Greene, 179–80.

44. Foner, 87; Reynolds, 58.

45. Quoted from Reynolds, 58–59.

46. Reynolds, 59.

47. An Observer in the Field, "The Anthracite Strike," in Harold W. Aurand, ed., *Coal Towns: A Contemporary Perspective, 1899–1923* (Lexington, Mass.: Ginn Custom Publishing, 1980), 17; James F. J. Archibald, "The Striking Miners and their Families," *Colliers* 30 (October 11, 1902): 6–7.

48. An Observer, "Anthracite Strike," in Aurand, 18.

49. Frank Norris, "Life in the Mining Region," *Everybody's Magazine* 7 (September 1902): 242.

50. Alice K. Fallows, "A Woman's Visit to the Coal Fields," *Outlook*, October 11, 1902, p. 351.

51. Leighton, 142.

52. Francis H. Nicols, "Children of the Coal Shadow," in Aurand, 21–22.

53. U.S., Department of Labor, *Report of the Anthracite Coal Commission*, Bulletin 41 (Washington, D.C.: U.S. Government Printing Office, 1903), quoted from reel 4 of transcript.

54. Ibid.

55. Ibid. The quoted statement and information on William Bardner may be found on reel 11 of transcript.

56. Reynolds, 94–95.

57. Leighton, 142.

58. All quotes from An Observer, "Anthracite Strike," 18–19.

59. Nicols, "Children," 25; An Observer, "Anthracite Strike," 19.

60. Nicols, "Children," 27–28.

61. Reynolds, 95.

62. Steward Culin, *A Trooper's Narrative* (Philadelphia: George W. Jacobs, 1903), 79–80.

63. All quoted statements from An Observer, "Anthracite Strike," 19.

64. *Report of the Anthracite Coal Commission*, reel 2.

65. *Report of the Anthracite Coal Commission*, 1898–1901.

66. Clarence Darrow, *The Story of My Life* (London: Watts, 1932), 390–91.

67. Quoted from Reynolds, 95.

68. Ibid.

69. Ibid.

70. Foner, 96.

71. Quoted from Reynolds, 96ff.; Foner, 96.

72. Robert H. Wiebe, "The Anthracite Strike of 1902: A Record of Confusion," *Mississippi Valley Historical Review* 48 (1961): 244.

73. Quoted from Foner, 97; Mary Harris Jones, *Autobiography of Mother Jones* (New York: Arno Press, New York Times, 1969).

74. Quoted from Foner, 97–98.

75. Quoted from Andrew Roy, *A History of the Coal Miners of the United States* (Westport, Conn.: Greenwood, 1970), 430. The following quoted statement by John Markle is found on p. 435.

76. The account of the conference appears in Reynolds, 96–97. The quoted statement appears on p. 97.

77. Foner, 98–99; Reynolds, 97.

78. Quoted from Reynolds, 98.

79. Cornell, chap. 8; Reynolds, 98.

80. Quoted from Gluck, 145.

81. Gluck, 146–47.

82. Reynolds, 99; the full transcript is found in U.S., Department of Labor, *Report of the Anthracite Commission*.

83. The statements quoted appear in Darrow, 354, 358, 363.

84. For a summation of the settlement and effects of the strike, see Wiebe, 249–51.

85. Wiebe, 251.

86. Darrow, 409.

87. Ibid., 406.

9. DECLINE

1. Liefer Magnusson, "Company Housing in the Anthracite Region of Penn-

sylvania," *U.S. Bureau of Labor Statistics Monthly Labor Review* 10 (May 1920): 185–95.

2. Richard Ramsey Mead, "An Analysis of the Decline of the Anthracite Industry since 1921" (Ph.D. diss., University of Pennsylvania, 1935), 12–16, 57–59, 92–98.

3. In his discussion of the reasons for anthracite's decline, Mead discounts the effects of labor conflicts. Harold K. Kanarek, in "Disaster for Hard Coal: The Anthracite Strike of 1925–1926," *Labor History* 15 (Winter 1974):44–62, blames the strikes of 1922 and 1925 for contributing to the public's disenchantment with hard coal.

4. Quoted from Harold K. Kanarek, "The Pennsylvania Anthracite Strike of 1922," *Pennsylvania Magazine of History and Biography* 99 (April 1975):208.

5. Ibid., 208–9.

6. Ibid., 210.

7. Samuel Gompers, "Miners' Cause Just," *American Federationist* 29 (April 1922):279; also quoted in Kanarek, 212.

8. A Pennsylvania law passed in 1897 stipulated that only miners with at least two years' of experience who passed an examination and received a certificate could dig anthracite. The certificate was held at the time by approximately 40,000 men. See Kanarek, *The Pennsylvania Anthracite Strike*, 212.

9. Kanarek, 214, 224; quoted from 215. See also the *New York Times* during this period regarding officials' sentiments on the use of alternative fuels.

10. The best account of the political maneuvering appears in Kanarek, 220–25.

11. Melvyn Dubofsky and Warren Van Tine, *John L. Lewis: A Biography* (New York: Quadrangle, New York Times, 1977), 102–5, 139. This is the best biography of Lewis.

12. The operators' position during the strike is described in *Coal Age*, August 20,

1925. On the position of the UMW, see Douglas Keith Monroe, "A Decade of Turmoil: John L. Lewis and the Anthracite Miners, 1926–1936" (Ph.D. diss., Georgetown University, 1977), 35. This is the best and most thorough account of the United Mine Workers, John L. Lewis, and the union struggles in the region during the 1920s and 1930s.

13. Dubofsky and Van Tine, 143.

14. Quoted from ibid.

15. *United Mine Workers Journal*, February 1, 1926; also quoted in Monroe, 39–40.

16. Dubofsky and Van Tine, 143.

17. *Wilkes-Barre Record*, February 13, 1926; also quoted in Monroe, 43.

18. Monroe, 44–45; quoted from Dubofsky and Van Tine, 143.

19. Monroe, 47–48.

20. John L. Lewis, *The Miners Fight for American Standards* (Indianapolis: Bell Publishing, 1925), 40–42.

21. For an excellent account of Lewis's rise to power and methods, see Dubofsky and Van Tine, especially chaps. 3 and 6.

22. Monroe, 78–80.

23. The violence and its causes are discussed in Ben M. Selekman, "Miners and Murder: What Lies Back of the Feud in Anthracite," *Survey*, May 1, 1928, 151–55; see also Monroe, 81–84.

24. Quoted from Monroe, 85. Lewis frequently used redbaiting against opponents within the UMW during the "Red Scare" days of the early 1920s. He apparently found the tactic useful even in 1928.

25. Monroe, 88–92.

26. Quoted from Monroe, 95.

27. Ibid., 96.

28. John Bodnar, *Anthracite People: Families, Unions, and Work, 1900–1940* (Harrisburg: Commonwealth of Pennsylvania, Pennsylvania Historical and Museum Commission, 1983), 3. Bodnar, a leading historian of Pennsylvania's working-class culture, is a pioneer in the use of oral history

in the Commonwealth. *Anthracite People*, a fascinating collection of interviews, provides a wealth of information on the peoples' attitudes and activities in the region. It is especially good on the period of UMW turmoil in the 1930s.

29. Interview with John Sarnoski in the Glen Lyon area in Bodnar, *Anthracite People*, quoted from p. 61.

30. Interview with Romaine Stewart in Bodnar, *Anthracite People*, quoted from p. 63.

31. Interview with Chester Brozena of Plymouth in Bodnar, *Anthracite People*, quoted from p. 54.

32. On Lewis's attitudes toward work equalization, see Monroe, 116. For an account of the short-lived rebellion at the convention, see Monroe, 125–31.

33. The contract terms are found in Monroe, 146–47.

34. The quoted statements appear in Monroe, 152, 154.

35. Interview with George Treski, quoted in Bodnar, *Anthracite People*, 6.

36. Quoted from Monroe, 155.

37. Ibid., 158–59.

38. Brozena interview in Bodnar, *Anthracite People*, quoted from p. 50.

39. Interview with Stanley Salva in Bodnar, *Anthracite People*, quoted from p. 67.

40. For an account of the strike, see the *Wilkes-Barre Record*, March 20–28, 1931. The quoted statement appears in Monroe, 187.

41. Monroe, 186–89.

42. *Wilkes-Barre Record*, July 21–24, 1931.

43. *Wilkes-Barre Record*, March 12, 1932; also Monroe, 203–5.

44. The strike is covered in the *Wilkes-Barre Record*, March 17–31, 1932. See also Monroe, 207–9.

45. Monroe, 181; Bodnar, *Anthracite People*, 3–5.

46. *Wilkes-Barre Record*, August 8, 1933; Monroe, 247.

47. Interview with Brozena in Bodnar, *Anthracite People*, quoted from p. 52.

48. Interview with Anthony Piscotty of Plymouth in Bodnar, *Anthracite People*, quoted from p. 75.

49. Interview with Leonard Wydotis in Bodnar, *Anthracite People*, quoted from p. 6.

50. Monroe, 248–49.

51. Ibid., 248–64, 286–90.

52. The *Wilkes-Barre Record* and *Times-Leader* and the *Scranton Times* of January and February 1934 all covered the strike.

53. Monroe, 294–98, 302, 304.

54. Ibid., 303–9.

55. Bodnar, *Anthracite People*, 8.

56. Interview with Stacia Treski in Bodnar, *Anthracite People*, quoted from p. 36.

57. Interview with Vincent Znaniecki in Bodnar, *Anthracite People*, p. 94.

58. Interview with Romaine Steward in Bodnar, *Anthracite People*, quoted from pp. 63–64.

59. Interview with William Everett in Bodnar, *Anthracite People*, quoted from pp. 81–83.

60. Monroe, 316.

61. *Wilkes-Barre Record*, October 28, 1935.

62. Monroe, 355.

63. Steve Nelson, James R. Barrett, and Rob Ruck, *Steve Nelson: American Radical* (Pittsburgh: University of Pittsburgh Press, 1981), 171–72.

64. Interview with Helen Hosey in Bodnar, *Anthracite People*, quoted from p. 10.

65. Interview with Vincent Znaniecki in Bodnar, *Anthracite People*, quoted from p. 87.

66. Interview with Brozena in Bodnar, *Anthracite People*, p. 48.

67. Interview with Margaret Fasulka, Wilkes-Barre, July 3, 1983, in the authors' files.

68. Bodnar, *Anthracite People*, 10–12; interview with Margaret Fasulka.

69. Interview with Jule Majikas, Wilkes-Barre, July 2, 1983, in the authors' files.

70. John Bodnar, *Workers' World: Kinship, Community, and Protest in the Industrial Society, 1900–1940* (Baltimore: Johns Hopkins University Press, 1982), 40 (interview with Helen Mack).

71. Interview with Frances Shergalis Sharpless, Harrisburg, August 1, 1983, in the authors' files; also see Bodnar, *Anthracite People*, 13.

72. For a fascinating account of the effort to organize the unemployed in the region, see Nelson, chap. 4. Also see interview with Steve Nelson, Easton, Pa., April 28, 1983, in the authors' files.

73. Nelson, 96.

74. Ibid., 115–17; interview with Nelson.

75. Nelson, 157.

76. Ibid., 160–61; interview with Nelson.

77. Nelson, 110.

78. Ibid., 163–64.

79. Ibid., 170–71. The story about burning the car and shooting the horse was told by Michael Komnath of Wilkes-Barre in an interview on November 22, 1984 (transcript in the authors' files).

80. Ibid., 177.

81. Ibid.

82. Monroe, 379, 368.

83. George A. Spohrer, "The Knox Mine Disaster: The Beginning of the End," April 19, 1969, in the authors' files.

84. Ibid., 32.

85. Donald L. Miller and Richard E. Sharpless, "The Ecological and Economic Impact of Anthracite Mining in Pennsylvania," in Shyamal K. Majumdar, ed., *Energy, Environment, and the Economy* (Philadelphia: Pennsylvania Academy of Science, 1981); for an excellent study of the decline of the region and recent efforts toward revitalization, see Dan Rose, *Energy Transition and the Local Community: A Theory of Society Applied to Hazleton, Pennsylvania* (Philadelphia: University of Pennsylvania Press, 1981); see also *Anthracite Task Force, 1977 Report* (Washington, D.C.: U.S. Department of Energy, 1977); T. Bakerman, "Anthracite Coal: A Study in Advanced Industrial Decline" (Ph.D. diss., University of Pennsylvania, 1956); U.S., Department of Energy, *Coal—Pennsylvania Anthracite 1978: Energy Data Report* (Washington, D.C.: U.S. Department of Energy, Energy Information Administration, 1980).

EPILOGUE

1. "The Home Folks Stand by Dan," *Time*, March 27, 1978, p. 20.

2. *Current Bibliography*, 1978, p. 134.

3. Ibid., 132.

4. Lucille Craft, "Anthracite's Troubled History," *Allentown Morning Call*, May 11, 1981.

5. George Crile, "The Best Congressman," *Harper's*, January 1975, p. 63.

6. Ibid., 66.

7. *Current Bibliography*, 133; Crile, 64.

8. The best account of Flood's activities in the wake of Hurricane Agnes appears in Crile. The quoted statements appear in Crile, 62, 65.

9. There are several accounts of the incident. The quoted passage appears in Crile, 61.

10. Ibid.

11. For excellent studies of politics in the region, and especially Schuylkill County, see William Gudelunas and William Shade, *Before the Molly Maguires* (New York: Arno Press, 1976); and Gudelunas's *The Rise of the Irish Factor in Anthracite Politics, 1850–1880*, Occasional Paper 3 (Pittsburgh: University of Pittsburgh, Pennsylvania Ethnic Studies Center, 1983); and

Gudelunas with Steven R. Couch, "Would a Protestant or Polish Kennedy Have Won? A Local Test of Ethnicity and Religion in the Presidential Election of 1960," *Ethnic Groups* 3 (1980):1–21.

12. Craft, "Anthracite's Troubled History."

13. Quoted in Ben Livingood, "Coal: King Again?" *Allentown Sunday Call-Chronicle*, May 10, 1981.

Index